The Joan Palevsky Imprint in Classical Literature

In honor of beloved Virgil—

"O degli altri poeti onore e lume . . ."

—Dante, *Inferno*

THE POEMS
OF CATULLUS

THE POEMS
OF CATULLUS

A BILINGUAL EDITION

TRANSLATED,

WITH COMMENTARY BY

PETER GREEN

UNIVERSITY OF

CALIFORNIA PRESS

BERKELEY   LOS ANGELES

LONDON

University of California Press
Berkeley and Los Angeles, California

University of California Press, Ltd.
London, England

First paperback printing 2007
© 2005 by Peter Green

Library of Congress Cataloging-in-Publication Data

Catullus, Gaius Valerius.
[Works. English & Latin. 2005]
   The poems of Catullus / translated, with commentary, by
Peter Green.—Bilingual ed.
        p.   cm.
   Includes bibliographical references and index.
   ISBN 978-0-520-25386-5 (pbk : alk.)
   1. Catullus, Gaius Valerius—Translations into English.
2. Elegiac poetry, Latin—Translations into English.   3. Love
poetry, Latin—Translations into English.   4. Epigrams,
Latin—Translations into English.   5. Rome—Poetry.
I. Green, Peter, 1924–.   II.   Title.

PA6275.E5G74   2005
874'.01—dc22   2004013920

Manufactured in the United States of America

14   13   12   11
10   9   8   7   6   5   4   3

Carin's, because of so much—
quare habe tibi quidquid hoc libelli
qualecumque—

They were real people, and we should do
our best to understand them in their own terms . . . with
as few anachronistic preconceptions as possible. It is hard to make
out what there is in the darkness beyond the window, but at least
we can try not to be distracted by our own reflections.

T. P. WISEMAN,
Catullus and His World: A Reappraisal

It is hard to say which is the greater danger at the current juncture:
to condemn Catullus too hastily on the grounds that he ought to have
conformed to a modern liberal ethics of human rights and personhood,
or to excuse him too hastily by the stratagem of positing, just behind
the persona, the presence of a "poet" who *did* conform to it.

DAVID WRAY,
Catullus and the Poetics of Roman Manhood

In bed I read Catullus. It passes my comprehension why Tennyson
could have called him 'tender'. He is vindictive, venomous, and
full of obscene malice. He is only tender about his brother
and Lesbia, and in the end she gets it hot as well.

HAROLD NICOLSON,
Diaries and Letters 1945–1962

At non effugies meos iambos.

CATULLUS, fr. 3

CONTENTS

PREFACE

In his elegantly combative book, *Catullus and His World: A Reappraisal* (1985), Peter Wiseman wrote: "Forty-four is probably a good age to stop writing about Catullus, if not already a bit late." Out of step as always, I find myself *beginning* to write about him when just two years short of the age of eighty. I can only plead that this vespertinal engagement comes as the conclusion to a lifelong love of his poetry—the epigrams and long works no less than the better-known "polymetrics"—culminating in a task as enjoyable as it was challenging: a fresh translation of the entire canon, into forms as near their originals as ingenuity, and the limitations of the English language, would permit.

I didn't really plan this book: like Harriet Beecher Stowe's Topsy, it just grew. One thing led to another. I translated one or two of the early poems for *Southern Humanities Review;* then someone bet me I couldn't do a version of 63, the Attis poem, into English galliambics, and that even if I did, no one would publish it. Having studied Tennyson's *Boadicea,* which showed that English galliambics not only were possible but could be made remarkably exciting, I took the bet and won it on both counts: my version was accepted, with most flattering speed, by *Arion.* After that there was no stopping me, not even the availability of a variety of earlier translations, none of which, it seemed to me, came near enough to conveying Catullus's (very un-English) style, rhythms, and diction to an audience unfamiliar with the original.

No one in their right mind (except egomaniac translators and fundamentally lazy readers) would actually prefer a translation, of poetry in particular, to the original; translation must always remain, in the last resort, a second-best crutch, something recognized, as early as 1568, by Roger Ascham in *The Scholemaster.* (This was not always the case, nor is it generally accepted even today: I have briefly sketched the historical antecedents below, pp. 24–30.) For this reason my version is a bilingual: the more often the reader is tempted to shift attention from right to left, from translation to text, the better I shall have succeeded in my aim. It is Catullus, not his various impresarios, whether translators, editors, or literary critics, who in the last resort merits the reader's attention.

So, who is my reader? I would like to think that the way this volume has been set up will attract as wide a readership as possible: the intelligent Latinless lover of literature who wants to get closer to a famous, moving, but difficult, elusive, and at times highly disconcerting poet; the student, at whatever level, from high school to university graduate, who is coming to Catullus through a slow mastering of the Latin language; the teacher—again at whatever level—who is guiding the student's footsteps.

It is for all of the above that the glossary and explanatory notes have been written. For these I have, on innumerable occasions, gratefully raided the works of my predecessors, above all those of Ellis, Fordyce, Godwin, Kroll, Lee, Quinn, Thomson, and Wiseman. The notes operate at a number of levels: each reader will pick and choose at need, from simple identifications to brief discussions of critical, historical, or textual problems. I am firmly convinced that the hypothetical general reader is far less scared or put off by notes and references than too many suppose. What one doesn't need one simply ignores. The selective bibliography and references cover enough current scholarship both to give a fair idea of what's going on in the field, and to provide leads into further work for those with the urge to pursue the discussion in greater detail.

My own aim has been descriptive rather than prescriptive throughout, especially where literary theory is concerned, regarding which, as a matter of policy, I carefully refrained, while engaged on my actual translation, from bringing myself up to date. When, in preparation for writing the notes and glossary, I did so, I found, to my encouragement, very few points at which I needed to revise my text or interpretation. (Like others, I have used Mynors's Oxford Classical Text as a kind of benchmark, largely because of the few conjectures it concedes; my own brief *apparatus criticus,* except in a few special instances, is restricted to the fairly numerous cases in which I diverge from it, and which are noted ad loc.).

On the other hand, I met with one or two revealing surprises, of which the most striking was David Wray's expounding, *as a novelty,* in his admirable study *Catullus and the Poetics of Roman Manhood* (2001), the idea of Catullus's attitudes, assumptions, and behavior being predicated—with modern anthropological parallels—on his background in an aggressively public and masculinized Mediterranean society that has changed very little in essence over the millennia. Perhaps because I lived in that society myself for the best part of a decade, it never occurred to me to think of

Catullus in any other way, or to find his many divergences from modern middle-class moral attitudes a cause for concern, much less embarrassment. It is in that relaxed and uncensorious spirit that I invite the reader to study and enjoy an ancient poet who can be, by turns, passionate and hilariously obscene, as buoyantly witty as W. S. Gilbert in a Savoy opera libretto, as melancholy as Matthew Arnold in "Dover Beach," as mean as Wyndham Lewis in *The Apes of God*, and as eruditely allusive as T. S. Eliot in *The Waste Land*.

Austin
Athens · Molyvos
Ikaria · Iowa City
1992—2003

ACKNOWLEDGMENTS

Acknowledgments are due to *Arion* and *Southern Humanities Review*, in the pages of which earlier versions of some of these translations first appeared. I owe a very great deal to Nicholas Poburko, the managing editor of the former, and Dan Latimer, the joint editor of the latter, for constructive criticism, enthusiastic acceptance, and persistent encouragement over a project which at times seemed to be taking for ever and getting nowhere: to both of them my grateful thanks. Other translations were commissioned by Professor Thomas K. Hubbard for *Homosexuality in Greece and Rome: A Sourcebook of Basic Documents* (2003).

A substantial amount of the notes and glossary was written in the Blegen Library of the American School of Classical Studies in Athens, an institution that combines unrivalled resources with a magical ambience peculiarly supportive of every kind of scholarly endeavor regarding the ancient world: my thanks to the School and its director, Professor Stephen Tracy, for appointing me a Senior Visiting Research Associate for fall 2002.

To the Main Library of the University of Iowa, with its extraordinarily rich holdings in classics and the humanities, my debt of gratitude continues to accumulate yearly; I must also record, once again, my thanks to its quietly efficient and speedy Interlibrary Loan Service, which my sometimes exotic requests have never yet defeated.

At the eleventh hour—almost literally—I came across Marilyn Skinner's brilliant and delightful monograph, *Catullus in Verona* (2003), which not only sharpened my understanding of the elegiac *libellus* at innnumerable points, but also demonstrated, to my considerable surprise, that modern literary theory can be made both exciting and fun. Whenever I disagreed with her (and I often did) I still invariably learned a great deal from each encounter.

Professor Susan Treggiari read my entire manuscript with a sympathetic but keenly critical eye, made numerous illuminating suggestions—gratefully adopted—and, more times than I care to think, saved me from the consequences of my own ignorance or wrongheadedness. I am also indebted to the sensible recommendations of the Press's anonymous referee. But my greatest long-term debt, as always, is to my wife—a legitimate occupant of the Iowan classical academic nest in which I remain an adjunct cuckoo—who knows far more about Catullus, and Roman history and literature generally, than I do, and whose brains I have picked ruthlessly throughout this entire project.

ABBREVIATIONS

Aesch.	Aeschylus, 525–456 B.C.E.
AJPh	*American Journal of Philology*
AnA	*Anzeiger für Altertumswissenschaft*
Appian	Appianos of Alexandria, fl. early 2nd cent. C.E.
BC	*Bella Civilia*
Apul.	Apuleius of Madaura, 125–c. 175 C.E.
Apol.	*Apologia*
A&R	*Atene & Roma*
Aristoph.	Aristophanes, c. 460–c. 385 B.C.E.
Athen.	*Athenaeum*
Aul. Gell.	Aulus Gellius, c. 125–200 C.E.
BICS	*Bulletin of the Institute of Classical Studies*
Boll. Stud. Lat.	*Bollettino di Studi Latini*
CA	*Classical Antiquity*
CB	*Classical Bulletin*
Cic.	Marcus Tullius Cicero, 106–43 B.C.E.
Ad Fam.	*Epistulae ad Familiares*
Ad Q. Fratr.	*Epistulae ad Quintum Fratrem*
Att.	*Epistulae ad Atticum*
Brut.	*Brutus*
Orat.	*Orator*
Pro Cael.	*Pro Caelio*
Tusc.	*Tusculanae Disputationes*
Vat.	*In Vatinium*
Verr.	*In Verrem*
CIL	*Corpus Inscriptionum Latinarum* (1863–)
CJ	*Classical Journal*

CM	*Classica et Mediaevalia*
CPh	*Classical Philology*
CQ	*Classical Quarterly*
CW	*Classical World/Weekly*
Demetr.	Demetrius, ? fl. late Hellenistic period, literary critic
De Eloc.	*De Elocutione (On Style)*
Dion. Hal.	Dionysius of Halicarnassus, fl. late 1st cent. B.C.E.
Eur.	Euripides, c. 480–407/6 B.C.E.
Androm.	*Andromache*
Med.	*Medea*
GIF	*Giornale Italiano di Filologia*
G&R	*Greece & Rome*
GR&ByS	*Greek Roman & Byzantine Studies*
Hist.	*Historia*
Hom.	Homer(os), fl. ? 8th century B.C.E.
Il.	*Iliad*
Od.	*Odyssey*
Hor.	Quintus Horatius Flaccus, 65–8 B.C.E. [Horace]
AP	*Ars Poetica*
Ep.	*Epistulae*
Sat.	*Satires[Sermones]*
HSCPh	*Harvard Studies in Classical Philology*
Hyg.	Hyginus, ? fl. 2nd century C.E.
Astr.	*Astronomica*
JRS	*Journal of Roman Studies*
Just.	M. Junianius Justinus [Justin], ? 3rd century C.E., epitomator of Pompeius Trogus
LCM	*Liverpool Classical Monthly*
LEC	*Les Études Classiques*
Livy	Titus Livius, 59 B.C.E.–17 C.E.
L-P	E. Lobel, D. L. Page, *Poetarum Lesbiorum Fragmenta.* Oxford 1955.
Lucr.	T. Lucretius Carus, c. 94–?51 B.C.E.
Macrob.	Macrobius Ambrosius Theodosius, fl. 5th century C.E.
Sat.	*Saturnalia*
Mart.	Marcus Valerius Martialis, c. 40–c. 102 C.E.

MH	*Museum Helveticum*
Mnem.	*Mnemosyne*
Nepos	Cornelius Nepos, biographer, c. 110–24 B.C.E.
Att.	*Atticus*
Ovid	Publius Ovidius Naso, 43 B.C.E.–18 C.E.
AA	*Ars Amatoria*
Am.	*Amores*
Her.	*Heroides*
Tr.	*Tristia*
PCPhS	*Proceedings of the Cambridge Philological Society*
Petron.	T. Petronius Arbiter, d. 66 C.E.
Sat.	*Satiricon*
Philol.	*Philologus*
Pind.	Pindar(os) of Thebes, 518–c. 438 B.C.E.
Isthm.	*Isthmian Odes*
Nem.	*Nemean Odes*
Plat.	Plato, 429–347 B.C.E.
Rep.	*Republic*
Plaut.	T. Maccius Plautus, d. 184 B.C.E.
Poen.	*Poenulus*
Plin.J.	Gaius Plinius Caecilius Secundus, 61–114 C.E.
Ep.	*Epistulae*
Plin.S.	Gaius Plinius Secundus, 23–79 C.E.
NH	*Natural History*
Plut.	Plutarch (L. Mestrius Ploutarchos), c. 50–c. 120 C.E.
Brut.	*Life of Brutus*
Caes.	*Life of Caesar*
Cic.	*Life of Cicero*
Pomp.	*Life of Pompey*
Rom.	*Life of Romulus*
Sull.	*Life of Sulla*
Porph.	Porphyry of Tyre, 234–305 C.E.
Prop.	Sextus Propertius, b. c. 50 B.C.E.
Ps.-Virg. Cat.	Pseudo-Virgil, *Catalepton* (in Appendix Vergiliana)
Quintil.	Marcus Fabius Quintilianus, c. 35–c. 95 C.E.
Inst. Orat.	*Institutio Oratoria*
QUCC	*Quaderni Urbinati di Cultura Classica*

RhM	*Rheinisches Museum*
Sall.	Gaius Sallustius Crispus, 86–35 B.C.E.
Cat.	*Bellum Catilinae*
Sen.	L. Annaeus Seneca, c. 50 B.C.E.–c. 40 C.E.
Controv.	*Controversiae*
SLLRH	*Studies in Latin Literature and Roman History*
SO	*Symbolae Osloenses*
Soph.	Sophocles, 496/5–406 B.C.E.
Phil.	*Philoctetes*
Suet.	Gaius Suetonius Tranquillus, C.E. 70–c. 130
De Gramm.	*De Grammaticis*
Div. Jul.	*Divus Julius [Life of Caesar]*
Syll.Class.	*Syllecta Classica*
Tac.	P.? Cornelius Tacitus, 56–c. 118 C.E.
Ann.	*Annales*
Dial.	*Dialogus de Oratoribus*
TAPhA	*Transactions and Proceedings of the American Philological Association*
Virgil	P. Vergilius Maro, 70–19 B.C.E.
Aen.	*Aeneid*
WJA	*Würzburger Jahrbücher für die Altertumswissenschaft*
WS	*Wiener Studien*

INTRODUCTION

LIFE AND BACKGROUND

We know very little for certain about Catullus himself, and most of that has to be extrapolated from his own work, always a risky procedure, and nowadays with the full weight of critical opinion against it (though this is always mutable, and there are signs of change in the air). On the other hand, we know a great deal about the last century of the Roman Republic, in which his short but intense life was spent, and about many of the public figures, both literary and political, whom he counted among his friends and enemies. Like Byron, whom in ways he resembled, he moved in fashionable circles, was radical without being constructively political, and wrote poetry that gives the overwhelming impression of being generated by the public affairs, literary fashions, and aristocratic private scandals of the day.

How far all these were fictionalized in his poetry we shall never know, but that they were pure invention is unlikely in the extreme: what need to make up stories when there was so much splendid material to hand? Obviously we can't take what Catullus writes about Caesar or Mamurra at face value, any more than we can Byron's portraits of George III and Southey in "The Vision of Judgement," or Dryden's of James II and the Duke of Buckingham in "Absalom and Achitophel." Yet it would be hard to deny that in every case the poetic version contained more than a grain of truth. If we treat Catullus's character-gallery of friends, enemies, and lovers (as opposed to his excursions into myth) as creative variations on an underlying basic actuality, we probably won't be too far from the truth.

So, first, dates. St. Jerome records Catullus's birth in Verona under the year 87 B.C.E., and his death in Rome either at the age of thirty or in his thirtieth year, in 57. His age at death is likely to be at least roughly correct: Ovid (*Am.* 3.9.61) also refers to his youth in this connection, and, as Fordyce (1961, ix) reminds us, "the age at which a man died was often recorded on his tombstone." On the other hand,

Jerome's date of 57 is demonstrably mistaken: in poems 11, 12, 29, 45, 55, and 113, Catullus refers to known events which show conclusively that he was alive as late as 54 (Skinner 2003, xx and 186 n. 4; Thomson's arguments [1997, 3–5] for 53/2 remain speculative). Nepos (*Att.* 12.4) notes that Catullus was dead by thirty-two, but gives no indication of the exact date. This has encouraged speculation. The generally accepted, and convincing, solution to this problem is that Jerome or his source confused the year of L. Cornelius Cinna's first consulship (87) with that of his fourth (84), and that Catullus's life can be dated 84–54. This makes him a couple of years older than his great friend and fellow poet, Calvus, and—if we accept the identification of "Lesbia" offered by Apuleius (*Apol.* 10)—ten years younger than his *inamorata* Clodia Metelli. It also makes him the contemporary of Lucretius, Cornelius Gallus, and just about every major protagonist, cultural or political, of Roman society during the fraught years of the late Republic.

Many of these leading figures he knew personally, and we catch tantalizing glimpses of them in his verse. During the winter intervals between his Gallic campaigns, probably from 58/7 onwards, Caesar was a regular guest of Catullus's father in Verona (Suet. *Div. Jul.* 73); the relationship survived Catullus's acidulous attacks (see 29, 54, 57, 93, with notes). This hints at disagreements between father and son; also, unless he had released his son from paternal control by a fictitious bill of sale *(emancipatio)*, Catullus's father still held him *in potestate,* so that Catullus would have been living in Rome on an allowance (Skinner 2003, xxi). That the family entertained Caesar, and (it would appear from 31) owned much if not all of the Sirmio peninsula, indicates very substantial assets.

Catullus's friends and acquaintances are such as we would expect from his background. Asinius Pollio (12), some eight years younger than Catullus, was to become a distinguished Augustan historian, like Quintilius Varus the friend of Virgil and Horace, and the builder of Rome's first public library. Catullus's dedicatee Cornelius Nepos was a prominent biographer. M. Caelius Rufus, quite apart from his role in *l'affaire* Lesbia, was one of Cicero's more entertaining correspondents. L. Calpurnius Piso (28, 47) may have been the original owner of the House of the Papyri in Herculaneum, with its collection of texts by Philodemus. Catullus's close friend Licinius Calvus was a prominent lawyer as well as a poet. The poet's relationship to Cicero remains enigmatic, largely on account of 49: how ironic was he being there? The relentlessly savaged Mamurra (29, 41, 57, 94, 105, 114, 115), labelled by Catullus "The Prick," was Caesar's very efficient chief supply officer in Gaul. How well Catullus knew Pompey is uncertain, but they must have been at least on speaking terms. L. Manlius Torquatus, whose epithalamium (wedding hymn) Catullus wrote, belonged to one of the oldest and most distinguished families in Rome. The cast of characters in the Catullan corpus may be embellished, but is certainly not invented.

Catullus's own family was provincial and, in all likelihood, equestrian: upper-class but not really aristocratic, well off through business connections but not wealthy by Roman standards, and certainly not part of the intensely political group, with a consular tradition going back several centuries, to which Clodia and her siblings belonged. (She was always a cut above Catullus socially, and at least until 56 had far more political clout.) In 57 Catullus went to Bithynia on the staff of C. Memmius (see 10.28), visiting en route the grave of his prematurely deceased and much-loved brother in the Troad (65, 68a and b, 101). He returned from this attachment in the spring of 56. Shortly before his death (? 54) he seems to have been contemplating another such posting, either with Caesar in Gaul or with the millionaire Crassus on his ill-fated Eastern campaign. Bearing in mind the brief lives of both brothers, the hacking cough to which Catullus seems to have been a martyr (44), his references—not necessarily or exclusively metaphorical—to a chronic and unpleasant malaise (76, ?38), his febrile intensity (50), and, not least, his intense and debilitating erotic preoccupations, it seems distinctly possible that tuberculosis (one of the great silent scourges of antiquity) ran in the family and was the cause of his death.

The old Chinese curse, "May you live in interesting times," certainly applies to the thirty-odd years of Catullus's existence. His first conscious years witnessed the civil war in Italy that left Sulla as dictator. Spartacus's slave revolt, not to mention the trial of Verres for gross abuse of office in Sicily, took place during his early adolescence. He probably arrived in Rome (which as an adult he regarded as his true home, 68a.33–36) when he was a little over twenty (63 B.C.E.), about the time of the Catilinarian conspiracy suppressed by Cicero. Shortly afterwards came the scandal caused by Clodius Pulcher's gate-crashing the women-only rites of the Bona Dea in Caesar's town house—about the same time as Catullus first made the acquaintance of the gate-crasher's already notorious sister.

In 60 came the formation of the first alliance between Caesar, Pompey, and the millionaire Crassus, and the beginning both of the Civil War (in Asinius Pollio's reasonable view, Hor. *Odes* 2.1.1–2) and of Caesar's inexorable climb to near-absolute power, a progress watched by Catullus and his friends with mounting alarm. (And Catullus had the chance to observe the great man at close quarters: it was now that Caesar's winter visits to the poet's father in Verona took place.) While Caesar campaigned in Gaul, Clodius and Milo organized rival street-gangs in the capital: Catullus's intermittent love-affair with the gangster-tribune's sibling (and reputed bedfellow) could never be really clear of politics.

Despite his protestations, he may not have been entirely sorry to leave for Bithynia in 57; Caelius Rufus had become Clodia's chief lover the year before. However, he dumped her during Catullus's absence abroad. Catullus returned to Rome soon after Caelius's trial, notable for Cicero's lethal exposure of Clodia (who had instigated the charges largely out of pique) to public ridicule of the worst kind. Catullus's own attitude to her seems to have vacillated. The year of his death saw renewed, violent rioting in Rome. One way and another, Britain or Syria may well have looked preferable at the time. *Dis aliter visum:* the gods and, probably, illness decided otherwise. Mulroy's suggestion (2002, xxvii) that Caesar could have had Catullus done away with makes no sense; had this happened, it would have been a scandal more notorious than Ovid's subsequent exile, and would have furnished Caesar's many enemies with some highly damaging propaganda against him, of which there is no trace.

LESBIA/CLODIA

Apuleius (*Apol.* 10) professed to identify, not only Catullus's "Lesbia," but also several other cryptonymic *inamorate* of the Augustan elegists (e.g., the "Cynthia" of Propertius). Where he obtained this information (perhaps from the literary section of Suetonius's *De Viris Illustribus*) is unknown. He claimed that Lesbia's real name was Clodia, but unfortunately failed to say which Clodia. It might, however, be argued that in the context this implied an obvious identification, much as the mention of Salamis in connection with the Greco-Persian Wars does not need a caveat explaining that the reference is not to the city on Cyprus. Certainly this is how it has been taken by most scholars from the Renaissance onwards: the assumption is that Catullus's lover was that notorious aristocratic lady Clodia Metelli, married until 59 to her cousin Q. Metellus Celer (see glossary s.v. Caecilius III), the target of Cicero's scathing and often ribald invective in his speech for Caelius. The cumulative evidence for this identification is in fact a good deal solider than that for many other firmly held beliefs about the ancient world.

The form "Clodia" rather than "Claudia" at once points to Clodia Metelli and her two sisters, who, when their firebrand brother P. Clodius Pulcher was trying to get himself adopted into a plebeian *gens*, likewise "went plebeian" by adopting the "populist" spelling of the family name. (Clodia Metelli was engaged in what Cicero termed a "civil war" against her conservative husband over this move: naturally Metellus opposed it [Cic. *Att.* 2.1.4–5].) The identity of "Lesbius" with Clodius (79 and note), and hence of "Lesbia" with Clodia, is virtually certain. From

68b.145–46, 83, and elsewhere we know that "Lesbia" was still married and living with her husband when her affair with Catullus began. Clodia Metelli's two sisters do not fit the bill: L. Lucullus had divorced one (for adultery) as early as 66/5; Q. Marcius Rex, the husband of the other (known as Tertia, and thus the youngest of the three) was dead before 61.

Moreover, as Quinn says (1972, 135), "the Clodia painted by Cicero in his speech in defence of Caelius is Lesbia to the life." Catullus himself, in that savagely bitter attack, 58 (one of several poems where Caelius is the addressee), speaks of "*our* Lesbia" *(Lesbia nostra)*, the woman who by then had been the lover of both, abandoning one only to be herself discarded by the other. (It is, incidentally, surprising—as Quinn [1972, 142–43] noted—how often scholars have, consciously or unconsciously, assumed, with middle-class romantic *pudeur*, that even a high-living aristocrat like Clodia would only indulge in *one relationship at a time*, that Caelius "replaced" Catullus, or vice versa, even though Catullus himself hints clearly enough at the simultaneity of her affairs, hoping, when depressed, for no more than to lead the pack: 68b.135ff.) She was one of the many things they had in common: his relationship with Caelius was an *odi et amo* one too. And Caelius Rufus did (often an argument against the identification of the character in 69) suffer from gout—in antiquity, because of wine drunk from lead-lined containers, a disease just as liable to affect young men as old (Mulroy 2002, xiv).

The development of a thesis rejecting the identification of Lesbia as Clodia Metelli has been, I suspect, primarily encouraged by attacks on the "biographical fallacy," and by a general determination—whether via "persona theory" (all apparent real-life details to be dismissed as fictional projections involving rhetorical topoi) or through amassing historical, and in particular chronological, objections—to relegate the declared love-life of Roman poets to the safer area of the literary imagination. The first of these techniques can safely be left for readers to adjust with the aid of common sense: the element of truth in it relates to the obvious and well-known fact that any writer, in any age, will embellish and fantasize on the basis of experience, and that this applies to Rome as much as any other society. Further, one of the instantly observable phenomena of Greek and Roman culture is that original invention, out of whole cloth as it were, in both cases came late and with difficulty. The tendency was always—certainly was still in Catullus's day—to work from life. A great deal—too much, I would argue—has been made of Catullus's declaration, in 16, that his poems (daring) bear no relation to his life (simon-pure). He was being attacked for his (often discernible) "feminine" qualities, and was defending himself, rather self-consciously, by making a loud macho noise in the best aggressive male tradition, determined to pose as a bigger hotshot penetrator than any of them. This strikes me as a rather weak platform on which to build a literary theory.

I am not impressed by the thesis, based on Catullus's metrical treatment of the first two syllables of the hendecasyllabic line (first adumbrated by Skutsch [1969], and well set out by Lee [1990, xxi–xxii]), according to which Catullus started by keeping to a strict spondaic base, but gradually began to admit trochaic and iambic bases as he went on. This depends on the fact that in 2–26 we find only four such resolutions—as many as in the ten lines of 1, the late dedication to Nepos—but in 28–60 no fewer than sixty-three. The trouble here, of course, is that the poems are in no sort of chronological order. Inevitably, efforts have been made to prove the theory by redating some of them to accommodate it, a circular argument which I find less than persuasive. There is also the fact that no poem can *irrefutably* be dated, on internal evidence, earlier than 56, while the fourteen which *are* securely datable all fall within the short period 56–54. Wiseman would like to down-date Catullus's relationship with Lesbia to that period also, which would mean discarding the identification of Lesbia as Clodia Metelli. I suspect this to be one of the theory's main attractions. But as Mulroy has demonstrated (2002, xiv–xvii), Wiseman's claim that 36 (datable to a point after Catullus's return from Bithynia in 56) proves his affair to have begun only in that year doesn't make sense. If "Lesbia" is making a vow in gratitude for Catullus's safe return from abroad, the clear implication is that the relationship had indeed begun *before* his departure.

I therefore accept, in broad outline, what is in fact the old and traditional account of Catullus's famous, intense, and (despite its brief moments of happiness) essentially ill-starred infatuation, together with its long-accepted chronology (with some variations, Schwabe's version [1862, 358–61]; for recent criticisms and corrections see Holzberg 2002, 19–21; Skinner 2003, xix–xxii). His *inamorata* was Clodia, second (?) daughter of Appius Claudius Pulcher, the wife of Q. Metellus Celer. They probably met for the first time in 62/1, during her husband's tour of duty as propraetor of Cisalpine Gaul. Clodia was then about thirty-three. We do not know how long she and Metellus had been married, but it may have been as much as fifteen years (her one child, her daughter Metella, could by then have been nearly nubile). Catullus was probably twenty-two or twenty-three—a good decade younger. Where did the meeting take place? Verona is a possibility. Even if governors' wives normally stayed in Rome, a woman like Clodia made her own rules, and as Caesar later stayed with Catullus's father when *en poste*, it is very likely that Metellus did so too.

On the other hand, we know from Cicero's correspondence that Clodia was in Rome for at least part of her husband's absence in the north: partly because of the somewhat scandalous reputation she was acquiring, but more specifically because Cicero himself was cultivating her as a useful political go-between. Metellus had taken to Gaul the army allotted to Cicero after his consulship in 63. His brother, Q. Metellus Nepos, was also making trouble for Cicero, who regularly wrote and visited Clodia at this time. (He also appealed to Pompey's wife Mucia.) We know that his main aim was to get Nepos off his back (Cic. *Fam.* 5.2.6), but he probably also found her a valuable source of political gossip. Amusingly, by the time Plutarch came to write his *Life* of Cicero, their relationship had been fantasized into a ploy by Clodia to marry the orator, with Cicero's wife Terentia worried by the frequent visits, and Cicero being driven in self-defense to turn against Clodius at the time of his trial in 61. Since Cicero was not only a good deal more *arriviste* than Catullus, but also a middle-class prude with a professed lack of interest in sex (Wiseman 1985, 43–44), this is improbable, to say the least. But the circumstances make it more than possible that Catullus's own relationship with Clodia began in Rome during this period, before Metellus's return to the capital late in 61. This would make sense of knowing epigrams such as 83 and 92.

It was in 59, as we have seen—nearly two years later—that Caelius made his own play for Clodia's favors. At some point during this period Catullus was also prostrated by the death of his brother, with which neglect by his lover seems in some odd psychological way to have become confused. In 57 he left for Bithynia, returning soon after Caelius's trial in 56 to a temporary reunion solicited (107, 109) by the now much-ridiculed and politically ineffectual (though still wealthy) Clodia. Two years later, after further bitter recriminations (e.g., 72, 75), the lady was forty and the poet was dead. We are left with the memory of a passionate dancer, a brilliant-eyed, intellectually dazzling *femme fatale*, who, if Caelius can be believed—and the remark does have the ring of truth about it—may have been sophisticatedly seductive in the salon, but was a provincial prude in bed (Quintil. 8.6.52). Though the tradition concerning her was, we need not doubt, exaggerated and distorted for political and personal ends, we are not therefore entitled to assume, as some have done, that it amounted to nothing but a collection of stale and stereotyped literary topoi with no basis in reality.

This should not be interpreted as meaning that I have not taken note of, and (I hope) made due allowance for what Maria Wyke well summarizes as the recent tendency to draw attention to "Lesbia's depiction in Catullan poetry as an instance of the instability of Roman concepts of femininity," as well as to "the troubled masculinity of the authorial narrator and its grounding in late republican culture." What we have here are indeed "not women but representations shaped by . . . most frequently, literary texts" (Wyke 2002, 2–3, 36). True enough; but also true as regards just about everything and everybody, male or female, retrieved for our scrutiny from the ancient world. There are no special exceptions.

One last note about the social mores of the case, on which Lyne (1980, chap. 1) is fundamental. By the time of the late Republic, theory and practice, as regards both marriage and extra-marital affairs, had become widely divergent, a problem that was soon to exercise Augustus and his advisers, to Ovid's ultimate discomfort. Theory, based on the ancient *mos maiorum*, the moral code of a nation of simple landown-ing farmers, regarded a virtuous wife as one who "kept house and span wool" *(domum seruauit, lanam fecit)*, whose skirt covered her ankles, and who showed noth-ing but her face in public. But—again in theory—Roman law allowed potentially for equality between husband and wife. The relationship, in law, was secular. Di-vorce, technically, was easy. A wife retained her property—that famous town house on the Palatine belonged to Clodia, not Metellus—and was not required to take her husband's name. In practice, however, marriage among upper-class, and especially among political, families tended to be dynastic, arranged by parental fiat, often when the principals were still children. Political and economic advantage, not passion, formed its guiding principle. Divorce was chiefly handy for the cynical rearrange-ment of alliances.

Inevitably, this system tended to promote the familiar double standard by which young men sought an outlet for their more unruly passions—and often for intellec-tual or artistic companionship as well—not in the home (though domestic slaves were always available there), but from the world of call-girls and *demi-mondaines* which, as always, was not slow to spring up in response to a steady demand. At the lowest level, Marcus Cato (second century B.C.E.) approved of youths working off their urges legitimately (but not, of course, too often: moderation in all things) by visits to the local whorehouse (Porph. and Ps.-Acron on Hor. *Sat.* 1.2.31–32). Eastern cam-paigns from then on imported exotic attractions in the form of Greek-educated mu-sicians, dancers, and high-class literary call-girls whose sexual favors—at a price—were packaged with cultural trimmings, and who often entered into long-term relationships with their clients: Sulla's Nicopolis and Pompey's Flora are nice cases in point (Plut. *Sull.* 2.4, *Pomp.* 2.3–4). They could also wield political power; Ci-cero gives a startling account of one Chelidon's activities during Verres' praetor-ship (Cic. *1 Verr.* 104, 135ff.).

How did the legitimate wife, the respectable *materfamilias*, respond to all this? At first, clearly, by taking steps to differentiate herself as far as possible from the socially disreputable *fille de joie* who met those of her husband's demands that she herself had been brought up to regard as not falling within a decent woman's province. Hence the whorehouse. But when the competition became more sophisticated and intelligent, from the late second century B.C.E. onwards, we can see a very different reaction developing. "As the Hellenizing life of pleasure grew and prospered, some ladies started to want their cut" (Lyne 1980, 13). They became witty and well read; they discovered that they, too, had sexual instincts and needs. When Clodia was in her late teens she had the remarkable example of Sempronia to encourage her. In 77 this scion of the Gracchi, and wife of the consul D. Iunius Brutus, had a reputation as an elegant and learned conversationalist, who could compose poetry as well as discuss it, was a skilled lyre-player and danced, as Sallust put it, "more elegantly than was necessary for a virtuous woman" (Sall. *Cat.* 25). Anything the *demi-mondaines* could do, she could do better. This included sex. She wanted so much of it, Sallust says, that she approached men more often than they did her. The tradition of the smart, adulterous wife was well established by the time Clodia entered the arena.

THE LITERARY CONTEXT

A generation after Catullus, Horace addressed a long literary epistle (*Epist.* 2.1) to Augustus, of which probably the best-remembered apothegm is "Captive Greece captured her fierce conqueror, and brought the arts to rustic Latium" *(Graecia capta ferum uictorem cepit et artis / intulit agresti Latio)*. Elsewhere (*AP* 268–69) he advises the would-be poet to study Greek models day and night. As he makes clear by demeaning it, a strong native mid-Italic tradition in fact already existed: hymns, possibly lays, and especially satire, *ad hominem*, biting, often obscene (*Epist.* 2.1.86–89, 145–55). Indeed, it was not till after the Punic wars, as he admits (i.e., about the mid-second century B.C.E.), that Rome began to take note of "what Sophocles and Thespis and Aeschylus could contribute" (162–63)—about the same time as Greek imports of another sort (see the previous section) were likewise beginning to make inroads on traditional Roman values. But it was Greece, he insists, that primarily dictated both genre and style to subsequent Latin literature. Ennius became the "second Homer" (50ff.), while Livius Andronicus translated the *Odyssey* into Roman Saturnians, lines scoffed at by Horace (158–60) and defined by stress rather than metre: "the King was in his countinghouse, counting out his money" is a rough equivalent. Both Ennius and Livius tried their hands at plays, as did Accius and Pacuvius. Despite the Hellenic inspiration, what emerged tended towards crude nationalistic propaganda. Naevius wrote—again in Saturnians—an epic, the *Carmen Belli Poenici*, on the First Punic War (264–241 B.C.E.). Ennius's *Annales*, in hexameters, annexed the Trojan War as a charter myth for the origins of the Roman people, thus creating a model for Virgil. Livius's *Odyssey* Romanized its original in many ways, not least in substituting local Latin deities for Homer's Greek ones, an innovation with a long and regrettable history. (It was still going strong, along with the general Latinization of Greek names, as recently as the nineteenth century.) These early literary efforts were already beginning to cause concern before Horace noted how embarrassing in many ways they were to the more sophisticated public of his day.

Nothing, it is safe to say, did more to bring about the fundamental changes in taste which Horace's attitude assumes than the group of poets now known, very loosely, as the Neoterics, who lived and wrote in the mid-first century B.C.E., during the final years of the Republic, and whose best-known and most representative members were perhaps Licinius Calvus (14, 50, 53, 96), Helvius Cinna (10, 95, 113), and Catullus himself. Their reaction to the tradition, sketched above, which they had inherited was a complex one. To begin with, they were all highly erudite and well read —not for nothing did Catullus attract the epithet *doctus*—and virtually bilingual in Greek. In one area, that of satirical epigram, they looked back to their own, old, outspoken native tradition, sharpening it with stylish Greek invective (ψόγος) borrowed from the iambographer Hipponax and his successors. For the most part, however, their Greek models were neither archaic nor classical, but rather the scholar-poets of the Hellenistic mid-third century B.C.E., above all Callimachus. It was from them that the Neoterics acquired their learned allusiveness; their distaste for long, sprawling, pompous and cliché-ridden poetry (epic in particular, which they modified into the shorter, offbeat version known to us as the epyllion, of which 64 is a splendid example); their obsession with brevity, originality, and aptness of phrase; their personal rather than public preoccupation; and their reexamination of traditional myths for unusual (and often pathological or aberrant sexual) features hitherto ignored, in particular as these related to the origins or causes *(aitia)* of traditional customs and practices.

In so doing they also took over some of the social elements implicit in this Hellenistic revolution, of course. It is a nice question to what extent they did so consciously, and how far, if at all, the conditions motivating Ptolemaic court poets— in particular the reversion to authoritarian government, and the disillusion with the heroic ethos generated by an increasing reliance on mercenaries for the conduct of wars—applied to these upper-class Roman intellectuals two centuries later, as they watched the old Republican senatorial regime sliding relentlessly towards a showdown between rival warlords backed by what were becoming, in effect, private armies. It is in this light that we need to consider such poems of Catullus's as 29, 52, 54, 57, or 93—while at the same time always bearing in mind that, even during the worst of public events, life goes on, often cheerfully enough despite everything, as the greater part of Catullus's collection makes abundantly clear. (Theophrastus's *Characters*, so bubbling over with the minutiae of Athenian daily life and business, was written c. 319, when the city was enduring a Macedonian occupation.) Gossip, dinner parties, love-affairs, literary rivalries, libellous *feuilletons*, passionate moments of self-dramatization: all are here. It is one of Catullus's great skills to make his reader, almost without realizing it, an invisible eavesdropper on this intensely alive social picture of a mere two millennia ago.

It was their older contemporary Cicero who described this group of young poets as "Neoterics" (οἱ νεώτεροι, "the younger ones" or "the innovators"), or "the new poets" *(poetae noui)*. He did not mean the label as a compliment (*Orat.* 161; *Tusc.* 3.45): certainly they never so described themselves. Clearly he thought of them as in some sense a school or a movement (Lyne 1978, 167–68). In 50 he sent Atticus a parody of a Neoteric hexameter, with its heavy spondaic fifth foot (see below, p. 40) involving an obscure quadrisyllabic name (*Att.* 7.2.1). He also referred slightingly to these "praise-singers of Euphorion" for writing off Ennius. Euphorion was a slightly later contemporary of Callimachus, with the same interest in recherché material and stylistic innovation (affected obscurity included), who strongly influenced Catullus's friend Cinna, as the latter's epyllion *Smyrna* suggests (95, with notes). Here was the Alexandrian answer to old-style epic, and Catullus's own *Marriage of Peleus and Thetis* (64, with notes), tells an identical story. It is worth noting that as far as genre and subject matter went, the Neoterics' Alexandrianism was largely confined to the epyllion, or mini-epic, and related forms (i.e., in Catullus's work, essentially the long poems, 61–66 and 68). But the influence of Callimachus (the one such Hellenistic mentor whom Catullus acknowledges by name) in matters of style, diction, erudite allusiveness, and structure (e.g., sophisticated ring composition), is apparent throughout Catullus's work, and clearly also permeated that of his friends, as even their few surviving fragments suggest.

In about 64, Cinna bought the Greek poet Parthenios of Nicaea, who had been captured and enslaved during the Third Mithridatic War, made him his family tutor, and freed him in honor of his formidable literary achievements. (He subsequently became Virgil's Greek tutor [Macrob. *Sat.* 5.17.18].) Parthenios must have been a powerful influence on the group, though in what precise way is still debated. Certainly he was a Callimachean; he also owed something to Euphorion. It is more than likely that he was directly responsible for importing the collected works of both poets to Rome. Perhaps more important for our assessment of Catullus, he took a strong interest in something which left Callimachus himself completely cold (Clausen 1982, 186–87): the celebration of heterosexual love. It is often claimed for Catullus that his intensely personal and uncomfortably acute cycle of poems on and to Lesbia are without precedent in the history of ancient literature. If we possessed Parthenios's three-book hexameter *Encomium* on his wife Arete (as we do his prose summaries of a wide range of exotic love stories culled from past literature, the *Erotika Pathemata*), that judgment might well need modification.

The Lesbia cycle is a natural consequence, if not a direct product, of a steadily more self-regarding and psychologically analytical trend in ancient literature, which we can see developing as early as Euripides, and which acquires nearly pathological dimensions at times among the Alexandrians. A direct line runs from Phaedra and Medea to Lesbia; our trouble lies in lacking too many of the intervening links. This is not to deny for one moment Catullus's original brilliance, merely to try and set it in historical context. Those somewhat clumsy amatory epigrams—plainly Hellenistic in derivation—written a generation or two before the Neoterics by poetasters such as Lutatius Catulus (consul in 102), or the lyric erotica of Laevius (in a variety of metres, with sometimes bizarrely innovative diction), both reveal the on-going influence of Alexandria—exercised through anthologies of epigram such as the *Garland* of Meleager no less than by Callimachus and his epigoni—and demonstrate, by contrast, the measure of Catullus's independent genius in transmuting such material.

It is also surely not a coincidence that Catullus himself and a number of his acquaintances, Cinna, Cornelius Nepos, Furius, Valerius Cato among others, were (like Virgil after them), though Roman citizens—and thus entitled to an equestrian or even a senatorial career—still natives of Cisalpine Gaul, "that remote, self-conscious, and highly developed province" (Fordyce 1961, xix) in what is now northern Italy: a region close enough to Rome to participate in its cultural traditions, yet distant enough to have its own native vocabulary and customs (some of Catullus's words, most famously *basium* for "a kiss," were Cisalpine imports), and to bring a robustly independent attitude to urban literary fashions. Verona in particular, at the junction of two important trade routes, had grown to great prosperity, and had attracted an infusion of highly placed settlers from the south (it is possible that Catullus's family was amongst them). Such immigrants were Janus-like: they looked north for wealth, south for political and social advancement (Wiseman 1985, 108ff.; Thomson 1997, 11), and tended to make their own rules. Skinner (2003, xii) suggests, persuasively, a divisive polarity between Catullus's Roman and Cisalpine selves, with Rome embodying all his poetic individualism, while Verona stood for family responsibilities and local tradition. On Catullus's "sense that the responsibilities of family and communal life were matters to be taken seriously," see also Wiseman (1987, 370).

But this independence also is in evidence when we look at the way Catullus and his Neoteric friends handled the Alexandrian, and more specifically the Callimachean, tradition which they used to mark themselves off from the post-Ennian traditionalists. The Greek hendecasyllabic line (cf. below, p. 33) was refashioned, in Catullus's and, later, Martial's hands, into a wonderful instrument for light, conversational *vers d'occasion*, reflecting to an uncanny degree the rhythms and casual oral rhetoric of Italian speech. Even in an erudite display of counter-epic principles such as 64, Catullus still remains everywhere in debt to the phraseology, verbal usages, and stylistic habits (such as alliteration) of the tradition he is so aggressively rejecting (cf. Fordyce 1961, xxi): what he concentrates on is the avoidance, at all costs, of long-windedness, heroic platitudes, and predictable mythic narrative. Homer (as Callimachus had seen) was supreme and inimitable; but the Homeric age had long ago vanished, and what had to be eradicated were the feeble and anachronistic efforts of Homer's latter-day imitators to revive it artificially.

The process of assimilation and recreation was a complex one, and I have here only touched on some of its salient points. To explore it further, and get a sense of an ancient literary movement in action, complete with feuds, manifestos, and polemic, the reader should turn to Catullus's own poems, in all their kaleidoscopic variety, aided by the material available in the glossary and explanatory notes. Beyond these, again, lies the world of scholarship and literary theory, both of which have been busy with Catullus's slim volume of poetry at least since the Renaissance, and which I have made accessible, via the bibliography, to anyone eager to pursue this aspect of the Catullan phenomenon further. What follows in the next section is the briefest possible account of Catullus's textual transmission, and the vicissitudes of interpretation he has undergone down the centuries—what Germans pithily label *Rezeptionsgeschichte*—for those who lack the time or inclination to embark on what can seem an endless, and often maddening, quest: "that imbroglio of problems," as Sir Ronald Syme once wrote (*C&M* 17 [1956], 131, cited by Quinn 1970, xii), "where dogma and ingenuity have their habitation, where argument moves in circles, and no new passage is in or out."

THE TEXT: ARRANGEMENT AND TRANSMISSION

In the period immediately following his death, Catullus's literary impact was enormous, and it is clear that he and Calvus (with whom he is almost invariably bracketed by ancient writers) were regarded as the best of the Neoterics (Fordyce 1961, xxii ff.; for those with Latin, Wiseman 1985, 246–62 offers an exhaustive appendix of all references to Catullus in ancient authors). Both Virgil and Horace show his influence again and again. Virgil picks up lines and uses them with only minimal changes: a nice example is Ariadne's dream of a happy marriage at 64.141—*sed conubia laeta, sed optatos hymenaeos*—which reappears in the *Aeneid* (4.316) as part of Dido's tirade, in not dissimilar circumstances, addressed to the departing Aeneas: *per conubia nostra, per inceptos hymenaeos*. Horace alludes contemptuously (*Sat.* 1.10.18–19) to "the ape whose only achievement is parroting Calvus and Catullus," but nevertheless proves adept at the game himself: his "sweetly laughing" *(dulce ridentem)* Lalage (*Odes* 1.22.23) comes straight from Catullus's Lesbia (51.5). Our great predecessors, as T. S. Eliot well knew, help those who help themselves. The surest mark of familiarity is parody: someone up in the Province seized on 4, Catullus's tribute to his cutter, and turned it into a very funny take-off (Ps.-Virg. *Cat.* 10) attacking an ex-muleteer with pretensions.

By the first century C.E., the chief interest in Catullus's poetry had become concentrated on the "polymetric" group, in particular on his light and witty hendecasyllables, though for Quintilian it was 84 and the over-aspirated Arrius which won most admiration (a *nobile epigramma*, he called it, *Inst. Orat.* 1.5.20). Martial, whose ideal was to rank second after Catullus (7.99, 10.78.14–16), and for whom Verona owed as much to Catullus as Mantua did to Virgil (14.195: no mean tribute), especially fancied 2, 3, 5, and 7, the kiss and sparrow poems, thus setting a fashion that is still with us today. "Give me kisses," he said, "but let them be Catullan: / If they turn out as many as he reckoned / I'll present you with the *Sparrow* of Catullus" (11.6.14–16). The double entendre is clear: was it borrowed? (see note to 2). Certainly Martial used Catullus as a precedent for outspokenness (1 *epist* 10–13). By way of contrast, he imposed a stricter spondaic rule (cf. p. 33) on the opening foot of the hendecasyllabic line. Indeed the elder Pliny, in the dedicatory epistle of his *Natural History* to Vespasian, citing 1.3–4 of Catullus's own dedication to Nepos, actually rearranged the wording of line 3 (writing *nugas esse aliquid meas putare* rather than *meas esse aliquid putare nugas*), in order, as he put it, to avoid the "somewhat harsh" *(duriusculum)* Catullan usage.

This popularity was not to last. It persisted into the second century—it was, of course, Apuleius to whom we owe the identification of Lesbia as Clodia Metelli—but thereafter the evidence rapidly dries up. Catullus was not, for obvious reasons, a school author; the "thirty headmasters and headmistresses" on whose solemn advice Fordyce's publishers persuaded him to omit no fewer than thirty-two poems in 1961 (Thomson 1997, 59 n. 79) can be seen as the epigoni of a well-established tradition. Even as early as Aulus Gellius's lifetime (born c. 125 C.E.), Catullus's text was in difficulties (Aul. Gell. 6.20.6 on 27.4; cf. Fordyce 1961, 158–59; Holford-Strevens 1988, 138). We are witnessing here the early stages of that disintegrating process so brilliantly described by Tom Stoppard in *The Invention of Love* (24–25):

> [A]nyone with a secretary knows that what Catullus really wrote was already corrupt by the time it was copied twice, which was about the time of the first Roman invasion of Britain: and the earliest copy that has come down to *us* was written about 1,500 years after that. Think of all those secretaries!—corruption breeding corruption from papyrus to papyrus, and from the last disintegrating scrolls to the first new-fangled parchment books, with a thousand years of copying-out still to come, running the gauntlet of changing forms of script and spelling, and absence of punctuation—not to mention mildew and rats and fire and flood and Christian disapproval to the brink of extinction as what Catullus really wrote passed from scribe to scribe, this one drunk, that one sleepy, another without scruple, and of those sober, wide-awake and scrupulous, some ignorant of Latin and some, even worse, fancying themselves better Latinists than Catullus—until!—finally and at long last—mangled and tattered like a dog that has fought its way home, there falls across the threshold of the Italian Renaissance the sole surviving witness to thirty generations of carelessness and stupidity: the *Verona Codex* of Catullus; which was almost immediately lost again, but not before being copied with one last opportunity for error. And there you have the foundation of the poems of Catullus as they went to the printer for the first time, in Venice 400 years ago.

There are occasional sightings during the Dark Ages. Catullus's epithalamium 62 shows up in a ninth century anthology, the *Codex Thuaneus (T)*, and thus becomes our oldest surviving text. About the same time, there are echoes of Catullus in verses by a monk of Brescia, Hildemar. A century later, in 965, Bishop Rather of Verona refers to his perusal of the "previously unread Catullus" (Fordyce 1961, xxvi). It has been conjectured that this was the one manuscript (now known as *V*, the *Codex Veronensis*) which, unknown for the next three hundred years, mysteriously and briefly, resurfaced c. 1290, again in Verona (under a barrel, if we can trust an epigram attached to the text) , only to be lost again, seemingly for ever, but not before a copy, *A*, had been made of it. *A*, too, was lost; but it was copied twice before vanishing, and one of these copies, *O*, the *Codex Oxoniensis* or "Oxford MS," made c. 1370, survives in the Bodleian Library at Oxford. The second copy, *X*, owned by

Petrarch and also now lost, was itself copied twice. These copies—G, the *Codex Sangermanensis* of 1375, and R, the *Codex Vaticanus Ottobonianus*, also fourteenth century—survive, and with O form the basis of our modern texts. (*T* and *V* are close enough to posit a common source.) Stoppard's rhetorical strictures are all too well justified; Goold (1989, 11) calculated that *V* contained at least a thousand scribal errors. But he also pays an amply justified tribute to the "enthusiasm and genius" of Italian Renaissance scholarship, which eliminated nearly seven hundred of them. By today, as he says, "we are approaching the limit of what we can hope to accomplish" (13). But as he admits, "in the matter of interpretation there is no end."

This is particularly true when we come to consider the vexed problem of the poems' ordering and arrangement. What we have, in our surviving manuscripts, is a rough categorization by metre and genre: (a) the "polymetrics," 1–60; (b) the somewhat mixed bag of the long poems 61–68, though 65–68 are in elegiacs, and must (see below) belong rather with (c), the elegies and epigrams (69–116). Such an arrangement is characteristic of the methods employed by Hellenistic scholars in Alexandria; it also reminds us of the standard edition of the satirist Lucilius in antiquity (Rudd 1986, 82), similarly arranged by metre and also, as it happens, in three books (papyrus rolls). It certainly dislocates anything we know about the chronology of individual poems. Was this deliberate or accidental? Above all, to what extent, if at all, does the sequence as it has come down to us represent Catullus's own choice? He died young: did he anticipate his own death? If, as I believe (above, p. 3), he was consumptive, and knew it, nevertheless in the last year of his life he would seem to have been planning another semi-official trip abroad as part of a governor's staff (see note to 11), and may well have died suddenly and unexpectedly, leaving much unfinished business behind. (This would cast doubts on Skinner's thesis [2003, xiii] that the elegiac *libellus* might have been "released to the public after Catullus's return to Verona, as a valedictory to his public and a retrospective pronouncement upon his completed body of work.") The dedicatory verses to Cornelius Nepos (1) would appear—though this has been challenged—to apply to the polymetric collection only (1–60), known in antiquity as "Catullus's *Passer* [Sparrow]" (Mart. 4.14.13–14; Skinner 1981), but we cannot even be certain that it included all of them; some were *vers d'occasion* which could have been assembled by a posthumous editor, and 58b, similarly, looks very much like an unfinished scrap harvested from the poet's papers after his death.

As Wray (2001, 53) rightly says, this "Catullan question" is "still with us and not likely to disappear soon." Earlier advocates of overall authorial disposition include that major dogmatist Wilamowitz (Quinn 1972, 284 n. 12); recent supporters range from Wiseman (1969, revised 1979) by way of Quinn (1972), Most (1981), Skinner (1988), Lee (1990), Martin (1992) to Dettmer (1997), whose study is by far the most thoroughgoing and elaborate to date. The most commonly advanced argument involves perceived significant correspondence (what German scholars so vividly term *Einklang*) between anything from individual words to lines, themes, concepts, whole poems, or even groups of poems, the symmetry being created by either ring composition or chiasmus (earlier and later elements balanced in the first, interlocking like an *X* in the second). A variant on this is the "triplet argument," noting cases where a pair of poems consonant in tone sandwich a violently contrasting one (see Jocelyn 1999 on 10–12 for a striking example), the argument being that only the poet himself could or would make such an arrangement. There is also the metrical argument referred to above (see p. 6), according to which Catullus relaxed his strictness over the first foot of his hendecasyllables as he went on, so that 27–58 and 1 are demonstrably later than 2–26. Quinn (1972, 16) even gets round the presence of evident fragments in the corpus by the highly modernist argument that the "illusion of work unfinished" could have been deliberate.

None of these claims, most of which remain, by the nature of the evidence, necessarily subjective, can be regarded as irrefutable. On the other hand, they have cumulatively succeeded in establishing the sensible position that Catullus was responsible for organizing at least *some* of his collected work before his death. Perhaps their most useful achievement is to make us consider (Skinner 2003, xxvi) "the visual and tactile experience of manipulating an ancient scroll and its effect upon cognitive apprehension of the emerging content." But how far this "would have created and sustained a linear dimension against which temporal reversions and fluctuations played in counterpoint" is debatable. Few would now argue (I certainly would not) for a posthumous editor sorting out an inchoate mass of material virtually from scratch. What is more, such evidence as there is points clearly to the polymetric group, 1–60, as most unambiguously displaying signs of authorial control and pattern making. As Thomson shrewdly remarks (1997, 6), the further one proceeds beyond this point, the less persuasive the theories become (see, e.g., Martin 1992, 36, for the supposed chiastic symmetry of 61–68) , inducing in the reader a "feeling of *decrescendo*," ending, for some, in pure chaos. The more elaborate patterns invariably demand some rearrangement or textual emendation; they also (as Quinn 1972, 9 conceded) "require an interest in puzzle-solving that no sensible poet expects of his readers." Thus what has emerged is a counter-theory claiming no more than partial arrangement by Catullus himself (generally restricted to all or some of the polymetrics), plus posthumous editorial work. Ellis (1876, 1–3) and Wheeler in the first of his Sather Lectures (1934, 4–32) were followed by (among others) Fordyce (1961, 409–10), Giardina (1974), Clausen (1976 and 1982, 193–97), Skinner (1981), Hubbard (1983), Goold (1989) and Thomson (1997, 6–11). With this group I find myself in substantial agreement. The Alexandrian aesthetic notion of *poikilia*, seemingly haphazard *variatio*, can only explain just so much.

Among the more substantial and useful arguments raised, one of the most helpful is the idea that the archetype, *V*, derived ultimately from three separate *libelli*, put together at a time, probably not before the second century C.E., when the papyrus roll was being replaced by the vellum codex, the ancestor of the modern book (Fordyce 1961, 410; Thomson 1997, 6–8). These *libelli* will have been (a) 1–60 (848 lines), (b) 61–64 (795 lines), and (c) 65–116 (646 lines). It is possible that they were labelled *hendecasyllabi, epithalamia,* and *epigrammata* respectively. While no one would deny that Catullus shows a passion for *internal* "structure and the complex interplay of symmetry and asymmetry" (Wray 2001, 53), how far he can be held, given his premature death, to have applied that passion *externally*, to the collection as a whole, must remain in serious doubt—though one regularly applied argument, that at 2,400-odd lines the Catullan corpus is too long for a single roll, has been convincingly challenged by modern paleographers (evidence collected by Skinner 2003, 187 n. 14). The heterogeneity and kaleidoscopic diversity of arrangement can be paralleled in no other Latin author.

Even in the polymetric collection it has been argued, with some plausibility, that 54, 55, 58b, and 60 are more likely to have been added by a posthumous editor than to have formed part of the original "Sparrow" collection dedicated to Nepos. It is, interestingly, a theoretical literary critic who has the last word here (though conceivably not quite in the way she meant), pointing out that "the poems offer just enough similarity to suggest patterns, and just enough anomaly to refuse any definite pattern" (Janan 1994, 143). She goes on, "The corpus lacks definitive context or details that clearly indicate a dominant order; whatever order there is to be, *we, the readers, must provide it*" (my emphasis). Precisely. In today's critical climate, as Skinner concedes (2003, xxvii), "interpretive premises can be classified as heuristic fictions, textual meanings be proclaimed dizzyingly indeterminate, discursive closure thought an impossibility, and the death of the author kept from his poems only through a conspiracy of silence."

In the next section I sketch, briefly, how those readers have read and reacted to Catullus's poetry since the Renaissance.

The brief surfacing of *V*, and its dissemination through *O*, *G*, and *R*, marked the end of Catullus's long flirtation with near-total oblivion. During the century between then and the first printed edition of 1472 (which also included the texts of Tibullus, Propertius, and the *Silvae* of Statius), manuscripts multiplied at the average rate of one a year. During this time various Italian humanists removed over four hundred of the more egregious textual errors that had accumulated during the collection's journey from antiquity through the Dark and Middle Ages. But it was with the advent of printing that Catullus's fame really took off; as Goold says (1989, 13), "The last five centuries have responded to him a good deal more than did ancient Rome."

This is significant. Catullus's is one of those classical texts that reached us, not by way of use in schools (which ensured regular copying, and was predicated on orthodoxy), but by luck and accident, through the back door. It thus joins such works as Petronius's *Satyricon*, or those puzzling extracanonical plays of Euripides (with Greek titles initially ranging between *E* and *I*), still with us today because just one volume of a collected edition happened to survive against odds. What unites all these survivals is their oddness, their unpredictability, their deviation from the norm— which suggests that if our literary heritage from the ancient world were more complete, our view of it might be radically different. Catullus in his own day was always a *recherché* taste: despite his cheerful obscenities, the walls of Pompeii and Herculaneum—so rich in other poetic tags, infallible indexes of literary popularity— have not yet yielded a single Catullan quotation.

Thus Catullus's true fame has been entirely posthumous, and this at once raises the question of how far, and in what ways, subsequent generations—as invariably happens—have reinvented him in their own image. Wray (2001, 3) argues, I think rightly, that the process has already begun in the Latin biographical notice composed in Venice for Wendelin von Speyer's 1472 *editio princeps* by a humanist hack with the enchanting name (Gaisser 1993, 26) of Geralamo Squarzafico:

> Valerius Catullus, lyric writer, was born at Verona during the 163rd */sic/* Olympiad, the year before the birth of Sallustius Crispus [i.e., 87 B.C.E.], in the terrible times of Marius and Sulla, on the day that Plotinus */sic/* first began the teaching of Latin rhetoric in Rome. He loved an aristocratic girl */puellam primariam/*, Clodia, whom he calls Lesbia in his poetry. He was somewhat lascivious */lasciviusculus/*. During his lifetime he had few equals in metrical expression */frenata oratione/*, and none who were superior. He showed especial charm in his light verse, but considerable gravity on serious

topics. He wrote love poems, and an epithalamium for Manlius. He died at Rome in his 30th year, and there was public mourning at his funeral.

There are obvious careless slips (the 163rd Olympiad for the 173rd, CLXIII rather than CLXXIII, and Plotinus for Plotius), while the detail about public grief at his funeral, otherwise unattested, might (if not just an imaginative addition) have been drawn from a Paduan manuscript, afterwards lost, of Suetonius's *De Poetis* (Wiseman 1985, 208). But the rest is lifted straight from St. Jerome's version of Eusebius's *Chronicle* (which it echoes verbally), reinforced with Apuleius's identification of Lesbia and judgments based on the poems themselves. What is striking is the germ of the modern Catullus we already glimpse here: Wray (2001, 4) hardly exaggerates when he speaks of "'our Catullus', intact and entire, 'biographical fallacy and all': life privileged over work, and the Lesbia poems . . . over the rest of the collection." Less than a century later (1552), Marc-Antoine de Muret, Montaigne's tutor, identified Lesbia as the sister of P. Clodius Pulcher. All the modern ingredients were thus already in place.

In a sense this is not surprising. Catullus's life and work, like those of all his contemporaries in the late Republic, *were* inextricably intertwined, and it would never have occurred to him to think otherwise—any more than he would refrain from embroidering the truth when dealing with the personal relationships which fill his pages. (Compare the instructive case of Byron.) The Lesbia poems *do* excite our biographical interest, and only a dishonest casuist would pretend otherwise. Yet for three centuries and more, the main result of Catullus's rediscovery was not the "Lesbia story" as such, which aroused virtually no interest, but rather the pilfering of his corpus (whether through translation or simple borrowings, sometimes hard to distinguish) by an extraordinarily wide range of poets. To look no further than the English-speaking world, these ranged from Wyatt to Walter Savage Landor, from Herrick to Swift, from Ben Jonson to Pope. All, it is worth noting (for reasons to be discussed later), have no interest whatsoever in conveying the *unfamiliarity* of this Roman poet (thus, it might be argued, confirming Janan's dictum, p. 18), but blithely transpose Catullus's themes, diction, and metrics wholeheartedly into those of their own day.

John Skelton, about 1505, took the two short sparrow poems (2 and 3), and turned them into a 1382-line extravaganza, the "Lament for Philip Sparrow," framed by the Catholic Mass for the Dead. The seventeenth century had a field day with the more light-hearted love poems: 5 was tackled by, among others, Crashaw, Thomas Campion, and Ben Jonson, who also tried his hand at 7; countless kisses were back in fashion with a vengeance, and no longer a sign of effeminacy (cf. 16 and note). But their addressee remained simply a name, and the name (perhaps because of its less than decorous associations) was not even a popular one (Wiseman 1985, 212). Phyllis, Chloris and Celia became all the rage with these poets. Abraham Cowley (whose titles, ranging from "Inconstancy" to "Love's Ingratitude" show an amorous depression almost as intense as Catullus's own) tackled 45, setting Acme at Septimius in jaunty rhyme: "Twice (and twice would scarce suffice) / She kist his drunken, rowling eyes . . . " (Poole and Maule, 1995, 271–72). The Augustan age which followed shows a shift in interest. Nicholas Amhurst's replacement for Lesbia, Cloe *(sic)*, in his imitation of 58, "turns up to ev'ry puppy in the town / and claps the *Temple* rake for half a crown." Pope borrowed a good deal more than the idea from 66 for his famous *jeu d'esprit,* "The Rape of the Lock," while in 1798 poem 45 was recast as a slashing, and very funny, anti-Whig parody which would have delighted the author of 29 and 57 (Poole and Maule 272–73). Romantic sex was out; politics, satire, and literary artifice were in.

Like all literary fashions, this one too was transient, a symptom merely of the society that produced it. By the close of the eighteenth century, populist nationalism was in the air; revolutions in France, America and Greece encouraged Promethean dreams of tyrannicide, subversion of authority, aspirations towards freedom. Old and new merged giddily in Byron, the quintessential rebel aristocrat, who combined Augustan wit, Gothic romanticism, radical politics, and a large appetite for forbidden fruits, mostly sexual. After several centuries of unquestioned dominance, Roman imperial authority was out, and—largely as a result of George Grote's hugely influential, and Whiggish, *History of Greece*—Athenian democracy, long spurned by Tory oligarchs as disruptive of all proper institutions, was very much in. The new fashion in literature was, not surprisingly, for high romanticism, from Keats, Shelley, and Coleridge on down to Tennyson. It followed that those Roman authors who were subversive, individualistic, antiauthoritarian, and (in the widest sense) romantic would now achieve the greatest, the most fashionable, popularity.

Who, one might ask, better fulfilled these conditions than the passionate young poet from Verona, whose soul-searching was of a sort with which romantics born two millennia later could (or felt they could) identify, whose life and work were defined by his ill-starred *grande passion* for a scornful aristocratic *femme fatale,* and who died, tragically young, possibly of what was coming to be viewed as the romantic disease *par excellence?* A nice hint of what was in the air can be gained from the youthful poems of W. S. Landor, published just after the French Revolution, in which he remarks on Rome's luck in having had a poet like Catullus to offset her

"Caesars and civil wars." Landor's "rebellious republicanism" (Wiseman 1985, 213) found a kindred spirit in Catullus. On the other hand, his very typical middle-class *pudeur* (another new characteristic of the age that marked a change from the Augustans and Byron) had a lot of trouble with Catullus's obscenity (Fitzgerald 1995, 60), a difficulty that was to continue throughout the nineteenth century and for the greater part of the twentieth, though in the end this fashion, too, proved itself transient. (I am reminded of all the pundits who during this period assured us, with great confidence and solemnity, that certain passages in Pepys's *Diary* could never, ever, be published.) Tennyson's "tenderest of Roman poets" was as much the product of selectivity, tacit censorship, and *parti pris* argument as any other version.

Catullus's evolution also depended to a very great degree (Wiseman 1985, 217–18, Wray 2001, 2, 18) on the new scholarship developed in Germany by Karl Lachmann and others during the nineteenth century, which not only put textual criticism on a scientific basis but revolutionized the study of ancient history, making it possible, as Wiseman says, "to reconstruct periods like the late Republic with a degree of sophistication hitherto unattempted." Swinburne (and Landor later in life) had picked on 63, the terrible Attis poem, as significant for the new age (an early hint here of *fin de siècle* perversion), while for Tennyson (not least in his *In Memoriam* mood) what mattered was the ultrafraternal passion of loss expressed by 101; but there can be little doubt that what chiefly shaped the course of public reaction to Catullus for over a century was the careful reconstruction of his biography, and *grande affaire*, by Ludwig Schwabe in *Quaestiones Catullianae* (1862), in particular the long section, "De Amoribus Catulli" (53–157), and the chronological table (358–61) embodying his findings.

Schwabe's central assumptions—that "Lesbia" was Clodia Metelli, and that her relationship with Catullus began in the late 60s—have come under sustained attack, from Wiseman and others. However, reexamination of the evidence, together with the findings of recent research (e.g., Mulroy 2002, xi ff.), has convinced me that in essence Schwabe was right, even if overdetailed schematization such as that of Stoessl (1977, modified 1983) remains untenable. I also suspect that a great deal of the impetus against Schwabe's construction (which in fact was better documented than many propositions in ancient history that have gone unchallenged) is due to an ingrained academic distaste (cf. Yale classicists' reactions to Erich Segal's fiction) for what that construction presents—a highly personal, and undeniably romantic, love story. The so-called biographical fallacy was called into being as a badly needed corrective for the various excesses of ad hominem biographical interpretations, sentimental, moralizing, or anachronistic (Wiseman 1985, 218ff., has some awful, and hilarious, examples) which tended to hold the field for about a century from 1870. The mistake—now in process of adjustment—was to confuse excess with definitional error, a process only encouraged by the general current trend that seeks to cut literature free from life altogether, and treat it as a self-generated exercise in the rhetoric of the imagination. This fashion, too, will pass.

It has become virtually *de rigueur* to bring in Yeats's famous poem, "The Scholars," when attempting to update Catullus for the modern era. Yeats dramatized the contrast between a young, love-sick poet and the bald, otherworldly, shuffling, elderly academics who presumed to judge and explain him ("Lord, what would they say / did their Catullus walk that way?"); his picture satirizes the appropriation of the passionate by the sexless. That was in 1919, when poets of the modernist movement, such as Pound, were beginning to turn their attention to the Roman elegists, and of course part of Yeats's satire is aimed at the middle-class, professional prudishness that still insisted on bowdlerizing Catullus's relatively mild obscenities. Amusingly, after half a century's complete freedom of expression (which translators exploited with sometimes misleadingly excessive gusto), scholars who tackle this aspect of Catullus's work (Fitzgerald 1995, 59–86 is a nice example) tend to exaggerate its importance, and betray their own residual embarrassment, by treating it with a portentous technical solemnity quite alien to the culture that produced it. It is, in fact, a characteristic upper-class Mediterranean phenomenon, exploited with aggressive and youthful panache, and singular only in its oral obsession. It shocked people like Cicero, and was meant to. Since Yeats's scholars shared many of Cicero's bourgeois pretensions, Catullus would probably be tickled to find that he had shocked them too. Personally, I rather enjoy it, and (I hope) in the same casual way that it was thrown off. With luck, that reaction will come through in my translation.

Both Wiseman (1985) and Wray (2001), the second in particular, provide an excellent survey of those changes in the academic reception of Catullus that have, over the past half century, steered Catullan criticism away from the personal, biographical concept of a romantic lyric poet ("rather like Keats in a toga," as one friend remarked to me), first to the modernist—but still essentially neo-Romantic—version pioneered by Kenneth Quinn (1959), and thereafter to the possibility of what Wray terms a "postmodern Catullus" (Wray 2001, 36ff.). Fascinating though I find this transitional process, and however skillfully it is deployed (Wray's analysis is a brilliant *tour de force*), it is not my concern here. What it reveals is, simply put, the latest of a series of cultural appropriations, earlier examples of which I have tried to sketch here as a way of placing Catullus in perspective against his historical *Nachleben*. The process is not one (as it is sometimes made out) of working towards a final true perception of Catullus, which involves rejecting all past theories as erroneous, but rather a hit-and-miss series of partial insights that light up now one, now another aspect of their subject, and in so doing emphasize its, his, in every sense classical complexity, depth, and variety. Far from hoping to present my readers with a new, and compelling, *appropriation* of Catullus, I want to set out this profoundly alien ancient poet, as far as I can, without modern accruals—with just historical background information, and a single step from English to Latin text—and let the reader make up his or her own mind. I am under no delusion that I have entirely escaped the appropriation process myself—an impossible endeavor—but at least I have striven to do so to the very best of my ability.

TRANSLATION AND ITS PROBLEMS

Appropriation brings me to the problem of translation, since this, historically considered, presents endless examples of appropriation in its most naked and unmistakable form. I have set out my general conclusions on this topic elsewhere (Green 1960, 1987, 1989) and do not need to repeat them here. But some points are worth stressing. To look no further than the English-speaking world, translations not only of Catullus but of all classical poets, Greek or Roman, have, from the Renaissance on (see Bolgar 1954, app. 2, 506–41, for a pre-1600 checklist) regularly evoked the idiom, verse forms, social prejudices, and moral flavor of the age translating them rather than those of their originals. In the preface on translation prefixed to his *Second Miscellany*, Dryden (Saintsbury ed., 1685, 281–82)—picking up an earlier suggestion of Denham's—justified his extensive anglicization of whatever ancient poet he tackled on the grounds that "my own [version] is of a piece with his, and that *if he were living, and an Englishman,* they are such as he would probably have written" (my emphasis). In the dedication to his *Aeneid* (1697), he repeated the principle. This encouraging license will explain just about everything, from Herrick's rhyming quatrains by way of Pope's stopped couplets to Jack Lindsay's 1929 version of 63, the Attis poem, in the stanza form employed by Swinburne for *Dolores.* Leaf through the *Oxford Book of Greek Verse in Translation* (1938), and you will find Ibycus done in the even more idiosyncratic stanza used by Andrew Marvell for his "Ode on the return of Cromwell from Ireland," and a truly bizarre *Odyssey,* by J. W. Mackail, entirely in the AABA quatrains best known from Edward Fitzgerald's *Rubaiyat of Omar Khayyam.*

Dryden's formula, and the various examples of homegrown pastiche to which it gave some sort of theoretical sanction, at once raise the crucial question of just who the putative readers might be that these versions were supposedly aimed at: of why, in the last resort, the translations were being made at all. As early as the Elizabethan age, Roger Ascham in *The Scholemaster* (1568/70) conceded that "even the best translation is for mere necessitie but an evill imped wing to flie withall, or a hevie stompe leg of wood to go withall." In other words, a *pis aller* for those unable to read Latin or Greek. Yet the vast majority of translations (and this is as true of Catullus as of any other ancient author) seem aimed at convincing the reader, against all the evidence, that he is dealing with a range of comforting native familiarities. Why? One major reason is surely the fact that, from the Renaissance to comparatively recent times, literary (as opposed to informational) translations have almost always had as their target other scholars and men of letters *who knew the original language*, and who would thus appreciate elegant pastiche.

This trend was constantly encouraged and enhanced by the educational practice of having students turn, say, Shakespearian soliloquies into Sophoclean-style Greek iambics, or Herrick and Crashaw into the light elegiac couplets perfected by Ovid. Granted such a discipline, the converse process would seem only logical. When, in 1966, Peter Whigham produced a version of 63 that reads like one of Pound's earlier *Cantos*, he was, *mutatis mutandis*, operating in the same centuries-old, restricted-access tradition (for his arguments in favor of this see Radice-Reynolds 1987, 216ff.). Opposition existed—for example, in 1856 F. W. Newman argued that the translator should attempt "to retain every peculiarity of the original so far as he is able, with the greater care, the more foreign it may happen to be" (cited by Savory 1968, 65)—but found, as always, few supporters. Today, however, Ascham's warning, so long neglected, is more apposite than ever: translations now are almost entirely for those who lack the original, so that the translator, like it or not—and many, anxious to show off their native skills, don't—bears an extra responsibility for conveying both the sense and the form of that original, however alien, to the very best of his or her ability.

As most translators are only too well aware, this, in poetry especially, is an uphill struggle all the way. But the impossibility of achieving perfection in such a task cannot serve as an excuse for abandoning it altogether. We may ultimately be reduced to compromise "equivalents" in most areas, but that is where we should end, not (see most recently Mulroy 2002, xxxiii ff.) the point from which we begin—an option which, however tempting for those after an easy fix, is in essence no more than a dilution of the Dryden principle. It is surprising how often scholars and translators back away from the challenge simply on account of its perceived difficulties.

When Patrick Wilkinson complained that there was no easy way of reproducing the Alcaic stanza in English, he evoked a stinging rebuke from J. B. Leishman (1956, 53; cf. Green 1960, 190) which is well worth repeating here:

> There certainly is not, for it was by no easy way that Horace produced it; neverthe-less, I am convinced that no translator can hope to achieve even moderate success un-less he attempts to reproduce it as closely as his language will permit, and refuses to deceive himself and others with vain notions of being able to invent 'some stanza that recalls the movement of the original'. For his business is not to 'recall' its movement to those who already know the original, and do not require to have it recalled, but to communicate it to those who cannot read the original for themselves . . . And I will insist that the syllabic pattern of the lines . . . can be reproduced exactly, and the move-ment of them very much more closely than has commonly (and, perhaps I may add, lazily) been supposed.

That has always been my guiding principle and inspiration throughout a long, some-times frustrating, but always exhilarating run-in with the Catullan collection.

The temptation to pastiche (not least for a classicist!) is, of course, more than understandable. To convey the subtleties of meaning presents a tough enough chal-lenge in itself. To find adequate parallel idioms is still harder: an alien tongue pro-duces alien thought patterns. *L'esprit de l'escalier* is not the spirit of the staircase, and a Greek who announces *"perà vréchei"* wants you to know, not that "It's raining over there," but that *he's* all right, Jack, and couldn't care less. Moreover words, as T. S. Eliot knew too well, "slip, slide, perish, / decay with imprecision, will not stay in place, / will not stay still." Poetry here offers especial difficulties. As L. W. Tancock reminds us, "the poet uses words differently from the prose-writer; words for him are colours, units in mosaics of sound," so that "a *similar* pattern or song may be produced which may have a similar effect," but will not be identical, "any more than a passage written for oboe will be the same when played on a harpsichord, though the notes may be the same" (Booth et al., 1958, 49). Indeed, to attempt a phonemic reproduction of the physical sound of a poem can lead (in Catullus's case) to the ab-surd grotesqueries of Celia and Louis Zukofsky's version of 78.9–10: "Worm with no impunity for aye, name to how many a cycle / nose can't—wait queer, Sis Fame'll liquidate your anus." In Catullus's case, on top of all these problems, the translator constantly has to deal with the kind of in-group, topical allusions, both public and private, endemic to a group of highly educated and politically conscious littérateurs.

All these difficulties—compounded for anyone trying to give readers a true sense of Catullus's original poetry, rather than using his work, in effect, as a springboard for native literary exercises—are grounded in language. There remains, however, one major area, central to any poet's creativity, which, for all its built-in hazards, does, like music, transcend language's crippling national restrictions: and that is the poem's rhythmic pattern, its metrical form. Paradoxically, in an era when monoglot readers are devouring classical translations in greater numbers than ever before, and thus need (cf. Leishman above) as close an approximation to the original texts as ingenuity can devise, this aspect of translation is almost universally neglected. The last, and so far as I can determine, the *only* previous complete English-language version of Catullus with every poem done, as near as could be managed, in an equivalent of its original metre was that by Robinson Ellis (1871). Yet the rhythm, the beat, of a poem constitutes its essential musical core. To take Catullus's dancing, jaunty hendecasyllables and transpose them, on the Dryden principle, into rhymed ballad stanzas or imagist free verse (more literary exercises for the *cognoscenti*) is to vitiate his originality and offer the reader a wholly misleading image.

Something, inevitably, must always be lost in the process of transposition; something, inevitably, of the translator's own literary context will cling to his version, however hard he may try to eliminate it (Ellis, for instance, like most littérateurs in the later nineteenth century, was clearly—and admittedly—under the spell of Swinburne). But must the loss always be so great? Current fashion, which systematically depreciates the author (sometimes virtually denying his—less often her—existence) in favor of those who interpret the author's work, whether as critics, translators, or readers at large, would probably (borrowing a trope from Stanley Fish) reply, "Yes, and a good thing too." My flat opposition to such a principle, coupled with the love I have maintained for the Catullan corpus ever since adolescence, and a desire to make the delights of that corpus as widely available as possible, must serve as the excuse both for producing yet another version of Catullus, and for the particular form it has taken.

Anyone even superficially acquainted with Latin or Greek is aware of the fundamental distinction between these languages and (among other modern tongues) English, when it comes to poetry: the former have both stress and metre, the latter stress only. In other words, Latin and Greek vowels possess fixed quantities, long or short, either by nature or by position (e.g., a short vowel lengthening before two juxtaposed consonants), and this creates a metrical schema independent of, and indeed contrapuntal to, accentual stress and ictus. In English, on the other hand, which has no fixed vowel quantities, and thus *only* accentual stress to work with, any attempt to reproduce classical metres is bound to suffer from two serious drawbacks: (a) the sole guide to both accentual stress and metrical schema will be the translator's ingenuity in shaping the line so that the reader instinctively emphasizes the right words; and (b) since this means that more often than not schema and stress pattern will be made to coincide, the contrapuntal effect that forms so attractive a feature of Latin or Greek verse is always in danger of being lost.

Unfortunately, this hazard particularly applies in the two most frequently encountered classical metres, the hexameter and the elegiac couplet (for a detailed discussion of these and all other metres employed by Catullus the reader should consult the following section). Why this should be so is virtually never discussed; but the reason—a very simple one—in fact constitutes the main challenge to any would-be metrical translator. In both hexameter and pentameter, the two main metrical building blocks, the dactyl (— ∪ ∪) and the spondee (— —), both have a long initial syllable. This produces a fast, naturally *falling* line, and directly militates against the inbuilt rhythmic pattern of English, which has a firm determination to climb uphill, always with short initial syllables, and most often in an iambic (∪ —) pattern, wherever possible: the lasting popularity of the blank verse line is no accident. Saintsbury (1906, vol. 3, 414, 417) saw the danger for an anglicized hexameter: "Good dactylic movements in English tip themselves up and become anapestic [i.e., — ∪ ∪ to ∪ ∪ —]," with extra syllables at the beginning of the line and partial suppression at the end. This tendency both produced too many short syllables (English has few naturally spondaic [— —] words), and led to a constant identification of metrical schema and stress pattern, thus eliminating the contrapuntal tension between them.

The notorious flatness of the English accentual or stress hexameter and pentameter is directly due to this accident of language, as Tennyson knew when he wrote a spoof in which metre and stress *were*, grotesquely, at odds: "These lame hexaméters, the strong-winged music of Homer . . . When did a frog coarsér croak upon our Helicón?" When indeed? Actually, quite often, and as early as the Elizabethan age, which saw a vigorous investigation into the possibility of acclimatizing classical metres to English. Sir Philip Sidney, in his *Arcadia,* experimented not only with hexameters and elegiacs, but also with hendecasyllables, sapphics, anacreontics, and asclepiads (cf. p. 36). The main advocates of the English hexameter were Gabriel Harvey and William Webbe, in his *Discourse of English Poetrie* (1586), and what they wanted to do, among other things, was, incredibly, to treat accentual English *as though it was* metrical Latin, and amenable to the same prosodic rules of length and positioning. If their hope was to restore contrapuntal tension to the line, they were disappointed. Only someone already conversant with the metrical rules of Virgil would understand what Richard Stanyhurst (1582) was after when he translated *Aen.* 4.304–8 thus:

Át lást sh(e) Aénéás thús, nót próvóked, asaúlteth.
Ánd thóghst thów, fáythlésse cóystrél, só smoóthlye to sháddow
Thy pácking práctíse? fróm my sóyle prívilie slíncking?
Shál nót my lyking, ne yet earst fayth plighted in handclaspe,
Nór Dídóes buriál from this crosse iournye withóld the?

Neither the numerous spondees (— —) in place of dactyls (— ∪ ∪), nor the elision of *she* in the first line, come naturally to the uninitiated reader looking for natural stress, and the result is merely grotesque: sequential stressed syllables simply do not come naturally in English. The same applies *a fortiori* to the pentameter. When Sidney attempted 70, his version of the last two lines was: "These be her woordes, but a womans wordes to a love that is eger / ín wyndes ór wátérs | strémes do requíre to be writ."

This determination to make English, against all the odds, behave like Latin had a long history: it was still the guiding principle behind Ellis's 1871 translation, and his preface (vii–xx) gives the most detailed theoretical outline of the system known to me. Yet even for classicists it remains no more than a perverse curiosity—apart from anything else, Latin is an inflected language, so that since object, subject, verb part and so on all are identifiably labelled, it can play hopscotch with word order in a way English can't—and has surely been one of the major factors militating against *any* attempt to convey an impression of Catullus's actual rhythmic patterns. On top of everything else, Ellis went in for coy archaisms, old-fashioned inversions, and obfuscatory bowdlerization: small wonder that no one tried matching the metres again after him.

Yet clearly this is a problem that any translator of Catullus has to solve somehow, since about one-third of his surviving work is in either elegiacs or hexameters. In my case, fortunately, I came to the task with a solution that I had been able to develop through extended work on both the hexameter (Juvenal, Apollonius Rhodius), and the elegiac couplet (Ovid). In the first case this meant building on the insights of Richmond Lattimore and Cecil Day Lewis, who, to quote my earlier formulation (Green 1987, 99):

saw that the way to produce some real stress equivalent to the hexameter was to go for the beat, the ictus, since this was native to English, and let the metre, within limits, take care of itself. They worked out a loose, flexible line (but varied on occasion with one stress or more) and a variable, predominantly feminine ending, that could take easy overrun, moved swiftly, and to a great extent countered the determination of the English language to climb uphill . . . This line at least catches the precipitate striding movement of the hexameter, while preserving its basic structure, including the caesura. What is sacrificed is the linguistically unattainable ideal of true metrical equivalence.

How well this device worked at its best can be seen in Lattimore's *Iliad* and Day Lewis's *Aeneid*, and I have been refining and developing it ever since.

The elegiac couplet poses some different problems in addition, while somewhat restricting the scope of one's resources for dealing with the hexameter alone (e.g., in the use of sweeping run-overs and enjambment). To get the contrast between hexameter and pentameter is the easiest part: keep the pentameter at least one stress shorter than the hexameter, and give it a masculine ending by setting a sharp emphasis on the final syllable, while always making sure the hexameter has a feminine, dissyllabic, ending. Even so, it becomes difficult to avoid a sense, in accentual English, of repetitive monotony, seeing that so many Greek or Latin elegiac couplets, like an English stanza, form self-contained sentences.

At the same time, the strongly marked, rocking-horse rhythm of the pentameter (analyzed pp. 40–41 below) tends, in English, to overstress the metrical schema. Thus the greatest danger in stress elegiacs comes from precisely what gives the metrical version of the genre such plangent grace: a series of unvarying stopped couplets, each rhythmically identical to the last. To avoid this I use overrun and enjambment far more than a Latin poet would, and also exploit rhythmic contrasts between the two lines of the couplet to the uttermost. This sometimes involves reducing the pentameter to three or, exceptionally, even two stresses, while extending the hexameter with an extra stress in override, so to speak, and occasionally cutting it back to a five-beat line. These are my only "equivalents," and in each case I have brought them as near the original as the mutual incompatibilities of Latin and English will allow.

When we turn to the so-called polymetric poems, most of the difficulties encountered above vanish, since the accentual patterns here are predominantly iambic ($\cup$ —) or anapestic ($\cup\cup$ —), and where a long initial syllable does predominate, at the beginning of the hendecasyllable, it can quite easily be arranged so that the reader stresses it instinctively. The secret, of course, is that the translator, working in a medium with no fixed quantities, must as far as possible create natural stresses in his prosody which mimic the required metrical schema, letting readers shape the line without assistance. (I count it as a kind of failure when I need to nudge the reader, as is sometimes unavoidable, with diacritical signs: an accent to indicate unanticipated stress, a vertical divider showing a break in the rhythm, caesura or diaeresis.) This process is helped by the polymetric metres, where there exists a far closer, less contrapuntal relationship between the metrical and the accentual schema (see next section). In addition, accentual English can on occasion absorb the extra light syllable that would not pass in strict metre; I have availed myself of this privilege as sparingly as possible, but on occasion it has proved invaluable. As Saintsbury remarked (1906, vol. 3, 392), "Prosody, like the excellent woman's children in George Eliot, 'can do with an extry bit.'"

Selver (1966, 68) was thus quite wrong when he described the Alcaic stanza as "far less adapted to English" than the hexameter or elegaic: as Tennyson knew and demonstrated, it can produce an English version of great power and beauty. This adaptability is also true, *a fortiori*, of the hendecasyllables in which a majority of Catullus's polymetrics were composed. Sidney's *Arcadia*, again, has some interesting early specimens, with only the occasional quantitative counterstress obtruding:

> Reason tell me thy minde, if here be reason,
> In this strange violénce, to make resistance,
> Where sweet graces erect the stately banner.

But it is Tennyson's hendecasyllabic *jeu d'esprit* that truly catches the light, witty, buoyant nature of the line:

> O you chorus of indolent reviewers,
> Irresponsible, indolent reviewers,
> Look, I come to the test, a tiny poem
> All composed in a metre of Catullus,
> All in quantity, careful of my motion,
> Like the skater on ice that hardly bears him,
> Lest I fall unawares before the people,
> Waking laughter in indolent reviewers . . .

It was also Tennyson who (a fact less widely known) worked out, in "Boadicea," a stress equivalent for the extraordinary galliambic metre of 63 (see p. 38), which, for once, demanded at least as much virtuosity from its Roman composer (who had to use a language with a surprising lack of short syllables) as it does from its English translator.

These have told us all their anger in miraculous utterances,
Thunder, a flying fire in heaven, a murmur heard aërially,
Phantom sound of blows descending, moan of an enemy massacred,
Phantom wail of women and children, multitudinous agonies . . .

Without this experiment of Tennyson's to guide me I might, I suspect, have given up on the Attis poem, the one complete surviving galliambic poem from the ancient world. The iambic-based poems, on the other hand, presented few problems in a language solidly based on the blank verse line and the alexandrine: the one real difficulty I had to face (again because of serial long syllables) lay in the line endings of the choliambic or scazon (pp. 33–34), and even here the challenge was far less demanding than in the elegiacs. So, now my task is completed, I feel I can at least say, with Tennyson,

Should I flounder awhile without a tumble
Thro' this metrification of Catullus
They should speak to me not without a welcome,
All that chorus of indolent reviewers . . .

Well, I've always been an optimist.

THE CATULLAN METRES

I. HENDECASYLLABLES (HEND)

An aeolic form (i.e., one with a central choriambic nucleus: — ∪ ∪ —), sometimes known as "Phalaecian" after the fourth century B.C.E. Greek poet Phalaecus, the hendecasyllabic line is not common in Greek lyric, though it does occur in tragic choral odes, and also in Attic drinking songs *(skolia)*. Nor is it found in surviving Roman literature till the last century of the Republic: it was Catullus and Calvus who popularized it. Forty-three of the first sixty poems in Catullus's corpus, the so-called polymetric group, are composed in this metre: its dancing, perky rhythm (as Tennyson saw) is ideal for witty squibs and *vers d'occasion*.

Normally (as its name implies) the hendecasyllable is a line of eleven syllables, but in 55 and 58b Catullus sometimes collapses the two central short syllables of the choriamb (— ∪ ∪ —) into one long one, thus producing a decasyllabic line. The basic structure is as follows (— = long syllable, ∪ = short syllable, / = stress):

/   /   /   /   /

—— | —∪∪— | ∪— | ∪— | —

—∪| — | | |∪

∪— |

∪∪∪ | [only at 55.10]

Thus the main building block is an aeolic choriamb, prefaced by either a spondee (— —) or, less commonly, a trochee (— ∪) or iamb (∪ —), and followed by two iambs plus a single variable-length syllable. Interestingly, Horace never employs this catchy, rhythmically haunting metre (see above, p. 14), but it proved extremely popular later with Martial and Statius, and is also found in Petronius. "Its insistent iambic second half gives it a colloquial, vernacular quality that evokes the comic stage and the rhythms of street language" (Garrison 1991, 174).

2. CHOLIAMBICS (CHOL)

The second most popular form in the polymetric group (used by Catullus for 8, 22, 31, 37, 39, 44, 59 and 60), this oddly graceless metre, the name of which means "lame iambics" (also known as *scazons*, or "limpers"), is a variant on the *iambic trimeter* or *senarius* (q.v. below), in which the final foot, reversing normal metrical stress, is a spondee or trochee rather than an iamb, thus creating an emphatic dull thud at closure. When, as in 8, all lines are end-stopped, the effect on the reader is of being mentally and emotionally jack-hammered. The form was traditionally ascribed to the late sixth century Greek iambic poet Hipponax, and regarded (Quinn 1970, xxxiii) as "a deformed or mutilated version of the ordinary iambic line," deliberately so, in order to mirror in symbolically appropriate fashion the vices and crippled perversions of mankind. Once again, it was Catullus and his friend Calvus who popularized the form in Roman literature. Consciously learned, *docti*, they discarded the varieties of scansion adopted by Hipponax himself (and followed, at Rome, by Varro). The line they constituted was a trimeter (an iambic *metron* consisted of two feet, which is why the line is known as a trimeter rather than a hexameter, containing as it does three *metra* rather than six) with a *caesura* (rhythmical break, ||, between words but in mid-foot) in either the third or fourth foot, and sometimes in both (Ellis 1876, xxv):

```
     1      2       3       4       5    6
     /      /       /       /       / / /
  ∪ — ∪ — | ∪ || — ∪ || — | ∪ — — ∪
  —     ∪∪∪ |  —| | —   ||      |        —
—∪∪          | — || ∪∪
```

Martial loosens up the line still further by allowing an anapest (∪ ∪ —) in the fourth
foot, and a tribrach (∪ ∪ ∪) in the third. Ellis (1876) doubts, probably with good
reason, whether Catullus would have allowed these resolutions.

3. IAMBIC TRIMETER AND SENARIUS (ITRIM, ISEN)

The iambic trimeter is the basic iambic line employed by Archilochus, and subse-
quently by the Greek tragedians in non-lyric dialogue. It consists (see above) of three
iambic *metra*, again with a caesura splitting the third and/or the fourth foot, and with
spondees regularly allowed in place of iambs in the first and third feet. Though it is
regularly represented in English by the blank verse line, its actual accentual equiv-
alent is the alexandrine (e.g., Dryden's "with necks in thunder clothed, and long-
resounding pace"), and I have used a flexible alexandrine for my versions of 4, 29,
and 52. Catullus's trimeters are in fact stricter than much of Greek tragic practice,
and far stricter than the trimeters both of Old Comedy and, in Latin, of the corre-
sponding metrics of Seneca and Petronius, where resolutions of long syllables into
anapests, dactyls, and tribrachs proliferate (cf. Raven 1965, 58). The schema is found
in Catullus only at 52:

```
     1      2      3      4      5      6
     /      /      /      /      /      /
  ∪ —  ∪ — | ∪ || — ∪ || — | ∪ — ∪ —
  —         | — ||                      ∪
```

The *senarius* (4, 29) is even stricter, keeping to the basic iambic pattern throughout.

4. IAMBIC TETRAMETER CATALECTIC (ITETCAT)

This was originally a "dialogue" metre, most notably in Greek Old Comedy (e.g.,
Aristoph. *Frogs* 905–70, the debate between Aeschylus and Euripides), and also
found—with free resolutions of vowel quantities—in Roman comedy, where it is
known as the *septenarius*. Tennyson—again—borrowed its catchy rhythmic pattern
for *Locksley Hall:*

In the Spring a livelier iris changes on the burnish'd dove;
In the Spring a young man's fancy lightly turns to thoughts of love.

Catullus uses it once only, for 25, and again tends to keep to the strict form, allowing variation only in the first and fifth feet. The line consists of four iambic *metra* (hence "tetrameter"), of which the last is catalectic (i.e., short of a final syllable). There is a natural break *(diaeresis)* between the second and third *metra*:

```
 1    2    3    4    5    6    7    8
 /    /    /    /    /    /    /
 ∪ — ∪ — | ∪ — ∪ — || ∪ — ∪ — | ∪ — ∪
 —                  || —                  —
```

The Latin *septenarius* regards the line as consisting of seven iambic feet plus an "overspill" (Lee 1990, 191).

5. GLYCONIC / PHERECRATEAN (GLYCPHER)

There are several other forms of aeolic verse with which Catullus experimented in addition to hendecasyllables (see section 1 above), though these remained out and away his favorite. All of them are structured round the central, rhythmically powerful building block ("Under the bridge, over the hill") of the choriamb (— ∪ ∪ —). In Greek lyric poetry, the most common form aeolic verse took was the *glyconic* line, in combination with its catalectic (shortened by one syllable) form, the *pherecratean:*

```
 /      /      /
 — ∪ | — ∪ ∪ — | ∪ — (glyconic)
 ∪ — |
 — — |

 /      /      /
 — ∪ | — ∪ ∪ — | — (pherecratean)
 ∪ —              ∪
```

Catullus uses this metrical combination twice, both times in strophe form. Poem 34, the hymn to Diana, has three glyconic lines followed by a pherecratean; 61, the long epithalamium for Manlius and Aurunculeia, follows the same pattern except that here we find four glyconic lines rather than three. At 61.25, uniquely, the short syllables of the choriamb in the pherecratean are resolved into one long syllable: *nutriunt umore*, — ∪ | ——— | —, the last syllable of *umore* being lengthened by position in relation to the first word *(quare)* of the next line. Similarly, in both poems the scansion is occasionally hypermetric (i.e., a final vowel of one line is elided with an opening vowel in the next: at 34.11 and 22, and at 61.115, 135, 140, and 227).

6. PRIAPEAN (PRIAP)

This metre is so named, not from any supposed erotic quality in its rhythm, but because during the Hellenistic period it was the recognized medium for hymns addressed to the ithyphallic garden god, Priapus. Catullus uses it once only, for 17: it simply consists of a long, slightly lumbering line—appropriate for dealing with a tottering bridge—formed from a glyconic followed by a pherecratean, with a strong natural break *(diaeresis)* between them:

$$— \cup | —\cup\cup — | \cup— || —\cup | —\cup\cup — | \cup$$
$$—| \qquad\qquad || \quad —| \qquad\quad |—$$

7. GREATER (OR SECOND) ASCLEPIAD (GRASCLEP)

The asclepiad is found as early as Sappho (who reportedly wrote the whole of her third book in greater asclepiads) and Alcaeus, but derives its name from the early Hellenistic epigrammatist Asclepiades of Samos (fl. 300–270). It is formed by inserting extra choriambic *metra* into a glyconic base: one for the "lesser" (or "first"), two for the "greater" (or "second"), with no substitutes or resolutions, and strong pauses *(diaereses)* both before and after the second choriamb:

$$/ \quad / \quad / \quad / \quad / \quad / \quad /$$
$$——| — \cup \cup — || — \cup \cup — || — \cup \cup — | \cup —$$

Catullus, who uses this metre only for 30, keeps the strict spondaic base, but—unlike Horace later (e.g., at *Odes* 1.11 and 18)—does not always observe the pauses (see, e.g., lines 11–12). The final syllable is often naturally short, but always lengthens positionally, in relation to the first word of the following line. This slow, syncopated, repetitive, drumbeat line is as hypnotic as the not dissimilar pattern of Ravel's *Bolero* (try it in von Karajan's classic blues-influenced version).

8. SAPPHIC STROPHE (SAPPH)

Catullus composed two poems in this metre, 11 and 51, the chronological book-ends, as it were, to his relationship with Lesbia (see notes ad loc.). Poem 51, an actual translation from some of Sappho's original Greek stanzas, closely follows her metrical usages and licenses (Ellis 1876, xxxvi), and we may assume that 11 does the same; whereas we later find Horace imposing stricter rules (cf. Raven 1965, 144). The Sapphic quatrain as Catullus reproduces it consists of three lines built, as always with aeolic verse, round a central choriamb (— ∪ ∪ —), and followed, for closure, by a shorter line known as an *adonean* or *adonic:*

$$
\overset{/}{—} \; \overset{/}{∪} \; \overset{/}{—} \; ∪ \; | \; \overset{/}{—} \; ∪ \; ∪ \; \overset{/}{—} \; | \; ∪ \; — \; —
$$
$$
— \, | \qquad\qquad\qquad\qquad ∪ \, (3\,x)
$$
$$
\overset{/}{—} \; ∪ \; ∪ \; \overset{/}{—} \; | \; ∪ \quad \text{(adonean)}
$$
$$
| \, —
$$

The adonean, as Garrison (1991, 175) reminds us, "gives the stanza a sense of closure because it is the normal rhythm at the end of a hexameter." (See section 10 below.)

The danger in creating an English equivalent is that of ignoring the contrapuntal choriambic rhythms, and thus producing a metrically quite different, briskly jaunty effect, as George Canning did in his famous political squib:

> Needy Knife-grinder! whither are you going?
> Rough is the road, your wheel is out of order—
> Bleak blows the blast;—your hat has got a hole in't.
>   So have your breeches.

Swinburne, on the other hand, caught the line's subtle syncopations and counter-stresses as well as anyone writing in an uninflected language could ever hope to do, as his poem, "Sapphics," from *Poems and Ballads* (1866) demonstrates:

> So the goddess fled from her place, with awful
> Sound of feet and thunder of wings around her;
> While behind a clamour of singing women
>   Severed the twilight.

Swinburne is not a poet much in favor these days, but he was a master metrist, and I am glad to acknowledge what I have learned from him.

9. GALLIAMBICS (GALL)

This extraordinary metre, used by Catullus only for that *tour de force*, poem 63, was in fact specially designed to accompany the ecstatic ritual of Cybele's acolytes, and its hammering rhythms, with their rat-a-tat line ending—Latin, with so many fewer short quantities than Greek, was a difficult language to adapt to its use—were peculiarly appropriate for the purpose. (For Tennyson's galliambic experiment in "Boadicea," see above, pp. 31–32.) Just how the line breaks down in metrical terms has been the subject of much debate. The most useful discussions are now those of Thomson (1997, 375–77) and Morisi (1999, 49–56). Thomson accepts the ancient metrician Hephaestion's explanation of the line as being, in essence, ionic: that is, based on the variants ∪ ∪ — — and — — ∪ ∪ (sometimes viewed as trisyllabic longs with resolution of the first or last syllable).

By the time Catullus came to use the form, variation from the basic first ionic (*a minore*, ∪ ∪ — —) had taken place by the process known as *anaclasis*, involving the reversal of the last syllable of one foot and the first of the next, so that in the first half of the line the original ionic pattern ∪ ∪ — — | ∪ ∪ — — had become ∪ ∪ —∪ | —∪ — —.

The basic form of Catullus's galliambic, then, is as follows:

$$\cup \cup - \cup \mid - \cup - - \parallel \cup \cup - \cup \mid \cup \cup \cup -$$
$$\cup\cup \qquad \mid \cup\cup$$

This accounts for the majority of the lines in 63, the top line representing about two-thirds of the whole, while the resolutions indicated in the second line are the most common variants, based on the general license either to resolve any one long syllable into two shorts, or, vice versa, to contract any two shorts into one long. Wherever possible, the machine-gun rattle of short syllables in the final catalectic *metron* is preserved. But the line can also be weighted and slowed down, for dramatic effect, with a plethora of long syllables, as at 73:

iam, iam dolet quod egi: iam, iamque paenitet:
$$- - \cup \mid - \cup - - \parallel - - \cup \mid - \cup -$$

Nevertheless, the most common variation goes in the other direction, with an expansion into short syllables, and a flutter of elided words, as at 63:

Ego mulier, eg(o) adulescens, eg(o) ephebus, ego puer
⏑ ⏑ ⏑ ⏑ ⏑ | ⏑ ⏑ ⏑ — — ‖ ⏑ ⏑ — ⏑ | ⏑ ⏑ ⏑ —

Again, the final syllable of the line, though often short by nature, is lengthened positionally against the opening syllable of the following line, hinting at the enjambed speed of the whole sequence. As Godwin (1995, 19) says, "a virtuoso performance . . . without loss of either sense or poetic feeling."

10. DACTYLIC HEXAMETER (HEX) AND THE ELEGIAC COUPLET (ELEG)

Catullus employs the dactylic hexameter for two of his long poems, 62 and 64, the latter by far the longest poem in the entire corpus, and the elegiac couplet (hexameter plus pentameter) for all poems after 64 (i.e., 65–116). The first is the metre employed by all epic poets from Homer onwards (e.g., at Rome, Virgil and Lucan), and satirists (e.g., Persius and Juvenal), while the second is that of every elegist (e.g., Propertius, Tibullus, and Ovid). Thus for many readers today there is a familiarity about the structure and form of the poems in the second half of Catullus's canon which they are not so liable to feel when confronted by the poems in the polymetric group.

The dactylic hexameter remained virtually unchanged from Homer's day. It had been introduced into Latin literature early, by Q. Ennius (239–169 B.C.E.), who used it for his *Annals*. Since it was also the accepted metre for didactic poetry (used, e.g., by Hesiod and Aratus), it was likewise employed by Catullus's exact contemporary Lucretius (?97–?51) for his versified exposition of Epicurean philosophy, the *De Rerum Natura*. As its name implies, it is a six-foot line, consisting almost entirely of dactyls ("fingers," — ⏑ ⏑ , so named from the one long and two short joints of the index finger), with the final sixth foot a spondee or trochee (— — or — ⏑), and all feet—except, normally, the fifth—resolvable into spondees:

1	2	3	4	5	6
/	/	/	/	/	/

— ⏑ ⏑ | — ⏑ ⏑ | — ‖ ⏑ ‖ ⏑ | — ‖ ⏑ ‖ ⏑ | — ⏑ ⏑ | — ⏑
— — — — [—] —

Latin being richer in long syllables than Greek (cf. above, section 9 ad init.), reso-
lution into spondees is more frequent among Roman poets: in particular, resolution
of the fifth foot, generally avoided by Greek writers, is a marked feature (as Cicero
noted) of Neoteric, and in particular of Catullus's, metrics (see, e.g., 64.78–80 for
three in a row; the resolution is occasionally found later as well, as in one of the most
beautiful lines of all Latin literature, Propertius's *sunt apud infernos tot milia for-
mosarum* [2.28.49]: "so many thousand beauties there are among the dead"). Before
such a spondaic fifth foot, the fourth is nearly always dactylic; there is also a ten-
dency, as the usage evolves, to have *only* a dissyllabic or trisyllabic word at the end
of the line.

The springy counterpoint of the dactylic hexameter (notoriously absent when
the strict form is reproduced in English), is achieved by a constant tension between
natural stress and metre. The most notable aspect of this is the *caesura*, a natural
rhythmic break in the line, always *between* words but *within* a metrical foot. Nor-
mally the caesura is located in either the third or the fourth foot of the hexamater,
and sometimes in both. It most often falls after the first long syllable, when it is known
as a "strong" caesura; when it occurs between the two short syllables of a dactyl (see
schema above) it is termed a "weak," and sometimes, especially in the fourth foot,
a "bucolic" caesura. It is interesting that in the metrics of the hexameter Catullus
shows a marked advance in sophistication over his contemporary Lucretius: the hexa-
meter as he handles it is virtually indistinguishable from that subsequently employed
by Virgil and his fellow Augustans (cf. Raven 1965, 90–103).

The dactylic hexameter is also employed as the first line in the so-called elegiac
couplet, the second being the (misleadingly named) pentameter, a pairing that, again,
has a long Greek history going back to archaic poets such as Archilochus and Solon,
and developed by Hellenistic epigrammatists. The pentameter is characterized by
two peculiar features: a rigid central break in the rhythm between metra *(diaeresis)*,
and inflexible dactylic restriction in the second half of the line. The result is a form
which, rather than consisting of five feet in any normally recognized sense, consists
of two sections, each containing two and a half feet:

```
   /        /        /    /        /        /
— ∪∪ | — ∪∪ | — || — ∪∪ | — ∪∪ | ∪
   —|      —|                        |—
```

The result is to give a neat sense of rhythmic closure to the couplet. Looked at an-
other way, the pentameter consists of two *hemiepes* (i.e., the opening of the hexam-

eter as far as a strong caesura in the third foot: e.g., *arma uirumque cano*). The sense of the hexameter frequently runs on into the pentameter, by the process known as enjambment; the pentameter, by contrast, almost never continues into the next hexameter, but is end-stopped (however, see 65.10–11 for an interesting exception).

In elegiac couplets, the central caesura of the hexameter tends to be stricter than in running hexameters, the strong third-foot variety predominating. The two- or three-syllable-word ending is likewise the general rule. Since the elegiac couplet was adapted for Roman usage rather later than the hexameter, we are faced with the intriguing paradox that, while Catullus's hexameters (see above) are extremely sophisticated and well fitted to the special characteristics of the Latin language, his pentameters, through adhering more closely to their Greek models, can seem, on occasion, remarkably crude when compared to those of, say, Ovid or Propertius. Catullus can stumble into a whole plethora of awkward elisions: see, for example, 73.6, where we find *quam modo qui m(e) un(um) atqu(e) unic(um) amic(um) habuit*, the elisions even (as at 77.4) extending over the central diaeresis, a practice sedulously avoided by the Augustans.

The most noticeable difference between Catullus's pentameters and those of his successors is his partiality for ending the line with words of anything between two and five syllables (for the latter see, e.g., *sodalicium* at 100.4). He once actually manages to do the entire second half of the line in a single seven-syllable word: 68.112, *Amphitryoniades*, a splendid Hellenistic conceit. He also once (76.8) produced a monosyllabic ending, *dictaque factaque sunt*. One has only to read this aloud to understand why it was outlawed by later elegists. By Ovid's day, a dissyllabic final word had become the rule. Catullus had in fact already begun to move in this direction since almost two-fifths of his pentameters do, in fact, have dissyllabic endings (Raven 1965, 106).

THE POEMS

1

Hend.   Cui dono lepidum nouum libellum
          arida modo pumice expolitum ?
          Corneli, tibi: namque tu solebas
          meas esse aliquid putare nugas
5   iam tum, cum ausus es unus Italorum
          omne aeuum tribus explicare cartis
          doctis, Iuppiter, et laboriosis.
          quare habe tibi quidquid hoc libelli
          qualecumque; quod, <o> patrona uirgo,
10   plus uno maneat perenne saeclo!

2A

Hend.   Passer, deliciae meae puellae,
          quicum ludere, quem in sinu tenere,
          cui primum digitum dare appetenti
          et acris solet incitare morsus,
5   cum desiderio meo nitenti
          carum nescio quid lubet iocari,
          et solaciolum sui doloris,
          credo, ut tum grauis acquiescat ardor:
          tecum ludere sicut ipsa possem
10   et tristis animi leuare curas !

2B

          tam gratum est mihi quam ferunt puellae
          pernici aureolum fuisse malum
          quod zonam soluit diu ligatam.

Who's the dedicatee of my new witty
booklet, all fresh-polished with abrasive?   — revision
You, Cornelius: for you always used to
feel my trivia possessed some substance,   — irony → not trivia
5   even when you dared—the lone Italian!—
that great three-decker treatment of past ages:
scholarly stuff, my god, and *so* exhaustive!
So take this little booklet, this mere trifle,
whatever it may be worth—and Patron Virgin,
10 let it outlast at least ~~one~~ generation!

                    └ focus on present not past

Sparrow, precious darling of my sweetheart,
always her plaything, held fast in her bosom,
whom she loves to provoke with outstretched finger
tempting the little pecker to nip harder
5   when *my* incandescent longing fancies
just a smidgin of fun and games and comfort   longing
for the pain she's feeling (I believe it!),
something to lighten that too-heavy ardor—
how I wish I could sport with you as she does,
10 bring some relief to the spirit's black depression!

2B

    . . . just as welcome to me as they say that golden
apple was, long ago, to the maiden runner,
which freed, at last, a girdle too long knotted.

3

Hend. Lugete, o Veneres Cupidinesque,
et quantum est hominum uenustiorum:
passer mortuus est meae puellae,
passer, deliciae meae puellae,
5   quem plus illa oculis suis amabat.
nam mellitus erat suamque norat
ipsam tam bene quam puella matrem,
nec sese a gremio illius mouebat,
sed circumsiliens modo huc modo illuc
10   ad solam dominam usque pipiabat;
qui nunc it per iter tenebricosum
illud, unde negant redire quemquam.
at uobis male sit, malae tenebrae
Orci, quae omnia bella deuoratis :
15   tam bellum mihi passerem abstulistis.
o factum male! o miselle passer !
tua nunc opera meae puellae
flendo turgiduli rubent ocelli.

4

ISen. Phaselus ille, quem uidetis, hospites,
ait fuisse nauium celerrimus,
neque ullius natantis impetum trabis
nequisse praeterire, siue palmulis
5   opus foret uolare siue linteo.
et hoc negat minacis Hadriatici
negare litus insulasue Cycladas
Rhodumque nobilem horridamque Thracia
Propontida trucemue Ponticum sinum,
10   ubi iste post phaselus antea fuit

4.8: Thracia *Thomson*, traciam *corr.* R, tractam *V*. 24: nouissime *V*, nouissimo *Ital.*

3

Mourn, Cupids all, every Venus, and whatever
company still exists of caring people:
Sparrow lies dead, my own true sweetheart's sparrow,
Sparrow, the pet and darling of my sweetheart,
5   loved by her more than she valued her own eyesight.
Sweet as honey he was, and knew his mistress
no less closely than a child her mother;
nor from her warm lap's safety would he ever
venture far, but hopping this and that way
10   came back, cheeping, always to his lady.
Now he's travelling on that dark-shroud journey
whence, they tell us, none of the departed
ever returns. The hell with you, you evil
blackness of Hell, devouring all that's lovely—
15   such a beautiful sparrow you've torn from me!
Oh wicked deed! Oh wretched little sparrow!
It's your fault that now my sweetheart's eyelids
are sore and swollen red from all her weeping.

*grief of
Lesbia,
anger of
Catullus*

4

That cutter that you see there, gentlemen, of mine
claims she was once the swiftest vessel of them all:
There was no hull afloat the thrust of which she'd not
outspeed, whether it was | with oars or under sail
5   as the occasion called for, either one.
And she denies the Adriatic's menacing
coast can deny this claim, or the Cycladic isles,
or noble Rhodes, or the | Propontis, bristling with
rough Thracian storms, or the | wild Pontic gulf, where she,
10   the destined future cutter, started out her life

comata silua; nam Cytorio in iugo
loquente saepe sibilum edidit coma.
Amastri Pontica et Cytore buxifer,
tibi haec fuisse et esse cognitissima
15   ait phaselus: ultima ex origine
tuo stetisse dicit in cacumine,
tuo imbuisse palmulas in aequore,
et inde tot per impotentia freta
erum tulisse, laeua siue dextera
20   uocaret aura, siue utrumque Iuppiter
simul secundus incidisset in pedem;
neque ulla uota litoralibus deis
sibi esse facta, cum ueniret a mari
nouissime hunc ad usque limpidum lacum.
25   sed haec prius fuere: nunc recondita
senet quiete seque dedicat tibi,
gemelle Castor et gemelle Castoris.

5

Hend.   Vivamus, mea Lesbia, atque amemus,
rumoresque senum seueriorum
omnes unius aestimemus assis !
soles occidere et redire possunt :
5   nobis cum semel occidit breuis lux
nox est perpetua una dormienda.
da mi basia mille, deinde centum,
dein mille altera, dein secunda centum,
deinde usque altera mille, deinde centum.
10   dein, cum milia multa fecerimus,
conturbabimus illa, ne sciamus,
aut ne quis malus inuidere possit,
cum tantum sciat esse basiorum.

as leaf-maned trees, which on | Cytórus's mountain ridge
would often whisper with soft-speaking foliage.
Pontic Amastris and | you, groved Cytórus's slopes,
to you this setting was, and still remains, well known,
the cutter says. In her | remote beginning she
claims it was on your summit that she stood, that your
waters were then the first to handsel her trim oars,
and from that moment on, through strait on hazardous strait
carried her master, whether from starboard or from port
beckoned the breeze, or came a strong and following wind,
a godsend, driving hard upon both sheets at once.
Nor were there any vows to dry-land deities
made for her when at last, her final voyage done,
she left the deep and reached this ever-limpid lake.
But that was long ago. Now she's laid up for good
in quiet retirement, dedicates herself to you,
twin Castor, and to you, great Castor's brother-twin.

15

20

25

5

Let's live, Lesbia mine, and love—and as for
scandal, all the gossip, old men's strictures,
value the lot at no more than a farthing!
Suns can rise and set ad infinitum—
for us, though, once our brief life's quenched, there's only
one unending night that's left to sleep through.
Give me a thousand kisses, then a hundred,
then a thousand more, a second hundred,
then yet another thousand then a hundred—
then when we've notched up all these many thousands,
shuffle the figures, lose count of the total,
so no maleficent enemy can hex us
knowing the final sum of all our kisses.

5

10

[handwritten margin notes:]
passion of the moment
infatuation
possession

6

Hend.   Flavi, delicias tuas Catullo,
        ni sint illepidae atque inelegantes,
        uelles dicere nec tacere posses.
        uerum nescio quid febriculosi
5   scorti diligis: hoc pudet fateri.
        nam te non uiduas iacere noctes
        nequiquam tacitum cubile clamat
        sertis ac Syrio fragrans oliuo,
        puluinusque peraeque et hic et ille
10   attritus, tremulique quassa lecti
        argutatio inambulatioque.
        nam nil ista ualet nihil tacere.
        cur ? non tam latera ecfututa pandas,
        ni tu quid facias ineptiarum.
15   quare, quidquid habes boni malique,
        dic nobis. uolo te ac tuos amores
        ad caelum lepido uocare uersu.

7

Hend.   Quaeris, quot mihi basiationes
        tuae, Lesbia, sint satis superque.
        quam magnus numerus Libyssae harenae
        lasarpiciferis iacet Cyrenis
5   oraclum Iouis inter aestuosi
        et Batti ueteris sacrum sepulcrum ;
        aut quam sidera multa, cum tacet nox,
        furtiuos hominum uident amores :
        tam te basia multa basiare
10   uesano satis et super Catullo est,
        quae nec pernumerare curiosi
        possint nec mala fascinare lingua.

6.12: nam nil ista ualet *Lachmann*, †nam inista preualet† *V*

6

Flavius, that sweetie of yours (Catullus speaking)
must be *totally* inelegant and unsmart—
you couldn't keep quiet otherwise, you'd *tell* me.
Fact is, it's just some commonplace consumptive
5   tart you're mad for, and you blush to say so.
Look, your nights aren't solitary: silence
won't help out when your own bedroom shouts it—
stinking Syrian perfume, all those garlands,
both your pillows, on each side of the bed, all
10 rumpled, *and* the gimcrack bedstead shaken
into sharp creaking, loud perambulation!
It's no good, no good *at all,* your saying
nothing. Why? You wouldn't look so fucked out
if you weren't up to some inept adventure.
15 So, whatever you've got there, nice or awful,
tell us! I'm *after you,* man, *and* your lovebird,
want to ensky you *both* in witty poems!

 ## 7

You'd like to know how many of your kisses
would be enough and over, Lesbia, fór me?
Match them to every grain of Libyan sand in
silphium-rich Cyrene, from the shrine of
5   torrid oracular Jupiter to the sacred
sepulchre of old Battus; reckon their total
equal to all those stars that in the silent
night look down on the stolen loves of mortals.
*That'*s the number of times I need to kiss you,   — passion /
10 *That'*s what would satisfy your mad Catullus—   infatuation
far too many for the curious to figure,
or for an evil tongue to work you mischief!

8

Chol.   Miser Catulle, desinas ineptire,
        et quod uides perisse perditum ducas.
        fulsere quondam candidi tibi soles,
        cum uentitabas quo puella ducebat
5   amata nobis quantum amabitur nulla.
        ibi illa multa cum iocosa fiebant,
        quae tu uolebas nec puella nolebat,
        fulsere uere candidi tibi soles.
        nunc iam illa non uolt: tu quoque inpote<ns noli>,
10   nec quae fugit sectare, nec miser uiue,
        sed obstinata mente perfer, obdura.
        uale, puella. iam Catullus obdurat,
        nec te requiret nec rogabit inuitam.
        at tu dolebis, cum rogaberis nulla.
15   scelesta, uae te, quae tibi manet uita ?
        quis nunc te adibit ? cui uideberis bella ?
        quem nunc amabis ? cuius esse diceris ?
        quem basiabis ? cui labella mordebis ?
        at tu, Catulle, destinatus obdura.

9

Hend.   Verani, omnibus e meis amicis
        antistans mihi milibus trecentis,
        uenistine domum ad tuos penates
        fratresque unanimos anumque matrem ?
5   uenisti. o mihi nuntii beati !
        uisam te incolumem audiamque Hiberum
        narrantem loca, facta, nationes,
        ut mos est tuus, applicansque collum
        iucundum os oculosque suauiabor.
10   o quantum est hominum beatiorum,
        quid me laetius est beatiusue ?

8

Wretched Catullus, stop this stupid tomfool stuff
and what you see has perished treat as lost for good.
Time was, every day for you the sun shone bright,
when you scurried off wherever *she* led *you*—
5   that girl you loved as no one shall again be loved.
There, when so many charming pleasures all went on,
things that *you* wanted, things *she* didn't quite turn down,
then for you truly every day the sun shone bright.
Now she's said *No,* so you too, feeble wretch, say *No.*
10   Don't chase reluctance, don't embrace a sad-sack life—
make up your mind, be stubborn, obdurate, hang tough!
So goodbye, sweetheart. Now Catullus *will* hang tough,
won't ask, "Where is she?" won't, since you've said *No,* beg, plead.
You'll soon be sorry, when you get these pleas no more—
15   bitch, wicked bitch, poor wretch, what life awaits *you* now?
Who'll now pursue you, still admire you for your looks?
Whom will you love now? Who will ever call you theirs?
Who'll get your kisses? Whose lips will you bite in play?
You, though, Catullus, keep your mind made up, *hang tough!*

[handwritten margin notes: rejection by Lesbia; Invective; endurance]

9

Dear Veranius, of all my close companions
by three hundred miles the foremost—have you
come back home to your household gods, to brothers
one in mind with you, to your aged mother?
5   *Yes, you're back!* The news makes me so happy—
I'll see you safe and sound, hear all your stories
of Spanish tribes and cities, what you did there,
told in your special style. I'll hug you to me,
rain kisses on your eyes and laughing face. Oh,
10   take all the fortunate men alive now—who, pray,
could be happier, more fortunate, than I am?

[handwritten margin note: joy for the return of his friend]

53

10

Hend.   Varus me meus ad suos amores
      uisum duxerat e foro otiosum,
      scortillum, ut mihi tum repente uisum est,
      non sane illepidum neque inuenustum.
5   huc ut uenimus, incidere nobis
      sermones uarii, in quibus, quid esset
      iam Bithynia, quo modo se haberet,
      et quonam mihi profuisset aere.
      respondi id quod erat, nihil neque ipsis
10   nec praetoribus esse nec cohorti,
      cur quisquam caput unctius referret,
      praesertim quibus esset irrumator
      praetor, nec faceret pili cohortem.
      'at certe tamen,' inquiunt 'quod illic
15   natum dicitur esse, comparasti
      ad lecticam homines.' ego, ut puellae
      unum me facerem beatiorem,
      'non' inquam 'mihi tam fuit maligne,
      ut, prouincia quod mala incidisset,
20   non possem octo homines parare rectos.'
      at mi nullus erat nec hic neque illic,
      fractum qui ueteris pedem grabati
      in collo sibi collocare posset.
      hic illa, ut decuit cinaediorem,
25   'quaeso', inquit 'mihi, mi Catulle, paulum
      istos commoda: nam uolo ad Serapim
      deferri.' 'mane,' inquii puellae,
      'istud quod modo dixeram me habere
      fugit me ratio: meus sodalis
30   Cinna est Gaius—is sibi parauit.
      uerum, utrum illius an mei, quid ad me ?
      utor tam bene quam mihi pararim.
      sed tu insulsa male et molesta uiuis,
      per quam non licet esse neglegentem.'

10

My friend Varus saw me lounging in the Forum,
dragged me off with him to meet his girlfriend.
"Little scrubber" was my first impression—
not unsmart, though, not entirely witless.
5   When we got there, conversation turned to
every kind of subject, and among them
how were things in Bithynia, what was happening,
had my posting brought me in a windfall?
I replied with the truth: not even praetors,
10   much less aides, could find even the slightest
hope of deals that would fatten their resources—
nót least whén said praetor was a fuckface
and didn't give a shit for his poor staffers.
"Well, at least," they said, "you must have picked up
15   some of what we hear's their major export—
litter-bearers?" Anxious to impress his
girlfriend, make her suppose I was a fat-cat,
"Sure," said I, "though I got a lousy province,
life wasn't all *that* bad for me—I somehow
20   found myself eight able-bodied porters."
(Truth was, neither here nor there so much as
one spent shag did I own, the kind who'd barely
manage to heft an ancient broken bed-leg.)
At this—predictable bitch—she said, "Catullus,
25   darling, please, please, lend me them—I only
need them a little while, I want a ride to
Serapis's temple." "Whoa," I told her, "what I
claimed just now that I had, I really hadn't,
my mind was slipping, actually it's my colleague
30   Cinna, first name Gaius, bought them—though why
shoúld *I* care who it is that they belong to?
I still use them just as though I owned them.
Not but what you're a bore, a walking pest, who
won't let pass even slight exaggerations."

11

Sapph. Furi et Aureli, comites Catulli,
siue in extremos penetrabit Indos,
litus ut longe resonante Eoa
tunditur unda,

5 siue in Hyrcanos Arabasue molles,
seu Sagas sagittiferosue Parthos,
siue quae septemgeminus colorat
aequora Nilus,

siue trans altas gradietur Alpes,
10 Caesaris uisens monimenta magni,
Gallicum Rhenum, horribiles uitro ulti-
mosque Britannos,

omnia haec, quaecumque feret uoluntas
caelitum, temptare simul parati,
15 pauca nuntiate meae puellae
non bona dicta.

cum suis uiuat ualeatque moechis,
quos simul complexa tenet trecentos,
nullum amans uere, sed identidem omnium
20 ilia rumpens;

nec meum respectet, ut ante, amorem,
qui illius culpa cecidit uelut prati
ultimi flos, praetereunte postquam
tactus aratro est.

11.11: uitro *McKie*, -que *V*

Furius and Aurelius, comrades of Catullus,
whether he'll penetrate the distant Indies
where the shore's slammed by far-resounding Eastern
    thunderous breakers,

5 or make for Hyrcania, or the queening Arabs,
or the Sacae, or the Parthians with their quivers,
or that flat delta to which the seven-channelled
    Nile gives its color,

or toil across high-towering Alpine passes
10 to visit the monuments of mighty Caesar,
the Gaulish Rhine, those rude back-of-beyonders
    the woad-dyed Britons—

All this, or whatever the high gods in heaven
may bring, you're both ready to face together;
15 just find my girl, deliver her this short and
    blunt little message:
                    — *anger.*

Long may she live and flourish with her gallants,
embracing all three hundred in one session,   — *shallow*
                                          life
loving none truly, yet cracking each one's loins
20 over and over.

Let her no more, as once, look for my passion,   *loss of*
which through her fault lies fallen like some flower   *innocence and*
at the field's edge, after the passing ploughshare's   *beauty*
    cut a path through it.

12

Hend.   Marrucine Asini, manu sinistra
non belle uteris: in ioco atque uino
tollis lintea neglegentiorum.
hoc salsum esse putas ? fugit te, inepte:
5   quamuis sordida res et inuenusta est.
non credis mihi ? crede Pollioni
fratri, qui tua furta uel talento
mutari uelit: est enim leporum
differtus puer ac facetiarum.
10   quare aut hendecasyllabos trecentos
exspecta, aut mihi linteum remitte,
quod me non mouet aestimatione,
uerum est mnemosynum mei sodalis.
nam sudaria Saetaba ex Hiberis
15   miserunt mihi muneri Fabullus
et Veranius : haec amem necesse est
ut Veraniolum meum et Fabullum.

13

Hend.   Cenabis bene, mi Fabulle, apud me
paucis, si tibi di fauent, diebus,
si tecum attuleris bonam atque magnam
cenam, non sine candida puella
5   et uino et sale et omnibus cachinnis.
haec si, inquam, attuleris, uenuste noster,
cenabis bene; nam tui Catulli
plenus sacculus est aranearum.
sed contra accipies meros amores
10   seu quid suauius elegantiusue est:
nam unguentum dabo, quod meae puellae
donarunt Veneres Cupidinesque,
quod tu cum olfacies, deos rogabis,
totum ut te faciant, Fabulle, nasum.

12

Your left hand, friend <u>Asinius</u>, you provincial,
works its <u>mischief</u> while we drink and gossip,
snitching napkins from distracted guests. You
think this trick is smart? So dumb, you can't see

5   just how <u>dirty</u> your game is, <u>how unlovely</u>?
Don't believe me? Then believe your brother
Pollio, who'd quite gladly pay good money
if he could stop your larceny—a sweetheart
chock-full of charm, that boy, and always witty.

10   Either, then, you give me back my napkin,
or else you'll get a scad of scathing verses.
It's not so much the price that's made me angry:
this was a gift, a memento from my comrade,
top-line real native hand-towels, that Fabullus—

15   and Veranius—sent me all the way from
Spain: so I must love them just as much as
sweet Veranius and my dear Fabullus.

[handwritten margin notes: "dumb prank" and "brother would be ashamed"]

13

You'll dine well, dear Fabullus, in my lodging
one day soon—*if* the gods look on you kindly,
if you bring along a good and lavish
dinner, not to mention an attractive

5   girl, plus wine and salt and witty stories.
If, I repeat, you bring this lot, old sweetheart,
you'll dine well. The thing is, your Catullus
has a purse that's full—of spiders' cobwebs.
Still, in return you'll get love undiluted—

10   ór something even tastier and smarter:
I'll contribute the unguent that the Cupids—
Venuses too—of passion gave my girlfriend.
Get one whiff of that, and you'll beseech the
gods to make you one big nose, Fabullus!

14A

Hend. Ni te plus oculis meis amarem,
iucundissime Calue, munere isto
odissem te odio Vatiniano:
nam quid feci ego quidue sum locutus,
5   cur me tot male perderes poetis ?
isti di mala multa dent clienti,
qui tantum tibi misit impiorum.
quod si, ut suspicor, hoc nouum ac repertum
munus dat tibi Sulla litterator,
10 non est mi male, sed bene ac beate,
quod non dispereunt tui labores.
di magni, horribilem et sacrum libellum !
quem tu scilicet ad tuum Catullum
misti, continuo ut die periret,
15 Saturnalibus, optimo dierum!
non non hoc tibi, salse, sic abibit.
nam, si luxerit, ad librariorum
curram scrinia, Caesios, Aquinos,
Suffenum, omnia colligam uenena,
20 ac te his suppliciis remunerabor.
uos hinc interea ualete abite
illuc, unde malum pedem attulistis,
saecli incommoda, pessimi poetae.

14B

Si qui forte mearum ineptiarum
lectores eritis manusque uestras
non horrebitis admouere nobis . . .

14a.16: salse *G*, false *OR*

More than my own eyes I love you, Calvus,
you great tease: were it not so, for that ghastly
gift of yours I'd hate you like—Vatinius!
What did I ever do or say to make you
5 finish me off with all these rotten poets?
May high gods heap troubles on that client
who sent you such a parcel of blasphemers!
Still, if (as I suspect) this new *recherché*
gift came to you from Sulla, Man of Letters,
10 I don't take it amiss, but am delighted,
seeing that all your work has not been wasted.
Great gods, *what* a *disgusting* little booklet,
and you carefully chose the time to send it
to your Catullus, so that you would kill him
15 on that best of all days, the Saturnalia!
No, you *won't* get away with this, you smart-ass—
first thing tomorrow morning I'll go round the
booksellers' stalls, buy Caesius, Aquinus,
Suffénus, all the poison on the market,
20 pay you back with a counterdose of torture.
Meanwhile, you lot, *out*—back where you hauled your
bad feet from, time's trash, appalling poets!

*friend poet sends
Catullus junk on purpose
to annoy him*

14B

If maybe there are some of you who'll read my
stupid ineptitudes, and won't recoil from
reaching out and laying hands upon us . . .

15

Hend.   Commendo tibi me ac meos amores,
        Aureli. ueniam peto pudentem,
        ut, si quicquam animo tuo cupisti,
        quod castum expeteres et integellum,
5   conserues puerum mihi pudice,
        non dico a populo—nihil ueremur
        istos, qui in platea modo huc modo illuc
        in re praetereunt sua occupati,
        uerum a te metuo tuoque pene
10   infesto pueris bonis malisque.
        quem tu qua lubet, ut lubet, moueto
        quantum uis, ubi erit foris paratum :
        hunc unum excipio, ut puto, pudenter.
        quod si te mala mens furorque uecors
15   in tantam impulerit, sceleste, culpam,
        ut nostrum insidiis caput lacessas,
        a tum te miserum malique fati !
        quem attractis pedibus patente porta
        percurrent raphanique mugilesque.

16

Hend.   Pedicabo ego uos et irrumabo,
        Aureli pathice et cinaede Furi,
        qui me ex uersiculis meis putastis,
        quod sunt molliculi, parum pudicum.
5   nam castum esse decet pium poetam
        ipsum, uersiculos nihil necesse est;
        qui tum denique habent salem ac leporem,
        si sunt molliculi ac parum pudici,
        et quod pruriat incitare possunt,
10   non dico pueris, sed his pilosis
        qui duros nequeunt mouere lumbos.

15

Let me commend me and my boyfriend to you,
Aurelius. I'm asking just one modest favor—
that if you've ever in your heart felt driven
to seek out something chaste and undeflowered,
you'll keep the boy safe for me, and well protected—
not from the public at large: no, I fear nothing
from folk going to and fro in the piazza,
brisk, preoccupied, minding their own business.
It's *you* that scare me, you and your great whanger,
a standing threat to boys both good and naughty.
Look, wag the damn thing where and how you fancy,
all you've a mind to out there, cocked and ready—
just leave *him* out of it, make one nice exception!
But should ill-will or mindless madness drive you
to such a state, you bastard, that you're willing
to practice low tricks on me and provoke me,
ah, *then* you'll feel my dire retaliation,
feet spread and strapped, back-passage widely gaping,
reamed all its length with radishes and mullets!

16

Up yours both, and sucks to the pair of you,
Queen Aurelius, Furius the faggot,
who dared judge *me* on the basis of my verses—
they mayn't be manly: does that make *me* indecent?
Squeaky-clean, that's what every proper poet's
person should be, but not his bloody squiblets,
which, in the last resort, lack salt and flavor
if *not* "unmanly" and rather less than decent,
just the ticket to work a furious itch up,
I won't say in boys, but in those hirsute
clods incapable of wiggling their hard haunches.

uos, quod milia multa basiorum
legistis, male me marem putatis?
pedicabo ego uos et irrumabo.

17

Priap. O Colonia, quae cupis ponte ludere longo,
   et salire paratum habes, sed uereris inepta
   crura ponticuli axulis stantis in recidiuis,
   ne supinus eat cauaque in palude recumbat:
5   sic tibi bonus ex tua pons libidine fiat,
   in quo uel Salisubsali sacra suscipiantur,
   munus hoc mihi maximi da, Colonia, risus.
   quendam municipem meum de tuo uolo ponte
   ire praecipitem in lutum per caputque pedesque,
10   uerum totius ut lacus putidaeque paludis
   liuidissima maximeque est profunda uorago.
   insulsissimus est homo, nec sapit pueri instar
   bimuli tremula patris dormientis in ulna.
   cui cum sit uiridissimo nupta flore puella
15   et puella tenellulo delicatior haedo,
   adseruanda nigerrimis diligentius uuis,
   ludere hanc sinit ut lubet, nec pili facit uni,
   nec se subleuat ex sua parte, sed uelut alnus
   in fossa Liguri iacet suppernata securi,
20   tantundem omnia sentiens quam si nulla sit usquam;
   talis iste meus stupor nil uidet, nihil audit,
   ipse qui sit, utrum sit an non sit, id quoque nescit.
   nunc eum uolo de tuo ponte mittere pronum,
   si pote stolidum repente excitare ueternum,
25   et supinum animum in graui derelinquere caeno,
   ferream ut soleam tenaci in uoragine mula.

 17.3: recidiuis *Nisbet*, rediuiuis *V*

Just because you've read about my countless
thousand kisses, you think I'm less than virile?
Up yours both, and sucks to the pair of you!

17

Dear Verona, so eager to   celebrate on your lóng bridge
ánd all ready for dancing there   if it weren't for the scary
legs of the wretched bridge itself   shored with tottering timbers
lest it fall on its back, collapse   supine into the marshes!
Máy a goód bridge be built for you   just the way that you'd like it,
strong enough even to carry the   Sálisubsálian dancers—
if you play one hysterical   jape for me, please, Verona!
Thére's this féllow-townsman of mine   whom I'd love to see booted
headlong into the muck below,   neck over crop, exactly
where in the whole of the spreading lake's   foully malodorous bog land
lies the deepest and filthiest   sheer vertiginous sinkhole.
"Mindless moron" describes the guy   —no more sense than a baby
two years old, snoozing rock-a-bye   snug on its father's arm, for
though he's wed to a girl he caught   right in her springtime glory,
and more skittish, this girl, than the   tenderest frisky kidling,
plus she needs to be guarded more   carefully than the ripest
grapes, yet he lets her play around   all she wants, doesn't mind it.
Nor's *he* willing to rise on his   own part, lies like an alder
felled, laid flat in the ditch by some   keen Ligurian axman,
no more conscious of things than if   *she* was just nonexistent.
There you have this dumb clod of mine—   sees zip, hears nothing, zero,
not one clue who the héll he is,   even if he exists, yet.
This is the guy I'd love to toss   off your bridge, pitch him headlong,
find out if he can shake himself   suddenly free of his stolid
sloth, leave his passive heart behind   stuck in the clinging mud, as
mules' iron shoes can get suckered off   by a voracious quagmire.

21

Hend.   Aureli, pater esuritionum,
        non harum modo, sed quot aut fuerunt
        aut sunt aut aliis erunt in annis,
        pedicare cupis meos amores.
5   nec clam: nam simul es, iocaris una,
        haerens ad latus omnia experiris.
        frustra: nam insidias mihi instruentem
        tangam te prior irrumatione.
        atque id si faceres satur, tacerem :
10   nunc ipsum id doleo. quod esurire
        a temet puer et sitire discet.
        quare desine, dum licet pudico,
        ne finem facias, sed irrumatus.

22

Chol.   Suffenus iste, Vare, quem probe nosti,
        homo est uenustus et dicax et urbanus,
        idemque longe plurimos facit uersus.
        puto esse ego illi milia aut decem aut plura
5   perscripta, nec sic ut fit in palimpsesto
        relata: cartae regiae, noui libri,
        noui umbilici, lora rubra membranae,
        derecta plumbo et pumice omnia aequata.
        haec cum legas tu, bellus ille et urbanus
10   Suffenus unus caprimulgus aut fossor
        rursus uidetur: tantum abhorret ac mutat.
        hoc quid putemus esse ? qui modo scurra
        aut si quid hac re scitius uidebatur,
        idem infaceto est infacetior rure,
15   simul poemata attigit, neque idem umquam

21.11: a temet *Froehlich*, †me me† *V*
22.5: palimpsesto *Ital.*, palimpseston *Marcilius*

21

You, Aurelius, big Daddy of all the hungers—
not just of these, but of every one hereafter
or heretofore, in past years or the future:
so you're bent on rogering my darling—
openly, too! You're with him, swapping stories,   5
sticking close up to him, trying every gambit . . .
No good, friend. If you're plotting to replace me
I'll fix *you* first, serve you a proper mouthful!
If you'd just dined when you did it I'd keep silent;
what really ticks me off is that the laddie   10
surely will learn from you that thirst and hunger.
So—lay off while you decently can, or else you'll
come to a messy end, mouth crammed to bursting!

22

That chap Suffenus, Varus, whom you know too well
is a delightful fellow, witty, quite urbane,
and *so* prolific, number one for churned-out verse—
ten thousand lines, I reckon—could be more—
he's written, not on palimpsest, like most plain folk: 5
no, *he* insists on royal papyrus, brand-new rolls,
new bosses, scarlet cords, expensive parchment wraps,
all pumiced smooth and levelled off, square-ruled.
But when you *read* it, then that same smart úrbáne mán
Suffenus seems a country lout, clod, clown,   10
he's so remote from what he was, *so* changed.
How explain this? One moment such a smart town wit,
or anything still more clever (could that be?),
he comes on hicker than a backwoods hick
the minute he tries a poem—yet this guy   15

aeque est beatus ac poema cum scribit:
tam gaudet in se tamque se ipse miratur .
nimirum idem omnes fallimur, neque est quisquam
quem non in aliqua re uidere Suffenum
20 possis. suus cuique attributus est error ;
sed non uidemus manticae quod in tergo est.

23

Hend. Furi, cui neque seruus est neque arca,
nec cimex neque araneus neque ignis,
uerum est et pater et nouerca, quorum
dentes uel silicem comesse possunt,
5 est pulcre tibi cum tuo parente
et cum coniuge lignea parentis.
nec mirum : bene nam ualetis omnes,
pulcre concoquitis, nihil timetis,
non incendia, non graues ruinas,
10 non facta impia, non dolos ueneni,
non casus alios periculorum.
atqui corpora sicciora cornu
aut siquid magis aridum est habetis
sole et frigore et esuritione.
15 quare non tibi sit bene ac beate?
a te sudor abest, abest saliua,
mucusque et mala pituita nasi.
hanc ad munditiem adde mundiorem,
quod culus tibi purior salillo est,
20 nec toto decies cacas in anno;
atque id durius est faba et lapillis,
quod tu si manibus teras fricesque,
non umquam digitum inquinare possis.
haec tu commoda tam beata, Furi,

23.23: possis *Ital.*, posses *V*

is never so happy as when composing verse,
thinks he's so marvelous, such a real fly boy.
Ah well, we all make that mistake—there's not
one of us whom you can't in some small way
20   see as Suffenus. Each reveals his inborn flaw—
and yet we're blind to the load on oúr ówn bácks!

23

You have, Furius, neither slave nor strongbox,
neither bugs nor spiders, no, nor kindling—
yet you do have a father and a stepmom,
teeth well up to chomping flints for dinner.
5   Oh, you get on splendidly with Daddy,
and with Daddy's beanpole of a bedmate—
not surprising, since you're all so healthy,
fine digestion, no persistent worries,
no damn conflagrations, no collapsing
10   buildings, no domestic crimes like murder
(poison, natch), no other kinds of danger:
plus, you've bodies dry as any bone, or
whatever's even drier, all because of
sun and cold and your near-starvation diet.
15   So, why shouldn't you be well and happy?
Sweat's unknown to you, you've no saliva,
no snot, no catarrh, no dripping sinus.
To this cleanliness add an even cleaner
asshole, than any saltcellar more polished,
20   *and* you shit less than ten times in a year, and
what comes out is as hard as beans or pebbles—
if you rubbed it in your hands it wouldn't
leave the least mess, even on one finger!
These rich blessings, Furius, please never

25 noli spernere nec putare parui,
    et sestertia quae soles precari
    centum desine: nam sat es beatus.

24

Hend. O qui flosculus es Iuuentiorum,
         non horum modo, sed quot aut fuerunt
         aut posthac aliis erunt in annis,
         mallem diuitias Midae dedisses
5   isti, cui neque seruus est neque arca,
         quam sic te sineres ab illo amari.
         'quid? non est homo bellus?' inquies. est:
         sed bello huic neque seruus est neque arca.
         hoc tu quam lubet abice eleuaque :
10   nec seruum tamen ille habet neque arcam.

25

ITetCat. Cinaede Thalle, mollior cuniculi capillo
            uel anseris medullula uel imula oricilla
            uel pene languido senis situque araneoso,
            idemque, Thalle, turbida rapacior procella,
5   cum diua Murcia ebrios ostendit oscitantes,
            remitte pallium mihi meum, quod inuolasti,
            sudariumque Saetabum catagraphosque Thynos,
            inepte, quae palam soles habere tamquam auita.
            quae nunc tuis ab unguibus reglutina et remitte,
10   ne laneum latusculum manusque mollicellas
            inusta turpiter tibi conscribilent flagella,
            et insolenter aestues, uelut minuta magno
            deprensa nauis in mari, uesaniente uento.

24.7: quid *O*, qui *GR*
25.5: Murcia *Putnam*, †mulier† *V;* ebrios *Green,* †aries† *V*
25.11: conscribilent flagella *Turnebus,* flagella conscribilent *V*

underestimate or despise, and please stop
nagging me for that hundred thousand, since you're
quite well-heeled enough as it is already.

24

Hey, Juventius, blossom, best of all your
blue-blood clan, not just the current crop but
every forebear, each remote descendant—
I'd prefer your shelling out a fortune
5   on that jerk (who's penniless and slaveless)
to the way you're letting the shit love you!
"What," you say, "he's not a dish?" A dish, yes,
but a dish that's penniless and slaveless—
pooh-pooh that all you like, and blow it off: still,
10   *still* he's got no slaves, and not a penny!

25

O queenie Thallus, softer than a furry little rabbit,
a goosey-woosey's marrow or the bottom of an earlobe,
an old man's languid penis with its cobwebby senescence—
yet also, Thallus, greedier than any fierce tornado
5   whenever heavenly sloth reveals the tipsy diners nodding:
just give me back that cloak of mine you pounced upon and pilfered,
the monogrammed set of face-towels too, and all those Spanish napkins,
which—idiot!—you keep on show as heirlooms: pray unglue them
this moment from your talons and return them to me, if you
10   don't want your fleecy little flanks and tender poofy paw-waws
all scribbled with the lash of whips, burned with a shameful branding,
on heat (not in your usual way), just like a little skiff that's
caught in a heavy storm at sea, a hurricane of gale force.

26

Hend.   Furi, uillula uestra non ad Austri
flatus opposita est neque ad Fauoni
nec saeui Boreae aut Apheliotae,
uerum ad milia quindecim et ducentos.
5   o uentum horribilem atque pestilentem !

27

Hend.   Minister uetuli puer Falerni
inger mi calices amariores,
ut lex Postumiae iubet magistrae
ebrioso acino ebriosioris.
10   at uos quo lubet hinc abite, lymphae,
uini pernicies, et ad seueros
migrate. hic merus est Thyonianus.

28

Hend.   Pisonis comites, cohors inanis,
aptis sarcinulis et expeditis,
Verani optime tuque mi Fabulle,
quid rerum geritis ? satisne cum isto
5   uappam frigoraque et famem tulistis ?
ecquidnam in tabulis patet lucelli
expensum, ut mihi, qui meum secutus
praetorem refero datum lucello ?
o Memmi, bene me ac diu supinum
10   tota ista trabe lentus irrumasti.
sed, quantum uideo, pari fuistis
casu: nam nihilo minore uerpa

28.5: uappam *Green*, uappa *V*

26

Your nice bijou cottage in the country,
Furius, stands exposed to draughts from neither
south, east, west, nor savage north: instead it's
faced with an *over*draft of fifteen hundred
5   plus—a wind most vile and pestilential!

27

You boy there, serving out the vintage *vino*—
mix me stronger and sharper-tasting cupfuls,
follow the lady of the revels' orders
(who's more drunk than the killer stuff she's drinking).
5   You, though, pure-water nymphs, can get the hell out—
ruination to wine you are, move over,
join the puritans. Here the wine is *un*mixed!

28

Dear Véránius, and you, my own Fabullus,
Piso's flacks, poor empty-handed staffers
loaded up with your piddling little backpacks—
how's life with you? Have you had your fill of
5   flat wine, cold, and hunger with that bastard?
Do *your* ledgers show a little profit
paid out, just like mine? When serving *my* chief
I'd chalk up my expenses as net income.
(Memmius, man, you really reamed me over,
10   force-fed me slowly with that giant whanger!)
Now, so far as *I* can see, you two have
met the selfsame fate, crammed by no lesser

farti estis. pete nobiles amicos!
at uobis mala multa di deaeque
15   dent, opprobria Romuli Remique.

29

ISen.   Quis hoc potest uidere, quis potest pati,
nisi impudicus et uorax et aleo,
Mamurram habere quod Comata Gallia
habebat uncti et ultima Britannia ?
5   cinaede Romule, haec uidebis et feres ?
et ille nunc superbus et superfluens
perambulabit omnium cubilia,
ut albulus columbus aut Adoneus?
cinaede Romule, haec uidebis et feres?
10   es impudicus et uorax et aleo.
eone nomine, imperator unice,
fuisti in ultima occidentis insula,
ut ista uestra diffututa mentula
ducenties comesset aut trecenties?
15   quid est alid sinistra liberalitas ?
parum expatrauit an parum elluatus est ?
paterna prima lancinata sunt bona,
secunda praeda Pontica, inde tertia
Hibera, quam scit amnis aurifer Tagus:
20   nunc Galliae timetur et Britanniae.
quid hunc malum fouetis ? aut quid hic potest
nisi uncta deuorare patrimonia ?
eone nomine, Urbis o piissimi,
socer generque, perdidistis omnia ?

29.23: o piissimi *Haupt*, †opulentissime† *V*

yárd yoursélves! Seek noble friends, they tell us!
May all gods (and goddesses) now serve out
15   those two blots on Romulus and Remus!

29

Who, pray, except some gamester, some voracious
and shameless gut would watch this, who could tolerate
Mamurra skimming all the cream from wildwood Gaul,
and Britain too, the world's | remotest outpost. Hey,
5   fag Romulus, can *you* put up with such a scene?
Now, I suppose, that ass—so arrogant-otiose—
will work his stud's routine through every bed around,
just like some cute white dove or young Adonis. Hey,
fag Romulus, can *you* put up with such a scene?
10   Then *you're* a shameless glutton *and* a gamester:
O military Supremo, was this then your aim,
while you were in that final island of the west,
to let this shagged-out prick, your crony, chomp his way
through twenty million, maybe thirty? What is that,
15   I ask you then, but clumsy open-handed waste?
You think he hasn't screwed | and chewed his fill? Just look:
first, his inheritance. This | he squandered. Next go off
all of his Black Sea pickings, and then, third, his loot
from Portugal—as gold-rich Tagus knows too well.
20   Now Gaul and Britain both are in the danger zone.
Why do you back this no-good? what's his function been
except to wolf rich oily patrimonies down?
Was it for *this*, you ultra-pious Roman pair,
father and son-in-law, you blew the takings, eh?

30

GrAsclep. Alfene immemor atque unanimis false sodalibus,
iam nil miseret, dure, tui dulcis amiculi ?
iam me prodere, iam non dubitas fallere, perfide ?
nec facta impia fallacum hominum caelicolis placent.
5   quod tu neglegis ac me miserum deseris in malis.
eheu, quid faciant, dic, homines cuiue habeant fidem?
certe tute iubebas animam tradere, inique, <me>
inducens in amorem, quasi tuta omnia mi forent.
idem nunc retrahis te ac tua dicta omnia factaque
10 uentos irrita ferre ac nebulas aereas sinis.
si tu oblitus es, at di meminerunt, meminit Fides,
quae te ut paeniteat postmodo facti faciet tui.

31

Chol. Paene insularum, Sirmio, insularumque
ocelle, quascumque in liquentibus stagnis
marique uasto fert uterque Neptunus,
quam te libenter quamque laetus inuiso,
5   uix mi ipse credens Thuniam atque Bithunos
liquisse campos et uidere te in tuto.
o quid solutis est beatius curis,
cum mens onus reponit, ac peregrino
labore fessi uenimus larem ad nostrum,
10 desideratoque acquiescimus lecto?
hoc est quod unum est pro laboribus tantis.
salue, o uenusta Sirmio, atque ero gaude;
gaudete uosque, o Lydiae lacus undae;
ridete, quidquid est domi cachinnorum.

31.13: gaudete *V,* gaudente *Bergk.*

30

Al-fé-nús! You forget *and* you play false those who've been true to you—
Have you *no* pity left hard though you are for your 'sweet intimate'?
No qualms when you betray, cheat and deceive *me*, faithless creature? Do
acts of treacherous men, impious deeds, please Heaven's occupants?
5 All this *you* disregard, leave me bereft, lost in my misery.
Oh, what *can* people do, you tell me that, whom can they trust? Because
you, yes *you*, that's for sure, wickedly made me give my soul to you,
drew me into your love, acting as though all would be safe for me.
Now it's *you* who pull back, leave all your words, all your past deeds to be
10 blown away by the winds, all unfulfilled, clouds of pure nothingness.
You've forgotten? The gods never forget— nor does Good Faith, who will
soon, too soon, after this make you regret all that you've done to me.

(31)  *homecoming*

Of all near-islands, Sirmio, and of islands
the jewel, of every sort that in pellucid
lakes or vast ocean fresh or salt Neptune bears—
how gladly, with what joy I now cast eyes
5 on you once more, can't believe I've left those flat,
endless Bithynian plains, can see your safe haven.
What greater bliss than when, cares all dissolved,
the mind lays down its burden, and, exhausted
by our foreign labors we at last reach home
10 and sink into the bed we've so long yearned for?
This, this alone makes all our toil worthwhile.
Greetings, sweet Sirmio, and rejoice, your master's
here: and rejoice, you too, you lakeside ripples,
and all you joys of home, break out in laughter.

32

Hend.   Amabo, mea dulcis Ipsitilla,
meae deliciae, mei lepores,
iube ad te ueniam meridiatum.
et si iusseris, illud adiuuato,
5   ne quis luminis obseret tabellam,
neu tibi lubeat foras abire,
sed domi maneas paresque nobis
nouem continuas fututiones.
uerum si quid ages, statim iubeto:
10   nam pransus iaceo et satur supinus
pertundo tunicamque palliumque.

33

Hend.   O furum optime balneariorum
Vibenni pater et cinaede fili
(nam dextra pater inquinatiore,
culo filius est uoraciore),
5   cur non exilium malasque in oras
itis ? quandoquidem patris rapinae
notae sunt populo, et natis pilosas,
fili, non potes asse uenditare.

34

GlycPher   Dianae sumus in fide
puellae et pueri integri:
<Dianam pueri integri>
puellaeque canamus.

32.5: luminis *O, Gratwick*, liminis *X*.

32

Please please *please*, my darling Ipsithilla,
oh my delicate dish, my clever sweetheart,
please invite me home for the siesta—
and, supposing that you *do* invite me, make sure
5 no one happens to bolt and bar your shutters,
and that *you* don't, on a whim, decide to
go off out: just stay home and prepare for
us nine whole uninterrupted fuckfests.
Fact is, if you're on, ask me *at once*, I've
10 lunched, I'm full, flat on my back and bursting
up, up, up, through undershirt and bedclothes!

33

Oh you cream of the con men in the bathhouse,
Pop Vibennius, and your son the bum-boy—
Dad may have a dirtier right hand, but
Junior's got a more voracious backside—
5 why not just sod off to exile in some
hellhole, since Dad's larcenies are public
knowledge, while *you*, son, cannot hawk your bristly
asshole, no, not even for a penny!

34

We in Díana's tutelage
chaste unwed boys and maidens are:
óf Diana as chaste unwed
boys and maidens let's sing now.

5   o Latonia, maximi
magna progenies Iouis,
quam mater prope Deliam
deposiuit oliuam,

montium domina ut fores
10   siluarumque uirentium
saltuumque reconditorum
amniumque sonantum:

tu Lucina dolentibus
Iuno dicta puerperis,
15   tu potens Triuia et notho es
dicta lumine Luna.

tu cursu, dea, menstruo
metiens iter annuum,
rustica agricolae bonis
20   tecta frugibus exples.

sis quocumque tibi placet
sancta nomine, Romulique,
antique ut solita es, bona
sospites ope gentem.

35

Hend.   Poetae tenero, meo sodali,
uelim Caecilio, papyre, dicas
Veronam ueniat, Noui relinquens
Comi moenia Lariumque litus.
5   nam quasdam uolo cogitationes
amici accipiat sui meique.
quare, si sapiet, uiam uorabit,
quamuis candida milies puella
euntem reuocet, manusque collo

5 Leto's daughter, by greatest Jove
   sired, yourself the great progeny
   whom your mother delivered there
   under the Delian olive,

   mistress-to-be of all mountain glens,
10 all green-burgeoning forestage,
   all remote and sequestered rides,
   every echoing river:

   women in pangs of childbirth call
   ón you as Juno Lucina, you're
15 potent at crossways, sometimes named
   Moon with counterfeit lustre.

   Measuring out in your monthly course,
   Goddess, the year's whole itinerary,
   you fill the farmer's rustic barns
20 with an abundant harvest.

   By whatever title you please
   be you reverenced, and as once
   long ago you were wont, protect,
   strongly, Romulus' scions.

35

   Would you kindly, papyrus, tell my comrade,
   sensitive bard Caecilius, to leave the
   ramparts of Novum Comum and its lakeside,
   make a visit across here to Verona?
5 Í'd líke hím to mull certain cogitations
   made by someone who's friend to him and me both—
   wherefore, if he's wise, he'll eat the distance,
   even though called back a thousand times by
   that cute girl from his journey, flinging both arms

10   ambas iniciens roget morari.
       quae nunc, si mihi uera nuntiantur,
       illum deperit impotente amore.
       nam quo tempore legit incohatam
       Dindymi dominam, ex eo misellae
15   ignes interiorem edunt medullam.
       ignosco tibi, Sapphica puella
       musa doctior; est enim uenuste
       Magna Caecilio incohata Mater.

36

Hend.   Annales Volusi, cacata carta,
       uotum soluite pro mea puella.
       nam sanctae Veneri Cupidinique
       uouit, si sibi restitutus essem
5   desissemque truces uibrare iambos,
       electissima pessimi poetae
       scripta tardipedi deo daturam
       infelicibus ustulanda lignis.
       et hoc pessima se puella uidit
10   iocose ac lepide uouere diuis.
       nunc o caeruleo creata ponto,
       quae sanctum Idalium Vriosque apertos
       quaeque Ancona Cnidumque harundinosam
       colis quaeque Amathunta quaeque Golgos
15   quaeque Durrachium Hadriae tabernam,
       acceptum face redditumque uotum,
       si non illepidum neque inuenustum est.
       at uos interea uenite in ignem,
       pleni ruris et inficetiarum
20   annales Volusi, cacata carta.

36.10: iocose ac lepide *Goold*, iocose lepide *V*

10　round his neck and beseeching him to linger—
　　she who, if the news I hear's the truth, is
　　dying of hopeless passion for him. Ever
　　since she perused his still unfinished opus
　　Dindymos' Mistress, flames have been consuming
15　all her inmost marrow. I don't blame you,
　　girl more well-read than Sappho's Muse: no doubt that
　　this work by Caecilius, his *Great Mother*,
　　is, quite true, most beautifully *un*finished.

[handwritten margin note: thoughts on another poet — needs polishing]

36

　　You, Volusius' *Annals*, crappy chapters,
　　please discharge this vow made by my girlfriend:
　　she to holy Venus and to Cupid
　　swore that, should she get me back, and if I
5　stopped unleashing my harsh iambics on her,
　　she'd serve up all the choicest writings of the
　　dead-worst poet to the crippled god for roasting
　　on funereal firewood. She, the dead-worst
　　girl herself, supposed this vow to all the
10　gods a witty joke, so now, O Thou formed
　　from the dark blue sea, who hauntest all Thy
　　holy sites like Idalium and Urii's
　　open roadstead, Ancona, reedy Cnidus,
　　Amathus too and Golgi, not to mention
15　Dyrrachium, famed Adriatic tavern—
　　note this vow as entered and discharged, and
　　not entirely charmless or unwitty.
　　You, though, meanwhile serve the fire as fuel,
　　one great load of countrified ineptness,
20　you, Volusius' *Annals*, crappy chapters.

37

Chol. Salax taberna uosque contubernales,
a pilleatis nona fratribus pila,
solis putatis esse mentulas uobis,
solis licere, quidquid est puellarum,
5   confutuere et putare ceteros hircos?
an, continenter quod sedetis insulsi
centum an ducenti, non putatis ausurum
me una ducentos irrumare sessores?
atqui putate: namque totius uobis
10 frontem tabernae sopionibus scribam.
puella nam mi, quae meo sinu fugit,
amata tantum quantum amabitur nulla,
pro qua mihi sunt magna bella pugnata,
consedit istic. hanc boni beatique
15 omnes amatis, et quidem, quod indignum est,
omnes pusilli et semitarii moechi;
tu praeter omnes une de capillatis,
cuniculosae Celtiberiae fili,
Egnati, opaca quem bonum facit barba
20 et dens Hibera defricatus urina.

38

Hend. Malest, Cornifici, tuo Catullo,
malest, me hercule, et laboriose,
et magis magis in dies et horas.
quem tu, quod minimum facillimumque est,
5   qua solatus es allocutione?
irascor tibi. sic meos amores?
paulum quid lubet allocutionis,
maestius lacrimis Simonideis.

37

Public house, bordello, and you, its habitués,
nine doors along from the felt-hatted Brethren—
you think your crowd the only ones with cocks, then?
the one lot licensed to fuck all the girlies,
5   while the rest of us are goats? Because there's one,
or maybe two, hundred of you dumbass fuckwits
sitting lined up here, you really suppose I wouldn't
dare fill two hundred cocksucking squatters' mouths?
Well, think again. *And* I'll cover the whole frontage
10 of your damn tavern with obscene graffiti—
for that girl of mine, now fled from my embraces,
once loved by me as none shall be, ever again,
for whose dear sake I fought great wars, now has
taken up residence here. All you smart and wealthy
15 buzzflies are mad for her, and so (to her discredit)
is every petty adulterer from the backstreets,
and you above all, king of the long-haired ponces,
product of Spain with all its teeming rabbits,
Egnatius, aping class with your thick, black beard and
20 flashing teeth scrubbed white with Spanish urine.

38

Life is really a bitch for your Catullus,
Cornificius, *and* (my god!) so *boring*,
and it keeps getting worse now, daily, hourly—
yet have you—it would take the slightest, simplest
5 effort—*offered him any consolation?*
I'm pissed off with you. *That* much for my love, then?
Please, please, spare me *some* small consolation,
words more tearful than the message on a gravestone!

39

Chol.   Egnatius, quod candidos habet dentes,
renidet usque quaque. si ad rei uentum est
subsellium, cum orator excitat fletum,
renidet ille; si ad pii rogum fili

5   lugetur, orba cum flet unicum mater,
renidet ille. quidquid est, ubicumque est,
quodcumque agit, renidet: hunc habet morbum,
neque elegantem, ut arbitror, neque urbanum.
quare monendum est <te> mihi, bone Egnati.

10   si urbanus esses aut Sabinus aut Tiburs
aut parcus Vmber aut obesus Etruscus
aut Lanuuinus ater atque dentatus
aut Transpadanus, ut meos quoque attingam,
aut quilubet, qui puriter lauit dentes,

15   tamen renidere usque quaque te nollem:
nam risu inepto res ineptior nulla est.
nunc Celtiber <es>: Celtiberia in terra,
quod quisque minxit, hoc sibi solet mane
dentem atque russam defricare gingiuam,

20   ut, quo iste uester expolitior dens est,
hoc te amplius bibisse praedicet loti.

40

Hend.   Quaenam te mala mens, miselle Rauide,
agit praecipitem in meos iambos?
quis deus tibi non bene aduocatus
uecordem parat excitare rixam ?

5   an ut peruenias in ora uulgi?
quid uis? qualubet esse notus optas?
eris, quandoquidem meos amores
cum longa uoluisti amare poena.

39.11: parcus *V*, pinguis *Lindsay*

satire: mildly makes fun of human
faults / social follies

invective: sharp, abusive
hostile speech;
tone of anger / outrage
at some percieved
harm, for example,
hypocrisy

39

Because Egnatius has those damn white teeth, he
flashes them everywhere. On the bench in court,
when counsel for the defense is coaxing tears, he
flashes them. Beside the pyre of a loving son, as
5   mama, grief-stricken, mourns her lost sole child, he
flashes them. Whatever's up, wherever, never
mind what he's doing, he flashes them. This sick urge
is, I would say, neither elegant nor well bred.
So I have to warn you, Egnatius, my good sir,
10 that even if you were Roman, or Sabine, or Tiburtine,
a thrifty Umbrian or an Etruscan fat-cat,
a swarthy Lanuvium sporting big buck teeth
or (to include my own people) a Transpadane, or
anyone who cleans his teeth with good pure water,
15 I'd *still* not want you flashing yours all round, since
nothing's more fatuous than a fatuous grin. *But*
actually you're a Spaniard, and on Spanish terrain
everyone hoards his night piss, which next morning
he uses to scrub off his teeth, *and* his sore red gums:
20 so the more brightly polished your nice white teeth, the
more stale piddle it proves that you've just knocked back.

40

Wretched Ravidus, what mistaken judgment
drives you headlong into my iambics?
What god, ill invoked by you, is getting
ready to conjure up a senseless quarrel?
5   What's your game, then? To be a vulgar byword,
get yourself known at all costs? *That* you will be,
since you've chosen to be my lover's lover—
and pay the long-term price for your intrusion!

41

Hend.   Ameana puella defututa
tota milia me decem poposcit,
ista turpiculo puella naso,
decoctoris amica Formiani.
5   propinqui, quibus est puella curae,
amicos medicosque conuocate :
non est sana puella, nec rogare
qualis sit solet aes imaginosum.

42

Hend.   Adeste, hendecasyllabi, quot estis
omnes undique, quotquot estis omnes.
iocum me putat esse moecha turpis,
et negat mihi nostra reddituram
5   pugillaria, si pati potestis.
persequamur eam et reflagitemus.
quae sit, quaeritis ? illa, quam uidetis
turpe incedere, mimice ac moleste
ridentem catuli ore Gallicani.
10   circumsistite eam, et reflagitate,
"moecha putida, redde codicillos,
redde, putida moecha, codicillos!"
non assis facit: o lutum, lupanar,
aut si perditius potest quid esse.
15   sed non est tamen hoc satis putandum.
quod si non aliud potest, ruborem
ferreo canis exprimamus ore.
conclamate iterum altiore uoce

42.13: facit *Halbertsma,* facis? *V.* 14: potest *Ital.,* potes *V*

41

Ameana, that fucked-out little scrubber,
just had the nerve to ask me for ten thousand.
(She's the one with the rather icky nose, the
bankrupt from Formiae's mistress.) Her relations,
those responsible for the creature's welfare,
really need now to call on friends—and doctors:
shé's clean out of her mind, that girl, and never
spot-checks her true cash value in the mirror.

42

Come, you hendecasyllables, in force now,
each last one of you, from every quarter—
this vile slut seems under the impression
I'm a walking joke, won't give me back my
writing tablets—really, can you beat it?
Let's go after her, call for their surrender!
Which one is she, you ask? The one you see there,
her with the vulgar stride, the quite revolting
stage-door laugh, the face like a French poodle's.
Close in round her now, demand in chorus:
"Rotten slut, give back the writing tablets!
Give back, rotten slut, the writing tablets!"
Not one farthing she cares, the filthy scrubber
(fill in any nastier name you think of).
Still, don't let's make this our final effort—
even though we can't do more, let's raise a
burning blush on the bitch's brazen face, so
all shout one more time, and even louder,

"moecha putida, redde codicillos,
20 redde, putida moecha, codicillos!"
sed nil proficimus, nihil mouetur.
mutanda est ratio modusque uobis,
siquid proficere amplius potestis:
"pudica et proba, redde codicillos."

43

Hend. Salve, nec minimo puella naso
nec bello pede nec nigris ocellis
nec longis digitis nec ore sicco
nec sane nimis elegante lingua,
5 decoctoris amica Formiani.
ten prouincia narrat esse bellam ?
tecum Lesbia nostra comparatur ?
o saeclum insapiens et infacetum !

44

Chol. O funde noster seu Sabine seu Tiburs
(nam te esse Tiburtem autumant, quibus non est
cordi Catullum laedere; at quibus cordi est,
quouis Sabinum pignore esse contendunt),
5 sed seu Sabine siue uerius Tiburs,
fui libenter in tua suburbana
uilla, malamque pectore expuli tussim,
non inmerenti quam mihi meus uenter,
dum sumptuosas appeto, dedit, cenas.
10 nam, Sestianus dum uolo esse conuiua,
orationem in Antium petitorem
plenam ueneni et pestilentiae legi.
hinc me grauedo frigida et frequens tussis

44.13: hinc *Green,* hic *V.* 17: ultu' *Muretus,* ulta *V*

"Rotten slut, give back the writing tablets!
20 *Give back, rotten slut, the writing tablets!"*
Still this gets us nowhere, she remains un-
moved, you'll need to change your tune and method.
Try this, then, see if it gets you further:
"Pure chaste maid, give back the writing tablets!"

43

Hi there, girl with a nose by no means tiny,
non-dark eyes and two *most* undainty ankles,
not-long fingers and undry lips, besides a
tongue that's far from overly refined—you
5   bankrupt from Formiae's mistress! Does the Province
spread the word that you're attractive? Do men
pick on *you* to compare my Lesbia with now?
Oh this tasteless age, ill bred and witless!

44

Our Country Place, which art Sabine—or maybe Tiburtine
(for those proclaim thee Tiburtine whose hearts hold no
malice towards Catullus, whereas those whose do
will bet the house thou art Sabine), but whichever
5   thou art, be it Sabine or maybe Tiburtine, I
was so glad to be settled in thy not quite urban
villa, convalescing from a bad chest cough
caught by my own damn fault, my own damn greed while
chasing invitations to expensive blowouts, for it
10 was through my determination to be Sestius' guest that
I came to read his speech attacking Antius'
candidacy, packed with poison, pestilential stuff,
and contracted a freezing cold and a chronic cough

quassauit usque, dum in tuum sinum fugi,
15 et me recuraui otioque et urtica.
quare refectus maximas tibi grates
ago, meum quod non es ultu' peccatum.
nec deprecor iam, si nefaria scripta
Sesti recepso, quin grauedinem et tussim
20 non mi, sed ipsi Sestio ferat frigus,
qui tunc uocat me, cum malum librum legi.

45

Hend. Acmen Septimius suos amores
tenens in gremio "mea" inquit "Acme,
ni te perdite amo atque amare porro
omnes sum assidue paratus annos,
5 quantum qui pote plurimum perire,
solus in Libya Indiaue tosta
caesio ueniam obuius leoni.'
hoc ut dixit, Amor sinistra ut ante
dextra sternuit approbationem.
10   at Acme leuiter caput reflectens
et dulcis pueri ebrios ocellos
illo purpureo ore suauiata,
"sic," inquit "mea uita Septimille,
huic uni domino usque seruiamus,
15 ut multo mihi maior acriorque
ignis mollibus ardet in medullis."
hoc ut dixit, Amor sinistra ut ante
dextra sternuit approbationem.
    nunc ab auspicio bono profecti
20 mutuis animis amant amantur.

45.6: Indiaue *Green*, Indiaque *V*

that shook me until I retreated to thy bosom
15 and cured myself with rest and nettle tea. Wherefore,
recovered now, I offer thee my heartfelt thanks
that thou didst not punish my misdeed—nor will
I complain, should I ever again be given frigid stuff
from Sestius' ghastly works, should it unload nasal
20 drip and a hacking cough, not on me but on Sestius,
for inviting me just when I've read his malignant brief!

45

Holding his girlfriend Acme close upon his
lap, Septimius said: "My darling Acme,
if I don't love you madly, if I'm not quite,
quite resolved to be constant all my lifetime,
5 insurpassably, desperately devoted,
in far Libya or burning India may I
meet up, solo, with a green-eyed lion!"
At these words, Love leftward as beforehand
rightward sneezed his approbation. Then sweet
10 Acme, gently tilting back her head and
with those rich red lips bestowing kisses
on her darling boy's besotted eyes, said:
"Thus, Septimius, *thus*, my life, my precious,
may we serve this single lord for ever,
15 while more strongly and fiercely day by day this
hot flame blazes through my melting marrow."
At these words, Love leftward as beforehand
rightward sneezed his approbation. Now from
this auspicious omen setting out, they
20 give and receive true love with equal passion.

love duet,
false love

own

involuntary

unam Septimius misellus Acmen
mauult quam Syrias Britanniasque:
uno in Septimio fidelis Acme
facit delicias libidinesque.
25 quis ullos homines beatiores
uidit, quis Venerem auspicatiorem ?

46

Hend. Iam uer egelidos refert tepores,
iam caeli furor aequinoctialis
iucundis Zephyri silescit aureis.
linquantur Phrygii, Catulle, campi
5 Nicaeaeque ager uber aestuosae:
ad claras Asiae uolemus urbes.
iam mens praetrepidans auet uagari,
iam laeti studio pedes uigescunt.
o dulces comitum ualete coetus,
10 longe quos simul a domo profectos
diuersae uarie uiae reportant.

47

Hend. Porci et Socration, duae sinistrae
Pisonis, scabies famesque mundi,
uos Veraniolo meo et Fabullo
uerpus praeposuit Priapus ille ?
5 uos conuiuia lauta sumptuose
de die facitis, mei sodales
quaerunt in triuio uocationes ?

Poor Septimius now rates Acme over
all the hoopla of Syria and Britain;
with Septimius only, faithful Acme
runs the gamut of all delights and pleasures.
25 Who, pray, ever saw two more triumphant
lovers, who a Venus more auspicious?

46 *themes: spring friendship journey*

Now spring fetches back the warmth, and winter's
chills die out; now raging equinoctial
storms are hushed by the west wind's pleasant breezes.
Leave these Phrygian plains, Catullus, leave the
5 lush green meadows of summer-hot Nicaea:
let's decamp, move to Asia's famous cities.
Now my heart's in a tizzy, yearns for action,
nów my feét jitter, eager to be going—
so goodbye to my band of pleasant colleagues:
10 though we made the long trip from home together,
widely varying routes will take us back now.

47

Socration and Porcius, Piso's pair of
left-hand men, the world's prize itch and gut-ache,
has that stripped prick, that damn Priapus chosen
you over dear Veranius and Fabullus?
5 Are *you* setting up smart expensive dinners—
in broad daylight too—while my companions
tramp the streets in their search for invitations?

48

Hend.   Mellitos oculos tuos, Iuuenti,
si quis me sinat usque basiare,
usque ad milia basiem trecenta
nec mi umquam uidear satur futurus,
5   non si densior aridis aristis
sit nostrae seges osculationis.

49

Hend.   Disertissime Romuli nepotum,
quot sunt quotque fuere, Marce Tulli,
quotque post aliis erunt in annis,
gratias tibi maximas Catullus
5   agit pessimus omnium poeta,
tanto pessimus omnium poeta,
quanto tu optimus omnium patronus.

50

Hend.   Hesterno, Licini, die otiosi
multum lusimus in meis tabellis,
ut conuenerat esse delicatos:
scribens uersiculos uterque nostrum
5   ludebat numero modo hoc modo illoc,
reddens mutua per iocum atque uinum.
atque illinc abii tuo lepore
incensus, Licini, facetiisque,
ut nec me miserum cibus iuuaret
10   nec somnus tegeret quiete ocellos,
sed toto indomitus furore lecto

48.4: mi umquam *Statius*, numquam *V*

48

Oh those honey-sweet eyes of yours, Juventius!
If they'd let me kiss them all I wanted
I'd go on three hundred thousand times, and
never feel I was getting near my limit,
5   even though our crop of osculations
ended tighter-packed than dried-out wheat ears.

49

Sweetest-spoken of Romulus' descendants, *Cicero*
past or present, Marcus Tullius, and all who   *sarcasm*
may yet follow in the distant future—
warmest thanks to you herewith from Catullus,
5   who's the worst of all poets, by as much the
worst of all living poets, as yourself are
best of all courtroom lawyers for your clients.

50

Being at leisure yesterday, we had great
fun, Licinius, with impromptu verses
(on agreement to be light and witty),
each alternately scribbling little squiblets,
5   playing around with every kind of metre,
matching jest with jest, vintage with vintage.
When I left I was só high on your dazzling
charm, Licinius, and your smart one-liners,
eating afforded me (ah poor me!) no pleasure,
10   sleep just *would not* quietly close my eyelids—
there I lay on my bed in mad excitement,

uersarer, cupiens uidere lucem,
ut tecum loquerer simulque ut essem.
at defessa labore membra postquam
15 semimortua lectulo iacebant,
hoc, iucunde, tibi poema feci,
ex quo perspiceres meum dolorem.
nunc audax caue sis, precesque nostras,
oramus, caue despuas, ocelle,
20 ne poenas Nemesis reposcat a te.
est uemens dea: laedere hanc caueto.

51

Sapph. Ille mi par esse deo uidetur,
ille, si fas est, superare diuos,
qui sedens aduersus identidem te
    spectat et audit

5 dulce ridentem, misero quod omnis
eripit sensus mihi: nam simul te,
Lesbia, aspexi, nihil est super mi
    <uocis in ore;>

lingua sed torpet, tenuis sub artus
10 flamma demanat, sonitu suopte
tintinant aures, gemina teguntur
    lumina nocte.

otium, Catulle, tibi molestum est:
otio exsultas nimiumque gestis:
15 otium et reges prius et beatas
    perdidit urbes.

51.8: <uocis in ore> *Ritter, lacuna V*

tossing, eager for morning, which would let me
be with you, talk with you. But when, exhausted
by such work, my limbs were sprawled across my
15 truckle bed, half dead from all the effort,
then I made this poem for you, sweetheart,
let it tell you the depth of my emotion.
Now please don't be thoughtless, don't despise our
prayers, we beg of you, precious, lest hereafter
20 Nemesis catches you, demands repayment:
she's a vehement goddess, don't provoke her.

 51

In my eyes he seems like a god's co-equal,   — *person sitting with*
he, if I dare say so, eclipses godhead,   *Lesbia is on par w/ god*
who now face to face, uninterrupted,
    watches and hears you

5   sweetly laughing—*that* sunders unhappy me from
all my senses: the instant I catch sight of
you now, Lesbia, dumbness grips my <voice, it
    dies on my vocal   *longing =*
                                               disease

cords>, my tongue goes torpid, and through my body
10 thin fire lances down, my ears are ringing
with their own thunder, while night curtains both my
    eyes into darkness.

Leisure, Catullus, is dangerous to you: leisure   *too much*
urges you into extravagant behavior: *responsibility*
15 leisure in time gone by has ruined kings and   *for love*
    prosperous cities.

52

ITrim Quid est, Catulle ? quid moraris emori ?
   sella in curuli struma Nonius sedet,
   per consulatum peierat Vatinius :
   quid est, Catulle ? quid moraris emori ?

53

Hend. Risi nescio quem modo e corona,
   qui, cum mirifice Vatiniana
   meus crimina Caluos explicasset,
   admirans ait haec manusque tollens,
 5 "di magni, salaputium disertum !"

54

Hend. Othonis caput (oppido est pusillum),
   uestri, Rustice, semilauta crura,
   subtile et leue peditum Libonis—
   si non omnia, displicere uellem
 5 tibi et Fufidio seni recocto . . .
   irascere iterum meis iambis
   inmerentibus, unice imperator?

54.2: uestri *Green*, †et eri† *V*; Rustice *Statius*, rustice *V*. 5: Fufidio *Bickel*, sufficio *V*. 7: ? add. *Green*.

52

What's left, Catullus? Why not die right here and now?
That pustule Nonius occupies a curule chair,
Vatinius falsely swears by his own consulship.
What's left, Catullus? Why not die right here and now?

53

Nice joke lately in court from some bystander:
when my Calvus had finished his quite brilliant
list of all Vatinius' misdemeanors,
this man cries, hands raised in admiration,
5   "Oh my god, an articulate cock-robin!"

54

 Caesar

Otho's bean (it's so tiny he's a pinhead),
your legs, Rusticus, never fully washed, and
Libo's smooth and crafty crepitations—
these at least, I would hope, will irritate both
5   you and Fufidius, that warmed-up oldie . . .   *overtones*
Going to lose your cool again because of
my oh-so-innocent iambics, super *Duce?*

55

Hend.	Oramus, si forte non molestum est,
[Dec.]	demonstres ubi sint tuae tenebrae.
	te Campo quaesiuimus minore,
	te in Circo, te in omnibus libellis,
5	te in templo summi Iouis sacrato.
	in Magni simul ambulatione
	femellas omnes, amice, prendi,
	quas uultu uidi tamen sereno.
	"adferte huc," sic ipse flagitabam,
10	"Camerium mihi, pessimae puellae!"
	quaedam inquit, nudum sinum reducens,
	"en hic in roseis latet papillis."
	sed te iam ferre Herculei labos est;
	tanto te in fastu negas, amice.
15	dic nobis ubi sis futurus, ede
	audacter, committe, crede luci.
	nunc te lacteolae tenent puellae ?
	si linguam clauso tenes in ore,
	fructus proicies amoris omnes.
20	uerbosa gaudet Venus loquella.
	uel, si uis, licet obseres palatum,
	dum uestri sim particeps amoris.

56

Hend.	O rem ridiculam, Cato, et iocosam,
	dignamque auribus et tuo cachinno!
	ride quidquid amas, Cato, Catullum :
	res est ridicula et nimis iocosa.
5	deprendi modo pupulum puellae

55.3: te in *Sillig,* te *V.* 9: adferte *Green,* huc *Lee,* †auelte† *V.* 11: sinum reducens *Avantiu*s, nudum reduc . . . *V*

Please come clean, if it isn't too much trouble—
Where's your hideout? Show us! We've been searching
high and low for you—on the lesser Campus,
round the Circus, in all the bookstores, even
5 up in the hallowed shrine of Jove Almighty.
Meanwhile down in Pompey's colonnade I've
been on at all the girlies, friend, although they
looked quite blank at my words. "Just hand him over,"
Í told every one of them. "Come on now,
10 bad bad girls, let me see Camerius pronto!"
"Here," said one, pulling down her dress, "you want him?
He's right here, in between my rosy titties!"
Oh my friend, putting up with you's a bore now,
you're so arrogant in your flat denials!
15 Tell us the place you're going to be, reveal it
bravely, blurt the truth out, trust in daylight.
Bosomy blondes have got you in their clutches?
If you seal your tongue in, clamp your lips shut,
that'll lose you all the fruits of passion—
20 Venus loves those rhetorical cadenzas.
Still, if such is your wish, keep mum—provided
I can stake out a claim to share your love now!

56

Cato, such a ridiculous and comic
Business, *well* worth your notice, sure to get a
Giggle, Cato: laugh, if you love Catullus!
So ridiculous, really too *too* comic—
5 I just caught my girlfriend's little slave boy

trusantem; hunc ego, si placet Dionae,
protelo rigida mea cecidi.

57

Hend.   Pulcre conuenit improbis cinaedis,
        Mamurrae pathicoque Caesarique.
        nec mirum: maculae pares utrisque,
        urbana altera et illa Formiana,
5   impressae resident nec eluentur:
        morbosi pariter, gemelli utrique,
        uno in lecticulo erudituli ambo,
        non hic quam ille magis uorax adulter,
        riuales socii et puellularum.
10   pulcre conuenit improbis cinaedis.

58A

Hend.   Caeli, Lesbia nostra, Lesbia illa,
        illa Lesbia, quam Catullus unam
        plus quam se atque suos amauit omnes,
        nunc in quadriuiis et angiportis
5   glubit magnanimos Remi nepotes.

58B

Hend. Non custos si fingar ille Cretum,
[Dec.] non Ladas ego pinnipesue Perseus,
        non si Pegaseo ferar uolatu,
        non Rhesi niueae citaeque bigae;
5   adde huc plumipedas uolatilesque,

57.9: socii et *V*, socii *Avantius*
58a.5: magnanimos *Ital.*, magnanimi *Voss*, magna amiremini *V*

Getting it up for her, and (Venus love me!)
Split *him*, tandem-fashion, with *my* banger!

57

They're well matched, that pair of shameless buggers,
Bitch-queens both of them, Caesar and Mamurra—
Why not? Both display the same disease-spots
(Caught in town by one, abroad by t'other),
5   Deep pocks, there for life, no scrubbing *them* out.
Twins indeed, both sharing the same sickness,
Two sort-of-well-read dwarfs on one cute couchlet,
Hotshots both as studs for married ladies,
Such close friends—but rivals after nymphets—
10 They're well-matched, that pair of shameless buggers.

[handwritten marginalia: belittling]

[handwritten marginalia: sexual insulted]

58A

Caelius, Lesbia—*our* dear Lesbia, *that* one,
that Lesbia whom alone Catullus worshipped
more than himself, far more than all his kinsfolk—
now on backstreet corners and down alleys
5   jacks off Remus's generous descendants.

[handwritten marginalia: she's just a mistress / slut]

58B

Even were I Crete's own brazen guardian,
or wing-footed Perseus, or that runner
Ladas, even should I hitch a ride on
Pegasus, ór were to drive the snow white mares of
5   Rhesus—yes, and throw in wings and feathers,

uentorumque simul require cursum,
quos iunctos, Cameri, mihi dicares:
defessus tamen omnibus medullis
et multis languoribus peresus
10   essem te, mi amice, quaeritando.

59

Chol.   Bononiensis Rufa Rufulum fellat,
uxor Meneni, saepe quam in sepulcretis
uidistis ipso rapere de rogo cenam,
cum deuolutum ex igne prosequens panem
5   ab semiraso tunderetur ustore.

60

Chol.   Num te leaena montibus Libystinis
aut Scylla latrans infima inguinum parte
tam mente dura procreauit ac taetra,
ut supplicis uocem in nouissimo casu
5   contemptam haberes, a nimis fero corde ?

61

GlycPher.   Collis O Heliconii
cultor, Vraniae genus,
qui rapis teneram ad uirum
uirginem, o Hymenaee Hymen,
5   o Hymen Hymenaee;

58b.10: mi amice *Scaliger*, mihi amice *V*

and insist on the speed of all the storm winds:
harness me up this lot, Camerius, still I'd
end worn out, just knackered to the marrow,
gnawed right down to the bone by sheer exhaustion
10 after this endless search for you, my comrade.

59

Rufa, Bologna lady, sucks dear Rufus' cock—
Menenius' wife, the one you've seen lots of times
out in the graveyards, snitching food off a pyre,
in pursuit of a loaf that's tumbled from the cinders,
5   or getting banged by some stubble-chinned corpse burner.

60

Was it a lioness up in the Libyan foothills
or Scylla barking from her nether groin who
bore you with so tough and harsh a mind-set
that you could scorn a suppliant's desperate cry
5   in his last, worst, crisis, ah too savage heart?

61

marriage hymn

epithalmium – wedding song

Hymen, dweller on Helicon's
slopes, Urania's progeny,
you who snatch off the ~~tender bride~~
to her husband, O Hymen, O

greek god of marriage

5   Hymen, o Hymeneal!

cinge tempora floribus
suaue olentis amaraci,
flammeum cape laetus, huc
huc ueni, niueo gerens
10   luteum pede soccum;

excitusque hilari die,
nuptialia concinens
uoce carmina tinnula,
pelle humum pedibus, manu
15   pineam quate taedam.

namque Iunia Manlio,
qualis Idalium colens
uenit ad Phrygium Venus
iudicem, bona cum bona
20   nubet alite uirgo,

floridis uelut enitens
myrtus Asia ramulis
quos Hamadryades deae
ludicrum sibi roscido
25   nutriunt umore.

quare age, huc aditum ferens,
perge linquere Thespiae
rupis Aonios specus,
nympha quos super irrigat
30   frigerans Aganippe.

ac domum dominam uoca
coniugis cupidam noui,
mentem amore reuinciens,
ut tenax hedera huc et huc
35   arborem implicat errans

Wreathe your temples with blossoms of
softly sweet-scented marjoram, *yellow*
don the ~~flame-tinted veil~~ and come
hither joyfully, snow white foot

10   shod in the yellow slipper.

Summoned now on this happy day,
join in singing the wedding hymn—
let your high-ringing voice be heard,
let your foot tap the beat, your hand   *customary*

15   brandish on high the pine torch.   *wedding torch*

This for Junia—lovely as   *bride* — *beautiful*
Venus, queen of Idalium,
on the way to her Phrygian   *groom*
judge—who'll marry with Manlius,

20   fair bride brought with fair omen,

like some myrtle of Asia, bright
shining with twigs all in bud—divine
nymphs, Hamádryads, nurture them
as their own favorite plaything, on

25   moisture of morning dewdrops.

Wherefore come, make your presence known,
hasten, leave the Aonian
caves of Helicon's rocky slopes
down which courses the cooling stream

30   from the spring Aganippe.

Call to her home the ~~bride-to-be~~
yearning for her new husband, and
bind her heart fast with love, as clings
ivy this way and that, as twine

35   tendrils around the tree trunk.

109

uosque item simul, integrae
uirgines, quibus aduenit
par dies, agite in modum
dicite, o Hymenaee Hymen,
40   o Hymen Hymenaee.

ut lubentius, audiens
se citarier ad suum
munus, huc aditum ferat
dux bonae Veneris, boni
45   coniugator amoris.

quis deus magis est ama-
tis petendus amantibus ?
quem colent homines magis
caelitum, o Hymenaee Hymen,
50   o Hymen Hymenaee ?

te suis tremulus parens
inuocat, tibi uirgines
zonula soluunt sinus,
te timens cupida nouos
55   captat aure maritus.

tu fero iuueni in manus
floridam ipse puellulam
dedis a gremio suae
matris, o Hymenaee Hymen,
60   o Hymen Hymenaee.

nil potest sine te Venus,
fama quod bona comprobet,
commodi capere, at potest
te uolente. quis huic deo
65   compararier ausit ?

You too now, you the still unwed
maidens, biding your time till a
like day dawns for you, on the beat
raise the chorus, "O Hymen, O

40   Hymen, O Hymeneal!"

Thus more gladly, on hearing him-
self called forth to perform his own
office, he'll bring his presence here,   *marriage*
lord of right-channelled passion and   *(societal*

45   conjugator of trúe love.   *expectations)*

There's no god to be sought after
more by lovers and loved ones—which
heavenly being will be worshipped by
mankind over you, Hymen, O

50   Hymen, O Hymeneal?

You all tremulous parents beg   *parents*
on their children's behalf; for you   *expected to*
                                                            be nervous
intact virgins ungirdle; you   *rite of passage*
capture each novice husband's keen

55   (ánd uneasy) attention.

Into a young man's fierce embrace   *- traditionalist*
you hand over the child in bloom
straight from the loving breast of her
mother, O Hymeneal, O

60   Hymen, O Hymeneal!

Lacking you Venus cannot gain
any profit that good repute
would approve of, but granted your
favor, can. Who'd have courage to

65   match himself with *this* godhead?

nulla quit sine te domus
liberos dare, nec parens
stirpe nitier; at potest
te uolente. quis huic deo
70   compararier ausit ?

quae tuis careat sacris,
non queat dare praesides
terra finibus: at queat
te uolente. quis huic deo
75   compararier ausit ?

claustra pandite ianuae.
uirgo ades. uiden ut faces
splendidas quatiunt comas ?

————————————

————————————

————————————

————————————

tardet ingenuus pudor,
80 quem tamen magis audiens,
        flet quod ire necesse est.

flere desine. non tibi Au-
runculeia periculum est,
ne qua femina pulcrior
85 clarum ab Oceano diem
        uiderit uenientem.

talis in uario solet
diuitis domini hortulo
stare flos hyacinthinus.
90 sed moraris, abit dies.
        <prodeas noua nupta.>

61.77: ades *Schrader*, adest *V*

Lacking you, there's no home can have
freeborn children, nor parents lean
on their offspring, but granted your
will, they can. Who'd have courage to
70   match himself with *this* godhead?

children as a blessing

Lands deprived of your sacred rites
cannot breed proper guards for their
frontiers, but if they're granted your
favor, can. Who'd have courage to
75   match himself with *this* godhead?

soldiers

Unbar, fling wide the doors! O bride,
you're here! See how the torches shake,
splendidly, their bright fire-manes!

———————————————

———————————————

———————————————

———————————————

Well-bred modesty holds her back:
80   *this* is the voice she hears, and now
        weeps because she must go. Oh,

dry your tears! There's no danger, Au-
runculeia, that any more
lovely woman will see the bright
85   morning light as the dawn ascends
        dazzlingly out of Ocean.

So in the well-stocked garden of
some rich owner the blossoming
hyacinth puts on its show. But you
90   linger: daylight is fading fast:
        new bride, come out and join us!

prodeas noua nupta, si
iam uidetur, et audias
nostra uerba. uiden ? faces
95   aureas quatiunt comas :
     prodeas noua nupta.

non tuus leuis in mala
deditus uir adultera,
probra turpia persequens,
100   a tuis teneris uolet
     secubare papillis,

lenta sed uelut adsitas
uitis implicat arbores,
implicabitur in tuum
105   complexum. sed abit dies:
     prodeas noua nupta.

o cubile, quod omnibus

—————————————

—————————————

—————————————

     candido pede lecti,

quae tuo ueniunt ero,
110   quanta gaudia, quae uaga
nocte, quae medio die
gaudeat! sed abit dies :
     prodeas noua nupta.

tollite, <o> pueri, faces:
115   flammeum uideo uenire.
ite concinite in modum
     "io Hymen Hymenaee io,
       io Hymen Hymenaee."

New bride, come out and join us, if
you're prepared now, and listen to
this our message. See how the bright
95   torches shake out their golden manes!
     New bride, come out and join us!

Your man isn't a fly-by-night   — *Catullus +*
stuck on some cheap adulteress,   *Lesbia*
chasing vicious delights: he won't
100 want to bed down away from your
     breasts, your delicate nipples.

No way: just as the pliant vine   *— stability/*
winds itself around neighbor trees   *attachment*
he'll be firmly enfolded in
105 your embrace. But day's fading fast:
     new bride, come out and join us!

Marriage bed, that for everyone

     ——————————————

     ——————————————

——————————————

     at the couch's white foot now,

what delights will your lord enjoy,
110 great and many, both in the quick   *— sex*
night and then at siesta time—
such delights! But day's fading fast:
     new bride, come out and join us!

Hey boys, raise high your torches—I
115 see the flame-colored veil approach!
All together in chorus now:
"Io Hymen Hymeneal, io,
     io Hymen Hymeneal!"

ne diu taceat procax
120   Fescennina iocatio,
nec nuces pueris neget
desertum domini audiens
    concubinus amorem.

da nuces pueris, iners
125   concubine! satis diu
lusisti nucibus: lubet
iam seruire Talasio.
    concubine, nuces da.

sordebant tibi uilicae,
130   concubine, hodie atque heri:
nunc tuum cinerarius
tondet os. miser a miser
    concubine, nuces da.

diceris male te a tuis
135   unguentate glabris marite
abstinere, sed abstine.
io Hymen Hymenaee io,
    <io Hymen Hymenaee.>

scimus haec tibi quae licent
140   sola cognita, sed marito
ista non eadem licent.
io Hymen Hymenaee io,
    io Hymen Hymenaee.

nupta, tu quoque quae tuus
145   uir petet caue ne neges,
ni petitum aliunde eat.
io Hymen Hymenaee io,
    io Hymen Hymenaee.

Time, high time, for the ribald and
120   cocksure bantering; time for the
boy toy, finding himself cut off
from his master's affections, to
hand out nuts to the children!
Scatter nuts to the kids, you limp
125   boy toy! Long enough now you've been
playing with nuts: but today you must
yield your rule to the marriage god:
boy toy, scatter your nuts now!

Till today you despised the rough
130   farm girls, boy toy, but now your cheeks
must be shaved by the barber, you
wretched, thrice wretched creature, you!
Boy toy, scatter your nuts now!

Scented bridegroom, it's rumored you're
135   finding it hard to abstain from your
nice smooth boys, but abstain you must:
Io Hymen, Hymeneal io,
<io Hymen Hymeneal!>

Yes, we realize you've only known
140   licit pleasures—but married men
aren't allowed the same privilege!
Io Hymen, Hymeneal, io,
io Hymen Hymeneal!

You too, bride, must take care you don't
145   shut the door on your husband's needs
lest he take his demands elsewhere—
Io Hymen, Hymeneal io,
io Hymen Hymeneal!

en tibi domus ut potens
150 et beata uiri tui,
quae tibi sine seruiat
<io Hymen Hymenaee io,
   io Hymen Hymenaee.>

usque dum tremulum mouens
155 cana tempus anilitas
omnia omnibus annuit.
io Hymen Hymenaee io,
   io Hymen Hymenaee.

transfer omine cum bono
160 limen aureolos pedes,
rasilemque subi forem.
io Hymen Hymenaee io,
   io Hymen Hymenaee.

aspice intus ut accubans
165 uir tuus Tyrio in toro
totus immineat tibi.
io Hymen Hymenaee io,
   io Hymen Hymenaee!

illi non minus ac tibi
170 pectore uritur intimo
flamma, sed penite magis.
io Hymen Hymenaee io,
   io Hymen Hymenaee.

mitte brachiolum teres,
175 praetextate, puellulae:
iam cubile adeat uiri.
io Hymen Hymenaee io,
   io Hymen Hymenaee.

Here stands your husband's home for you—
150   see how wealthy and grand it is!
Let it serve you as mistress now,
Io Hymen, Hymeneal io,
    io Hymen Hymeneal!

—ánd till white-haired senility   *forever*
155   with its tremulous headpiece keeps
nod, nod, nodding at everything,
Io Hymen, Hymeneal io,
    io Hymen Hymeneal!

Líft yoúr golden feet with all best
160   omens over the threshold and
pass through the polished entrance-way—
Io Hymen, Hymeneal io,
    io Hymen Hymeneal!

See inside, how on purple-draped   *sexual*
165   couch your husband reclines, his whole   *references*
heart and mind now intent on you—
Io Hymen, Hymeneal io,
    io Hymen Hymeneal!

—since for him no whit less than for
170   you there burns in his innermost
self that flame, but more secretly:
Io Hymen, Hymeneal io,
    io Hymen Hymeneal!

You, boy page, must release the girl
175   bride's slim arm, since it's time for her
now to come to the marriage bed —
Io Hymen, Hymeneal io,
    io Hymen Hymeneal!

<uos> bonae senibus uiris
180 cognitae bene feminae
collocate puellulam.
  io Hymen Hymenaee io,
    io Hymen Hymenaee.

iam licet uenias, marite:
185 uxor in thalamo tibi est,
ore floridulo nitens,
alba parthenice uelut
  luteumue papauer.

at, marite, ita me iuuent
190 caelites, nihilo minus
pulcer es, neque te Venus
neglegit. sed abit dies:
  perge, ne remorare.

non diu remoratus es:
195 iam uenis. bona te Venus
iuuerit, quoniam palam
quod cupis cupis, et bonum
  non abscondis amorem.

ille pulueris Africi
200 siderumque micantium
subducat numerum prius,
qui uestri numerare uolt
  multa milia ludi.

ludite ut lubet, et breui
205 liberos date. non decet
tam uetus sine liberis
nomen esse, sed indidem
  semper ingenerari.

You, good wives, so well known to your
180 aged husbands, must settle the
bride child in her position now—
Io Hymen, Hymeneal io,
io Hymen Hymeneal!

Time now, bridegroom, for you to come:
185 here's your wife in the bridal bed,
face as bright as a flower in bud—
white parthenium blossom or
golden yellowish poppy.

Yet—so help me the heavenly
190 host!—you, bridegroom, are no whit less
beauteous, no way neglected by
Venus: bút daylight's ebbing fast,
come on quickly, don't linger.

Ah now, *you* didn't linger long:
195 here you are! May good Venus give
you support, since your longing for
what you long for is plain, and you
don't conceal your good passion.

All the sand grains of Africa,
200 every one of the glittering
constellations he first must count,
he who wants to enumerate
all your thousands of love plays.

Play as pleasure dictates, and soon
205 give us children: so old a name
shouldn't go short of heirs, it's not
right, no, they should renew themselves
out of the same stock forever.

[handwritten marginal note: personal reference]

Torquatus uolo paruulus
210 matris e gremio suae
porrigens teneras manus
dulce rideat ad patrem
    semihiante labello.

sit suo similis patri
215 Manlio et facile insciis
noscitetur ab obuiis,
et pudicitiam suae

    matris indicet ore.
talis illius a bona
·220 matre laus genus approbet,
qualis unica ab optima
matre Telemacho manet
    fama Penelopeo.

claudite ostia, uirgines:
225 lusimus satis. at boni
coniuges, bene uiuite et
munere assiduo ualentem
    exercete iuuentam.

62

Hexam.   Vesper adest, iuuenes, consurgite: Vesper Olympo
exspectata diu uix tandem lumina tollit.
surgere iam tempus, iam pinguis linquere mensas,
iam ueniet uirgo, iam dicetur hymenaeus.
5   Hymen o Hymenaee, Hymen ades o Hymenaee!

Cernitis, innuptae, iuuenes? consurgite contra;
nimirum Oetaeos ostendit Noctifer ignes.

61.216: obuiis *Pleitner*, omnibus *V*

What I want is a tiny Tor-
210 quatus, held on his mother's lap,
stretching out little hands to his
father, prettily smiling with
    tiny lips semiparted;

child

May he come to resemble his
215 father Manlius, easily
recognized by all comers and
in his features proclaiming the
    chastity of his mother.

patrimony: inheritance, birthright, legacy

May such praise (from his mother's worth)
220 offer proof of his high descent—
just as once from Penelope,
peerless mother, Telemachus
    got unmatchable honor.

privacy

Close the doors, you unmarried girls:
225 playtime's over for us. You good
married couple, live happy and
exercise your youth's vigor in
    constant bouts of its duty.

62

The youths: The evening star's here: stand up, men. High in the heavens
now at long last it's brought up its long-awaited brightness.
Time for us too to be up, to leave these rich-spread tables.
Now the bride will be coming, the wedding song will be sung:
5   Hymen O Hymeneal, come Hymen O Hymeneal!

The girls: You see the young men, maidens? Stand up then and face them—
night's harbinger must be showing his heavenly radiance.

sic certest; uiden ut perniciter exsiluere ?
non temere exsiluere, canent quod uincere par est.
10 Hymen o Hymenaee, Hymen ades o Hymenaee !

Non facilis nobis, aequales, palma parata est;
aspicite, innuptae secum ut meditata requirunt.
non frustra meditantur: habent memorabile quod sit;
nec mirum, penitus quae tota mente laborant.
15 nos alio mentes, alio diuisimus aures;
iure igitur uincemur: amat uictoria curam.
quare nunc animos saltem conuertite uestros;
dicere iam incipient, iam respondere decebit.
Hymen o Hymenaee, Hymen ades o Hymenaee!

20 Hespere, quis caelo fertur crudelior ignis ?
qui natam possis complexu auellere matris,
complexu matris retinentem auellere natam,
et iuueni ardenti castam donare puellam.
quid faciunt hostes capta crudelius urbe ?
25 Hymen o Hymenaee, Hymen ades o Hymenaee !

Hespere, quis caelo lucet iucundior ignis ?
qui desponsa tua firmes conubia flamma,
quae pepigere uiri, pepigerunt ante parentes,
nec iunxere prius quam se tuus extulit ardor.
30 quid datur a diuis felici optatius hora ?
Hymen o Hymenaee, Hymen ades o Hymenaee !

Hesperus e nobis, aequales, abstulit unam.

———————————————

———————————————

namque tuo aduentu uigilat custodia semper,
nocte latent fures, quos idem saepe reuertens,
35 Hespere, mutato comprendis nomine Eoüs.

Yes for sure—did you see how quickly they jumped up? They
didn't do that for nothing: so now we must match their song—
10   Hymen O Hymeneal, come Hymen O Hymeneal!

The youths: There's no prize guaranteed for us, my comrades. Observe
how the girls are recalling their well-conned verses! Practice
has clearly made perfect, they've got something striking to offer—
small wonder, with all the hard work they've been putting in!
15   We may have heard the words, but our minds were elsewhere.
If we lose it'll serve us right, to win needs practice—
so now, at least, focus your minds, pay strict attention:
they're about to begin their song, and we'll have to answer it,
Hymen O Hymeneal, come Hymen O Hymeneal!

20   *The girls:* What crueller fire spans the sky than you, O star of evening?
You can tear a daughter from the arms of her mother,
from her mother's arms tear a clinging daughter,
hand over a chaste maiden to some sex-hot youngster—
could a foeman be more brutal at a city's capture?
25   Hymen O Hymeneal, come Hymen O Hymeneal!

The youths: What *happier* fire, O star, illuminates the heavens?
With your flame you bring fulfillment to the marriage contract
pledged beforehand by parents, pledged by would-be
husbands, yet not made good till your fiery light has risen.
30   What better gift have the gods than this most happy hour?
Hymen O Hymeneal, come Hymen O Hymeneal!

The girls: The evening star, my companions, has taken off one of us . . .
< . . . . >

The youths: < . . . . >
for ever at your advent watchmen are on the lookout,
thieves lurk at night, but you often, in your recurrence
35   as morning star—different name—can catch them red-handed.

at lubet innuptis ficto te carpere questu.
quid tum, si carpunt, tacita quem mente requirunt ?
Hymen o Hymenaee, Hymen ades o Hymenaee !

     Vt flos in saeptis secretus nascitur hortis,
40   ignotus pecori, nullo conuolsus aratro,
quem mulcent aurae, firmat sol, educat imber;
multi illum pueri, multae optauere puellae:
idem cum tenui carptus defloruit ungui,
nulli illum pueri, nullae optauere puellae:
45   sic uirgo, dum intacta manet, dum cara suis est;
cum castum amisit polluto corpore florem,
nec pueris iucunda manet, nec cara puellis.
Hymen o Hymenaee, Hymen ades o Hymenaee!

     Vt uidua in nudo uitis quae nascitur aruo,
50   numquam se extollit, numquam mitem educat uuam,
sed tenerum prono deflectens pondere corpus
iam iam contingit summum radice flagellum;
hanc nulli agricolae, nulli coluere iuuenci:
at si forte eadem est ulmo coniuncta marita,
55   multi illam agricolae, multi coluere iuuenci:
sic uirgo dum intacta manet, dum inculta senescit;
cum par conubium maturo tempore adepta est,
cara uiro magis et minus est inuisa parenti.
58b   < Hymen o Hymenaee, Hymen ades o Hymenaee!>

     Et tu ne pugna cum tali coniuge, uirgo.
60   non aequom est pugnare, pater cui tradidit ipse,
ipse pater cum matre, quibus parere necesse est.
uirginitas non tota tua est, ex parte parentum est,
tertia pars patrist, pars est data tertia matri,
tertia sola tua est: noli pugnare duobus,
65   qui genero sua iura simul cum dote dederunt.
Hymen o Hymenaee, Hymen ades o Hymenaee!

62.54: marita *T*, marito *V*

Yet girls enjoy concocting their false complaints about you:
so what? They may complain, but at heart it's you they long for.
Hymen O Hymeneal, come Hymen O Hymeneal!

The girls: Like a flower that blossoms unseen in some high-fenced garden,
40   unknown to the flock, not ripped up by the ploughshare,
caressed by the breeze, sun-strengthened and shower-nurtured,
and many there are have desired it, boys and girls equally,
yet when its bloom fades, nicked off by a sharp thumbnail,
none there are to desire it, neither boys nor girls.
45   So a virgin, while still untouched, remains dear to her family,
but when with body defiled she loses chastity's blossom
to boys and girls alike she's no longer desirable.

The youths: Like the unwed vine that grows in an empty field,
50   and can never climb, never bear ripe grape-clusters,
but—frail body sagging under its groundward load—
all but touches its roots with its bowed-down topmost tendril—
no husbandman has worked on it, nor any oxen,
whereas one that's married up to its marital elm gets
55   worked on by many oxen, many husbandmen.
So too with an untouched virgin: she grows old untended,
but when in the fullness of time she makes a fitting marriage
she's more precious to her man and less tedious to her parents.
58b   Hymen O Hymeneal, come Hymen O Hymeneal!

And you, young lady, never fight with such a husband.
60   It's not proper to fight the one to whom your own father gave you,
your own father and mother, to whom you owe submission.
Your maidenhead's not all your own, in part it belongs to
your parents: one third's your father's, one third your mother's;
only one third is your own. Don't fight against the couple
65   who bestowed on their son-in-law their own rights with your dowry.
Hymen O Hymeneal, come Hymen O Hymeneal!

63

Gall.   Super alta uectus Attis celeri rate maria,
        Phrygium ut nemus citato cupide pede tetigit
        adiitque opaca siluis redimita loca deae,
        stimulatus ibi furenti rabie, uagus animis,
5   deuolsit ili acuto sibi pondera silice,
        itaque ut relicta sensit sibi membra sine uiro,
        etiam recente terrae sola sanguine maculans,
        niueis citata cepit manibus leue typanum,
        typanum tuum, Cybebe, tua, mater, initia,
10   quatiensque terga tauri teneris caua digitis
        canere haec suis adorta est tremebunda comitibus.
        "agite ite ad alta, Gallae, Cybeles nemora simul,
        simul ite, Dindymenae dominae uaga pecora,
        aliena quae petentes uelut exules loca
15   sectam meam exsecutae duce me mihi comites
        rapidum salum tulistis truculentaque pelagi,
        et corpus euirastis Veneris nimio odio;
        hilarate erae citatis erroribus animum.
        mora tarda mente cedat: simul ite, sequimini
20   Phrygiam ad domum Cybebes, Phrygia ad nemora deae
        ubi cymbalum sonat uox, ubi tympana reboant,
        tibicen ubi canit Phryx curuo graue calamo,
        ubi capita Maenades ui iaciunt hederigerae,
        ubi sacra sancta acutis ululatibus agitant,
25   ubi sueuit illa diuae uolitare uaga cohors,
        quo nos decet citatis celerare tripudiis."
        simul haec comitibus Attis cecinit notha mulier,
        thiasus repente linguis trepidantibus ululat,
        leue tympanum remugit, caua cymbala recrepant,
30   uiridem citus adit Idam properante pede chorus.
        furibunda simul anhelans uaga uadit animam agens
        comitata tympano Attis per opaca nemora dux,
        ueluti iuuenca uitans onus indomita iugi;
        rapidae ducem sequuntur Gallae properipedem.
35   itaque, ut domum Cybebes tetigere lassulae,

63

Over deep seas Attis, carried on a rapid catámaran,
eagerly with hurrying footsteps sought that forest in Phrygia,
penetrated the tree-thick coverts, the goddess' shadowy habitat,
and there, by furious madness driven, wits adrift in insanity,
5   seized a keen flint, slashed away the weight of his groin's double complement;
and when she felt the members left her shorn of all their virility
dropping still a spatter of fresh-shed | blood on the ground as she sped along,
quickly with snow white hand she seized the lightweight rat-a-tat tympanum—
yours the tympanum, O Cybébé, yours, great Mother, the mysteries—
10   and on the hollow drum-skin beat a | táttoo with delicate fingertips,
making this passionate invocation, body convulsed, to her followers:
"On together with me, you Gallae, seek the high forests of Cybelé,
on together, you roving herd of the Dindyménian Dómina,
who like exiles in pursuit of new and alien territory,
15   following me as leader, comrades to my orders obedient
bore the salt sea's tidal swiftness, its rough oceanic truculence,
and now have all unmanned your bodies | from too great hatred of venery—
by your impetuous wanderings let your | mistress' heart be exhilarate!
Purge your spirits of slow reluctance, and all together now follow me
20   to the Phrygian home of great Cybébé, the goddess' Phrygian forest groves,
where the sound of cymbals echoes, and the sharp rattle of kettledrums,
where the Phrygian player's deép notes boom from the curve of his basset-horn,
where the maenads, ivy-garlanded, toss their heads in mad ecstasy,
where with shrilling ululations they act out their ritual ceremonies,
25   where the goddess's roving troupers long have flitted perégrinant—
there is where we now must hasten with our impetuous sarabands!"
As soon as Attis, woman no woman, had uttered these words to her followers
an instant cry went up from the quivering | tongues of the ululant revellers,
echoing cymbals clashed, there thudded the light tattoo of the tambourines,
30   as headlong to leafy Ida hastened with scurrying footfall her company.
Leading them, breathless, pressing onward, gasping her heart and spirit up,
threading thick woodlands Attis wandered, the drumbeat still her accompaniment,
like some heifer, as yet unbroken, fleeing the collar's grim discipline,
while the Gallae crowded hotly after their swift-footed pacesetter.
35   So when they reached Cybébé's precinct, swooning-exhausted, woman-faint,

nimio e labore somnum capiunt sine Cerere.
piger his labante languore oculos sopor operit;
abit in quiete molli rabidus furor animi.
sed ubi oris aurei Sol radiantibus oculis
40   lustrauit aethera album, sola dura, mare ferum,
pepulitque noctis umbras uegetis sonipedibus,
ibi Somnus excitam Attin fugiens citus abiit;
trepidante eum recepit dea Pasithea sinu.
ita de quiete molli rapida sine rabie
45   simul ipsa pectore Attis sua facta recoluit,
liquidaque mente uidit sine quis ubique foret,
animo aestuante rusum reditum ad uada tetulit.
ibi maria uasta uisens lacrimantibus oculis,
patriam allocuta maestast ita uoce miseriter.
50   "patria o mei creatrix, patria o mea genetrix,
ego quam miser relinquens, dominos ut erifugae
famuli solent, ad Idae tetuli nemora pedem,
ut aput niuem et ferarum gelida stabula forem,
et earum omnia adirem furibunda latibula,
55   ubinam aut quibus locis te positam, patria, reor?
cupit ipsa pupula ad te sibi derigere aciem,
rabie fera carens dum breue tempus animus est.
egone a mea remota haec ferar in nemora domo?
patria, bonis, amicis, genitoribus abero?
60   abero foro, palaestra, stadio et gyminasiis?
miser a miser, querendum est etiam atque etiam, anime.
quod enim genus figuraest, ego non quod obierim?
ego mulier, ego adolescens, ego ephebus, ego puer,
ego gymnasi fui flos, ego eram decus olei:
65   mihi ianuae frequentes, mihi limina tepida,
mihi floridis corollis redimita domus erat,
linquendum ubi esset orto mihi Sole cubiculum.
ego nunc deum ministra et Cybeles famula ferar?
ego Maenas, ego mei pars, ego uir sterilis ero?
70   ego uiridis algida Idae niue amicta loca colam?
ego uitam agam sub altis Phrygiae columinibus,
ubi cerua siluicultrix, ubi aper nemoriuagus?

shot with huge effort, breadless, empty, soon they collapsed into somnolence.
Tides of slumber, slow and languorous, closed their eyes, rippled over them:
in soft repose there ebbed to nothing all their minds' rabid delirium.
But when the Sun with his golden orb and eyes of sharp-dazzling radiance
40 lightened the pale white empyrean, harsh earth, the sea's liquid riotousness,
chasing away Night's gloomy shadows, his fresh steeds' hooves briskly clattering,
then Sleep arose from Attis wakened, fled away swiftly, precipitate,
sought comfort in the trembling bosom | óf the goddess Pasíthea.
So after slumber, now abandoned by her frenzied paroxysm,
45 Attis reflected on the deed that she herself had initiated,
saw where she was, what things she'd lost, mind purged to diaphanous clarity.
Back to the shore she forced her footsteps, heart full of simmering bitterness,
and there, as she gazed with tear-filled eyes at the ocean's lonely immensity,
thus she addressed her distant homeland, in saddest accents and piteously:
50 "Ah, dear country that shaped my being, country that bore and delivered me,
which to my misery I abandoned—like some runaway minion
fleeing his master—and pressed on hotfoot to Ida's wildwooded forestry,
passed the snowline, made my way to the wild beasts' frost-riven ádyta,
reaching as far, in my mad frenzy, as their remotest covert—ah where,
55 where, in which quarter, O my country, must I now look for your territory?
My eyes, unbidden, long to turn their | gaze upon you, motherlandwards,
while, for this too-brief space, my mind stays | free of its savage insanity.
Ah, am I doomed to these alien forests, far from what's home, what's familiar—
absent from country, from my possessions, from friends and those who engendered me
60 absent from forum and from palaestra, from race-course and from gymnasium?
Ah wretch, ah wretch, whose life henceforward is nothing but wailing and misery!
What variation of human figure exists that I haven't appropriated?
This I, now woman, was I the ephebe, the child; this I the young teenager,
this I the gymnasium's finest flower, the glory of oil-smooth athleticism.
65 For me all thresholds were warm, for me all hallways were crowded with visitors,
for me the house was a riot of posies, of flowers all looping and garlanded,
when the sun came up and the time was on me to rise and abandon my bedchamber.
Am I now to be known as the gods' own handmaid, the serving girl of great Cybelé?
Shall *I* be a maenad, I but a part of me, I unmanned to sterility?
70 Am I to dwell on verdant Ida's chill and snow-clad escarpments? Shall
I waste my remaining lifespan under | the lofty columns of Phrygia,
there with the hind that roams the forest, there with the boar in his timberland?

iam iam dolet quod egi, iam iamque paenitet."
roseis ut huic labellis sonitus <citus> abiit,

75 geminas deorum ad aures noua nuntia referens,
ibi iuncta iuga resoluens Cybele leonibus
laeuumque pecoris hostem stimulans ita loquitur.
"agedum," inquit "age ferox <i>, fac ut hunc furor < agitet<,
fac uti furoris ictu reditum in nemora ferat,

80 mea libere nimis qui fugere imperia cupit.
age caede terga cauda, tua uerbera patere,
fac cuncta mugienti fremitu loca retonent,
rutilam ferox torosa ceruice quate iubam."
ait haec minax Cybebe religatque iuga manu.

85 ferus ipse sese adhortans rabidum incitat animo,
uadit, fremit, refringit uirgulta pede uago.
at ubi umida albicantis loca litoris adiit,
teneramque uidit Attin prope marmora pelagi,
facit impetum. illa demens fugit in nemora fera;

90 ibi semper omne uitae spatium famula fuit.

dea, magna dea, Cybebe, dea domina Dindymi,
procul a mea tuos sit furor omnis, era, domo:
alios age incitatos, alios age rabidos.

64

Hexam.   Peliaco quondam prognatae uertice pinus
dicuntur liquidas Neptuni nasse per undas
Phasidos ad fluctus et fines Aeeteos,
cum lecti iuuenes, Argiuae robora pubis,

5 auratam optantes Colchis auertere pellem
ausi sunt uada salsa cita decurrere puppi,
caerula uerrentes abiegnis aequora palmis.
diua quibus retinens in summis urbibus arces

63.85: rabidum *Schwabe*, rapidum *V*

Now, ah now, what I've done appalls me; now, ah now, I repent of it!"
As from those rose red lips there issued with arrowy speed her sharp utterance,
75   bringing a new report to the ready ears of the gods, those keen listeners,
Cybelé then, unyoking the reins that harnessed the lions to her chariot pole,
goaded the left one, the cattle killer, kindling its wrath with her urgency:
"Go now, my fierce one, go, pursue him, plague him with savage dementia,
make the stroke of his frenzy drive him back to the groves of my habitat,
80   he who yearns so overfreely to shake off my mastering dominance!
Flog your back with your tail in fury, lash yourself into rabidity,
roar till each hidden covert reechoes your fierce and terrifying utterance—
go, my fierce one, toss the tawny | mane on your neck's muscularity!"
So spoke Cybébé in rage, with one hand | slipped the yoke pin. The beast took off
85   in a feral fury, driven wild by its self-incitement to savagery,
sprang on roaring, paws in motion sending the brushwood skittering.
But when it neared the sea-damp shoreline, the bright white stretch of the littoral,
and there saw delicate Attis standing by the sea's marbled infinity,
it charged. Demented, she scuttled headlong back to the wild woods, a fugitive,
90   there to remain for ever, a lifelong | slave girl, a feminine acolyte.

Goddess, great goddess, O Cybébé, goddess, mistress of Díndymos,
far from my own house be all your | furies, Lady, and madnesses—
whip up others into frenzy, goad on others to ecstasy!

64

Once on a time pine trees from Pelion's summit
are said to have swum through Neptune's crystal ripples
to the breakers of Phasis and Aeëtes' territory,
when chosen young men, the strong core of Argive manhood,
5   eager to filch that gilded hide from the Colchians,
dared in their swift vessel to traverse the briny shoals,
sweeping blue, deep-sea vistas with their blades of fir-wood.
For them the goddess whose realm's in high citadels

ipsa leui fecit uolitantem flamine currum,
10   pinea coniungens inflexae texta carinae.
illa rudem cursu prima imbuit Amphitriten;
quae simul ac rostro uentosum proscidit aequor
tortaque remigio spumis incanuit unda,
emersere feri candenti e gurgite uultus
15   aequoreae monstrum Nereides admirantes.
illa, atque <haud> alia, uiderunt luce marinas
mortales oculis nudato corpore Nymphas
nutricum tenus exstantes e gurgite cano.
tum Thetidis Peleus incensus fertur amore,
20   tum Thetis humanos non despexit hymenaeos,
tum Thetidi pater ipse iugandum Pelea sensit.
o nimis optato saeclorum tempore nati
heroes, saluete, deum genus! o bona matrum
23b   progenies, saluete iter<um saluete bonarum!>
uos ego saepe, meo uos carmine compellabo.
25   teque adeo eximie taedis felicibus aucte,
Thessaliae columen Peleu, cui Iuppiter ipse,
ipse suos diuum genitor concessit amores;
tene Thetis tenuit pulcerrima Nereine ?
tene suam Tethys concessit ducere neptem,
30   Oceanusque, mari totum qui amplectitur orbem ?
     quae simul optatae finito tempore luces
aduenere, domum conuentu tota frequentat
Thessalia, oppletur laetanti regia coetu:
dona ferunt prae se, declarant gaudia uultu.
35   deseritur Scyros, linquunt Pthiotica Tempe
Crannonisque domos ac moenia Larisaea,
Pharsalum coeunt, Pharsalia tecta frequentant.
rura colit nemo, mollescunt coꞁla iuuencis,
non humilis curuis purgatur uinea rastris,

64.14: feri *V*, freti *Schrader*. 23b: progenies, saluete iter<um> *ex schol.*, iter<um saluete,
bonarum> *Peerlkamp*

herself made the craft that flew with the gentlest breeze,
10   conjoining pine-wood strakes to the curve of its hull—
the hull that was first to handsel those untouched waters.
And the moment its prow sheared through their wind-whipped surface,
and waves glistened spume white from the twist of the oar blades,
wild shy faces emerged from the foaming eddies,
15   deepwater Nereïds, in wonder at this portent.
That was the day, never matched, when mere mortals witnessed
marine nymphs rising up from the dappled sea surge,
mother-naked to breasts and below. It was then that Peleus—
so goes the story—burned up with love for Thetis,
20   then that Thetis did not reject a human marriage,
then that the Father himself felt Peleus and Thetis should wed.
O born in those days most missed through later ages,
you heroes, hail, gods' scions! noble offspring
23b   of noble women, all hail! I shall have occasion
to invoke you often in the course of my poem,
25   and you first and foremost, so blest by beatitude's torches,
bulwark of Thessaly, Peleus, to whom Jove himself, no less,
himself, though Sire of the Gods, resigned his loved one.
Did Thetis, most lovely of Nereïds, then embrace you?
Did Tethys permit you to wed her granddaughter,
30   and Ocean, who rings the whole globe with his waters?
When in due course this most eagerly awaited
wedding day dawns, guests from every distant quarter
of Thessaly throng the house, the palace is crowded
with a rejoicing multitude. All bear gifts, their faces
35   beam pleasure. Scyros is empty, they've deserted Phthiotic
Tempe, the houses of Crannon, the ramparts of Lárissa,
converging on Phársalus, packing Pharsalian rooftops.
Fieldwork's abandoned, draught oxen's necks get flabby,
no curved rake clears the weeds from the low-set ground vines,

40   non glebam prono conuellit uomere taurus,
     non falx attenuat frondatorum arboris umbram,
     squalida desertis rubigo infertur aratris.
     ipsius at sedes, quacumque opulenta recessit
     regia, fulgenti splendent auro atque argento.
45   candet ebur soliis, collucent pocula mensae,
     tota domus gaudet regali splendida gaza.
     puluinar uero diuae geniale locatur
     sedibus in mediis, Indo quod dente politum
     tincta tegit roseo conchyli purpura fuco.

50   haec uestis priscis hominum uariata figuris
     heroum mira uirtutes indicat arte.
     namque fluentisono prospectans litore Diae,
     Thesea cedentem celeri cum classe tuetur
     indomitos in corde gerens Ariadna furores,
55   necdum etiam sese quae uisit uisere credit,
     utpote fallaci quae turn primum excita somno
     desertam in sola miseram se cernat harena.
     immemor at iuuenis fugiens pellit uada remis,
     irrita uentosae linquens promissa procellae.
60   quem procul ex alga maestis Minois ocellis,
     saxea ut effigies bacchantis, prospicit, eheu,
     prospicit et magnis curarum fluctuat undis,
     non flauo retinens subtilem uertice mitram,
     non contecta leui uelatum pectus amictu,
65   non tereti strophio lactentis uincta papillas
     omnia quae toto delapsa e corpore passim
     ipsius ante pedes fluctus salis alludebant.
     sed neque tum mitrae neque tum fluitantis amictus
     illa uicem curans toto ex te pectore, Theseu,
70   toto animo, tota pendebat perdita mente.
     a misera, assiduis quam luctibus externauit
     spinosas Erycina serens in pectore curas,
     illa tempestate, ferox quo ex tempore Theseus
     egressus curuis e litoribus Piraei
75   attigit iniusti regis Gortynia templa.

40 no teams now split the sod with deep-thrusting ploughshares,
no pruning hook lessens the shade of leaf-thick trees, while
the ploughs, deserted, are scarved with rust's scaly tetter.
But Peleus' seat, for the whole of its opulent rearward
length is a shining delight of gold and silver,
45 gleaming ivory thrones, cups glinting on their tables,
the entire house glittering proudly with royal treasure,
and there at its heart is set the goddess's own bridal
couch, all smoothly inlaid with Indian ivory,
its purple drapery dipped in the mollusc's blushing dye.

50 This coverlet, decorated with antique human figures,
portrays in marvelous art the brave deeds of heroes.
There, gazing out from Dia's surf-loud shoreline,
eyes fixed on Theseus as he and his swift vessels
dwindle away to nothing, with uncontrollable passion
55 filling her heart, not yet able to credit the witness
of her own eyes, roused that moment from treacherous slumber,
Ariadne finds herself left on the lonely strand, poor creature,
while her heedless young lover vanishes, oar strokes flailing
the shallows, scattering broken promises galewards.
60 Him from afar, there on the wrack-strewn beach, eyes
agonized, Minos' daughter, a stony bacchant, watches,
ah, watches, in breaking waves of grief unbounded,
lost the fine-woven net from her golden tresses,
lost the light garment veiling her torso, lost the
65 rounded breast-band that gathered her milk white bosom—
all of them, slipped from her body every which way, now
at her feet had become the salty ripples' playthings.
But at this moment neither net nor floating garment
were noticed by her: she with her whole heart, Theseus,
70 whole mind, whole spirit, was concentrated on *you.*
Ah wretched creature, in whose breast She of Eryx planted
such thorny cares, whom She crazed with never-ending sorrows
from the day and hour when Theseus, that bold gallant,
setting forth from the curving shoreline of Piraeus
75 arrived at the Cretan palace of that unjust monarch.

nam perhibent olim crudeli peste coactam
Androgeoneae poenas exsoluere caedis
electos iuuenes simul et decus innuptarum
Cecropiam solitam esse dapem dare Minotauro.
80   quis angusta malis cum moenia uexarentur,
ipse suum Theseus pro caris corpus Athenis
proicere optauit potius quam talia Cretam
funera Cecropiae nec funera portarentur.
atque ita naue leui nitens ac lenibus auris
85   magnanimum ad Minoa uenit sedesque superbas.
hunc simul ac cupido conspexit lumine uirgo
regia, quam suauis exspirans castus odores
lectulus in molli complexu matris alebat,
quales Eurotae progignunt flumina myrtus
90   auraue distinctos educit uerna colores,
non prius ex illo flagrantia declinauit
lumina, quam cuncto concepit corpore flammam
funditus atque imis exarsit tota medullis.
heu misere exagitans immiti corde furores
95   sancte puer, curis hominum qui gaudia misces,
quaeque regis Golgos quaeque Idalium frondosum,
qualibus incensam iactastis mente puellam
fluctibus, in flauo saepe hospite suspirantem!
quantos illa tulit languenti corde timores!
100   quanto saepe magis fulgore expalluit auri,
cum saeuum cupiens contra contendere monstrum
aut mortem appeteret Theseus aut praemia laudis!
non ingrata tamen frustra munuscula diuis
promittens tacito suscepit uota labello.
105   nam uelut in summo quatientem brachia Tauro
quercum aut conigeram sudanti cortice pinum
indomitus turbo contorquens flamine robur,
eruit (illa procul radicitus exturbata
prona cadit, late quaeuis cumque obuia frangens),
110   sic domito saeuum prostrauit corpore Theseus

64.89: progignunt *Ital.*, pergignunt *V*, praecingunt *Baehrens*

For long ago, the tale goes, in thrall to a pestilential
cruel demand for atonement after Androgeos' murder,
the city of Cecrops would send the pick of her young men,
the flower of her maidens, as a feast for the Minotaur.
80 With this evil hanging heavy over her narrow ramparts,
Theseus chose, for the sake of the Athens he loved, to
expose his own body rather than suffer these dead,
these living dead, to be shipped to Crete like cattle.
So trusting to his light vessel and following breezes
85 he came to haughty Minos and his palatial abode.
Him, the instant that with eyes of desire the royal
virgin spied him, though still confined to a single
sweet-scented bed and her mother's soft embraces,
like myrtle brought forth by the waters of Eurotas
90 or the dappled colors that vernal breezes conjure,
she did not lower her smoldering gaze from him till
through the length of her body the flame was kindled
deep at the core, and blazed up in her inmost marrow.
Ah, wretchedly stirring wild passions, ruthless at heart,
95 Sacred Boy, you who mingle joy with sorrow for mortals,
and you, Lady, ruler of Golgi and leaf-thick Idalium,
on what rough surges you tossed that girl, mind flaring,
as over and over she sighed for the blond stranger:
what looming terrors with heavy heart she suffered,
100 how often she turned paler than gold's bright splendor
when Theseus, hot to contend with the savage monster,
courted either death or the rewards of glory!
Yet the giftlets she offered the gods, the vows she pledged
with silent lips—these were not in vain, not unpleasing.
105 For as on the peaks of Taurus, branches thrashing,
an oak or coniferous pine with gum-sweating cortex
has its strength wrenched round by a twister's all-powerful
blast, is torn up roots and all, crashes prostrate
all its great length, smashes everything in a wide swathe,
110 so Theseus brought down the monster, mastered its body

nequiquam uanis iactantem cornua uentis.
inde pedem sospes multa cum laude reflexit
errabunda regens tenui uestigia filo,
ne labyrintheis e flexibus egredientem
115 tecti frustraretur inobseruabilis error.
sed quid ego a primo digressus carmine plura
commemorem, ut linquens genitoris filia uultum,
ut consanguineae complexum, ut denique matris,
quae misera in gnata deperdita lamentata est,
120 omnibus his Thesei dulcem praeoptarit amorem:
aut ut uecta rati spumosa ad litora Diae
<uenerit,> aut ut eam deuinctam lumina somno
liquerit immemori discedens pectore coniunx?
saepe illam perhibent ardenti corde furentem
125 clarisonas imo fudisse e pectore uoces,
ac tum praeruptos tristem conscendere montes,
unde aciem <in> pelagi uastos protenderet aestus,
tum tremuli salis aduersas procurrere in undas
mollia nudatae tollentem tegmina surae,
130 atque haec extremis maestam dixisse querellis,
frigidulos udo singultus ore cientem:
"sicine me patriis auectam, perfide, ab aris,
perfide, deserto liquisti in litore, Theseu?
sicine discedens neglecto numine diuum,
135 immemor a! deuota domum periuria portas?
nullane res potuit crudelis flectere mentis
consilium? tibi nulla fuit clementia praesto,
immite ut nostri uellet miserescere pectus?
at non haec quondam blanda promissa dedisti
140 uoce mihi, non haec miseram sperare iubebas,
sed conubia laeta, sed optatos hymenaeos,
quae cuncta aerii discerpunt irrita uenti.
nunc iam nulla uiro iuranti femina credat,

64.119: lamentata est *Conington*, leta *V*, laeta<batur> *Lachmann*
64.140: miseram *Ital.*, misere *V*. 148: meminere *Cʒwalina*, metuere *V*

as it butted its horns in vain against airy emptiness,
then walked back out unhurt, in a cloud of glory, guiding
his fallible footsteps with that one slender thread, lest
during his emergence from the Labyrinth's windings
115 its deceptively mazed confusion should frustrate his purpose.
But why should I digress still further from my major
theme by relating how this daughter put behind her
her father's face, her consanguineous sister's
embraces, a mother lost in grief for her wretched offspring,
120 opting above all these for Theseus' sweet sweet love?
Or how aboard his vessel she came to Dia's surf-creamed
beaches, or how there he left her, eyes slumber-weighted,
to take himself off and vanish, a fickle-hearted husband?
Often (they tell us) heart burning, wild with passion,
125 she'd pour forth shrill cries fetched up from her innermost breast,
and then in her misery would scramble up steep mountains
from where she could see further across the sea's vast motion;
then, again, would rush into the briny's toppling breakers,
light skirt hitched up, exposing her naked thighs,
130 and in the abyss of her sorrow heaving cold little sobs,
face streaked with tears, would cry: "Is *this* the way, then,
that—after taking me far from my ancestral altars—
you leave me on this lonely beach, perfidious, Theseus?
135 Is *this* the how you vanish, the gods' will all neglected?
in blank indifference to divinity's own ruling
as you carelessly carry homeward your damnable perjuries?
Was there nothing that could deflect your cruel mind's
set purpose? Had you no compassion on hand
to nudge your hard heart into feeling pity for me?
140 These aren't the smooth-spoken promises you once made me,
this was not what you led my poor heart to expect,
but rather wedded bliss, the marriage I so yearned for—
all of which the intangible winds are shredding, making void.
Henceforth let no woman trust a man's sworn promise,

nulla uiri speret sermones esse fideles;
145 quis dum aliquid cupiens animus praegestit apisci,
nil metuunt iurare, nihil promittere parcunt:
sed simul ac cupidae mentis satiata libido est,
dicta nihil meminere, nihil periuria curant.
certe ego te in medio uersantem turbine leti
150 eripui, et potius germanum amittere creui,
quam tibi fallaci supremo in tempore dessem.
pro quo dilaceranda feris dabor alitibusque
praeda, neque iniacta tumulabor mortua terra.
quaenam te genuit sola sub rupe leaena,
155 quod mare conceptum spumantibus exspuit undis,
quae Syrtis, quae Scylla rapax, quae uasta Carybdis,
talia qui reddis pro dulci praemia uita ?
si tibi non cordi fuerant conubia nostra,
saeua quod horrebas prisci praecepta parentis,
160 attamen in uestras potuisti ducere sedes,
quae tibi iucundo famularer serua labore,
candida permulcens liquidis uestigia lymphis,
purpureaue tuum consternens ueste cubile.
sed quid ego ignaris nequiquam conqueror auris,
165 externata malo, quae nullis sensibus auctae
nec missas audire queunt nec reddere uoces ?
ille autem prope iam mediis uersatur in undis,
nec quisquam apparet uacua mortalis in alga.
sic nimis insultans extremo tempore saeua
170 fors etiam nostris inuidit questibus auris.
Iuppiter omnipotens, utinam ne tempore primo
Cnosia Cecropiae tetigissent litora puppes,
indomito nec dira ferens stipendia tauro
perfidus in Creta religasset nauita funem,
175 nec malus hic celans dulci crudelia forma
consilia in nostris requiesset sedibus hospes!
nam quo me referam? quali spe perdita nitor?

64.164: conqueror *Ital.*, conquerar *V.* 174: in Creta *O*, in Cretam *V*

or hope that he'll ever be true to his given word,
145 for as long as his lustful heart is bent on possession
he'll shrink from no oath, stop short at no promises,
but the moment the urge of his ardent mind is sated
he forgets all he's said, breaks oaths without a tremor.
The truth is, when you were spinning in death's vortex
150 *I* pulled you clear, chose rather to lose a brother
than to fail you, you liar, when your need was greatest:
and in return I'll be left as a carcass for kites and jackals
to tear asunder, I'll get no proper burial. What
lioness was it whelped you under some lonely rock, what
155 sea conceived you, spat you up in the breakers' spume,
what Syrtes, what ravening Scylla, what bleak Charybdis,
that you should make such return for your precious life?
If you failed to find marriage with me to your proper liking
through dread of an old-style father's merciless precepts,
160 you still could have brought me to your ancestral home,
to be your slave, to serve you with adoration,
washing your white-soled feet in crystal water, or
spreading and dressing your bed with a purple coverlet.
Oh, why do I uselessly plead to the indifferent breezes,
165 grief-stricken though I am? Being unendowed with senses
they can neither hear nor answer the words I utter—
while *he* by now has made nearly half his voyage,
and there's no other mortal in sight here on this lonely
wrack-strewn beach. That's cruel Fortune for you:
170 when we're down she kicks us, grudges hearers for our complaints.
Almighty Jove, how I wish in those early days no
Cecropian vessels had beached on Cnossos' strand,
nor, bearing ghastly tribute for a bull yet unmastered,
had that perfidious sailor ever thrown hawser out on
175 a Cretan quayside, or evilly | masking his cruel purpose
with a sweet show, had stayed as guest in our house, for
where now can I turn? I'm undone, I háve no récourse.

Idaeosne petam montes? at gurgite lato
discernens ponti truculentum diuidit aequor.
180 an patris auxilium sperem? quemne ipsa reliqui
respersum iuuenem fraterna caede secuta?
coniugis an fido consoler memet amore?
quine fugit lentos incuruans gurgite remos?
praeterea nullo colitur sola insula tecto,
185 nec patet egressus pelagi cingentibus undis.
nulla fugae ratio, nulla spes: omnia muta,
omnia sunt deserta, ostentant omnia letum.
non tamen ante mihi languescent lumina morte,
nec prius a fesso secedent corpore sensus,
190 quam iustam a diuis exposcam prodita multam
caelestumque fidem postrema comprecer hora.
quare facta uirum multantes uindice poena
Eumenides, quibus anguino redimita capillo
frons exspirantis praeportat pectoris iras,
195 huc huc aduentate, meas audite querellas,
quas ego, uae misera, extremis proferre medullis
cogor inops, ardens, amenti caeca furore.
quae quoniam uerae nascuntur pectore ab imo,
uos nolite pati nostrum uanescere luctum,
200 sed quali solam Theseus me mente reliquit,
tali mente, deae, funestet seque suosque."
has postquam maesto profudit pectore uoces,
supplicium saeuis exposcens anxia factis,
annuit inuicto caelestum numine rector;
205 quo motu tellus atque horrida contremuerunt
aequora concussitque micantia sidera mundus.
ipse autem caeca mentem caligine Theseus
consitus oblito dimisit pectore cuncta,
quae mandata prius constanti mente tenebat,
210 dulcia nec maesto sustollens signa parenti
sospitem Erectheum se ostendit uisere portum.
namque ferunt olim, classi cum moenia diuae
linquentem gnatum uentis concrederet Aegeus,
talia complexum iuueni mandata dedisse:

Should I make for the mountains of Ida? There's a wide gulf lying
between, and the waters of a rough sea passage
180   divide us. Can I look for my father's help, when I left him
to follow a young man stained with the blood of my brother?
Can I solace myself with a faithful husband's love when
he's running away from me, urging tough oars through the water?
On top of which there's not | one single house on this lonely
185   island, it's ringed by breakers, offers no loophole.
There's no way of escape, no hope, and, everywhere, silence:
everywhere's emptiness, everything signals death.
Yet my eyes shall not fade and grow still in dissolution,
nor the senses secede from my exhausted body,
190   till I've petitioned the gods for a befitting forfeit
for this betrayal, in my last hours have prayed that heaven
will keep faith. So, you whose vengeful exactions
answer men's crimes, you Furies whose snake-wreathed brows
announce the wrath gusting up from your secret hearts, I
195   summon you here to me now: give ear to the complaints
which I in my misery am forced to dredge up from the inmost
core of my being—helpless, burning, blinded
by mindless frenzy. But since they're the true products
of my private heart, don't let my grief all go for nothing:
200   rather in just such a mood as Theseus abandoned me
to my lonely fate, let him, goddesses, | now doom both himself and his!"
After she'd poured out this speech from her grief-stricken heart,
desperately seeking requital for such heartless treatment,
the Celestial Ruler nodded in final and absolute
205   assent, and at that gesture both earth and turbulent
ocean shook, and the firmament quaked with its glittering stars.
But Theseus himself, his mind a seedbed of blind darkness,
with forgetful heart let slip all the various commandments
that up to that moment he'd constantly kept in mind,
210   failed to hoist the happy signal for his grieving father
that would show he'd come safely in sight of Erechtheus' harbor.
For when Aegeus, they say, was entrusting to the winds his
son and his son's fleet on departure from Athens's ramparts,
he embraced the young man and gave him these instructions:

215　"gnate mihi longa iucundior unice uita,
　　　gnate, ego quem in dubios cogor dimittere casus,
　　　reddite in extrema nuper mihi fine senectae,
　　　quandoquidem fortuna mea ac tua feruida uirtus
　　　eripit inuito mihi te, cui languida nondum
220　lumina sunt gnati cara saturata figura,
　　　non ego te gaudens laetanti pectore mittam,
　　　nec te ferre sinam fortunae signa secundae,
　　　sed primum multas expromam mente querellas,
　　　canitiem terra atque infuso puluere foedans,
225　inde infecta uago suspendam lintea malo,
　　　nostros ut luctus nostraeque incendia mentis
　　　carbasus obscurata dicet ferrugine Hibera.
　　　quod tibi si sancti concesserit incola Itoni,
　　　quae nostrum genus ac sedes defendere Erecthei
230　annuit, ut tauri respergas sanguine dextram,
　　　tum uero facito ut memori tibi condita corde
　　　haec uigeant mandata, nec ulla oblitteret aetas;
　　　ut simul ac nostros inuisent lumina collis,
　　　funestam antennae deponant undique uestem,
235　candidaque intorti sustollant uela rudentes,
　　　quam primum cernens ut laeta gaudia mente
　　　agnoscam, cum te reducem fors prospera sistet."
　　　haec mandata prius constanti mente tenentem
　　　Thesea ceu pulsae uentorum flamine nubes
240　aereum niuei montis liquere cacumen.
　　　at pater, ut summa prospectum ex arce petebat,
　　　anxia in assiduos absumens lumina fletus,
　　　cum primum inflati conspexit lintea ueli,
　　　praecipitem sese scopulorum e uertice iecit,
245　amissum credens immiti Thesea fato.
　　　sic funesta domus ingressus tecta paterna
　　　morte ferox Theseus, qualem Minoidi luctum

64.237: fors *Dousa*, aetas *V.* 243: inflati *V*, infecti *Sabellicus*

215 "My only son, dearer to me than long life, my son
whom I'm forced to send forth to a perilous destiny,
though but lately restored to me in my extreme old age:
since my ill luck and your most fervid valor
now against my will take you from me—my dim old eyes
220 have not yet had their fill of my son's dear features—
I shall not send you forth gladly, with a rejoicing heart,
nor allow you to carry the signs of a fortunate destiny,
but shall first express my many heartfelt complaints,
fouling my old white hairs with handfuls of earth and dust,
225 and then hang your wanderer's mast with black-dyed sailcloth,
so that our grief and burning resentment of mind
may be declared by canvas darkened with Spanish rust.
But if She who dwells in sacred | Itónus, the bestower
of security on our race and the seat of Erechtheus,
230 should grant you to stain your right hand with bull's blood, then
take good care that your heart lays up and remembers
these commands of mine; keep them fresh, let time not erase them.
The instant your eyes catch sight of our hilly coastline,
let the yardarms lower all their funereal canvas
235 and the braided sheets haul up white sails as replacements
to let me know for certain, as early as may be,
bringing joy to my heart, the bright lot of your safe return."
These precepts, hitherto kept most constantly in mind,
now, like clouds whipped away from some snowy mountain top
240 by the gale's blast, abandoned Theseus. But his father,
scanning the horizon from the acropolis' summit,
anxious eyes worn out with constant weeping,
no sooner had glimpsed the canvas of the bellying sail
than he flung himself headlong from the height of the rock face,
245 believing Theseus destroyed by an unrelenting fate.
Thus when he entered the house now in mourning for his father's
death, haughty Theseus was himself faced with such grief

obtulerat mente immemori, talem ipse recepit.
quae tum prospectans cedentem maesta carinam
250   multiplices animo uoluebat saucia curas.

     at parte ex alia florens uolitabat Iacchus
cum thiaso Satyrorum et Nysigenis Silenis,
te quaerens, Ariadna, tuoque incensus amore.
cui Thyades passim lymphata mente furebant
255   euhoe bacchantes, euhoe capita inflectentes.
harum pars tecta quatiebant cuspide thyrsos,
pars e diuolso iactabant membra iuuenco,
pars sese tortis serpentibus incingebant,
pars obscura cauis celebrabant orgia cistis,
260   orgia quae frustra cupiunt audire profani;
plangebant aliae proceris tympana palmis,
aut tereti tenuis tinnitus aere ciebant;
multis raucisonos efflabant cornua bombos
barbaraque horribili stridebat tibia cantu.

265   talibus amplifice uestis decorata figuris
puluinar complexa suo uelabat amictu.
quae postquam cupide spectando Thessala pubes
expleta est, sanctis coepit decedere diuis.
hic, qualis flatu placidum mare matutino
270   horrificans Zephyrus procliuas incitat undas,
Aurora exoriente uagi sub limina Solis,
quae tarde primum clementi flamine pulsae
procedunt leuiterque sonant plangore cachinni,
post uento crescente magis magis increbescunt,
275   purpureaque procul nantes ab luce refulgent:
sic tum uestibulo linquentes regia tecta
ad se quisque uago passim pede discedebant.
quorum post abitum princeps e uertice Pelei
aduenit Chiron portans siluestria dona:

64.254: cui Thyades *Skutsch*, qui tum alacres *V.* 276: uestibulo *Schrader* uestibuli *V*

as by his thoughtless mind he'd left for Minos' daughter—
who, gazing in sorrow after his vanishing vessel,
250 and wounded at heart, now pondered a mass of troubles.

But in another quarter young Iacchus went winging by
with his band of Satyrs and Nysa-bred Sileni,
searching for you, Ariadne, for you aflame with passion.
All about him with frenzied mind spun the crazy maenads,
255 screaming *"euhoe, euhoe,"* heads jerking madly,
some of them brandishing thyrsi with sheathed tips,
some tossing around the limbs of a dismembered
bullock, some decking themselves with writhing serpents,
others at secret rituals with hollow caskets—
260 rituals which the profane desire in vain to share.
Some again with flattened palms were beating on drumheads
or drawing thin rattle and clash from the rounded bronze.
Many were blowing horns, a raucous booming clamor,
while barbarous pipes skirled out their ghastly themes.

265 Such were the figures most amply adorning the coverlet
that lay the whole width of the couch, veiled and encompassed it.
So after Thessaly's youth had satisfied their eager
urge to inspect it, they now | stood aside for the sacred gods.
Here, just as a calm sea's riffed by the matutinal
270 breath of the west wind, that catches the curling ripples
as dawn comes up at the threshold of the vagrant sun,
so that slowly at first, impelled by the gentle breeze,
they advance, to break with laughter's light plangency,
but then, as the wind increases, swell, swell in volume
275 and surging afar reflect the reddish sunlight,
so, pouring forth from the portals of the royal palace,
the crowd now scattered, each to his own abode.
Then, when they all were gone, there arrived, first, Chiron,
from Pelion's ridges, bearing gifts of the forest:

280　nam quoscumque ferunt campi, quos Thessala magnis
　　　montibus ora creat, quos propter fluminis undas
　　　aura parit flores tepidi fecunda Fauoni,
　　　hos indistinctis plexos tulit ipse corollis,
　　　quo permulsa domus iucundo risit odore.
285　confestim Penios adest, uiridantia Tempe,
　　　Tempe, quae siluae cingunt super impendentes,
　　　Haemonisin linquens Dryasin celebranda choreis,
　　　non uacuos: namque ille tulit radicitus altas
　　　fagos ac recto proceras stipite laurus,
290　non sine nutanti platano lentaque sorore
　　　flammati Phaethontis et aerea cupressu.
　　　haec circum sedes late contexta locauit,
　　　uestibulum ut molli uelatum fronde uireret.
　　　post hunc consequitur sollerti corde Prometheus,
295　extenuata gerens ueteris uestigia poenae,
　　　quam quondam silici restrictus membra catena
　　　persoluit pendens e uerticibus praeruptis.
　　　inde pater diuum sancta cum coniuge natisque
　　　aduenit caelo, te solum, Phoebe, relinquens
300　unigenamque simul cultricem montibus Idri:
　　　Pelea nam tecum pariter soror aspernata est,
　　　nec Thetidis taedas uoluit celebrare iugalis.
　　　qui postquam niueis flexerunt sedibus artus,
　　　large multiplici constructae sunt dape mensae,
305　cum interea infirmo quatientes corpora motu
　　　ueridicos Parcae coeperunt edere cantus.
　　　his corpus tremulum complectens undique uestis
　　　candida purpurea talos incinxerat ora,
　　　at roseae niueo residebant uertice uittae,
310　aeternumque manus carpebant rite laborem.
　　　laeua colum molli lana retinebat amictum,
　　　dextera tum leuiter deducens fila supinis

64.287: Haemonisin, *Heinsius*, †Minosim† *V*, Edonisin *Arkins;* Dryasin *Lee*, †doris† *V*, claris
　　　Ital.

280 for whatever flowers Thessaly grows, in the plain or on lofty
mountains, or beside the river's rippling passage,
nurtured by the west wind's warm and fecund breath,
all these he brought, in individual arrangements,
and the house laughed, happy in their fragrant perfume.

285 Next came Peníos, setting out from verdant Tempe,
Tempe enclosed above by overhanging woodlands,
the haunt of Haemonian dryads who dance in their honor;
nor was he giftless, for he came bearing tall, uprooted
beeches and stately laurels, straight in the stem,

290 together with nodding plane trees, and the lithe poplar
sisters of cindered Phaëthon, and tall airy
cypresses. These he set, all widely interwoven,
about the palace, to make a soft green leafy archway
for its portals. There followed him fox-hearted Prometheus,

295 bearing the scars, now faded, of that ancient punishment
he once endured, limbs stapled to flint by metal shackles,
suspended over the void from a dizzying precipice.
Then the Father of Gods with his holy wife and children
arrived from heaven, leaving you only, Phoebus,

300 along with your sibling, haunter of Idrus' mountains,
since you and your sister both equally scorned Peleus
and would not attend the wedding of him and Thetis.
When the guests had settled themselves on the white-backed seating
the tables were piled high with an array of dishes;

305 and meanwhile, old bodies prey to infirmity's tremors,
the trio of Fates began their prophetic chanting.
Each wore a long white robe that enfolded her tremulous
frame and fell to her ankles, purple-bordered; the three
had bandeaux of roses on their snow-white heads,

310 while their hands were properly busy with their unending labor,
the left gripping the distaff, all shrouded in soft wool,
while the right, first, teased out the threads with upturned

formabat digitis, tum prono pollice torquens
libratum tereti uersabat turbine fusum,

315 atque ita decerpens aequabat semper opus dens,
laneaque aridulis haerebant morsa labellis,
quae prius in leui fuerant exstantia filo :
ante pedes autem candentis mollia lanae
uellera uirgati custodibant calathisci.

320 haec turn clarisona pectentes uellera uoce
talia diuino fuderunt carmine fata,
carmine, perfidiae quod post nulla arguet aetas.

o decus eximium magnis uirtutibus augens,
Emathiae tutamen, Opis carissime nato,

325 accipe, quod laeta tibi pandunt luce sorores,
ueridicum oraclum: sed uos, quae fata sequuntur,
currite ducentes subtegmina, currite, fusi.
adueniet tibi iam portans optata maritis
Hesperus, adueniet fausto cum sidere coniunx,

330 quae tibi flexanimo mentem perfundat amore
languidulosque paret tecum coniungere somnos,
leuia substernens robusto brachia collo.
currite ducentes subtegmina, currite, fusi.
nulla domus tales umquam contexit amores,

335 nullus amor tali coniunxit foedere amantes,
qualis adest Thetidi, qualis concordia Peleo.
currite ducentes subtegmina, currite, fusi.
nascetur uobis expers terroris Achilles,
hostibus haud tergo, sed forti pectore notus,

340 qui persaepe uago uictor certamine cursus
flammea praeuertet celeris uestigia ceruae.
currite ducentes subtegmina, currite, fusi.
non illi quisquam bello se conferet heros,
cum Phrygii Teucro manabunt sanguine <campi,>

345 Troicaque obsidens longinquo moenia bello,
periuri Pelopis uastabit tertius heres.

64.313: prono *Kraggerud*, prono in *V* ; 320: pectentes *Statius*, pellentes *V*

fingers and formed them, then twisting with down-turned thumb
spun the spindle, balanced on its rounded whorl,

315   while constantly with their teeth they nibbled and smoothed the work,
and to their thin lips nipped-off wool tufts adhered
which before were excrescences on the even thread line,
while before their feet the soft fleeces of bright white wool
were stored in little baskets of woven osier.

320   They now, still carding their fleeces, in clear articulate tones
poured forth in god-inspired song these prophecies—
a song no future age would accuse of falsehood.
"O you who augment high achievement with great virtues,
Emathia's safeguard, most dear to the son of Ops,

325   accept what the Sisters reveal for you on this auspicious
day, a true oracle. But you which the fates follow,
run, drawing the weft out, run, you spindles!
Soon, soon there will come for you, granting all bridegrooms' longings,
Hesperus: that beneficent | star will be accompanied

330   by the partner who'll steep your awareness in mind-bending love
and be eager to share with you the sleep of exhaustion,
smooth arms pillowed beneath your sturdy neck.
Run, drawing the weft out, run, you spindles!
No house has ever embodied such a passion,

335   no love has ever joined lovers in such a compact,
as is the concord uniting Thetis and Peleus.
Run, drawing the weft out, run, you spindles!
There shall be born to you the fearless Achilles,
known to his foes not by back but by valiant front, who,

340   time and again victorious in the long-range footrace,
will outstrip the flame-swift tracks of the fleeting roebuck.
Run, drawing the weft out, run, you spindles!
Not one hero exists who'll be his equal in warfare
when the plains of Phrygia run with Teucrian blood

345   and in that long, long war and siege, Troy's ramparts
shall fall to the third in line from perjured Pelops.

currite ducentes subtegmina, currite, fusi.
illius egregias uirtutes claraque facta
saepe fatebuntur gnatorum in funere matres,
350 cum incultum cano soluent a uertice crinem,
putriaque infirmis uariabunt pectora palmis.

    currite ducentes subtegmina, currite, fusi.
namque uelut densas praecerpens messor aristas
sole sub ardenti flauentia demetit arua,
355 Troiugenum infesto prosternet corpora ferro.

    currite ducentes subtegmina, currite, fusi.
testis erit magnis uirtutibus unda Scamandri,
quae passim rapido diffunditur Hellesponto,
cuius iter caesis angustans corporum aceruis
360 alta tepefaciet permixta flumina caede.

    currite ducentes subtegmina, currite, fusi.
denique testis erit morti quoque reddita praeda,
cum teres excelso coaceruatum aggere bustum
excipiet niueos perculsae uirginis artus.

365   currite ducentes subtegmina, currite, fusi.
nam simul ac fessis dederit fors copiam Achiuis
urbis Dardaniae Neptunia soluere uincla,
alta Polyxenia madefient caede sepulcra;
quae, uelut ancipiti succumbens uictima ferro,
370 proiciet truncum summisso poplite corpus.

    currite ducentes subtegmina, currite, fusi.
quare agite optatos animi coniungite amores.
accipiat coniunx felici foedere diuam,
dedatur cupido iam dudum nupta marito.

375   currite ducentes subtegmina, currite, fusi.
non illam nutrix orienti luce reuisens
377 hesterno collum poterit circumdare filo,
379 anxia nec mater discordis maesta puellae
380 secubitu caros mittet sperare nepotes.

64.351: putriaque *Heinsius*, putridaque *V*
64.378: *del. Bergk*

Run, drawing the weft out, run, you spindles!
His virtues preeminent and most noble deeds
mothers shall ofttimes confess at their own sons' obsequies,
350   letting fall loose unkempt locks from their old white crowns
and with weak hands beating tattoo on their withered breasts.
Run, drawing the weft out, run, you spindles!
Just as a reaper, culling close-packed wheat ears
under a burning sun harvests the umber fields,
355   so with fierce steel shall he lay low his Trojans.
Run. drawing the weft out, run, you spindles!
Witness to his great virtues shall be Scamander's water,
discharging every way in the swift Hellespont.
He'll choke its flow with piles of slaughtered bodies,
360   warm its deep channel with that slaughter's blood.
Run, drawing the weft out, run, you spindles!
Final witness shall be his recompense even in death
when stacked in a lofty barrow his rounded sepulchre
receives the snow-white limbs of a slaughtered virgin.
365   *Run, drawing the weft out, run, you spindles!*
For as soon as Fortune grants the exhausted Achaeans
the means to loose Neptune's bonds from that Dardanian city,
his high tomb will be drenched with the blood of Polyxena,
and she, like a victim undone by the two-edged steel,
370   shall slump down there, knees folding, a headless body.
Run, drawing the weft out, run, you spindles!
Come, therefore, unite the loves your hearts have longed for,
let your consort accept the goddess in happy compact,
and the bride be given at last to her ardent bridegroom.
375   *Run, drawing the weft out, run, you spindles!*
Her nurse, revisiting her tomorrow at sunrise,
377   won't be able to circle her neck with yesterday's ribbon,
379   nor shall her anxious mother, saddened by her cross daughter's
380   bedding apart, fail to hope for dear grandchildren."

currite ducentes subtegmina, currite, fusi.
talia praefantes quondam felicia Peleo
carmina diuino cecinerunt pectore Parcae.
praesentes namque ante domos inuisere castas
385   heroum, et sese mortali ostendere coetu,
caelicolae nondum spreta pietate solebant.
saepe pater diuum templo in fulgente residens,
annua cum festis uenissent sacra diebus,
conspexit terra centum procumbere tauros.
390   saepe uagus Liber Parnasi uertice summo
Thyiadas effusis euantis crinibus egit,
cum Delphi tota certatim ex urbe ruentes
acciperent laeti diuum fumantibus aris.
saepe in letifero belli certamine Mauors
395   aut rapidi Tritonis era aut Amarunsia uirgo
armatas hominum est praesens hortata cateruas.
sed postquam tellus scelere est imbuta nefando
iustitiamque omnes cupida de mente fugarunt,
perfudere manus fraterno sanguine fratres,
400   destitit extinctos gnatus lugere parentes,
optauit genitor primaeui funera nati,
liber uti nuptae poteretur flore nouellae,
ignaro mater substernens se impia nato
impia non uerita est diuos scelerare penates.
405   omnia fanda nefanda malo permixta furore
iustificam nobis mentem auertere deorum.
quare nec talis dignantur uisere coetus,
nec se contingi patiuntur lumine claro.

64.382: Peleo *Goold*, Pelei *V*. 387: residens *Baehrens*, reuisens *V*

64.395: Amarunsia *Baehrens*, ramunsia *O*. 402: uti nuptae *Maely*, ut innuptae *V*; nouellae
    Baehrens, nouercae *V*

Run, drawing the weft out, run, you spindles!
Predicting, far in the past, such blessings for Peleus
did the Fates from divine breast thus utter their chants, since
in those days, when pious belief was not yet held in scorn,
385   Heaven's denizens used to visit the chaste dwellings
of heroes in person, show themselves at mortals' meetings.
Often the Father of Gods, there in his gleaming temple,
when his annual feast day came round, with its sacred rites,
would watch while a hundred bulls were poleaxed for him.
390   Often wandering Bacchus from Parnassus' peaks would
drive his howling maenads, loose hair flying,
while the people of Delphi, all leaving town together,
would joyously welcome the god with smoking altars.
Often, too, during war's deadly struggle, Mavors
395   or speedy Triton's Lady or the Virgin of Amarynthus
would be there to cheer on mere mortals' armed battalions.
But after Earth was imbued with unspeakable wrongdoing
and all sent justice packing from their covetous thoughts,
brothers now drenched their hands with the blood of brothers,
400   sons ceased to lament their parents' demise, a father
would hope for the premature death of his son, thus being
free himself to enjoy the bloom of son's teenage bride,
while an impious mother, couched supine | under her ignorant son
did not let her impiety scruple to outrage the household's
405   domestic gods. By confusing | good and bad in an evil frenzy
we alienated the gods' once-tolerant understanding,
which is why they neither deign to be present at such meetings
nor let themselves be exposed to open daylight.

65

Eleg.   Etsi me assiduo confectum cura dolore
        seuocat a doctis, Hortale, uirginibus,
    nec potis est dulcis Musarum expromere fetus
        mens animi, tantis fluctuat ipsa malis—
5   namque mei nuper Lethaeo gurgite fratris
        pallidulum manans alluit unda pedem,
    Troia Rhoeteo quem subter litore tellus
        ereptum nostris obterit ex oculis.
        <nunquam ego te potero posthac audire loquentem?>
10   numquam ego te, uita frater amabilior,
    aspiciam posthac ? at certe semper amabo,
        semper maesta tua carmina morte canam,
    qualia sub densis ramorum concinit umbris
        Daulias, absumpti fata gemens Ityli—
15   sed tamen in tantis maeroribus, Hortale, mitto
        haec expressa tibi carmina Battiadae,
    ne tua dicta uagis nequiquam credita uentis
        effluxisse meo forte putes animo,
    ut missum sponsi furtiuo munere malum
20   procurrit casto uirginis e gremio,
    quod miserae oblitae molli sub ueste locatum,
        dum aduentu matris prosilit, excutitur,
    atque illud prono praeceps agitur decursu,
        huic manat tristi conscius ore rubor.

66

Eleg.   Omnia qui magni dispexit lumina mundi,
        qui stellarum ortus comperit atque obitus,
    flammeus ut rapidi solis nitor obscuretur,
        ut cedant certis sidera temporibus,

---

65. 9: suppl. *Palmer, lacuna V*

65

Despite my being exhausted by long-standing sorrow,
and kept by care, Hortalus, from the Maids of Art,
my imagination unable to bring to birth sweet issues
of the Muses, so storm-tossed with trouble as it is—
5   for of late a ripple from Oblivion's vortex
lapped over my brother's foot, left it deadly pale,
and the Troad has snatched him from our sight, interred him
under the dead weight of the Rhoetean shore.
<Shall I never henceforth be able to hear you speaking?>
10 Shall I never, brother dearer to me than life
see you again? But for sure I shall cherish you always,
always make songs that are saddened by your death,
like those sung under the dense and shady branches
by the Daulian nightingale mourning Itylus' fate—
15 and yet, amid such sorrows, Hortalus, I send now,
translated for you, these verses by Battus' son,
in case you supposed your words had been vainly given
to the winds' vagaries and had slipped my mind,
as an apple (sent as a gift, on the sly, by her fiancé)
20 bounces out from a chaste young lady's lap—
poor dear, she forgot she'd tucked it away in the folds of
her nice soft dress—when she jumps up as mother comes in.
Out it pops, drops down, and keeps on rolling,
while she goes pink with embarrassment and guilt.

66

He who distinguished all the lights in the vault of heaven,
   who mastered the rising and setting of the stars,
the way the sun's scorching incandescence is darkened,
   how at set times the stars recede,

5   ut Triuiam furtim sub Latmia saxa relegans
        dulcis amor gyro deuocet aereo:
    idem me ille Conon caelesti in limine uidit
        e Beroniceo uertice caesariem
    fulgentem clare, quam multis illa dearum
10   leuia protendens brachia pollicita est,
    qua rex tempestate nouo auctus hymenaeo
        uastatum finis iuerat Assyrios,
    dulcia nocturnae portans uestigia rixae,
        quam de uirgineis gesserat exuuiis.
15 estne nouis nuptis odio Venus ? anne mariti
        frustrantur falsis gaudia lacrimulis,
    ubertim thalami quas intra limina fundunt ?
        non, ita me diui, uera gemunt, iuerint.
    id mea me multis docuit regina querellis
20   inuisente nouo proelia torua uiro.
    at tu non orbum luxti deserta cubile,
        sed fratris cari flebile discidium?
    quam penitus maestas exedit cura medullas!
        ut tibi tunc toto pectore sollicitae
25 sensibus ereptis mens excidit! at <te> ego certe
        cognoram a parua uirgine magnanimam.
    anne bonum oblita es facinus, quo regium adepta es
        coniugium, quo non fortius ausit alis ?
    sed tum maesta uirum mittens quae uerba locuta es !
30   Iuppiter, ut tersti lumina saepe manu!
    quis te mutauit tantus deus? an quod amantes
        non longe a caro corpore abesse uolunt?
    atque ibi me cunctis pro dulci coniuge diuis
        non sine taurino sanguine pollicita es,
35 si reditum tetulisset. is haut in tempore longo

---

66. 7: limine *Heinsius*, numine *V*
66.15: mariti *Green*, parentum *V*
66.21: at *X*, et *V*
66.28: quo . . . fortius *Muretus*, quod . . . fortior *V*
66.30: tersti *Avantius*, tristi *V*

how She of the crossways takes off to rocky Latmos
    lured by sweet love from her circuit in the sky—
that same Conon observed me at heaven's threshold,
    a lordly lock from Berenice's crown
brightly refulgent, that she vowed to an assortment
10   of goddesses, smooth arms outstretched,
at the time when the King, strengthened by his new marriage,
    was off to despoil Assyria's borderlands,
still bearing sweet traces of the nighttime struggle
    he'd waged for her virgin trophy. Is it true
15 that new brides hate Venus? Or are the tears pretended
    with which they frustrate a hopeful husband's joys,
those copious sobs inside the bridal chamber?
    So help me the gods, their grief is feigned, not real.
This, my Queen's constant lamentations taught me
20   while her bridegroom was off at the wars—
Or were you, deserted, grieving not for your widowed bed,
    but for a dear brother's sad going? Oh how
deeply sorrow gnawed into your unhappy marrow,
    how anxiety then flooded your breast
25 as reason fled, and you | were bereft of your senses! Truly
    I knew you were proud, assertive, even as a child.
Have you forgotten the brave act that won you a royal
    marriage, braver than any other would have dared!
What sad words you spoke when seeing off your man, ah
30   heavens, the times you had to wipe tears from your eyes!
What god had the greatness to change you? Or was it that lovers
    cannot bear to be far from the body they love?
That was when, for your dear husband's sake, you vowed me—
    not without bull's blood spilt—to all the gods
35 if he brought off a safe return. In little time he'd added

captam Asiam Aegypti finibus addiderat.
quis ego pro factis caelesti reddita coetu
    pristina uota nouo munere dissoluo.
inuita, o regina, tuo de uertice cessi,
40   inuita: adiuro teque tuumque caput,
digna ferat quod si quis inaniter adiurarit :
    sed quis se ferro postulet esse parem ?
ille quoque euersus mons est, quem maximum in oris
    progenies Thiae clara superuehitur,
45   cum Medi peperere nouum mare, cumque iuuentus
    per medium classi barbara nauit Athon.
quid facient crines, cum ferro talia cedant?
    Iuppiter, ut Chalybon omne genus pereat,
et qui principio sub terra quaerere uenas
50   institit ac ferri stringere duritiem !
abiunctae paulo ante comae mea fata sorores
    lugebant, cum se Memnonis Aethiopis
unigena impellens nutantibus aera pennis
    obtulit Arsinoës Locridos ales equos,
55   isque per aetherias me tollens auolat umbras
    et Veneris casto collocat in gremio.
ipsa suum Zephyritis eo famulum legarat,
    Graiia Canopitis incola litoribus.
hic liquidi uario ne solum in limine caeli
60   ex Ariadnaeis aurea temporibus
fixa corona foret, sed nos quoque fulgeremus
    deuotae flaui uerticis exuuiae,
uuidulam a fletu cedentem ad templa deum me
    sidus in antiquis diua nouum posuit.
65   Virginis et saeui contingens namque Leonis
    lumina, Callistoe iuncta Lycaoniae,
uertor in occasum, tardum dux ante Boöten,

66.42: quis *Green*, qui *V*
66.59: hic liquidi *Friedrich*, †hi dii uen ibi† *V;* limine *Ital.*, numine *V*
66.63: fletu *Ital.*, fluctu *V*
66.66: Callistoe *Parth.*, *Courtney*, calixto *V*, Callisto *Mynors*

captive Asia to Egypt's lands,
　for which great deeds I discharge my original promise
　　with this new offering to the celestial host.
Against my will, O Queen, was I parted from your crown then,
40　against my will, I swear by you and your head.
May this oath, if falsely sworn, bring condign retribution—
　yet who can claim to be a match for steel?
Even that mountain (than which in those parts none greater),
　scoured by the clear north wind, was overthrown
45　when the Medes opened up a new sea, when a barbarian
　warrior host through mid-Athos sailed their fleet.
What, then, can hair achieve when the high hills yield to iron?
　Jove, let the Chalybes perish, root and branch,
with the man who first pioneered the underground quest for
50　veins of ore, who drew out and hardened steel!
Lately bereft of me, my sister locks were mourning
　my fate, when, beating the air with vibrant wings,
lo, Ethiopian Memnon's sibling, Locrian
　Arsinoë's winged horse, who gathered me up
55　and bore me off through the darkening empyrean
　to set me down in Venus' virtuous lap.
The Queen in person, Greek settler on Canopus' shores,
　she of Zephyrion, had sent her own acolyte
to fetch me, and—lest in the clear sky's motley texture
60　the golden crown from Ariadne's brow
should alone have its fixed place, but rather that we also
　should shine there, votive spoils of a golden head—
all tear-damp as I was, on my way to the gods' dwellings,
　the goddess set me, a new star, among the old:
65　now abutting the lights of Virgo and savage Leo,
　and a near neighbor of Callisto, Lycaon's child,
I round to my setting, ahead of tardy Boötes

qui uix sero alto mergitur Oceano.
sed quamquam me nocte premunt uestigia diuum,
70   lux autem canae Tethyi restituit,
(pace tua fari hic liceat, Ramnusia uirgo,
      namque ego non ullo uera timore tegam,
nec si, me infestis discerpent sidera dictis,
      condita quin uere pectoris euoluam)
75 non his tam laetor rebus, quam me afore semper,
      afore me a dominae uertice discrucior,
quicum ego, dum uirgo quidem erat muliebribus expers
      unguentis, una uilia multa bibi.
nunc uos, optato quas iunxit lumine taeda,
80   non prius unanimis corpora coniugibus
tradite nudantes reiecta ueste papillas,
      quam iucunda mihi munera libet onyx,
uester onyx, casto colitis quae iura cubili.
      sed quae se impuro dedit adulterio,
85 illius a mala dona leuis bibat irrita puluis:
      namque ego ab indignis praemia nulla peto.
sed magis, o nuptae, semper concordia uestras,
      semper amor sedes incolat assiduus.
tu uero, regina, tuens cum sidera diuam
90   placabis festis luminibus Venerem,
unguinis expertem non siris esse tuam me,
      sed potius largis effice muneribus
sidera cur iterent: "utinam coma regia fiam!"—
      proximus Hydrochoi fulgeret Oarion!

66.74: *uere V*, *ueri cod. Berol.*
66.77: quidem erat muliebribus *Skutsch*, quondam fuit omnibus *V*
66.78: uilia *Lobel*, milia *O*
66.93: cur iterent *V*, corruerint *Lachmann;* 'utinam . . . fiam' *Simpson, Kidd*

who merges with deep Ocean barely and late.
Yet though by night the deities' footsteps trample
70   over me, and the dawn returns me to grey
Tethys—here, saving your grace, let me speak, Rhamnusian
     Maiden: I shall not conceal the truth through fear,
not though the stars should rend me with angry reproofs, but
     lay bare in truth those secrets my breast conceals—
75   I get less joy from my luck than torment at being
     severed, forever severed, from my mistress' head,
whence, while she was maiden still, and with no knowledge
     of married perfumes, I drank many frugal scents.
Now you brides, when the longed-for light of the torches
80   has conjoined you, don't yield your bodies to like
minded spouses, don't throw back your dresses, don't bare your nipples
     till the onyx jar has poured me out a sweet
libation—*your* onyx jar, you who keep the bed's chastity.
     But the woman who offers herself to unclean
85   adultery—ah, let *her* ill gifts be fruitless, swallowed
     by the casual dust, for I covet no rewards
from the unworthy. No, rather, O brides, may eternal
     concord and love forever dwell in your homes.
And you, O Queen, when you gaze on the constellations,
90   and propitiate divine Venus with festal lights,
do not let me, who am yours, lack my share of unguents,
     but rather by your generous gifts ensure
that the stars declare: "Would that *I* were a royal tress!"—Orion
     would then shine out bright right next to Aquarius!

67

Eleg.   O dulci iucunda uiro, iucunda parenti,
       salue, teque bona Iuppiter auctet ope,
    ianua, quam Balbo dicunt seruisse benigne
       olim, cum sedes ipse senex tenuit,
5   quamque ferunt rursus gnato seruisse maligne,
       postquam est porrecto pacta marita sene.
    dic agedum nobis, quare mutata feraris
       in dominum ueterem deseruisse fidem.

    "Non (ita Caecilio placeam, cui tradita nunc sum)
10   culpa mea est, quamquam dicitur esse mea,
    nec peccatum a me quisquam pote dicere quicquam:
       uerum istuc populi ianua quicque facit,
    qui, quacumque aliquid reperitur non bene factum,
       ad me omnes clamant: ianua, culpa tua est."

15   Non istuc satis est uno te dicere uerbo,
       sed facere ut quiuis sentiat et uideat.

    "Qui possum? nemo quaerit nec scire laborat."

    Nos uolumus: nobis dicere ne dubita.

    "Primum igitur, uirgo quod fertur tradita nobis,
20   falsum est. non illam uir prior attigerat,
    languidior tenera cui pendens sicula beta
       numquam se mediam sustulit ad tunicam;
    sed pater illius gnati uiolasse cubile
       dicitur et miseram conscelerasse domum,
25   siue quod impia mens caeco flagrabat amore,
       seu quod iners sterili semine natus erat,

67.6: est *V*, es *Aldine;* pacta *Badian,* facta *V*
67.12: istuc *Heyse,* †istius *V;* populo *Ital.,* populi *V;* quicque *Munro,* qui te *V*
67.20: attigerat *Ital.,* attigerit *V*

67

Catullus: O delight to a pleasant husband, delight to a parent,
    greetings, and may Jove grant you good increase,
house door: you, people say, served Balbus with devotion
    back then when the old man ruled the roost himself,
5 but (or so it's alleged) served his son with mean reluctance
    when the boy got wed—after Daddy was laid out.
So, talk. Explain. Why do they say you've altered,
    broken faith with your old master? Tell me all.

House door: It's not—so please Caecilius, now my owner—
10   any fault of mine, although it's said to be,
nor can anyone claim I did anything improper.
    But you know what folk say, "Blame the door for everything"—
whenever some peccadillo is discovered,
    a chorus goes up at once: "Door, that's *your* fault!"

15 *Catullus:* That's not good enough—just your bare assertion:
    you need to make people feel it, see it as fact.

House door: How? No one asks me, or bothers to look for answers.

Catullus: *I* want to, so tell me, don't be shy.

House door: All right, then. First, the tale | that she came here as a virgin
20   is a lie. It's true she'd never been touched
by her previous husband, whose prick was softer than beetroot
    and never got up as far as his midshirt;
but it's said that his father raided sonny boy's bed space
    and did violence to his unhappy home,
25 either because blind passion created a bonfire
    in his impious mind, or the boy was simply inert,

ut quaerendum unde <unde> foret neruosius illud,
    quod posset zonam soluere uirgineam."

Egregium narras mira pietate parentem,
30   qui ipse sui gnati minxerit in gremium!

"Atqui non solum hoc dicit se cognitum habere
    Brixia Cycneae supposita speculae,
flauus quam molli praecurrit flumine Mella,
    Brixia Veronae mater amata meae,
35 sed de Postumio et Corneli narrat amore,
    cum quibus illa malum fecit adulterium.
dixerit hic aliquis: qui tu istaec, ianua, nosti,
    cui numquam domini limine abesse licet,
nec populum auscultare, sed hic suffixa tigillo
40   tantum operire soles aut aperire domum?
saepe illam audiui furtiua uoce loquentem
    solam cum ancillis haec sua flagitia,
nomine dicentem quos diximus, utpote quae mi
    speraret nec linguam esse nec auriculam.
45 praeterea addebat quendam, quem dicere nolo
    nomine, ne tollat rubra supercilia.
longus homo est, magnas cui lites intulit olim
    falsum mendaci uentre puerperium."

68A

Eleg.   Quod mihi fortuna casuque oppressus acerbo
    conscriptum hoc lacrimis mittis epistolium,
naufragum ut eiectum spumantibus aequoris undis
    subleuem et a mortis limine restituam,
5 quem neque sancta Venus molli requiescere somno

67.37: qui *Ital.*, quid? *V*

his seed sterile, meaning that somehow, from somewhere, a stiffer
    key had to be found to unlock her virgin zone.

Catullus: Mind-boggling piety this, an egregious parent
30   you're describing, a man who'd piss in his own son's lap!

House door: And yet—so says Brescia, perched below Swan Hill's watchtower,
    lapped by the lazy Mella's golden flow,
Brescia, much-loved mother of my own Verona—
    she knows all this well, and in addition tells tales
35 of love affairs with Cornelius and Postumius,
    the shabby adultery she committed with both.
Here someone may say, "Door, how can you possibly *know* this
    when you're stuck at your master's threshold, can never leave,
can't listen to public gossip, stand rooted under
40   the lintel, can only open and shut the house?"
Well, I often heard her having furtive discussions,
    alone with the maids, about those escapades of hers,
naming the names I told you, clearly not supposing
    I possessed either ears or tongue.
45 What's more, she mentioned a person I'd rather not name, lest
    he raises his ginger eyebrows. He's a tall
fellow who once was cited in a big lawsuit—
    a case of false childbirth, a mendacious womb.

68A

That it's to me, now you're weighed down by harsh ill fortune,
    that you send this little message, penned in tears—
begging for help when you're shipwrecked, tossed up by the creaming
    breakers, seeking rescue from the threshold of death,
5 granted no healing sleep by holy Venus, abandoned

desertum in lecto caelibe perpetitur,
nec ueterum dulci scriptorum carmine Musae
    oblectant, cum mens anxia peruigilat:
id gratum est mihi, me quoniam tibi dicis amicum,
10   muneraque et Musarum hinc petis et Veneris.
sed tibi ne mea sint ignota incommoda, Manli,
    neu me odisse putes hospitis officium,
accipe, quis merser fortunae fluctibus ipse,
    ne amplius a misero dona beata petas.
15 tempore quo primum uestis mihi tradita pura est,
    iucundum cum aetas florida uer ageret,
multa satis lusi: non est dea nescia nostri,
    quae dulcem curis miscet amaritiem.
sed totum hoc studium luctu fraterna mihi mors
20   abstulit. o misero frater adempte mihi—
tu mea tu moriens fregisti commoda, frater,
    tecum una tota est nostra sepulta domus,
omnia tecum una perierunt gaudia nostra,
    quae tuus in uita dulcis alebat amor.
25 cuius ego interitu tota de mente fugaui
    haec studia atque omnes delicias animi.
quare, quod scribis Veronae turpe Catullo
    esse, quod hic quisquis de meliore nota
frigida deserto tepefactet membra cubili,
30   id, Manli, non est turpe, magis miserum est.
ignosces igitur si, quae mihi luctus ademit,
    haec tibi non tribuo munera, cum nequeo.
nam, quod scriptorum non magna est copia apud me,
    hoc fit, quod Romae uiuimus: illa domus,
35 illa mihi sedes, illic mea carpitur aetas;
    huc una ex multis capsula me sequitur.
quod cum ita sit, nolim statuas nos mente maligna
    id facere aut animo non satis ingenuo,
quod tibi non utriusque petenti copia posta est:
40   ultro ego deferrem, copia siqua foret.

68a.11, 30: Manli *Ital.*, Mali *V*

alone in your single bed, with no
comfort from the Muses, impervious to the writings
   of ancient worthies while your anxious mind
keeps wakeful—this gives me pleasure, since you call me friend, ask
10   for gifts of both poetry and love.
But to make quite sure you're not unaware of my troubles,
   Manlius, or think I dismiss the duties of a guest,
let me tell you what waves of misfortune I too am overwhelmed by
   to stop you asking this wretch for cheerful gifts.
15   From the day when I first put on the white gown of manhood,
   when my budding years were in their enchanted spring,
I played to the limit. The goddess who duly mingles
   cares with sweet bitterness is not unaware of me.
But from all pursuits of that kind the death of my brother
20   has debarred me through grief.—*O brother, snatched away*
from unhappy me, by dying | you broke my well-being, brother,
   our whole house is buried along with you,
with your going all our joys together perished,
   which, while you were still alive, your sweet love fed!—
25   Since his passing I've entirely cleared my mind of
   all my old interests and frivolous thoughts,
so when you write now that it's a shame for Catullus
   to be in Verona, since here the better sort
have to warm their cold members in a lonely bedroom—
30   that, Manlius, calls for pity, "a shame" it's not.
You will, then, forgive me if I cannot provide you
   with gifts of which grief has bereft me. No can do.
And the fact that I don't have a store of writers with me
   is because I live in Rome, my home is there,
35   my roots—it's where my whole life is spent. One book box,
   one only, of all I own, has followed me here.
And that being so, I'd not, like you to think me either
      hostile minded or disingenuous for not
having got you each of the things you asked for: gladly
40   would I provide them, were they there to be found.

Eleg. Non possum reticere, deae, qua me Allius in re
   iuuerit aut quantis iuuerit officiis,
  ne fugiens saeclis obliuiscentibus aetas
   illius hoc caeca nocte tegat studium:
45 sed dicam uobis, uos porro dicite multis
   milibus et facite haec carta loquatur anus.
  <sic per opus nostrum crescat sua fama per annos>
   notescatque magis mortuus atque magis,
  nec tenuem texens sublimis aranea telam
50   in deserto Alli nomine opus faciat.
  nam, mihi quam dederit duplex Amathusia curam,
   scitis, et in quo me torruerit genere,
  cum tantum arderem quantum Trinacria rupes
   lymphaque in Oetaeis Malia Thermopylis,
55 maesta neque assiduo tabescere lumina fletu
   cessarent tristique imbre madere genae.
  qualis in aerii perlucens uertice montis
   riuus muscoso prosilit e lapide,
  qui cum de prona praeceps est ualle uolutus,
60   per medium densi transit iter populi,
  dulce uiatori lasso in sudore leuamen,
   cum grauis exustos aestus hiulcat agros,
  ac uelut in nigro iactatis turbine nautis
   lenius aspirans aura secunda uenit
65 iam prece Pollucis, iam Castoris implorata,
   tale fuit nobis Allius auxilium.
  is clausum lato patefecit limite campum,
   isque domum nobis isque dedit dominae,
  ad quam communes exerceremus amores.
70   quo mea se molli candida diua pede
  intulit et trito fulgentem in limine plantam
   innixa arguta constituit solea,

68b.47: suppl. Green, *lacuna V.* 63: ac *Palladius, Mynors;* hec *O,* hic *X*

I cannot stay reticent, goddesses, as to how Allius
    helped me, or in what kindnesses his help
consisted, lest fleeting time with its years of oblivion
    bury deep in blind night his care for me.
45   No, I shall tell you, and you thereafter tell countless
    thousands, making this paper speak in its old age.
    <Thus through my work let his fame with time be augmented>
    and yet greater renown accrue to him in death,
nor, weaving her fine-spun web, let the lofty spider
50   work her way over Allius' neglected name.
For you know the trouble made for me by deceitful Venus,
    and the way in which she held me to the fire
when I was as burning hot as Sicilian Etna
    or the spring at Thermopylae's Hot Gates,
55   and my sad eyes were worn out with excessive weeping,
    my cheeks forever soaked by that bitter rain.
Just as glittering from the heights of some airy mountain
    a stream comes jetting over mossy stone,
spills down sheer rock-face into the valley below it
60   and makes its way across a much-travelled road,
sweet respite for the wayfarer, tired and sweating,
    when the scorched ploughland's cracked with heavy heat,
or as for sailors storm-tossed by a black tornado
    a gently breathing tailwind supervenes
65   after their desperate prayer to Castor and Pollux—
    such was the help that Allius gave to us.
He opened up énclosed land with a spacious driveway,
    provided a house for my mistress and for me
where we could sink ourselves in our mutual passion.
70   Hither my refulgent goddess with light step
came, set her gleaming foot on the worn threshold
    with a tiny squeak of her sandal. So in time past

coniugis ut quondam flagrans aduenit amore
    Protesilaëam Laodamia domum
75 inceptam frustra, nondum cum sanguine sacro
    hostia caelestis pacificasset eros.
nil mihi tam ualde placeat, Ramnusia uirgo,
    quod temere inuitis suscipiatur eris.
quam ieiuna pium desideret ara cruorem,
80   docta est amisso Laodamia uiro,
coniugis ante coacta noui dimittere collum,
    quam ueniens una atque altera rursus hiems
noctibus in longis auidum saturasset amorem,
    posset ut abrupto uiuere coniugio,
85 quod scibant Parcae non longo tempore abesse,
    si miles muros isset ad Iliacos.
nam tum Helenae raptu primores Argiuorum
    coeperat ad sese Troia ciere uiros,
Troia (nefas!) commune sepulcrum Asiae Europaeque,
90   Troia uirum et uirtutum omnium acerba cinis,
quaene etiam nostro letum miserabile fratri
    attulit. ei misero frater adempte mihi,
ei misero fratri iucundum lumen ademptum,
    tecum una tota est nostra sepulta domus,
95 omnia tecum una perierunt gaudia nostra,
    quae tuus in uita dulcis alebat amor.
quem nunc tam longe non inter nota sepulcra
    nec prope cognatos compositum cineres,
sed Troia obscena, Troia infelice sepultum
100   detinet extremo terra aliena solo.
ad quam tum properans fertur <lecta> undique pubes
    Graeca penetralis deseruisse focos,
ne Paris abducta gauisus libera moecha
    otia pacato degeret in thalamo.
105 quo tibi tum casu, pulcherrima Laodamia,
    ereptum est uita dulcius atque anima
coniugium: tanto te absorbens uertice amoris
    aestus in abruptum detulerat barathrum,
quale ferunt Grai Pheneum prope Cyllenaeum

incandescent with love for her husband came Laodamia
    to the house that Protesiláüs had begun—
75 in vain, since as yet the blood of no sacred victim
    had appeased the Celestial Lords.
(May I want nothing so much, Rhamnusian Maiden,
    that I embark on it rashly, without their consent!)
Just how much the starved altar craves its pious, bloody
80 diet, Laodamia learned from her husband's loss,
being forced to relinquish her embracement of his person
    before a second winter after the first
had with its drawn-out nights so sated her avid passion
    that she could survive with her marriage cut off short—
85 something the Fates well knew would not be long in coming
    if he went for a soldier against Ilium's walls.
For then it was, upon Helen's rape, that the Argive leaders
    began to be roused against Troy—
Troy the ill omened, joint grave of Europe and Asia,
90 Troy, of men and the manly most bitter ash,
which likewise brought to my brother a pitiable
    death. Oh brother, cruelly snatched away
from unhappy me, poor brother, bereft of happy daylight,
    our whole house is buried along with you,
95 with your going all our joys together perished,
    which, while you were alive, your sweet love fed,
and whom, now so far away, not among familiar
    tombs or near kindred's ashes laid to rest,
but in Troy the obscene, ill-fated Troy sepultured
100 at the ends of the earth an alien land now holds.
Thither then speeding, the finest | young men from every quarter
    of Greece forsook, they say, hearth and home
to stop Paris freely enjoying the adulteress he'd stolen
    at leisure, in bed with her, undisturbed.
105 And so it chanced then, most beautiful Laodamia,
    that you were bereft of something dearer than life
or breath—your marriage. Sucked down by passion's vortex
    you found yourself plummeting into a sheer abyss
like that the Greeks tell of near Cyllenean Pheneus

110 siccare emulsa pingue palude solum,
    quod quondam caesis montis fodisse medullis
     audit falsiparens Amphitryoniades,
    tempore quo certa Stymphalia monstra sagitta
     perculit imperio deterioris eri,
115 pluribus ut caeli tereretur ianua diuis,
     Hebe nec longa uirginitate foret.
    sed tuus altus amor barathro fuit altior illo,
     qui tamen indomitam ferre iugum docuit.
    nam nec tam carum confecto aetate parenti
120 una caput seri nata nepotis alit,
    qui, cum diuitiis uix tandem inuentus auitis
     nomen testatas intulit in tabulas,
    impia derisi gentilis gaudia tollens
     suscitat a cano uolturium capiti:
125 nec tantum niueo gauisa est una columbo
     compar, quae multo dicitur improbius
    oscula mordenti semper decerpere rostro,
     quam quae praecipue multiuola est mulier.
    sed tu horum magnos uicisti sola furores,
130 ut semel es flauo conciliata uiro.
    aut nihil aut paulo cui tum concedere digna
     lux mea se nostrum contulit in gremium,
    quam circumcursans hinc illinc saepe Cupido
     fulgebat crocina candidus in tunica.
135 quae tamen etsi uno non est contenta Catullo,
     rara uerecundae furta feremus erae,
    ne nimium simus stultorum more molesti.
    saepe etiam Iuno, maxima caelicolum,
    coniugis in culpa flagrantem contudit iram,
140 noscens omniuoli plurima furta Iouis.
    atqui nec diuis homines componier aequum est,
141a <nec mala quot Iuno quantaue nos patimur,
141b nec mihi de caelo descendit "Tolle mariti,>

68b.139: contudit *Herzberg*, concoquit iram *Lachmann*, cotidiana *V*
68b.141A–B: lacunam indicauit *Marcilius*, 141A: suppl. *Goold*, 141B: suppl. *Green*

110   as draining a swamp and drying its rich soil out,
       and which Amphitryon's falsely ascribed offspring
         is said to have dug after piercing and opening up
       the mountain's marrow, when | at his inferior master's
         behest he skewered those monstrous Stymphalian birds
115   with shafts unerring, that more | gods might throng heaven's gateway
         and Hebe not suffer a long virginity.
       But your deep love ran far deeper than that sinkhole,
         teaching you, still untamed, to bear the yoke.
       More precious this, than to | an age-worn parent his only
120   daughter rearing a late-born grandson at last,
       the heir now finally found for grandfather's riches,
         set down by name and witnessed in the will,
       to mockingly block some distant cousin's unseemly
         hopes, and drive off the vulture from that white head.
125   Nor has any dove, ever, so much enjoyed her snowy
         partner (though said with unmatched shamelessness
       to harvest more kisses, nonstop, biting and billing,
         than the most promiscuous woman). You alone
       outstripped the outsize passions of these creatures
130   once settled with that fair-haired fellow of yours.
       Well, my own darling conceded her little or nothing
         when she ended up in my lap,
       and Cupid was fluttering all round her in the background,
         bright and cute in his saffron tunic. Yet
135   although the lady's not satisfied with one Catullus only
         she's modest enough, I can stand the occasional lapse—
       being a stupid, jealous bore will get me nowhere.
         Besides, even Juno, Celestial number one,
       often banked down fiery rage at her husband's peccadilloes
140   when she learnt of all-lusting Jupiter's multiple tricks.
       Yet to match up gods with mortals is hardly proper,
141a   <nor can we equal all Juno's grievous wrongs,
141b and no voice from heaven told me "Shoulder a husband's,>

ingratum tremuli tolle parentis onus!"
nec tamen illa mihi dextra deducta paterna
　　fragrantem Assyrio uenit odore domum,
145　sed furtiua dedit mira munuscula nocte,
　　ipsius ex ipso dempta uiri gremio.
quare illud satis est, si nobis is datur unis
　　quem lapide illa diem candidiore notat.

hoc tibi, quod potui, confectum carmine munus
150　pro multis, Alli, redditur officiis,
ne uestrum scabra tangat rubigine nomen
　　haec atque illa dies atque alia atque alia.
huc addent diui quam plurima, quae Themis olim
　　antiquis solita est munera ferre piis.
155　sitis felices et tu simul et tua uita,
　　et domus in qua olim lusimus et domina,
et qui principio uobis me tradidit, Alli,
　　a quo sunt primo mi omnia nata bona,
et longe ante omnes mihi quae me carior ipso est,
160　lux mea, qua uiua uiuere dulce mihi est.

69

Eleg.　Noli admirari, quare tibi femina nulla,
　　Rufe, uelit tenerum supposuisse femur,
non si illam rarae labefactes munere uestis
　　aut perluciduli deliciis lapidis.
5　laedit te quaedam mala fabula, qua tibi fertur

68b.148: diem *Ital.*, dies *V*
68b.156: in qua olim *Ital.*, <ipsa> in qua *Ital.alii*
68b.157: uobis *Wiseman*, nobis *V;* me tradidit *Scaliger,* †terram dedit† *V;* Alli *Green,* †aufert† *V.*
68b.158: primo mi omnia *Haupt*, primo omnia *V*

shoulder a doddering father's thankless load!"
And anyway she never came to me on her own father's
    arm, to a house fragrant with Assyrian scent,
145   but for one miraculous night brought me stolen presents
    filched from her, yes, her husband's, yes, ah, lap.
So it's enough if for me alone is reserved that
    day she designates with a *whiter* stone.

This gift, then, such as it is, comprised in a poem,
150   a return for your many kindnesses, I send now
lest today or tomorrow or the next or the next day after
    should touch your name, Allius, with its scabrous rust.
To it the gods will add all the blessings that Themis
    once brought back to the pious in olden times.
155   May you both be happy, you and your love together,
    and the house where once I and my mistress played,
and he who first introduced me to you, Allius,
    from whom, for me, all good things had their start,
and she above all, far dearer to me than myself, my
160   star, who by living makes my own life sweet.

69

No need to wonder why no woman's willing,
    Rufus, to spread her soft thighs under you,
though you sap her resistance with expensive dresses
    or rare and translucent gems.
5   You're done in by unkind tittle-tattle, which alleges

ualle sub alarum trux habitare caper.
hunc metuunt omnes, neque mirum: nam mala ualde est
    bestia, nec quicum bella puella cubet.
quare aut crudelem nasorum interfice pestem,
10   aut admirari desine cur fugiunt.

70

Eleg.   Nulli se dicit mulier mea nubere malle
    quam mihi, non si se Iuppiter ipse petat.
dicit: sed mulier cupido quod dicit amanti,
    in uento et rapida scribere oportet aqua.

71

Eleg.   Si cui iure bono sacer alarum obstitit hircus,
    aut si quem merito tarda podagra secat,
aemulus iste tuus, qui uestrum exercet amorem,
    mirifice est apte nactus utrumque malum.
5   nam quotiens futuit, totiens ulciscitur ambos:
    illam affligit odore, ipse perit podagra.

72

Eleg.   Dicebas quondam solum te nosse Catullum,
    Lesbia, nec prae me uelle tenere Iouem.
dilexi tum te non tantum ut uulgus amicam,
    sed pater ut gnatos diligit et generos:
5   nunc te cognoui: quare etsi impensius uror,

71.4: apte *Ital.*, a te *V*

your armpit's valley is home to a rank goat.
This everyone fears, and no wonder: it's a nasty creature
    with which *no* pretty girl would share a bed.
So either kill off this brutal plague of noses
10   or stop being puzzled why girls run away.

My woman declares there's no one she'd sooner marry
    than me, not even were Jove himself to propose.
She declares—but a woman's words to her eager lover
    should be written on running water, on the wind.

← women can't
cynical   be trusted

71

If the damnable goat in the armpits justly hurt anyone,
    or limping gout ever rightfully caused pain,
that rival of yours, busy humping your shared lover,
    by contracting both maladies wonderfully fits the bill:
5 Every time that he fucks, he punishes both parties:
    the odor sickens her, the gout slays him.

You told me once, Lesbia, that Catullus alone understood you,
    That you wouldn't choose to clasp Jupiter rather than me.
I loved you then, not just as the common herd their women,
    but as a father loves his sons and sons-in-law.
5 Now, though, I *know* you. So yes, though I burn more fiercely,

passionate

to love more
and to
    cherish less

multo mi tamen es uilior et leuior.
qui potis est, inquis? quod amantem iniuria talis
cogit amare magis, sed bene uelle minus.

73

Eleg.   Desine de quoquam quicquam bene uelle mereri
    aut aliquem fieri posse putare pium.
omnia sunt ingrata, nihil fecisse benigne
    <prodest,> immo etiam taedet obestque magis;
5 ut mihi, quem nemo grauius nec acerbius urget,
    quam modo qui me unum atque unicum amicum habuit.

74

Eleg.   Gellius audierat patruum obiurgare solere,
    si quis delicias diceret aut faceret.
hoc ne ipsi accideret, patrui perdepsuit ipsam
    uxorem et patruum reddidit Harpocratem.
5 quod uoluit fecit: nam, quamuis irrumet ipsum
    nunc patruum, uerbum non faciet patruus.

75

Eleg.   Huc est mens deducta tua mea, Lesbia, culpa
    atque ita se officio perdidit ipsa suo,
ut iam nec bene uelle queat tibi, si optima fias,
    nec desistere amare, omnia si facias.

yet for me you're far cheaper, lighter. "How,"
you ask, "can that be?" It's because such injury forces
a lover to love more, but to cherish less.

73

Stop trying to earn the goodwill of any person, or supposing
there has to be someone, somewhere, who keeps faith.
Ingratitude's universal. Past acts of kindness bring you
nothing, are rather a bore and an obstacle—
5   so for me, whom no one pressures more, or more sharply,
than he who lately called me his "sometime friend."

74

Gellius had heard that Uncle was wont to admonish
all those the least bit *risqué* in word or deed.
To avoid this himself he reamed Uncle's wife, thus making
Uncle a hush-hush Holy Child.
5   What he wanted, he got: now if he stuffs it in Uncle's
open mouth, well, Uncle won't say a word.

75

My mind has been brought so low by your conduct, Lesbia,
and so undone itself through its own goodwill
that now if you were perfect it couldn't like you,
nor cease to love you now, whatever you did.

feels humiliated
but can't give
her up

76

Eleg.   Siqua recordanti benefacta priora uoluptas
      est homini, cum se cogitat esse pium,
   nec sanctam uiolasse fidem, nec foedere in ullo
      diuum ad fallendos numine abusum homines,
5   multa parata manent in longa aetate, Catulle,
      ex hoc ingrato gaudia amore tibi.
   nam quaecumque homines bene cuiquam aut dicere possunt
      aut facere, haec a te dictaque factaque sunt.
   omnia quae ingratae perierunt credita menti.
10   quare iam te cur amplius excrucies?
   quin tu animum offirmas atque istinc teque reducis,
      et dis inuitis desinis esse miser ?
   difficile est longum subito deponere amorem,
      difficile est, uerum hoc qua lubet efficias:
15   una salus haec est, hoc est tibi peruincendum,
      hoc facias, siue id non pote siue pote.
   o di, si uestrum est misereri, aut si quibus umquam
      extremam iam ipsa in morte tulistis opem,
   me miserum aspicite et, si uitam puriter egi,
20   eripite hanc pestem perniciemque mihi,
   quae mihi subrepens imos ut torpor in artus
      expulit ex omni pectore laetitias.
   non iam illud quaero, contra me ut diligat illa,
      aut, quod non potis est, esse pudica uelit :
25   ipse ualere opto et taetrum hunc deponere morbum.
      o di, reddite mi hoc pro pietate mea.

76.3: foedere in ullo *Ital.*, foedere nullo *V.* 11: animum *Statius,* animo *V*

If a man derives pleasure from recalling his acts of kindness,
    from the thought that he's kept good faith,
never broken his sworn word, nor in any agreement
    exploited the gods' favor to deceive
5 mortals, then many delights still wait for you, Catullus,
    through the long years, from this most thankless love;   *not mutual*
for whatever generous things men can say or do to
    their fellows, these you have both said and done.
Yet the sum of them, entrusted to an ungrateful spirit,
10 is lost. Then why torment yourself any more?
Why not make a firm resolve, regain your freedom,
    reject this misery that the gods themselves oppose?
It's hard to abruptly shrug off love long established:
    hard, but this, somehow, you must do.
15 Here lies your only hope, you must win this struggle: *wants to*
    this, possible or not, must be your goal.   *stop loving her*
O gods, if it's in you to pity, or if you've ever rendered   *but can't*
    help at the last to those on the verge of death,   *wants to be*
look down on my misery, and if I've lived life cleanly,   *free*
20 pluck out of me this destruction, this plague,
which, creeping torpor-like into my inmost being
    has emptied my heart of joy.
I no longer ask that she should return my love, or—
    an impossibility—agree to be chaste.
25 What I long for is health, to cast off this unclean sickness.
    O gods, if I have kept faith, please grant me this!

77

Eleg.   Rufe mihi frustra ac nequiquam credite amice
      (frustra? immo magno cum pretio atque malo),
  sicine subrepsti mi, atque intestina perurens
      ei misero eripuisti omnia nostra bona?
5 eripuisti, eheu, nostrae crudele uenenum
      uitae, eheu nostrae pestis amicitiae.

78A

Eleg.   Gallus habet fratres, quorum est lepidissima coniunx
      alterius, lepidus filius alterius.
  Gallus homo est bellus: nam dulces iungit amores,
      cum puero ut bello bella puella cubet.
5 Gallus homo est stultus, nec se uidet esse maritum,
      qui patruus patrui monstret adulterium.

78B

Eleg.   . . . sed nunc id doleo, quod purae pura puellae
      suauia comminxit spurca saliua tua.
  uerum id non impune feres: nam te omnia saecla
      noscent et, qui sis, fama loquetur anus.

79

Eleg.   Lesbius est pulcher. quid ni? quem Lesbia malit
      quam te cum tota gente, Catulle, tua.
  sed tamen hic pulcher uendat cum gente Catullum,
      si tria notorum suauia reppererit.

77.5, 6: eheu *Baehrens*, heu heu *corr.* R, heu *V*

77

Rufus, I thought you my friend. In vain, and to no purpose.
    In vain? No, worse: to my great cost and harm.
Is *that* how you sidled up on me, an acid corroding
    my innards, stole from me all I hold most dear?
5   Yes, *stole*, alas: cruel poison in my lifeblood,
    the cancer, alas, of that friendship we once had.

78A

Gallus has brothers: one's fixed with a really dishy
    wife, the other has a quite dishy son.
A neat fellow, Gallus: he sets up this sweet liaison,
    lets the neat girl shack up with the neat boy.
5   A stupid fellow, Gallus: he can't see he's a married
    uncle parading avuncular cuckoldry.

78B

. . . but what irks me now is that your filthy saliva
    has soiled the pure kisses of a pure girl.
You won't get away scot-free, though. All future ages
    shall know you, and ancient Fame tell what you are.

79

Lesbius is—pretty. How not so? for Lesbia prefers him
    to you, Catullus, and your whole family tree—
which tree Mr. Pretty can sell off, Catullus included,
    if *he* gets even *three* kisses from his "friends."

80

Eleg. Quid dicam, Gelli, quare rosea ista labella
   hiberna fiant candidiora niue,
  mane domo cum exis et cum te octaua quiete
   e molli longo suscitat hora die?
5 nescio quid certe est: an uere fama susurrat
   grandia te medii tenta uorare uiri?
  sic certe est: clamant Victoris rupta miselli
   ilia, et emulso labra notata sero.

81

Eleg. Nemone in tanto potuit populo esse, Iuuenti,
   bellus homo, quem tu diligere inciperes,
  praeterquam iste tuus moribunda ab sede Pisauri
   hospes inaurata pallidior statua,
5 qui tibi nunc cordi est, quem tu praeponere nobis
   audes, et nescis quod facinus facias ?

82

Eleg. Quinti, si tibi uis oculos debere Catullum
   aut aliud si quid carius est oculis,
  eripere ei noli, multo quod carius illi
   est oculis seu quid carius est oculis.

80

How explain, Gellius, why those oh-so-rosy
    lips of yours turn whiter than winter snow
when you leave home in the morning, *and* when you wake from
    a peaceful siesta in the mid-afternoon?
5 Something's undoubtedly up. Is it true, the whisper
    that you gobble the swollen hugenesses of mid-
maledom? That's it, for sure. Poor Victor's ruptured
    groin shouts it, *and* the milked sperm-stains round your lips.

81

Amid all those crowds, Juventius, was there *no one,*
    not *one* smart stud to tempt you into love
except that guest of yours from some seaside snooze-pit,
    his complexion more bilious than a bust's stale gilt,
5 who's now your darling, whom you've the rind to value
    over *us?* A factitious fuckup, don't you think?

82

Quintius, if you're really keen for Catullus to owe you
    his eyes, or anything (is there?) dearer than eyes,
don't deprive him of what's far dearer to *him* than eyes—or
    anything dearer than eyes.

83

Eleg.   Lesbia mi praesente uiro mala plurima dicit:
        haec illi fatuo maxima laetitia est.
        mule, nihil sentis? si nostri oblita taceret,
          sana esset: nunc quod gannit et obloquitur,
5   non solum meminit, sed, quae multo acrior est res,
         irata est. hoc est, uritur et loquitur.

84

Eleg.   Chommoda dicebat, si quando commoda uellet
        dicere, et insidias Arrius hinsidias,
        et tum mirifice sperabat se esse locutum,
          cum quantum poterat dixerat hinsidias.
5   credo, sic mater, sic liber auunculus eius,
         sic maternus auus dixerat atque auia.
        hoc misso in Syriam requierant omnibus aures:
          audibant eadem haec leniter et leuiter,
        nec sibi postilla metuebant talia uerba,
10   cum subito affertur nuntius horribilis:
        Ionios fluctus, postquam illuc Arrius isset,
         iam non Ionios esse sed Hionios.

85

Eleg.   Odi et amo. quare id faciam, fortasse requiris?
        nescio, sed fieri sentio et excrucior.

83

Lesbia keeps insulting me in her husband's presence:
    this fills the fatuous idiot with delight.
Mule, you've no insight. If she shut up and ignored me
    that'd show healthy indifference; all these insults mean
5 is, she not only remembers, but—words of sharper import—
    feels angry. That is, the lady burns—and talks.

[margin notes: conflicted / wants to believe / its out of love]

84

Arrius *aspirates:* "chommodore" when trying to articulate
    "commodore," while "insidious" came out "*hin*sidious"—
imagining that he'd spoken up with wondrous impact
    by delivering "hinsidious" full force.
5 His mother, I gather, as well as his (free-born) uncle
    and both maternal grandparents talked that way.
When he was posted to Syria, our ears all got a respite,
    heard these same words smoothly and lightly pronounced,
without any lingering fear of such verbal mishandlings—
10 then, suddenly, there arrived the horrible news:
the Ionian Sea, after Arrius had arrived, was
    Ionian no longer, but *Chi*onian.

[margin notes: over compensation / trying to / fit into / roman society / trying to seem / high-class; snobbery]

85

I hate and love. You wonder, perhaps, why I'd do that?
    I have no idea. I just feel it. I am crucified.

[margin notes: imprisoned / by feelings / conflict]

86

Eleg.   Quintia formosa est multis. mihi candida, longa,
       recta est: haec ego sic singula confiteor.
    totum illud formosa nego: nam nulla uenustas,
       nulla in tam magno est corpore mica salis.
5   Lesbia formosa est, quae cum pulcherrima tota est,
       tum omnibus una omnis surripuit Veneres.

87

Eleg.   Nulla potest mulier tantum se dicere amatam
       uere, quantum a me Lesbia amata mea est.
    nulla fides ullo fuit umquam in foedere tanta,
       quanta in amore tuo ex parte reperta mea est.

88

Eleg.   Quid facit is, Gelli, qui cum matre atque sorore
       prurit et abiectis peruigilat tunicis?
    quid facit is, patruum qui non sinit esse maritum?
       ecquid scis quantum suscipiat sceleris?
5   suscipit, o Gelli, quantum non ultima Tethys
       nec genitor Nympharum abluit Oceanus:
    nam nihil est quicquam sceleris, quo prodeat ultra,
       non si demisso se ipse uoret capite.

87.3: umquam in *Palladius,* umquam *V*

86

Many find Quintia beautiful. For me she's fair-complexioned,
    tall, of good carriage. These few points I concede.
But overall beauty—no. There's no genuine attraction
    in that whole long body, not one grain of salt.
5   It's Lesbia who's beautiful, and, being wholly lovely,
    has stolen from all of the others their every charm.

87

No woman can say she's truly been loved as much as
    my Lesbia has been loved by me: there's no   *One way love*
guarantee so strong ever figured in any contract
    as that found, on my part, in my love for you.

88

What's that man doing, Gellius, who has the hots for mother
    and sister too, who's up all night in the buff?
What's he doing, who won't let Uncle be a husband?
    Are you aware how great a crime he commits?
5   His offense, Gellius, is one that neither remotest
    Tethys nor nymph-breeding Ocean can wash away:
for there's no more heinous crime he could commit, not even
    were he with down-stretched head to gobble himself.

89

Eleg.   Gellius est tenuis : quid ni ? cui tam bona mater
        tamque ualens uiuat tamque uenusta soror
    tamque bonus patruus tamque omnia plena puellis
        cognatis, quare is desinat esse macer?
5   qui ut nihil attingat, nisi quod fas tangere non est,
        quantumuis quare sit macer inuenies.

90

Eleg.   Nascatur magus ex Gelli matrisque nefando
        coniugio et discat Persicum haruspicium:
    nam magus ex matre et gnato gignatur oportet,
        si uera est Persarum impia religio,
5   gnatus ut accepto ueneretur carmine diuos
        omentum in flamma pingue liquefaciens.

91

Eleg.   Non ideo, Gelli, sperabam te mihi fidum
        in misero hac nostro, hoc perdito amore fore,
    quod te cognossem bene constantemue putarem
        aut posse a turpi mentem inhibere probro;
5   sed neque quod matrem nec germanam esse uidebam
        hanc tibi, cuius me magnus edebat amor.
    et quamuis tecum multo coniungerer usu,
        non satis id causae credideram esse tibi.
    tu satis id duxti: tantum tibi gaudium in omni
10   culpa est, in quacumque est aliquid sceleris.

90.5: gnatus *V*, gratus *L. Mueller*

89

Gellius is lean. Well, of course—his mother's *so-o-o* generous,
   and fighting fit, and his sister's *such* a dish,
and his uncle's so generous too, and the house just crammed with girlies—
   all relatives—so, why wouldn't he be lean?
5 If he hits on nothing but what's taboo to hit on,
   there's more than enough to keep him lean, you'll find.

90

Let a Magus be born of Gellius' | and his mother's unholy
   congress, and learn Persian divining skills—
for the Magus must needs be child of a son and his mother
   if the Persians' impious religion tell it true—
5 so their offspring can worship the gods with established chant while
   rendering down a fat caul in the flames.

91

Why did I hope you'd be loyal to me, Gellius, over
   this miserable, this foredoomed love of ours?
Not through knowing you well, or thinking you constant
   or able to keep your mind off indecent thoughts,
5 but because I saw that she | for whom great love devoured me
   was neither your mother nor your full
sister; and though you and I had long enjoyed close friendship
   I didn't think you'd find *that* sufficient cause.
You did, though. Such pleasure you get from any misdeed
10 in which there lurks even a whiff of crime.

92

Eleg.   Lesbia mi dicit semper male nec tacet umquam
        de me: Lesbia me dispeream nisi amat.
       quo signa? quia sunt totidem mea: deprecor illam
        assidue, uerum dispeream nisi amo.

93

Eleg.   Nil nimium studeo, Caesar, tibi uelle placere,
        nec scire utrum sis albus an ater homo.

94

Eleg.   Mentula moechatur. Moechatur mentula ? Certe.
       Hoc est quod dicunt: ipsa olera olla legit.

95

Eleg.   Zmyrna mei Cinnae nonam post denique messem
        quam coepta est nonamque edita post hiemem,
       milia cum interea quingenta Hortensius uno
        <uerba uolubiliter scribit inepta die>.
5   Zmyrna sacras Satrachi penitus mittetur ad undas,
        Zmyrnam cana diu saecula peruoluent.
       at Volusi annales Paduam morientur ad ipsam
        et laxas scombris saepe dabunt tunicas.
       parva mei mihi sint cordi monimenta <sodalis>,
10   at populus tumido gaudeat Antimacho.

95.4: suppl. *Green, lacuna V.* 5: sacras *Morgan*, canas *V*, cauas *Ital.;* 9–10: sep. as 95b *Statius*,
    Mynors; sodalis *Aldine, lacuna V*

92

Lesbia's always bad-mouthing me, never stops talking of me.
    That means Lesbia loves me, or I'll be damned.
What proves it? I'm just the same still—praying nonstop
    to lose her. But *I* love *her* still. Or I'll be damned.

93

barbed couplets ↓ *pointed two-line attack*

I've no great urge to find favor with you, Caesar, nor to
    discover whether, as man, you're black or white.

doesn't care what caesar thinks

94

Prick's an adulterer. "Adulterer, Prick?" For certain:
    The pot picks its own potherbs, as they say.

95

Smyrna, my Cinna's opus, is published at last, nine harvests
    and nine long winters after she was begun,
while Hortensius meantime scribbles five hundred thousand
    <ill-chosen words, never pausing, in one short day.>
5   *Smyrna* will travel as far as Satrachus' sacred streambed;
    when the ages are hoary, *Smyrna* will still be read—
unlike Volusius' *Annals,* that'll die by Padua's river,
    their only regular use to wrap cheap fish.
Dear to my heart is my comrade's small monument—let the
10   vulgar enjoy their bloated Antimachus.

Eleg. Si quicquam mutis gratum acceptumue sepulcris
      accidere a nostro, Calue, dolore potest,
    quo desiderio ueteres renouamus amores
      atque olim missas flemus amicitias,
5   certe non tanto mors immatura dolori est
      Quintiliae, quantum gaudet amore tuo.

97

Eleg. Non (ita me di ament) quicquam referre putaui,
      utrumne os an culum olfacerem Aemilio.
    nilo mundius hoc, nihiloque immundius illud,
      uerum etiam culus mundior et melior :
5   nam sine dentibus est. os dentis sesquipedalis,
      gingiuas uero ploxeni habet ueteris,
    praeterea rictum qualem diffissus in aestu
      meientis mulae cunnus habere solet.
    hic futuit multas et se facit esse uenustum,
10   et non pistrino traditur atque asino?
    quem siqua attingit, non illam posse putemus
      aegroti culum lingere carnificis ?

98

Eleg. In te, si in quemquam, dici pote, putide Vetti,
      id quod uerbosis dicitur et fatuis.
    ista cum lingua, si usus ueniat tibi, possis
      culos et crepidas lingere carpatinas.
5   si nos omnino uis omnes perdere, Vetti,
      hiscas: omnino quod cupis efficies.

97.5: os *Froehlich,* hic *V,* hoc *cod. Vat. lat. 1608*
98.1, 5: Vetti *Statius,* Victi *V*

96

If anything pleasant or welcome, Calvus, can befall the
    mute sepulchre in consequence of our grief,
from the yearning with which we renew our ancient passions
    and weep for friendships long since cast away,
5 surely it's not so much grief that's felt by Quintilia
    at her premature death, as joyfulness in your love.

97

I didn't, god help me, think it mattered whether
    I put my nose to Aemilius' mouth or ass,
neither being cleaner or dirtier than the other;
    but his ass in fact is cleaner, not so crass—
5 *no teeth*, for starters. His mouth's a cemetery inside:
    headstone grinders, gums like old wagon-leather.
What's worse, that grin of his yawns about as wide
    as a mule's cunt splits for pissing in hot weather,
and he screws all the girls, thinks he's got charm and class—
10 the mill wheel's the place for him, let him go grind
grain, forget pussy! Any woman who makes a pass
    at *him* would lick a sick hangman's rank behind.

98

Against you if against anyone, rot-breath Vettius,
    the complaints about gaping chatterers can be laid.
With that furred tongue of yours you could, had you occasion,
    lick assholes, or the soles of peasants' boots.
5 If you want to destroy us all totally, Vettius, you just need to
    open wide: you'll score a complete success.

99

Eleg.   Surripui tibi, dum ludis, mellite Iuuenti,
          suauiolum dulci dulcius ambrosia.
       uerum id non impune tuli: namque amplius horam
          suffixum in summa me memini esse cruce,
5   dum tibi me purgo nec possum fletibus ullis
          tantillum uestrae demere saeuitiae.
       nam simul id factum est, multis diluta labella
          guttis abstersti mollibus articulis,
       ne quicquam nostro contractum ex ore maneret,
10   tamquam commictae spurca saliua lupae.
       praeterea infesto miserum me tradere amori
          non cessasti omnique excruciare modo,
       ut mi ex ambrosia mutatum iam foret illud
          suauiolum tristi tristius elleboro.
15   quam quoniam poenam misero proponis amori,
          numquam iam posthac basia surripiam.

100

Eleg.   Caelius Aufillenum et Quintius Aufillenam
          flos Veronensum depereunt iuuenum,
       hic fratrem, ille sororem. hoc est, quod dicitur, illud
          fraternum uere dulce sodalicium.
5   cui faueam potius? Caeli, tibi: nam tua nobis
          perspecta est igni tum unica amicitia,
       cum uesana meas torreret flamma medullas.
          sis felix, Caeli, sis in amore potens.

99.8: abstersti *O*, abstersisti *Avantius;* mollibus *Lee*, omnibus *V*
100.6: est igni tum *Palmer*, est igitur *O*, ex igni *Schöll*

99

Juventius, honey-pot, I snatched from you while you were playing
    a tiny kiss, sweeter than ambrosia's sweet.
But no way did I get it for free: an hour or longer,
    as I recall, you had me nailed on the cross
5   while I made abject apologies, yet all my weeping
    didn't abate your cruelty one jot.
Oh, the instant I'd done it you dabbed your lips with water,
    raised a soft hand and knuckled them clean, to ensure
no trace of my mouth should remain, as though expunging
10   the filthy saliva of some pissed-on whore.
Since then, what's more, you've never quit making my love life
    a living hell, tormenting me every which way,
so that soon my poor kisslet turned from sweet to bitter,
    ambrosia no longer, but hellebore.
Well, since such is the penalty for my ill-starred passion,
15   henceforth I will *never* snatch another kiss!

100

Caelius and Quintius, the flower of Verona's manhood,
    over Aufillenus and Aufillena have lost their heads—
for the brother the one, for the sister the other. This has to be that
    sweet sibling comradeship we hear about.
5   Which should I favor? You, Caelius, for your special
    friendship with me was tempered by fire at a time
when that crazy flame was scorching through my marrow.
    So, good luck, Caelius: may you be potent in love.

101

Eleg.   Multas per gentes et multa per aequora uectus
         aduenio has miseras, frater, ad inferias,
    ut te postremo donarem munere mortis
         et mutam nequiquam alloquerer cinerem.
5   quandoquidem fortuna mihi tete abstulit ipsum,
         heu miser indigne frater adempte mihi,
    nunc tamen interea haec, prisco quae more parentum
         tradita sunt tristi munere ad inferias,
    accipe fraterno multum manantia fletu,
10   atque in perpetuum, frater, aue atque uale.

102

Eleg.   Si quicquam tacito commissum est fido ab amico,
         cuius sit penitus nota fides animi,
    meque esse inuenies illorum iure sacratum,
         Corneli, et factum me esse puta Harpocratem.

103

Eleg.   sodes mihi redde decem sestertia, Silo,
         deinde esto quamuis saeuus et indomitus :
    aut, si te nummi delectant, desine quaeso
         leno esse atque idem saeuus et indomitus.

104

Eleg.   Credis me potuisse meae male dicere uitae,
         ambobus mihi quae carior est oculis?
    non potui, nec, si possem, tam perdite amarem:
         sed tu cum Tappone omnia monstra facis.

101

A journey across many seas and through many nations
    has brought me here, brother, for these poor obsequies,
to let me address, all in vain, your silent ashes,
    and render you the last service for the dead,

5   since fortune, alas, has bereft me of your person,
    my poor brother, so unjustly taken from me.
Still, here now I offer those gifts which by ancestral custom
    are presented, sad offerings, at such obsequies:
accept them, soaked as they are with a brother's weeping,

10   and, brother, forever now hail and farewell.

[handwritten margin note: senus grief]

102

If a trustworthy friend has ever passed on a secret
    to one whose loyalty was fully known,
you'll find me, Cornelius, no less strongly committed
    to their ethos—and silent as any Holy Child.

103

Either please repay me those ten big ones, Silo,
    (which done, you can be as bloody as you please),
or, if the money's your pleasure, kindly desist from
    being a pimp *and* bloody, all at once.

104

Do you *really* believe I could have cursed my darling,
    whom I cherish more than both my eyes? No way:
I couldn't, nor, if I could, would my love be so desperate—
    but you and Tappo make shockers of everything.

105

Eleg.   Mentula conatur Pipleium scandere montem:
       Musae furcillis praecipitem eiciunt.

106

Eleg.   Cum puero bello praeconem qui uidet esse,
       quid credat, nisi se uendere discupere?

107

Eleg.   Si quicquam cupidoque optantique optigit umquam
       insperanti, hoc est gratum animo proprie.
    quare hoc est gratum nobis quoque, carius auro,
       quod te restituis, Lesbia, mi cupido.
5   restituis cupido atque insperanti, ipsa refers te
       nobis. o lucem candidiore nota !
    quis me uno uiuit felicior, aut magis hace
       optandam uita dicere quis poterit?

108

Eleg.   Si, Comini, populi arbitrio tua cana senectus
       spurcata impuris moribus intereat,
    non equidem dubito quin primum inimica bonorum
       lingua exsecta auido sit data uulturio,
5   effossos oculos uoret atro gutture coruus,
       intestina canes, cetera membra lupi.

107.7: hace *Ribbeck,* hac est *O,* me est *X.* 8: optandam *Ribbeck,* optandus *V*

105

Prick does his best to mount the heights of Pipla:
   Muses with dainty forklets toss him off.

[handwritten annotations in right margin, crossed out]

106

Seeing an auctioneer with some fetching young creature
   One can only assume the lad's desperate to sell—himself.

107

If anything ever came through for one who so longingly
   yearned for it, yet without hope—that's balm for the soul.
So, there's balm for us too, than gold more precious,
   Lesbia, in this: that you've brought yourself back to me
5 and my yearning for you: yes, back to my hopeless yearning,
   to me, by your own choice. O brighter than white
day! Who lives happier than I do? Who can argue
   that life holds any more desirable bliss?

[handwritten: Changing relationship]

108

[handwritten: invective]

[handwritten: invective]

If public judgment, Cominius, should ensure that your hoary
   old age, soiled by impure habits, was cut short,
I personally don't doubt but that some greedy vulture
   would, first, be fed your severed tongue, and then
5 your eyes would be pecked out and eaten by a black-throat
   crow, your guts scoffed by dogs, the rest by wolves.

[handwritten: bitter]

[handwritten: dismembered words]

109

Eleg. Iucundum, mea uita, mihi proponis amorem
      hunc nostrum inter nos perpetuumque fore.
  di magni, facite ut uere promittere possit,
      atque id sincere dicat et ex animo,
5 ut liceat nobis tota perducere uita
      aeternum hoc sanctae foedus amicitiae.

110

Eleg. Aufillena, bonae semper laudantur amicae:
      accipiunt pretium, quae facere instituunt.
  tu, quod promisti, mihi quod mentita inimica es,
      quod nec das et fers saepe, facis facinus.
5 aut facere ingenuae est, aut non promisse pudicae,
      Aufillena, fuit: sed data corripere
  fraudando officiis, plus quam meretricis auarae est,
      quae sese toto corpore prostituit.

111

Eleg. Aufillena, uiro contentam uiuere solo,
      nuptarum laus ex laudibus eximiis:
  sed cuiuis quamuis potius succumbere par est,
      quam matrem fratres efficere ex patruo.

112

Eleg Multus homo es, Naso, neque tecum multus homo <est qui>
      descendit: Naso, multus es et pathicus.

111.4: efficere ex patruo *Ital.*, ex patruo . . . *V*
112.1: <est qui> *Scaliger*, <est quin> *Schwabe*

109

You're suggesting, my life, that this mutual love between us
   can be a delight—*and* in perpetuity?
Great gods, only let her promise be in earnest,
   let her be speaking truly, and from the heart,
5 so that we can maintain, for the rest of our life together,
   our hallowed friendship through this eternal pact!

wants long, stable relationship

110

Aufillena, obliging girlfriends invariably get golden
   opinions: their actions bring their own reward.
But you, who broke your promise to me, I count as
   hostile: you grab without giving. That's a crime.
5 Either you're frank and do it, or, if you're modest,
   Aufillena, you never promised. But to rake in
gifts, then not honor your bargain—that's much worse than
   a greedy whore whose whole body is on the take.

111

That a woman, Aufillena, be content to live with
   one man is high praise for brides;
yet rather than mothering cousins by Dad's brother
   to put out for *anyone* is fine, just fine.

112

You're such a macho guy, Naso, yet few other macho guys seek your
   company. How so? Naso, you're macho—and a queen.

113

Eleg. Consule Pompeio primum duo, Cinna, solebant
   Mucillam: facto consule nunc iterum
  manserunt duo, sed creuerunt milia in unum
   singula. fecundum semen adulterio.

114

Eleg. Firmano saltu non falso Mentula diues
   fertur, qui tot res in se habet egregias,
  aucupium omne genus, piscis, prata, arua ferasque.
   nequiquam: fructus sumptibus exsuperat.
  5 quare concedo sit diues, dum omnia desint.
   saltum laudemus, dum modio ipse egeat.

115

Eleg. Mentula habet iuxta triginta iugera prati,
   quadraginta arui: cetera sunt maria.
  cur non diuitiis Croesum superare potis sit,
   uno qui in saltu tot bona possideat,
  5 prata arua ingentes siluas altasque paludes
   usque ad Hyperboreos et mare ad Oceanum?
  omnia magna haec sunt, tamen ipsest maximus ultro,
   non homo, sed uero mentula magna minax.

113.2: Mucillam *Pleitner*, mecilia *V*
114.6: modio *Richmond*, modo *V*
115.1: iuxta *Scaliger*, instar *V*
115.5: altasque paludes *Fordyce*, saltusque paludesque *V*

113

In Pompey's first consulship, Cinna, little Mucia had a couple
    of fellows. Now he's consul a second time
the two are still there, but for each one a thousand rivals
    have come springing up. Highly fecund, adultery's seed.

114

Report doesn't lie about Prick's wealth on his Firmum
    property—it's just crammed with desirable things:
game birds of every kind, fish, hunting, pasture, ploughland.
    No use, though: his assets are dwarfed by what he spends.
5   So, I'll concede that he's rich, even with zero credit—
    let's praise the property, though he's skint himself.

115

Prick owns over thirty units of hot pasture,
    forty under his plough, plus main galore.
How can he not outstrip the wealth of Croesus
5   when one estate contains so much good stuff,
meadow and arable, great forests, endless marshes,
    right to the Hyperboreans' and Ocean's shore?
All these are biggish items, but himself's the biggest—
    no man, but rather a pompous portentous PRICK.

116

Eleg.   Saepe tibi studioso animo uenante requirens
        carmina uti possem uertere Battiadae,
    qui te lenirem nobis, neu conarere
        tela infesta <meum> mittere in usque caput,
5   hunc uideo mihi nunc frustra sumptum esse laborem,
        Gelli, nec nostras hic ualuisse preces.
    contra nos tela ista tua euitabimus ictu,
        at fixus nostris tu dabi[s] supplicium.

116.2: uertere *Palmer*, mittere *V.* 7: ictu *Green*, amictu *Ital.*, †amitha *O*

116

Though often with studious mind attempting to render
    Callimachus' pregnant verses for your delight,
to ease you up on us and stop you forever trying
    to lob your hostile missiles at my head,
5   I see now that all this labor of mine was wasted,
    Gellius, that our pleas were all in vain.
Blow matching blow, we'll parry your shots against us—
    but you'll be skewered by ours, and pay the price.

EXPLANATORY NOTES

For named persons or places, unless otherwise stated, consult the glossary.

1   The "little booklet" raises the vexed question of arrangement and organization: did Catullus order the poems as we have them, or was this done after his death by editors? See introd. pp. 16–18. It is often argued that the overall length of Catullus's corpus, being too great for a single book (an argument, it seems, that will no longer stand: see below on 1–2) means that this dedication will have been to a smaller selection only, perhaps to some or all of the lyrical poems—the so-called polymetrics—represented by 1–60. However, Quinn cleverly suggests (1972, 19) that Catullus's reference to Nepos's three volumes may have hinted at Catullus's own three *libelli:* the long group (61–68) and the elegiacs (69–116) as well as the polymetrics. Many critics (e.g., Syndikus 1984, 74; Batstone 1998) see this dedicatory poem as a metaphorical proclamation of the Callimachean / Neoteric ideal: all elegance, learning, and polish. Despite Wiseman (1979, 169 with n. 14) and the numerous earlier scholars he cites, I remain skeptical. Cornelius Nepos—learned, concise, painstaking, innovative—has been described (Tatum 1997, 485) as Catullus's "ideal reader." He was also, with his exploration of universal history, a Transpadane, like Catullus, "poised to stride . . . into the domain, social and cultural, of the senatorial class" (which had hitherto monopolized the genre of large-scale historiography). Tatum sees both men, illuminatingly, as "Alexandrian in literary sensibilities and Italian in origin," with the second factor at least as important as the first. Wiseman (1979, 143–74) brilliantly demonstrates how rhetorically interwoven Roman poetics and historiography were, and thus how appropriate it was for Catullus to dedicate his work to Nepos.

1–2   The "book" was a papyrus roll, its ends smoothed with abrasive: it was wound onto a rod with a knob protruding at either end to facilitate scrolling from page to page. Its average length was between seven hundred and one thousand one hundred lines: Catullus's collection is over two thousand. However, recent paleographical research (see Skinner 2003, 187 n. 14) suggests that the Catullan corpus could, in fact, have been issued on a single outsize scroll.

8–10   It is Catullus's Muse, virginal and playful—but which one, for a collection of self-styled trivia?—who, in typically Roman fashion, also becomes his patron.

9   Endless unnecessary attempts have been made to improve this line textually: the latest effort (Gratwick 2002) produces *qualecumque quid. Patro <ci>ni ergo,* a line which for syntactical and metrical awkwardness deserves a special Bubonis Farti Palma, or Latin Stuffed Owl Award.

2   Lesbia's sparrow is too firmly entrenched, both by Catullus and by its subsequent history, to dislodge, but was probably in fact a blue rock thrush, popular as an Italian pet, real sparrows being dowdy, mean, and virtually untamable (Fordyce 1961, 88). Nevertheless, evidence for the *passer* and other birds as pets goes back as far as the plays of Plautus in Rome (as well as featuring in the *Greek Anthology*), and the sparrow, as we know from Sappho, was sacred to Aphrodite (the poem, incidentally, parodies the formal structure of a hymn to a goddess). It also (as Chaucer was aware) enjoyed a reputation for lechery—one reason why, ever since the Renaissance, a running debate, still open, has gone on as to whether this poem contains an obscene double entendre, since *passer* and its modern Italian descendant *passero* are both found as a slang term for the penis. This being so, it is hard to believe that Catullus did not at least let the ambiguity cross his mind, with the thought that it might also cross that of his reader; Martial (7.14., 11.6.15–16) certainly took it that way. That Catullus was playing with this ambiguity in both 2 and 3 is well argued by Holzberg (2002, 61–67). See also Genovese 1974, though his equation of the *passer* with a winged-phallus amulet is less convincing. Gaisser's romantic suggestion (1993, 242–43) that such a notion would rob Catullus's poem of its "affective and sentimental element" is seriously anachronistic. Cf. Thomas 1993, 131–42. For a detailed attack on the double entendre theory, see Jocelyn 1980.

2B   Despite various attempts to link this fragment to 2, Thomson (1997, 205–206) is right in his assertion that the syntax makes it impossible—one more reason for rejecting Mulroy's suggestion (2002, 4) that if we accept the sexual double entendre, Catullus could be implying that he's thrilled when Lesbia masturbates him. But to accept this, we also (line 9) would have to believe he could lament the impossibility of doing the job himself. For the myth alluded to, see glossary s.v. Atalanta.

3   If 2 takes off from a hymn, Catullus here neatly fuses the Greek concept of the dirge with that highly Hellenistic genre, the epitaph, and under both we find (Quinn

1970, 96) "a delicately ironical, graceful love poem, wary of any sentimentality."
It is also unique. As Fordyce says (1961, 92), "the simple emotion which turns the
lament for the dead pet into a love lyric, and makes commonplace and colloquial
language into poetry, owes nothing to any predecessor." Nor was the effect re-
peatable: neither Ovid's elegy on Corinna's parrot (*Am.* 2.6) nor John Skelton's
Lament for Philip Sparrow come near Catullus's subtlety, charm—and wry humor.
The last two lines (Krostenko 2001, 262) reveal the true reason for Catullus's grief:
the bird's demise had upset Lesbia. At 16 Goold's emendation of an emendation
(*quod* for the second *o*), welcomed by, among others, Quinn (1972, 85–86), may
get rid of the hiatus and expressly blame the sparrow for Lesbia's grief, but is un-
necessary to the sense and ruins the line's rhetorical balance.

4   Unlike some modern scholars, I am inclined to accept the thesis (first proposed by
Ellis) that Catullus himself is the master *(erus)* at Sirmio, and that the cutter or
yacht is the one in which he sailed home in 56, after service in Bithynia, through
the Hellespont, across the Aegean, up the Adriatic, and thence by way of the Po
and the Mincio to the Lago di Garda (Fordyce 1961, 97–98). This would date the
poem to spring 56 or later. Gordon Williams (1968, 190–94) suggests that what is
being shown off here is a commemorative fresco of the cutter, an attractive idea,
but pure speculation. The cutter itself is represented as providing the poet with
his information, and comes across (Quinn 1970, 101) as an "old garrulous slave . . .
proud of a successful career of faithful service." (For another instance of a talk-
ative domestic appurtenance, see 67 and note.) The poem was neatly parodied in
one of the minor works ascribed to Virgil (*Cat.* 10), describing the activities of a
muleteer called Sabinus.

5   The affair with "Lesbia mine" (1) is now presented as an ongoing, open scandal,
vulnerable to gossip and "old men's strictures." 10–13: The Latin verb *con-
turbabimus* belongs to technical phraseology indicating "fraudulent bankruptcy
with concealment of assets" (Fordyce 1961, 107). The object in this case is to frus-
trate jealous attempts at hexing *(inuidere)* Catullus and Lesbia by means of the evil
eye. Just as knowledge of a secret name or possession of a victim's nail parings or
hair clippings could, on the principle of the part for the whole, be used against their
owner, so Catullus affects to believe that an accurate tally of his and his lover's
kisses (over which Catullus "flicks his abacus like an accounts clerk," (Wiseman
1985, 139) may confer a similar power (cf. 7.12). The danger of observant eyes
goes beyond the *mal'occhio;* public Mediterranean scrutiny is pitiless and can be
lethal (Wray 2001, 143ff.) On the Greek island where I once lived there was a pop-
ular saying: "Wherever you go, remember there are three pairs of eyes watching
you, and only one of them is a goat's." There is a useful analysis by Segal (1968);
Greene (1998, 202–25) has some useful insights but suffers from feminist overkill.

6   Flavius is reluctant to show off his new girlfriend. The reader is left to guess that
     he's scared of Catullus poaching her. Catullus, applying a common literary topos
     to the affair, assures his friend that he merely wants to confer poetic immortality
     on him and his lover. Since he succeeded in this object better than he could have
     dreamed, the little squib acquires an ironic flavor in retrospect. The girl is *febricu-*
     losi, which I translate as "consumptive"; the impression Catullus wants to convey
     is of someone thin and feverish in appearance. In fact she was probably suffering
     from malaria (Wray 2001, 156 with references).

7   We can picture Lesbia—Clodia Metelli, if it was indeed she—reading or hearing
     5, and asking, amusedly, "All right, then, how many kisses *would* satisfy you?" Cf.
     Lyne 1980, 43–47, a sensitive and sympathetic analysis, pointing out in detail how
     "the ingredients of the poem (humour, urbanity, extravagance, warmth, and a touch
     of sentimentality), and the proportion and ordering of those ingredients, must al-
     low valuable insight into the personalities of both Catullus and Lesbia and into
     how the two interact." This poem, together with 2, 2a, 3, and 5, clearly belongs
     to an early stage in her affair with Catullus, c. 61/60 B.C.E. Cf. Greene 1998, 5.

   4 Silphium (probably asafetida) was a famous heal-all in antiquity (Plin. *NH*
     22.101–103), and Cyrene's main export; its juice was recommended to help diges-
     tion, reverse baldness, and cure everything from gout to dropsy. But what Catul-
     lus may well have had in mind here (as Professor Treggiari reminds me) are its al-
     leged contraceptive qualities: cf. J. M. Riddle, 1991, Oral contraceptives and
     early-term abortifacients during classical antiquity and the Middle Ages, *Past &*
     Present 132: 3–32.

11–12 Again we see Catullus's nervousness about his relationship being hexed by ill-wish-
     ers (cf. 5.10–13). Who, one wonders, might they have been? The censorious old
     men? Some rival? Even Lesbia's husband?

8   Despite the caveats of Godwin (1999, 123), I agree with Fordyce (1961, 110) and
     others (e.g., Quinn 1970, 115) that, just as the preceding poems mark an early phase
     in Catullus's relationship with Lesbia, so this one was written at a much later stage,
     when the affair had reached a point of bitter recrimination. (Whatever the arrange-
     ment of the poems may have been, it was certainly not chronological.) Godwin's
     efforts to see it *solely* as a literary construct, with Catullus artfully distancing him-
     self both from the (unnamed) *puella* and from his own "persona as lover-poet"
     are as misguided as the fashion he aims to supplant, i.e., reading it as biographical
     evidence and nothing else. The triple-thud line endings of the choliambic metre
     (see introd. p. 33), together with the absence of enjambment, are extraordinarily
     effective in conveying the notion of reiterated determination. For the speaker's frac-
     tured identity and conflicted persona see Greene (1998, 2–8), who, however, un-

derestimates the possibilities of this poem treated simply as a dramatic monologue (well analyzed on these terms, Strong Catullus vs. Weak Catullus, by Lyne 1980, 47–51).

9   For Veranius, Fabullus, and the chronology of their tours of duty in Macedonia and Spain see glossary s.vv. The construction is deft and economical; as Quinn says (1970, 119), "by the time we reach the end . . . we know all we need to know about Veranius and what he meant to Catullus."

10   The light anecdotal tone suggests Roman satire (e.g., Horace, *Sat.* 1.9) rather than a Hellenistic model such as the mime, though Quinn (1972, 224) is absolutely right to insist that the incident "all has the ring of something that actually happened, and happened the way Catullus tells it." Catullus tells a good story against himself, while progressively revising his opinion of Varus's girlfriend, who is too sassy to stick to her prescribed role in a man's world. Skinner (1989, 7ff.), seeing this, makes an interesting but rather overworked case for a subtext attacking "the essential unfairness of the Roman status system" (19) through an urbane and witty illustration of the abuse of power in a hierarchical society. The date must be soon after Catullus's return from Bithynia early in 56.

12–13   The praetor (provincial governor) is a "fuckface" *(irrumator)* because he stops his staff from doing well at the expense of the locals; but see, for example, 29, where Catullus complains about Caesar's staff making a killing in Gaul, Spain, and Britain. He doesn't object to the practice as such, but to its not being available for the enrichment of himself and his friends. At best, he is against *excessive* public greed.

26   On Serapis see glossary s.v.; the cult was popular in Rome in Catullus's day as a source of healing, and *incubatio* (i.e., sleeping overnight in the precinct, with attention from the god in a dream) was much practiced as a cure, just as we know it to have been in the Greek cult of Asclepius.

11   Perhaps the bitterest of the late Lesbia poems: contrast with the violent delineation of Lesbia's *nostalgie de la boue* the sad image of Catullus's love as a crushed flower, with its echo of Sappho (fr. 105.4–6 L–P, cf. Forsyth 1990/1, 457ff.). Note that Catullus now will not even address Lesbia personally, but sends a message (Macleod 1973a, 303) via Furius and Aurelius, well described by Skinner (2003, 83) as "the Rosencrantz and Guildenstern types" who later recur in the Juventius sequence (15–26). However, the variety of interpretations it has evoked (for a representative sample see Greene 1998, 118 n. 14) is itself significant. Putnam (1982) and Greene (1998, 26–32) deal best with Lesbia's alleged emasculation of the speaker, and "the conflict between the utilitarian civilizing forces of men and the innocence

of the natural world" (Greene 34). For a resolutely commonsensical overview, see Fredericksmeyer (1993). It cannot be a coincidence that this final repudiation of his faithless lover by Catullus returns to the metre (the Sapphic stanza, cf. introd. p. 37) in which what was clearly his first poem to her, 51, was written, and which he employs nowhere else. The poem's reference to Caesar's crossing of the Rhine and invasion of Britain, as well as to Egypt and Parthia (the restoration by Gabinius of Ptolemy XII Auletes to the throne of Egypt, the ill-fated expedition under Crassus), all events in 55, suggest a date either then or early in 54—which makes it, intriguingly, contemporary with that very different *jeu d'esprit*, 45. Also, its very specific references to Catullus's own possible upcoming ventures abroad (Quinn 1972, 173–75) strongly suggest that he was then contemplating another staff attachment, either with Caesar (as Cicero's brother Quintus and his protégé Trebatius were to do), or with Crassus in the East.

12   Like many a famous man since, Asinius Pollio (q.v. glossary) seems to have had a black sheep brother. The importance attached to table napkins in Roman literature (not only by Catullus) becomes more understandable when we remember that until forks were introduced, about the time of the Renaissance, everyone, Romans included, ate with their fingers. Thus napkins served not only as handkerchiefs and sweat rags (*sudaria*, 14), but also, to a far greater extent than today, to remove grease and similar remnants from a diner's hands between courses. This does not entirely explain why they should have been a favorite target (cf., e.g., 25) of light-fingered guests. For the correlation of social mores and literary elegance in this clever put-down see Krostenko (2001, 241–46, 251–52).

13   The poetical dinner invitation was a familiar topos in Greek and Roman literature, often accompanied by professions of poverty-based simplicity. Catullus gives it a fresh twist by telling his guest to bring his own food and wine as well as a girlfriend; all he himself will supply as host is the scent of *his* lover, who smells so sexy that Fabullus will wish he was all nose. The phallic joke is unmistakable; so is the nature of the smell (convincingly identified by Littman 1977). If Catullus is too poor (in theory) for food and wine, he certainly can't afford expensive perfume. Amusingly, this was *not* one of the poems that Fordyce omitted from his edition on the grounds (1973, v) that they "do not lend themselves to comment in English." Kirkpatrick, too (1998, 303–305), misses the point in his supposition that what the girl brings with her is simply a great new aphrodisiac.

14   Calvus (q.v. glossary) has sent Catullus a seasonal gift: a collection of bad (i.e., for them, old-fashioned non-Neoteric) poetry, the ancient equivalent, as Catullus would see it, of D. B. Wyndham Lewis's wonderfully awful anthology, *The Stuffed Owl*. The occasion was the Saturnalia (15), a holiday which began on 17 Decem-

ber, many of the customs connected with which (e.g., the exchange of presents and masters waiting on their servants) were later transferred to Christmas.

14B   This fragment—not even a complete sentence, but the protasis of an unfinished conditional clause—is one of the most cogent arguments (despite Wiseman 1969, 7–10) against the thesis that Catullus arranged his own collection as we have it, or at the very least that a posthumous editor did not tamper with that arrangement. It bears no conceivable relation to either 14 or 15, and is sometimes explained as surviving from a kind of second preface, to rather more daring (or obscene) poems (Wiseman 1969, Godwin 1999, 133). But this (like so much Catullan scholarship) is pure speculation: cf. Thomson (1997, 247). A fragment of a poem that became mutilated during transmission? A scrap preserved from Catullus's workshop by an "unintelligently conscientious" editor (Fordyce 1961, 139)? We simply cannot tell.

15   The tone is at once lightheartedly casual and explicitly gross: Catullus asks Aurelius (q.v. glossary) to look after his, Catullus's, boyfriend—perhaps Juventius, in any case an adolescent—and to refrain, notorious cocksman that he is, from making a pass at the boy himself. This has to be a parody of such a formal request *(commendatio)*: "no more unsuitable person for Catullus to entrust his boyfriend to could be imagined: he is willfully putting the lamb in the jaws of the wolf" (Macleod 1973a, 29; cf. Carratello 1995, 32–33). Commentators (e.g., Quinn 1970, 140–41) aren't sure how to take the jocular violence. Does he or doesn't he mean it all? The warning was probably real, the threats were surely comic exaggeration. Yet the treatment described at line 19—anal insertion of radishes and, more seriously, mullets (with the barbs, which made removal torture) as a recognized punishment for adultery—was traditional, and known at least as early as the fifth century B.C.E. (Aristoph. *Clouds* 1083 with scholia; cf. Mulroy 2002, 15). The process also included the singeing of anal hair.

16   The contrast between, and intermingling of, coarse threats and literary theory is striking, but opaque (Buchheit 1976, 332ff. takes it as a poetic manifesto). Again, commentators are fairly heavy-handed here, especially over the first and last lines, which are surely no more than a baroque extension of the kind of threat typified in English by the phrase, "Fuck you," without any suggestion of actual sexual intercourse. For the reinforcement of masculine feelings of superiority via verbs such as *paedico* ("bugger") and *irrumo* ("mouth-fuck") see Wray 2001, chapters 4–5. Though we do not need to posit a real-life situation here (Godwin 1999, 134), I should be surprised were Catullus not, in fact, responding to the obvious charge of slight effeminacy and immodesty (all that explicit stuff, those kisses) by pointing out that he's as masculine as you please, and would be happy to prove it on his

critics. Poem 16, as Krostenko reminds us (2001, 277ff.) "encapsulates the hazards [Catullus] encountered in formulating a new view of erotics, poetics, and the social world in Roman society." It is, nevertheless, elusive in detail; its train of thought "wavers or weaves between the poles of poetic reality and literal reality" (Batstone 1993, 154–55). Wray (2001, 185–86) suggests that in his distinction between a writer's life and his work, Catullus may have had in mind Archilochos, "the most conspicuous example known to antiquity of a holy poet who wrote dirty poems." Had Catullus survived a few more years he could have justified himself by the example of Octavian, as Martial (11.20) did later, citing a political squib by the future Augustus that is as obscene as anything Catullus ever wrote. Furius and Aurelius are portrayed as naïve critics, who deserve the kind of *ad hominem* treatment characterizing their own attitude to Catullus and his poetry. Cf. Pedrick 1993, 182–87; Macleod 1973b, 300–301; and my note on 48, to which this poem must allude.

17   Catullus is irritated with a local husband for not taking better care of his attractive and sexy young wife, and wants him tossed off the rickety bridge he so resembles into the swamp below. There is classic Mediterranean mockery here: the bridegroom who can't get his wife pregnant is a traditional target for public scorn (Wray 2001, 135ff., with modern parallels). There was apparently an ancient ritual in Rome which involved throwing sexagenarians off a bridge (Catullus's would-be victim seems to have been elderly); see Quinn 1970, 146. One possible reason was to secure the river's continued tolerance of the bridge. Quinn suggests, ingeniously, that "perhaps a ducking, while magically restoring the bridge to health and strength, will make a new man of the husband too." It is doubtful, however, whether the quaint details of archaic local custom had any significance for Catullus except to provide color and perhaps, (as Akbar Khan [1969] suggested), hint at sexual double entendre, on which see also Rudd (1959, 205ff.) and Genovese (1974, 122).

[18–20] The break in numerical sequence between 17 and 21 commemorates the removal from the canon of three short poems first added in 1554 by Muretus (M.-A. Muret), but subsequently rejected as spurious. Some, most recently Mulroy (2002, 17–18) retain 18, a short Priapean dedication, as genuine.

21   Aurelius's hungers *(esuritionum)* include most things for which one can have an appetite, above all food, money, and sex. This squib has to be read along with 15 in particular, though 16 similarly illuminates the jocular threats, which bear the same relation to a genuine physical *irrumatio* as do the slang phrases, "Sucks to you," or "X sucks."

7–8   Catullus will make Aurelius look a fool (? with this poem) first.

9–10   A puzzle. Catullus frequently (23, 24, 26) twits both Furius and Aurelius with poverty: Godwin (1999, 137; cf. Thomson 1997, 258) argues that his complaint is that "Aurelius is too poor to feed the boy properly." But surely the hunger here, too, is sexual, and what Catullus is suggesting is that if Aurelius was doing this on a full stomach—i.e., if he'd already satisfied his ravenous appetite—Catullus would treat it as a harmless flirtation, but as it is, he's scared that Aurelius may encourage the boy to develop (10–11) the same kind of violent appetites as he has himself. Cf. Carratello (1995, 33–35).

22   Catullus here uses the Hellenistic device of a letter to a friend to convey literary criticism—and the "limping iambics" (*choliambics* or *scazons*, see introd. p. 33) indicate that he is serious (Thomson 1997, 259). Suffenus, like Hortensius (95.3), is a poet of the old school, in the expansive Ennian tradition. He writes far too much (3–5: the great Neoteric sin); he equates luxurious accessories with quality (5–8); he is ridiculously pleased with his own efforts (17). And watch out: when he's off literature he's a decent man (1–2; cf. Krostenko 2001, 268–70), and we all, could we but see it, to some extent share his faults (18–21). At line 21 the "load on our own backs" refers to a fable of Phaedrus (no. 75), in which Jupiter hangs two bagfuls of faults on mortals: those of other people in front, where they can see them, but their own on their backs, out of sight. For the details of book production (5–9) see note to 1.

23   This spoof on the familiar Stoic topos of the intangible riches accruing to the poor philosopher includes advantages both normal (good health, digestion, lack of worries, 7–8) and bizarre (clean backside, hard dry turds). "The dryness of Furius's body is both metaphor and metonym of his financial distress" (Wray 2001, 74). But the whole poem is leading, unexpectedly, up to the refusal of a loan (26–27)—Furius has all the proper wealth he needs!

24   The first of the (attributed) Juventius poems. The joke, to our taste, is a little sour: as usual, Catullus is having fun at the expense of Furius's poverty (Krostenko 2001, 272 with n. 94), and what he is in effect telling Juventius (the family was old and distinguished) is, "Don't give the bastard your love, he can't afford you; just leave him a tip, he needs it."

4   Though Midas and his golden touch are familiar from Greek literature, this is the earliest surviving allusion to them in Rome.

25   It is virtually impossible to convey in English the full force of Catullus's contemptuous invective here, "especially the liquid diminutives conveying *mollitia* (effeminacy)" (Thomson 1997, 266), as he draws a nice contrast between Thal-

lus's softness and his rapacity. Once again, as in 12, napkins, of an expensive sort, are the pilferer's objective.

26   Most critics stress the pun in line 2: *opposita* can mean both "facing," "exposed to," and "mortgaged" (one of those ambiguities that give the translator a headache). But the real point, yet again, is Furius's poverty. His *uillula* (line 1) is diminutive, his mortgage is trifling (and the loan he asks for in 23 is nearly seven times that, Thomson 1997, 269). The last line, then, is sharply ironical.

27   Probably a simple drinking poem (often compared to those of Anacreon in the Greek tradition) rather than the elaborate metaphor for poetry postulated by Wiseman (1969, 7–8). The adjective *amariores* in line 2 must mean "stronger," i.e., with less water in it, rather than "more bitter" (bitterness would be an unusual desiderandum in wine). For a detailed oenological discussion, see Thomson 1997, 272.

28   For all characters mentioned (and for the chronology of Veranius's and Fabullus's service abroad), see glossary s.vv. The date of this poem will be shortly after Catullus's return from Bithynia in the spring of 56. The implications of a strict governor's leaving slim pickings for his staff contrast nicely with Catullus's reproaches in 29 against Mamurra, whose profiteering in Gaul and Britain had become a public scandal. For Catullus's politicization of sexual imagery (and vice versa) see the neat analysis by Skinner (1979, 137–40). Being "reamed over" by Memmius financially is the equivalent of oral rape (9–10). Cf. Wray 2001, 174.

29   This poem—the first of several in which we meet Mamurra—is addressed to Caesar and Pompey, the "father and son-in-law" of the final line (24), which dates it to before the death of Julia (Caesar's daughter, Pompey's wife) in 54, and probably to late in 55, between the first and second expeditions into Britain, "when talk of fortunes to be made from British plunder was in the air" (Fordyce 1961, 160), and false rumors of the island's supposedly vast mineral wealth had not yet been exploded. I agree with Neudling (1955, 89–90), Skinner (1979, 145–46 with earlier references), and Godwin (1999, 144) that lines 1–10 are addressed to Pompey, 11–20 to Caesar, and the coda (21–24) to the two together. Mamurra is thus the creature of them both.

29 and 57 (q.v.) look like the attacks which, Caesar claimed, left "ineradicable stains" on his character (Suet. *Div. Jul.* 73), though he and Catullus were subsequently reconciled, and Quinn (1970, 256) adduces strong chronological arguments that the poem which occasioned complaint and reconciliation was 57 (q.v. note), probably datable to 58/7. In 29 the emphasis is on the corrupt exploitation of

privilege by subordinates, aided and abetted by the state's new autocrats (Skinner 1979, 144–48).

3   "Wildwood Gaul" *(Gallia Comata)* is Transalpine Gaul, where Roman habits and culture have not yet caught on.

5   For Pompey's reputation as a *cinaedus* (passive homosexual)—*pace* Kroll (1922, 54), Fordyce (1961, 161), and others who identify "Queenie Romulus" as Caesar— see, for example, Calvus ap. Sen. *Controv.* 7.4.7; Plut. *Pomp.* 48.7; cf. Cic. *Ad Q. Fratr.* 2.3.2. Holzberg (2002, 107) has a balanced discussion (but leaning towards Caesar). The sarcastic use of the name Romulus, applied to ambitious, and particularly to ultra-Republican, politicians, was widespread: Cicero, for example, was known as "the Romulus from Arpinum."

11   "That final island of the west," a highly inaccurate description, refers to Britain.

13   Mamurra was later (94, 105, 114, 115) given the transparent nickname, "Prick" *(Mentula)*, by Catullus; it may have been this line which suggested it.

18   The allusion is to the loot acquired by Pompey and his troops during the final Eastern campaign against Mithradates VI of Pontus in 64/3.

19   Here Caesar is the target. He campaigned in Lusitania (Portugal) as propraetor of Further Spain in 61, and made a very good thing out of it (Plut. *Caes.* 12). Spain was long Rome's chief source of gold.

24   The allusion is to what some contemporaries, Catullus included—not to mention many modern scholars—saw as "the breakdown of the republican system under the recently renewed first triumvirate" (Thomson 1997, 281). That this was a considerable exaggeration has been well argued by Gruen (1974, 90ff. and elsewhere).

30   For Alfenus see glossary s.v. We do not know what the erotic trouble was over which Catullus found him wanting; to connect it with Lesbia is mere speculation. But the message is clear enough. As in business, so in love, the investment of capital demands honest trading, and the gods who monitor *fides* (good faith) take a dim view of those who tempt you to committal and then back out of the deal (cf. Wiseman 1985, 123). The delightful syncopated Greater Asclepiadean metre (cf. introd. p. 36) forces Catullus, as Kroll (1989, 56) nicely puts it, "to walk on stilts" ("auf Stelzen zu gehen"). Theocritus's *Idyll* 30, the lament of an elderly pederast over a boy with whom he's become obsessed, is in the same metre and has a rather similar tone.

31   On Sirmio, see glossary s.v. and also the notes to poem 4. This famous and charming poem has produced some surprisingly costive annotation, which present readers are spared. At first sight it might seem odd for so happy a theme to be treated in grumping choliambics (cf. introd. p. 33); Llewellyn Morgan (*PCPhS* 46 (2000)

99ff.) suggests that Catullus may have been trying to suggest the footsore weariness of the homecoming traveller.

2–3   Catullus is simply making a distinction between fresh and salt water deities.

5–6   Another allusion to Catullus's return home from service on the governor's staff in Bithynia (q.v.); the poem must thus be dated not earlier than spring 56.

13   Few commentators can be bothered to explain why the lake's waves are regarded as Lydian: it is because the local Etruscans were believed to have immigrated from that part of Asia Minor (Livy 5.33, Tac. *Ann.* 4.55; cf. Godwin 1999, 148).

32   This neat spoof (analysis in Krostenko 2001, 266–67, with n. 86), with its comic appeal for instant gratification—Catullus is on his bed after lunch (not breakfast, as Quinn [1970, 187ff.] supposes)—requires us to imagine a note hand-delivered, while the sender nurses a serious erection (11–12). Heath (1986, 28ff.) seems, quaintly, to assume that Catullus's asking Ipsithilla to ride him would have been regarded as proof of his nasty nature. Note the invented word *fututiones* (8: "fuck-fest;" Godwin [1999, 149] has "fuckifications," ingeniously pseudo-grandiose, but over-heavy in English). Literary allusiveness finds a place even here: Zeus engaged with Mnemosyne nine nights in a row to engender the Muses (Aveline 1994, 122–23). The joke, *pace* Gratwick (2000, 549), is not so shameless as to preclude autobiography.

33   For the prevalence of thefts in bathhouses, seemingly a perennial nuisance (despite the slaves whose job it was to safeguard property, often themselves the pilferers), see Ellis (1886, 88). The father steals; the son (now too old for the job, 7, despite his "more voracious backside," *culo . . . uoraciore*) puts out. The poem is a splendid example of mean and elegantly phrased aggression (Wray 2001, 119ff. has a refreshingly honest take on this). Catullus's *urbanitas* is here simply the urban sophisticate's superior command of rhetorical invective.

34   This short hymn to Diana is not generally thought to have been written for performance, certainly not for any specific occasion, but rather, like Horace's similar hymns to Diana (*Odes* 3.22) and Diana jointly with Apollo (*Odes* 1.21), to be read. However, Wiseman (1985, 95–101) makes a very persuasive case for its having been commissioned soon after 58—when Rome's grain supply was reorganized under the *lex Clodia*, and Delos, as a key entrepôt, was made tax-exempt by the *lex Gabinia Calpurnia*—for celebration of that event on the island. The combination of legendary sanctity (Delos as the birthplace of Apollo and Diana/Artemis) with the importance for Romans of plentiful, available grain is clear from the second law as much as from the hymn. The syncretism of Diana, Juno (with two epithets) and Hecate (via Artemis) is a characteristically Roman feature.

35   For Caecilius, Verona, and Novum Comum, see glossary s.vv. The poem must postdate 59, since it was in that year that Comum was resettled under the *lex Vatinia* with five thousand veterans, and received its new name (Appian, *BC* 2.26; Suet., *Div. Jul.* 28). Again, we do not know the occasion, but the main object, it would seem, was to imagine the impact of Caecilius's Neoteric *epyllion* about Cybele the Mistress of Beasts on the girl he was leaving behind. Once again (cf. 4, 42, 67), an inanimate object (this time the writing material) is treated as a messenger and informant.

36   When would Lesbia angle for Catullus's return rather than vice versa? Almost certainly late in 58, on his return from Bithynia, in the aftermath of the Caelius trial that had destroyed her political influence and left her, verging on forty, a public laughing-stock. Thomson (1997, 296) calls this poem "the union of Love and Wit at its most complete." Lesbia (not named, but unmistakable) has vowed, rather vaguely, if her disenchanted lover quits abusing her in verse and comes back to her, to burn the work of the "worst poet" *(pessimi poetae)*. Since this obviously refers to Catullus himself (he repeats the phrase in 49: it must have rankled), it is not at all clear why this should be an inducement to his return, but only Fordyce (1961, 179) seems to have been bothered by the illogicality. In any case the vagueness allows Catullus to suggest, mischievously, Volusius's shitty *Annals* —recommended for wrapping fish in 95—as an alternative. The wit and elegance of Catullus's own poem should (it is implied) suffice to get him off the hook. Cf. note to 42. Wray (2001, 75) links this and the following poem: "Poem 36 is a shit poem aimed at Volusius, Poem 37 is a piss poem aimed at Egnatius." He also stresses, rightly, the exotic Hellenistic erudition and technical poetic fireworks of 11–15, a demonstration to Volusius of how verse really should be written.

37   The "felt-hatted Brethren" are Castor and Pollux, whose temple stood on the south side of the Forum. The popular assumption (based, I suspect, on a misreading of Cic. *Pro Cael.* 48: see, e.g., Kroll 1922, 69–70; Quinn 1972, 135; Goold 1989, 243) is that Catullus's bordello nine doors down was in fact Clodia's town house on the Palatine, complete with casual lovers and hangers-on, but this is topographically impossible: Catullus very specifically locates it "among the 'old shops' *[tabernae ueteres]* on the southwest side of the Forum, soon to be swept away by the building of the Basilica Julia" (Wiseman 1985, 26). Wray reminds us solemnly (2001, 82) that Catullus's threats of retaliation (6–8 in particular) are "wild hyperbole" (yet no more than what's attributed to Lesbia at 11.17–20). On the other hand, the improbable accusation against Egnatius in line 20 (repeated at 39.17–21) gets confirmation from both Diodorus Siculus (5.33.5) and Strabo (3.4.16, C.164). Lesbia's association with him "calls her own taste into question" (Arkins 1982, 88). Note the intriguing near repetition of 8.5 in the very different context of 37.12.

38   What was Catullus's trouble here? Physical illness? Emotional worry? Literary irritation? We simply cannot tell, and it's possible that we're dealing with colorful Mediterranean exaggeration anyway (Wray 2001, 100–101). The appeal was not unusual (cf. 68a for Catullus's response to a similar approach by Manlius). Members of the tight-knit Neoteric group seem to have taken it for granted that their friends' problems were also their own. Cornificius was certainly younger than Catullus (he was quaestor in 48), which suggests that this was a fairly late poem. The words *meos amores* (6) also make it possible that he was, or had been, Catullus's boyfriend.

39   As Quinn (1970, 208) speculates, the way this poem builds up to its comic dénouement suggests that the joke is new, and that we have here an earlier shot at Egnatius than that in 37. Katz (2000, 338–48) rather mischievously suggests that at line 20 Catullus, with his repeated -*st*- clusters, may have been joking in terms of *dental fricatives:* a delightful linguists' pun, even if anachronistic.

40   It is only at the end of this short attack that we learn the reason for Catullus's annoyance: Ravidus has been after Catullus's lover. The lover is unnamed, and impossible even to guess the sex of (cf. 24, 38), let alone to identify. There is a clear reminiscence here of a similar attack by Archilochos (172 West), an epode addressed to Lykambes, the hoped-for father-in-law who decided that this foul-mouthed poet was better kept out of the family, and broke off Archilochos's engagement to his daughter.

41   4: The "bankrupt from Formiae" (cf. 43.5) was Mamurra. Quinn (1970, 214–15) and Godwin (1999, 160) both point out the pun at 7–8: Ameana is obsessed with one kind of *aes* (brass or bronze), i.e., bronze coins, money, but doesn't check in the other, a polished bronze mirror *(aes imaginosum)*, to see what she looks like. A Yorkshireman would recognize *brass* as covering both, but there is no satisfactory American equivalent. Was Ameana a call-girl or, like Sallust's Sempronia (*Cat.* 24–25), one of those extravagant upper-class ladies "prostituting themselves to meet their enormous expenses"? Quinn (1972, 235–36) opts for the second option, and I would agree. Catullus affects to regard her asking price as evidence of insane self-delusion. Cf. Wray 2001, 71–72.

42   Part of the joke here is the exploitation of formal rhetoric: the poem is a comic *flagitatio*, a traditional form of *Volksjustiz* in which an aggrieved party sought to regain property or other rights by exposing the offender (a thief, perhaps, or debtor) to withering public ridicule. The custom was still alive in Plautus's day; see *Pseud.* 357ff. The circumstances (if we are dealing with a real incident) in which the (unnamed) girl got hold of, and kept, Catullus's writing tablets are obscure, though

it is (of course) tempting to connect this incident with the lover's threat in 36, to burn the works of the "worst poet." Yet as Quinn (1970, 217) wisely reminds us, "the fact that certainty is impossible should warn us that we are letting our curiosity extend beyond what Catullus has fixed as the relevant data for his poem." Scansion and vocabulary are both reminiscent of the comic stage (Goldberg 2000, 481–83).

43 Since the girl addressed is again (5) the mistress of the Formian bankrupt, i.e., Mamurra, it is reasonable to identify her as Ameana. Various allusions in Roman poetry suggest that masculine preferences in women favored dark eyes, small noses, tiny feet, and long elegant fingers. For other preferences, see 86 and note. The unrefined tongue (4) could refer to a provincial accent, awkward locutions, a taste for oral sex, or all of the above. What low taste, Catullus says, these Veronese provincials have!

44 Lee (1990, 160) well describes this poem as "a parody in scazons of a *soterion* or thank-offering to a God for deliverance." The mock-religious tone appropriate to prayer is unmistakable: this is also why Catullus is so anxious (1–5) to make sure the farm is properly addressed (Quinn 1970, 221). The parody also, I suspect, makes gentle fun of that "frigid" or chilly hyperbole which Catullus attributes to Sestius (10–21), and from which he affects to have caught his cold and cough (on which see introd. p. 3). The *locus classicus* for a discussion of this kind of rhetorical frigidity is Demetr. *De Eloc.* 114–27, and Godwin (1999, 162) has an excellent note on it. Its essence seems to be wrapping up a trivial topic in portentous language—exactly what Catullus does here in order to puncture Sestius's highflown pretensions.

45 As elsewhere, what Catullus celebrates here is mutual love and commitment: not, at the time, a very Roman concept (Wiseman 1985, 117–18; cf. Lyne 1980, 33f.). The reference to "all the hoopla of Syria and Britain" (22) suggests a date fairly late in 55, when Crassus was off to the first and Caesar about to carry out his follow-up invasion of the second (which would mean that this delightful poem was written at the same time as the bitter valediction of 11). But as Godwin (1999, 165) rightly points out, the names were often used generically for East and West respectively. Tight symmetry of structure is matched by neat alliterative effects at which a translator can only hint.

8–9 The confusion over who gets a favorable sneeze, on which side when, depends on an ambiguity in the Latin which I have tried to reproduce; but since *all* the omens are favorable it hardly matters. The most common interpretation is that Love gives each lover *two*, one to the right, one to the left, which they, facing each other, will see differently. On classical sneeze-omens in general, see Fordyce 1961, 205–206.

46   The spring in question is most probably that of 56, immediately prior to Catullus's return to Italy from Bithynia (10, 31). No one who has at last been posted home after a long overseas tour in the wartime armed services, or has even finally caught that holiday train at the end of a boarding-school term, will fail to recognize the gleeful, almost incredulous relief of lines 4–8.

47   Like Quinn (1970, 231), we may wonder at what point it was that Catullus's two friends fell out of official favor; it sounds as though the scene here described is in Rome, after Piso's return there from Macedonia in the summer of 55. For an analysis see Pedrick (1993, 180–82); like Skinner (1979, 141), she sees Veranius and Fabullus being set up by Catullus as *unsuccessful* parasites.

48   The "innumerable" (actually 300,000) kisses mentioned here are clearly those that evoked the tut-tuttery and charges of effeminacy that Catullus was at pains to repudiate in 16: cf. Thomson (1997, 231). All those kisses, but nothing more serious, more assertive of masculine dominance? The metaphor at 5–6 is, as Godwin (1999, 168) says, intriguing: "The associations of the crop of corn are ones of fullness, ripeness, pleasure, sunshine."

49   This little poem has occasioned much speculation, in the first place because of its famous addressee, but perhaps even more on account of its oddly elusive and ironic tone (Svavarsson 1999, 131ff.). What was the occasion? And what, in fact, was Catullus thanking Cicero *for?* As Quinn points out (1999, 233–34), when Cicero returned from exile in September 57 Catullus was away in Bithynia, and in fact only returned to Rome in the spring of 56—just about the time (April) of Cicero's defense of Catullus's rival in love, M. Caelius Rufus, with its unforgettable, and lethal, attack on Clodia Metelli. It is highly unlikely that this poem does not, in some sense, represent payback time.

       Thomson (1997, 322–23, recapitulating an earlier article) neatly suggests that Cicero has sent Catullus one of his own poems, and that Catullus is saying, in effect, I may be a bad poet, but at least I *am* a poet; you're a distinguished lawyer, but a poet you're not. (Cicero seems to have been both vain and touchy about his attempts at poetry, which, to judge by the line Juvenal cites at 10.122, were excruciatingly bad). The last line also contains a nice ambiguity in *omnium patronus*, which could be taken as "everybody's lawyer"—a nice crack at his habit of successively defending and prosecuting the same man (e.g., Vatinius; see Quinn 1970, 235), as changing circumstances and his own benefit required.

50   A charming (yet, as always, carefully contrived) glimpse of Neoteric poets at play. For C. Licinius Calvus see glossary s.v. The poem may well be an early one: there is a slight awkwardness and formality still—not to mention the excitement

of novelty—in Catullus's relationship with him (Thomson 1997, 324; cf. Quinn 1970, 236). Did they meet in a tavern? They use Catullus's writing tablets (2), so they are not *chez* Calvus; Catullus has to leave (7), so they are not in his house either. The excitement and insomnia are very convincing: there are also unmistakable erotic undertones in the language (Macleod 1973a, 294). They met during the day, and Catullus was too worked up later to eat. We can picture them writing alternate lines on the same tablet, each more *recherché*, allusive, and improper than the last.

51   Wilkinson's idea that this free translation of three stanzas from a well-known Sappho poem was Catullus's first shot in his courting of Lesbia/Clodia has a lot going for it. Looked at in this way, it is a cautious enquiry, despite the naming of the addressee as "Lesbia" (7: not in Sappho). If the lady returned his feelings (or at least wanted to take things further) she would know what he meant; otherwise it was simply a poetic translation sent by one literary aficionado for the enjoyment of another, and nothing (of course) to do with present company (cf. Quinn 1972, 56–58). In the latter case, "Lesbia" was simply the "girl of Lesbos" apostrophized by Sappho; but if Clodia wanted the cryptonym, it was there waiting for her. The speaker's envy of the (probably licit) freedom possessed by this addressee's companion to enjoy her company is at least consonant with a scenario in which Catullus is commemorating his first encounter with Clodia, probably in 61/0, and at home, in her husband's company.

13–16   The fourth and final stanza is a puzzle. It corresponds to nothing in Sappho's Greek (the fourth stanza of which, with its acute physical symptoms, Catullus simply omits), and it is, to say the least, startling to find a crypto-declaration of love followed up, as Fordyce (1961, 219) well puts it, by the reflection, "Your trouble, Catullus, is not having anything to do." Of the two main current theories, one suggests that this stanza—perhaps like 2b and 14b—ended up, by scribal vagary, attached to a poem where it did not belong; the other, perhaps more psychologically plausible, argues that Catullus added this note of depressed self-recrimination much later, when the affair had gone very sour, or was already over (cf. Quinn 1972, 58–59). See also 11 and note ad loc. Finamore (1984, 11ff.) rightly links the *otium* (leisure) of 50 with that of 51. But why is Catullus's life as a leisured gentleman of private means troublesome *(molestum)* to him in this context? Could it be because his non-participation in the political power-game to which the Clodii and their peers were committed was what—even more than his social provinciality—put Clodia far beyond his reach? Even for the most dissolute of the young well-born politicos, "the pursuit of *otium* was no more than a brief period of social irresponsibility" (Quinn 1972, 215). Harrison (2001, 164–66) takes a similar line when he contrasts Catullus's "indoor erotic *otium*" with the "outdoor rigour of other more 'manly' activity" (a common Latin topos), and cites the case of Paris and Helen as a comparable mythic example which Catullus probably had in mind. And look at 52, 53, and 54—nothing but *negotium*, political life, there.

52   Probably datable to 55 or 54 (Fordyce 1961, 221) but not on that account, or because of the rhetorical question in the first and last line, to be used as evidence for the actual date of Catullus's death (Thomson 1997, 332). On the triumvirs' creatures so contemptuously attacked, see glossary s.vv. Vatinius and Nonius. Vatinius's boils and tumors were also targeted by Cicero (*Vat.* 4.10.39); he got his own back by describing Cicero as "our consular buffoon" (*consularis scurra*, Macrob. 2.1.12).

53   There were no fewer than three prosecutions of Vatinius, in 58, 56, and 54. For his running feud with C. Licinius Calvus, see Gruen (1974, 271–72 with n. 40). It is virtually impossible to determine which of them occasioned this squib, though Thomson (1997, 332–33) reminds us that in 58 (which he favors) Calvus was only about twenty-three (cf. Tac. *Dial.* 34.7). For his diminutive size, see glossary s.v. and Sen. *Contr.* 7.4.7.

   5   *Salaputium* is a correction, but a plausible one, from the passage of Seneca referred to above. The word is otherwise unknown, but etymologically seems to mean something like "jumped-up little prick" (Quinn 1970, 248); cf. Bickel (1953, 94–95). Thomson argues that *disertum* has predicative force (supply *est*), and translates (1997, 333), "The little runt can make a speech!"

54   Clearly "some unsavoury followers of Pompey and Caesar" (Thomson 1997, 334) are being attacked; but the references are uncertain, and there are textual difficulties. Rhetorically, the first three lines must catalogue three successive victims and their faults. This means finding an identity for the gentleman in line 2 with unwashed legs, and *rustice* is in the MSS. For what little can be guessed about Otho, Rusticus, and Libo, see glossary s.vv. Fufidius (5) is Bickel's guess (1949, 13–20) for the otherwise unattested *Sufficio* of the MSS. The last two lines (6–7) are often printed as a separate fragment (e.g., by Thomson 1997, 335), but this is unnecessary; making the apostrophe to Caesar a question helps.

55   The *terminus post quem* is dictated by the allusion to Pompey's portico (6), dedicated in 55 and subsequently a smart rendezvous (Ovid, *AA* 1.67, 3.387). The elusive Camerius reminds us of Flavius in 6, but he has gone one step further and completely vanished. As Quinn says (1970, 250), "alert, ironical concern for a friend who shows signs of having got involved with a girl is a common theme in Roman personal poetry." Stopping one's friends from making fools of themselves is the excuse; but curiosity and possible poaching show up pretty often too. The hendecasyllables are not strict: Catullus experiments with — — — as a replacement for — ∪ ∪ — to vary the pace.

3   What "lesser Campus"? We cannot be certain. The most likely candidate (Fordyce 1961, 226) is the "other campus" referred to by Strabo (5.3.8, C. 236) as adjacent to the Campus Martius, with the usual complement of porticoes and shrines. Cf. Wiseman (1987, 176–86, 219–21).

4   This is the Circus Maximus, located in the valley between the Palatine and Aventine hills, near the Forum. *Libellis* to mean "bookshops" (first suggested by Scaliger in 1577 and supported by Arkins [1994, 211–26] as "metonymy of a Greek kind" for *in librariis tabernis*) strains the Latin, but no better explanation has been proposed; it requires an even greater leap of faith to take *libellis* in the sense of "placards" or "public notices," and to credit Catullus with the conceit that Camerius should be sought on the missing persons list.

56   Modern nervousness about child molestation may mean that contemporary readers fail to find this anecdote quite such a hilarious joke as Catullus himself professes to do. Quinn, indeed (1970, 254), describes it as "hair-raising," in the circumstances perhaps an unfortunate epithet.

6   *Pro/telo*–one word or two? Clearly, both: Catullus's stiff cock is indeed a weapon (two words); and since he sodomizes the boy during the latter's act of masturbation, sex takes place "tandem-fashion" (one word). Catullus is partial to portmanteau words (as Lewis Carroll's Humpty-Dumpty would describe them) and subtle puns.

57   If Quinn is right (and his chronological arguments have much force), this poem can probably be dated to a point after Caesar's return from Spain in 61, but before 58, when he and Mamurra were in Rome together prior to leaving for Gaul. But when was the reconciliation? Suetonius (*Div. Jul.* 73) notes that after it Caesar *resumed* the visits to Catullus's father's house "that he had been in the habit of making" (*sicut consuerat*). The most obvious period for these visits was during Caesar's Gallic command (58–49), when Caesar came south every winter but was debarred (as an army commander) from entering Italy proper; Verona would offer a convenient compromise. If the first such visit was in the winter of 58/7, it would make sense to date the reconciliation to the second of Quinn's two alternatives, i.e., 56/5, when the visits had been established (and thus could be resumed), and Catullus was back from Bithynia (having published the libel before he left).

   Though Thomson (1997, 340–41) is right to play down the accuracy of the sexual charges, Caesar's reputation as a whole-hogging bisexual (Suet. *Div. Jul.* 52) certainly will have encouraged such attacks. But to be at one and the same time a passive homosexual (1–2, 10) and a nymphet fancier (9) is stretching it, though there is evidence of Caesar's liking for young girls (Suet. *Div. Jul.* 50). Skinner (1979, 144) argues that Catullus's real attack is against corruption in the chain of command: "Caesar, the commanding officer who would normally be expected to police his own functionaries, is tarred with the same brush as his henchman."

3–6   Most commentators take these "disease-spots" and "deep pocks" as moral and metaphorical. I am not so sure: I suspect that the implication is in fact of some kind of venereal disease occasioned by indiscriminate coupling.

7   Catullus contrives to mock the pair's literary as well as their sexual habits. A *lecticulus* was not only a bed but also a study couch, and Caesar prided himself as a grammarian no less than as a historian, politician, and general. For Mamurra's literary aspirations, see 105 and Godwin 1999, 179.

58A   Whether the accusation is literally true or not is impossible to determine; certainly it is not impossible, and history offers comparable cases. This, among the bitterest of Catullus's reflections on his former lover, must be dated to a period after his return from Bithynia, and also (if we grant that Lesbia is Clodia Metelli) after her break-up with her other lover, M. Caelius Rufus, that is, to 56 or 55. This would postdate the famous prosecution of Caelius (April 56) and his defense by Cicero, itself in large part a calculated attack on Clodia. Caelius (Quintil. *Inst. Orat.* 8.6.53, picking up Cic. *Pro Cael.* 23) referred to her at this time as a "two-bit *[quadrantaria]* Clytemnestra," and her apparent disappearance from the social scene after that prosecution failed is consonant with the kind of public low-life behavior that Catullus etches so dramatically. His invocation of Caelius, indeed, is all too apposite: *You've had her too,* the implication goes, *you know what I'm talking about.*

5   Perhaps (as a friend once suggested to me) only scholars from a habitually circumcised society could get *glubit* wrong (for some nice waffling examples see Quinn 1970, 260). The word is used of skinning or stripping, and thus here of Clodia—Mrs. Palm personified—giving her well-connected (and of course uncircumcised) boyfriends quick hand-jobs in back alleys: *nostalgie de la boue* indeed (Arkins 1994, 216). For the act, see Juv. 6.238 *(praeputia ducit)*.

58B   Clearly an unfinished draft or fragment. It is addressed to Camerius, whom we met in 55, and its theme, similarly, is an elaboration on the difficulty of running him down. Some (e.g., Goold) see it as a misplaced part of that poem, but the suggested joins are awkward: better to treat it as an afterthought or first draft, still unfinished, and, with its heavily Alexandrian treatment of a slight theme, both witty and subversive. For the mythological allusions see glossary s.vv. "Crete's own brazen guardian" (1) was the bronze giant Talos, a creation of Hephaistos, who ran round the coast of Crete thrice daily, keeping strangers at bay. It is interesting (and does not seem to have attracted notice) that the examples Catullus gives are all of extraordinary *speed*, as though Camerius were in view and had to be chased, rather than mysteriously hidden and needing to be found.

59　As Quinn points out (1970, 262), Catullus's first words could be a *graffito*. He cites several apposite ones (*CIL* 4.1427, 2402, 2491), the last of which actually addresses someone called Rufa: "Bless you, Rufa, you give such good head" *(Rufa ita uale quare bene felas)*. Even the activity is identical; if this is a coincidence, it must be accounted a remarkable one.

2–4　Not content with obliging her lover in the matter of oral sex, adulterous Rufa also raids funeral pyres for food-offerings (hence is presumptively poor, and thus, in Catullus's book, risible).

5　Undoubtedly (though some would deny it) when Rufa gets "banged" *(tunderetur)* by the cremator, sex is involved. It is also common (Thomson 1997, 346; Godwin 1999, 181; Quinn 1970, 263 is more cautious) to take "half-shaved" *(semirasus)* as an indication that this individual was a runaway slave, whose head was half shaved to facilitate recognition. I have never been able to understand this. Who did the shaving, and, more importantly, when? Presumably the owner, after the slave was recaptured (and was thus no longer a runaway). To shave a slave because he *might* run away is hardly less improbable than doing it while he was actually on the lam. Yet these are the only alternatives. And anyway, how long would it take hair to grow out once the runaway was free? Or what was to stop him shaving the rest of his head and passing himself off as an Egyptian priest? Far more persuasive is Professor Treggiari's suggestion to me, which I have adopted in my translation: "On the whole, I think some feature which ought to make him unattractive to women should be meant, and a rough chin seems more likely than a half-shaved scalp."

60　A cento of traditional mythic examples of hard-heartedness (cf. 64.155–58, elaborated later by Virgil, *Aen.* 4.365–67, Dido to Aeneas). The rhetorical cliché had been worked hard since Homer's day (*Il.*16.33–35, Patroclus to Achilles), and Euripides (*Med.* 1341–43) has Jason refer to Medea as "a lioness more savage than Scylla." Weinreich (1959, 75–76), Lieberg (1966, 115), and Wiseman (1985, 156–57) all take the addressee to be Lesbia: possible, but by no means certain.

2　As Quinn nicely puts it (1970, 264), "Roman poets tend to make [Scylla] a kind of monstrous mermaid somehow ending in a bunch of yelping dogs." But the way Catullus has this creature bark from her groin is his own twist: as Wiseman (1985, 157) suggests, "it reminds us of sex and shamelessness"—and thus, he would argue, by implication, of Lesbia.

61　The first of the central group of Catullus's long poems, between his shorter lyrics and elegiacs. Early scholarly efforts to divide the corpus into books by category are mistaken. As Goold points out (1989, 248), there are no such divisions cited in antiquity, and it seems clear that from the start, whether by Catullus's design or posthumous editorial whim, the collection was issued as a single unit. Poem 64 is the centerpiece, and though 61–64 would have made a book roll (810 lines), their positioning precludes this possibility.

61, like 62 and 64.323–81, is a wedding hymn: in this case a Greek-style lyric, Alexandrian in inspiration, but imbued throughout with exclusively Roman ritual (e.g., the throwing of nuts, the Fescennine raillery 124ff., and the threshold ritual at 159–61). Catullus combines the principles of Hellenistic poetry with the special themes proper to Roman wedding songs. The ritual involving Hymen has good Greek ancestry, yet Hymen himself is strongly Romanized, in both dress and function. The narrator throughout is Catullus himself, who delivers, first, an invocation to Hymen the god of marriage (with interspersed remarks to the bridesmaids), followed by apostrophes or addresses to bride, groom, and, finally, the two of them as a wedded couple. On the identity of bride and groom see glossary s.vv. Manlius Torquatus and Aurunculeia.

Fordyce (1961, 236)—supported by Wiseman (1985, 199)—is right to point out that Catullus, as compère, master of ceremonies, and commentator, omits many crucial details: nothing about the wedding feast, for instance, or "the sacrifices, the peculiarities of the bride's dress [on which see the details amassed by Treggiari 1991, 163 and Fedeli 1983, 155], the ritual acts performed by the bride at the door of her new home, and by the bridegroom as soon as she entered it." But such considerations do not necessarily preclude the performance of this hymn on the actual occasion of the wedding. Also, as Treggiari says (1991, 161), "we must be careful not to assume that every upper-class wedding incorporated all the small religious rites which are attested."

Nevertheless, serious arguments have been brought against such a performance. Quite apart from the omission of numerous key ritual elements in the ceremony, Philodemus, writing about 50 B.C.E., observes that the singing of epithalamia has virtually died out (De Mus. ed. Kemke 68.37–40)—though if anyone preserved the tradition, one might suppose, it would be a wealthy aristocrat of ancient lineage such as Manlius Torquatus. Nor (Thomson 1997, 348) is the poem fully dramatized; to a great extent it is a descriptive monologue. And though the shift of scene (150ff.) to the bridegroom's house is not a diriment impediment to actual performance, it is certainly awkward: "attempts to synchronize the lines with the stages of the ceremony are quite unconvincing" (Fordyce 1961, 230; cf. Godwin 1995, 100). Godwin's summing-up may ultimately come closest to the truth: "a literary artifact which incorporates the elements of a Roman wedding and comments on them in a mock-realistic manner"—but also, surely, for the personal delectation of Manlius (cf. 68) and his bride. Yet ambiguities and ironies suggest themselves here too. Would Manlius (with the excuse of Fescennine license or not) have taken Catullus's comments on his marked partiality for boys (125–41) entirely in good part? Would Aurunculeia have welcomed the reminder that she needed to retain all her sexual charms to keep her husband from straying (97–101, 144–46)?

6–10   Why Hymen should be instructed to appear dressed as a Roman bride, complete with wreath, bridal veil, and yellow shoes, has never been satisfactorily explained; that this was not a mere quirk on Catullus's part is shown by Ovid, *Her.* 21.165–68, where the same phenomenon appears. Note also the "high-ringing" *(tinnula)* voice attributed to the god.

15   Pine torches were so familiar a feature of a wedding that their Latin term *(taedae)* came to mean "marriage" *tout court*. Yet Festus (282.22ff. L) pointed out that at a Roman wedding the torches were in fact made from hawthorn.

21–25   Myrtle had a special (and appropriate) association with Venus: in Greek myth it was used to crown Aphrodite after she won the Judgment of Paris. "Asia" here probably refers to the coastal area of Lydia in Asia Minor, around the estuary of the Maeander river.

61–75   "There is no Greek precedent for this patriotic motif. We are in the world of *proles* and *propago* [offspring], where the importance of marriage is to provide citizens to defend the Republic" (Wiseman 1985, 112–13).

76–78   There are clear echoes here of Callimachus: see *Hymn* 2.4–7.

78b–e   To fill these missing verses G. B. Pighi wrote:

> cur moraris? Abit dies:
> prodeas, noua nupta!
>
> Neue respicias domum
> quae fuit tua, neu pedes . . .

which may be translated:

> Why delay? Daylight's nearly gone!
> New bride, come out and join us!
>
> Don't look back at the house that till
> now was yours, do not let your feet
> [falter through well-bred modesty], etc.

87–90   The image of the hyacinth instantly recalls Sappho's picture (fr. 105c L–P) of that flower trodden down by indifferent herdsmen, and reminds us (as Catullus does more than once) of Sappho's barely concealed view of marriage as "a brutal execution" (Edwards 1992, 182).

97ff.   It is hard to resist the suspicion that Catullus meant the bridegroom's indifference to adultery to be linked to his penchant for pederasty (subsequently stressed, 121–41).

119–20   The "ribald and cocksure bantering" known as "Fescennine fun" *(Fescennina iocatio)* was probably derived from *fascinum* (the evil eye), and designed as an apotropaic against ill-wishers or malevolent fortune. It was a regular feature of

Roman weddings: see Fordyce (1961, 248), who notes the similar abusive songs (for an identical purpose) sung at a general's triumph. This section highlights Catullus's originality.

127   The marriage god here is not Greek Hymen but Roman Talassio, of which name both Livy (1.9.12) and Plutarch (*Rom.* 15.2–3, *Pomp.* 4.3) offer an (obviously *ex post facto*) etiological explanation. During the rape of the Sabine women, the servants of a wealthy Roman named Talassius, acting on his instructions, seized and carried off a particularly beautiful girl. In response to questions as to whom she was destined for, they called out *"Talassio!"* "For Talassius!"

129–33   This stanza reminds us that a Roman marriage was—in a psychological if not a civic sense—a coming-of-age ceremony, and not only for the protagonists: even boy toys have to grow up.

159–61   The wish is for the bride to avoid the bad omen which would be caused by her stumbling (liminally) at her husband's threshold. Though carrying a bride over it is a tradition in many cultures to ensure good luck, Catullus appears to envisage her performing this minor *rite de passage* unaided. Cf. 68b.70–71 and note.

164–66   For a modern reader, the fact that the bridegroom had not accompanied the bride in the procession, but was awaiting her in his house, is odd enough. (He went ahead of the bride's party with his own group: Treggiari 1991, 166). But there is also the larger question of what he is doing, what couch he is on, and where it is located. One now largely discarded theory (cf. Fordyce 1961, 250; Thomson 1997, 360) is that he was still reclining at dinner; but the wedding feast had already been held, at the house of the bride's parents, before her ceremonial escorting *(deductio)* to her new abode (Treggiari 1991, 166–67). The actual marriage bed, not surprisingly, was in an inner room, and the husband was admitted to it only when the bride was ready. What, then, was the couch in the entrance hall *(atrium)*? Perhaps the *lectus genialis*, the marriage bed only in a symbolic sense (Treggiari 1991, 168, confirmed by Prop. 4.11.85–86), where the bridegroom would formally accept his new wife to share his home "with water and fire" *(aqua et igni accipere,* cf. Fordyce 1961, 251; Fedeli 1983, 111–13).

199–203   Cf. 5.7–13 and 7.3–8, where Catullus similarly pictures the innumerability of lovers' kisses in terms of sand grains or stars.

214–18   Again, the notion of wishing the happy couple a child which, by resembling its father, proves its mother's fidelity, may strike a reader today as being in dubious taste; but the convention has an ancestry going back at least to Hesiod's day (*WD* 235).

62   Catullus's second epithalamium differs from the first in several ways. To begin with, it is not even ostensibly written for a specific occasion. It also concentrates on a

stage of the ritual that 61 notably omits, that is, the immediate aftermath of the wedding feast, held in the house of the bride's parents before the escorting *(deductio)* of the bride to her husband's house. The time is sunset: the traditional setting, with the appearance of the evening star *(Hesper* or *Vesper)*, for a Greek or Roman wedding. The custom of both boys and girls taking part in the feast and subsequent ritual goes back at least to Aeschylus (fr. 43; cf. Kroll 1922, 122); in Greece the sexes were separated, in Rome not. Despite line 32 (which simply records her change of status), we may picture the bride as being present, or at least in the house, prior to her *deductio*. Meanwhile the boys' and girls' choirs compete in a sung impromptu exchange, on virginity versus marriage, in which (as so often in real life) while the girls make the best points (Godwin 1995, 114) and the boys mouth social platitudes, it is still the male cliché-mongers who have the last word. I am not convinced by Goud's efforts (1995, 23ff.) to force a strict amoebean symmetry on the exchange, much less by his argument that it is the girls who have the final word. See Fraenkel (1955), Wiseman (1985, 119), Jenkyns (1982, 51).

The poem, after "snatches from the talk of the young people," lines 1–19 (Quinn 1970, 276), consists entirely of this hymeneal singing match, of the sort made familiar by Theocritus (e.g., *Idylls* 4, 5, 8, 10) and, after Catullus, Virgil (*Eclogues* 3 and 7); like those examples, it is amoebean (i.e., a responsive dialogue) and written in hexameters (introd. pp. 39–40). It was also, interestingly, anthologized in the ninth century C.E. and thus offers us a text half a millennium older than that of any other poem in the corpus.

1, 7   The Latin speaks of "Olympus" and "Oetean fires," but commentators, rightly, have taken these as simple poetic particularizations (the rhetorical trope known as synecdoche) of, respectively, the heavens and a western sunset, rather than as indicating the location of the epithalamium. There is also the minor detail that Mts. Oeta and Olympus are, roughly, one hundred miles apart.

11–18   The boys (Quinn 1970, 276) "can see that the girls are getting their song ready, though they cannot hear what the girls are saying."

20–24   The "cruelty" of an ancient marriage was an undeniable fact. Primitive notions of hygiene and obstetrics made the chance of dying young, and agonizingly, an all too real risk for these brides. Euripides' Medea declared that she would rather fight three front line engagements than give birth once (*Med.* 248–51: the entire speech on the perils of marriage, from 230, is a formidable indictment), and from Sappho onwards there is a sense in which the epithalamium is also a potential dirge. It is these risks, contrasted with the mindless sexual drive of the young male, that justify Catullus's telling comparison with the rape and pillage when a city falls (24). As Wiseman says (1985, 119), "The ancient world lived closer than we do to the reality of sacked cities and raping soldiers [though recent affairs in the Balkans have considerably narrowed the gap], and some parts of Italy had suffered that reality only thirty years before."

27–30   A touch here of Roman legalism. What is being fulfilled is the contract agreed upon earlier, at the betrothal ceremony *(sponsio, pactio nuptialis)*, between the bridegroom-to-be and the bride's parents. See the excellent and full account in Treggiari (1991, 138–45).

39–47   A beautiful and delicate simile, with echoes of Sappho in the sense of fragility and transitoriness in the blossoming flower (Quinn 1970, 280), but also facing the brutal social fact that in the marriage market (and not only there) virginity was an essential prerequisite. The nick of a thumbnail (43) offers a savage image of carelessness and unthinking defloration.

62–65   The selling-off of the girl's virginity (in which she has only one-third ownership) to a prospective husband will not have had the same jolting effect on a Roman audience as it does on us. Yet even Kroll (1922, 129) betrays a certain unease when remarking that Catullus's distribution of entitlement is "half in jest" *(halb scherzhaft)*, as does Quinn (1970, 282) when he claims that "the argument from arithmetic, though very Roman, is hardly seriously intended." But Treggiari, the expert on Roman marriage, accepts the notion at face value (1991, 177).

63   This poem is unique in several ways. It is the only surviving work from the ancient world in the galliambic metre (see introd. p. 38), with its hypnotic rat-a-tat rhythm, evoking the tambourines of the Great Mother's eunuch priests who used it. It is a psychological *tour de force* quite unlike any other Greek or Roman poem known to us, pinpointing with nightmarish precision the hopeless horror of a well-connected Greco-Roman youth who, in an exalted moment of antisexual ecstasy, has effectively severed himself (in every sense) from his own country and society, as well as from the masculine status that defined his existence (cf. Skinner 1993, 111–12). Religious frenzy leads to self-mutilation and, ultimately, enslavement. Inevitably, attempts have been made (most persuasively by Highet [1957, 25ff.]; see also Morisi 1999, 40–41; Lefèvre 1998, 308ff.) to read into the poem the impact of Catullus's emotional thralldom to Lesbia. As Wiseman (1974, 54) well put it, "his passion was as insane as Attis' *furor*, the knifestroke that cut it like a flower in the meadow left him as unmanned as Attis, and like Attis all he got was slavery to a *domina*." This, of course, though psychologically shrewd, remains purely speculative, as does the equally plausible notion which sees in Catullus's allegory of emasculation and despair the dilemma of intelligent Romans caught in the incipient death throes of the late Republic, watching ambitious men—a Caesar, a Mamurra—subverting its principles, yet powerless to stop them (Skinner 1993, 117).

For various theories seeking to explain Catullus's motivation in writing this poem—for example, as a hymn for the Megalensia festival (!), or a translation of a lost work by Callimachus, or through homosexual influences (!), or as an attempt at a highly literary joke (about as funny, I'd have thought, as Kingsley Amis including Kipling's "Danny Deever" in an anthology of humorous verse)—see Näsström (1989, 23–27). Most suggestive, perhaps, despite the attendant difficulties, is the theory that sees Attis's act as "an aborted ephebic transition" (Skinner 1993, 113), the rejection of development into "a fully functioning adult male." See also Clay (1995, 143ff.) for the repudiation of sex involved in this "failed passage from adolescence to adulthood." What this theory fails to take into consideration, of course, is the powerful religious/ecstatic element in the scenario.

The cult of the Great Mother (Cybelé) had been installed in Rome in 204 B.C.E., at a crucial point during the war against Carthage, but was never comfortably assimilated to Roman mores. Lucretius (2.574–643) gives a vivid description of the annual procession by the priests of the cult, with its strange Eastern music and ecstatic features; but the cult itself was hedged about with restrictions, and Roman citizens were debarred from participation in it (Dion. Hal. 2.19.4–5). Though Catullus is plainly familiar with the Attis epigrams in the *Greek Anthology* (6.217–220), he does not concern himself with the central myth of the cult (concerning Attis as the youthful consort of Cybelé: see Fordyce 1961, 261–62; Morisi 1999, 23–25; Clay 1995, 198ff.; Godwin 1995, 121–22) except for two key details: its Phrygian location, and the crucial fact of castration. As regards the latter, while Anatolian Attis as consort was either forcibly emasculated as a punishment for infidelity, or did the job himself in despair at the failure of his marriage, Catullus's Greek protagonist does so in a fit of exaltation, with a view to serving the goddess in an accepted role (i.e., as a priest, a Gallus—or, to emphasize emasculation, Galla), and only after his irrevocable act suffers agonies of remorse.

Though the key to the psychological dilemma of 63 is lost, it would be hard to argue, given the unique nature of the narrative, that such a dilemma did not exist: on its interiorization see Perutelli 1996, 255ff. What we read has all the vivid horror and disjunctive motion of the worst kind of nightmare—a tribute to Catullus's extraordinary creative and metrical skills, but still, in the last resort, a baffling puzzle. Cf. Thomson 1997, 372–75. For those readers with Italian, Luca Morisi's exemplary new edition of the poem provides an excellent guide.

44ff.   Note that the group of companions who have accompanied Attis to this point, the Gallae, are simply forgotten when no longer needed; we see no more of them. In general, background details are reduced to the absolute essential minimum. Whereas Attis's first speech (12–26) is addressed to them, his second (50–73) ignores them completely, concentrating nostalgically on his own solitude and misery. The homesickness of the desperate is a common feature in ancient literature (Godwin 1995, 128). Morisi 1999, 36–38 (cf. Perutelli 1996, 259) sees this Attis-Catullus as a figure in search of his own true identity, sexual and general. The notion of sexual ambiguity is also pursued by Traina (1994, 189ff.).

76ff.　In both literature and the visual arts Cybelé is represented as riding in a chariot drawn by a pair of lions: see, for example, Soph. *Phil.* 400, Lucr. 2.600–601, Virg. *Aen.* 3.113. For her cult in Rome, see Beard 1994, 164ff.

88–90　Lachmann corrected *tenerum* (88) and *ille* (89) of *V* to *teneram* and *illa* in acknowledgment of Attis's feminized status. Like Mynors, I have accepted these emendations; like Mynors (who commented in his *apparatus criticus*, "an recte, dubitari potest"—"whether correctly, may be doubted"), I am far from sure of them. I have a suspicion that the MS tradition may have been right: that after Attis's declaration of repentance (73) her/his masculine sense of self may have been suggested by Catullus as returning—which would make the fate spelled out at 89–90 even more pathetic. Godwin (1995, 131) points out the ambiguity of *fera* (89): instead of the usually accepted neuter adjective qualifying *nemora* ("wild woods"), it could equally well be a noun ("wild beast") in apposition to Attis, who would thus, in her/his demented state, become a mere animal. Cf. also Arkins 1994, 216–17.

64　At 408 lines this is by far the longest poem in the Catullan corpus. Tightly structured in eight chiastic sections (Martin 1992, 157), it is generally described as an epyllion, that is, a mini-epic, and its allusions to Homer and Apollonius Rhodius (see Clare 1966 and Stoevesandt 1994/5) do nothing to discourage such an interpretation. The term is not found used thus in antiquity (in fact it scarcely occurs at all) and was first adopted by a German scholar in the mid-nineteenth century. However, it has become too useful, and popular, to discard. We know of other such short narratives in the Greek and Roman literary tradition: Callimachus's *Hekale*, the *Hylas* (*Idyll* 13) of Theocritus, Cinna's *Smyrna* (95), an *Io* by Calvus. The Aristaeus episode in Virgil's *Georgics* (4.315–558) is another example of the genre, a poem-within-a-poem not unlike the Ariadne episode here in 64. These epyllia generally take the main narrative facts for granted (thus presuming a highly literate audience): both in Alexandria and later among the Roman Neoterics they stress arcane mythological allusions, concise phraseology, subjective characterization, and the use of *ecphrasis*, i.e., narrative extrapolated from visual iconography, as here with the tapestry (50–264) that provides the springboard for the entire Ariadne episode (long and detailed analysis in Dyer 1994, especially 243ff.).

　　This episode, complete in itself, is 214 lines long, thus occupying over half of the total narrative (for structural theories see Blusch 1989, and Cupaiuolo 1994). It seems designed to provide a link to the marriage of Peleus and Thetis by hinting, through Ariadne's rescue by Bacchus, at the benefits to be got from a divine spouse. Yet, as always with Catullus, there are ambiguities. Peleus and Thetis had anything but a happy wedded life (see glossary s.vv.); Ariadne's rescue by Bacchus looks uncommonly like a rape (see below on 251–64). Further, from time immemorial mortals had been warned against overreaching themselves in aspirations to the divine: "Do not attempt to climb the sky," the lyric poet Alcman warned, "or to marry Aphrodite." Tragedy, in the shape of the yet unborn Achilles' career, lurks behind almost every line of the all-too-prophetic wedding song sung by the Fates (303–83). Catullus's readers and hearers, who knew the mythic background of these episodes much better than we do, must have been acutely aware of their grim undercurrents (well analyzed by Stoevesandt 1994/5, 167ff.). And even in his own terms Catullus surprises us with two passages (22–30 and 384–408) reminding us that the old heroic days when gods consorted with—and on rare occasions married—mortals are over. The gods have withdrawn from earth in disgust at human degeneracy, and (the implication is clear) there will never be another such marriage as that of the mortal hero Peleus to Thetis the sea nymph, with the gods turning up in force as wedding guests. The loss of innocence is a recurrent theme in Catullus (Petrini 1997, 16–17).

Catullus deals with the divine guest list in a disquieting and unusual way. Apollo and Artemis (in his version only) disdainfully refuse to attend the wedding (299–302), apparently out of contempt for Peleus, a mere mortal marrying above his station; but Catullus's readers would remember another possible reason, and not a pleasant one: cf. glossary s.v. Apollo. (It has also been argued [Thomson 1997, 427] that the divine siblings qua sun and moon are symbolically absent from what will prove a dark and stormy union.) It is, ominously in every sense, the Fates, rather than the Muses, who sing the hymeneal. And why, surprisingly at first sight, is Prometheus on the guest list (294–97)? Because he warned Zeus that Thetis was destined to bear a son greater than his father, something that made Zeus back off his own earlier pursuit of Thetis with some alacrity (27), and urge her marriage to a mortal. Omissions, too, are telling. One uninvited guest who, we know, showed up in the myth as generally told, but whom Catullus does not mention, is Eris (Strife), whose mischief on this occasion led to a quarrel between goddesses, the Judgment of Paris, and, ultimately, the Trojan War (Thomson 389–90), in which the child of the marriage being celebrated was destined to play a crucial part—and to end by losing his life. Though modern efforts to see the entire epyllion in ironic and antiheroic terms are clearly mistaken, and there is plenty of sheer sensuous exuberance in the description of palatial wealth and luxury (for the vividness of Catullus's sensual evocations, not only visual and aural, but also odorous, as at 87–90 and 184 for example, see Rees 1994, 75ff. and cf. Jenkyns 1982, 150), Catullus takes care that we never forget the dark shadows behind the narrative and in the future of its protagonists (cf. Putnam 1961, 192ff.).

Lastly, though we should beware of facile biographical inferences, it cannot have escaped Catullus's consciousness—indeed, he must have been acutely aware of the dilemma it presented—that Clodia Metelli (assuming her identity with Lesbia), though by spring 59 a widow, still remained, even more importantly, "socially far above him" (Treggiari 1991, 304), and thus, in view of Rome's rigid class hierarchy (not to mention the ambitious marital politicization of the Claudii as a clan), virtually beyond his reach as a potential wife. It cannot have been pure coincidence that when he came to write his epyllion he chose a mythical topic where hypergamy, for once, came off; at the same time, being a realist, he saw, all too clearly, the dangers to which such a match would, inevitably, be exposed (Putnam 1961, 198–99): the whole poem is obsessed by marriages, and not, for the most part, happy ones (Edwards 1992, 193ff.).

1–11 This proem offers a neat pastiche of myth: the central reference is to the legend of Jason and the Argonauts, who sailed eastward to Colchis at the furthest point in the Black Sea to get the Golden Fleece ("that gilded hide," 5) from King Aeëtes—and, though Catullus does not say so (but his audience would not need reminding), also to steal his daughter Medea, who, like Ariadne with Theseus, would give crucial aid to the leader of the adventurers, Jason, and (again like Ariadne) end up betrayed by him. Note the (typically Hellenistic) use of rhetorical synecdoche, where a part—here the material: pine trees, fir wood—is used for the whole, or for the finished product, a ship's oars (1, 7). In the same way, by metonymy (change of name or title) in Catullus's Latin text (1) Amphitrite, Poseidon/Neptune's wife, stands for the deep sea as such.

21, 26–27 The reason that Zeus/Jupiter approved the marriage, and withdrew his own bid for Thetis, was of course, the threat caused by the prophecy that Thetis's son would be more powerful than his father (see above).

35 "Scyros" (Siros *O*, Syros *X*), already read by Renaissance scholars, is clearly correct (Arkins 1994, 217), and Meineke's emendation "Cieros," accepted by Mynors, is unnecessary.

39–41 Despite Quinn's reassurances on the speed of rusting in the open (1970, 308), it does look very much as though Catullus is mocking a popular literary theme here: as Godwin says (1995, 142), "the length of time it takes to attend a wedding is hardly enough to see all this ruin in the fields."

43ff. Are we meant to feel envy and admiration for all this opulence in Peleus's establishment, or (if Catullus is addressing good Neoteric Epicureans) disgust (as at Lucr. 2.20–36)? Or a mixture of the two? Cf. Godwin 1995, 142.

50–266 The extended *ecphrasis*—during which the wedding of Peleus and Thetis is put on hold—describes (Dyer 1994, 227ff.), on the basis of a tapestry spread over the bridal bed, the seduction, abandonment, and divine rescue of Ariadne. Note that her dealings with Theseus are not recounted in chronological sequence, but as a series of vivid snapshots: we begin with Ariadne's abandonment (50–70), go back to their first encounter and the dispatch of the Minotaur (71–115), proceed to their flight together and her abandonment on Dia (116–31), are regaled with her curses on Theseus (132–70), followed by a flashback to the start of his expedition and arrival on Crete (171–76). Further imprecations (177–201) are promptly answered by Zeus/Jupiter (202–206), and followed by Theseus's omission to change his sails, thus precipitating his father's death (207–48), and, finally, Ariadne's own "rescue" by Bacchus (252–64). Ironically, the silent figures on the tapestry, Ariadne herself in particular, talk their heads off, while the living characters of the wedding, whether human or divine, say nothing—till the Fates begin their prophesying at 323 (Godwin 1995, 144–45).

95–96 The address is to Cupid and his mother, Aphrodite/Venus.

105 The name of the mountain range, Taurus ("Bull"), neatly anticipates Theseus's victory over the Minotaur. Further, the pine tree's epithet, "cone-bearing" *(conig-eram)*, is virtually indistinguishable from *cornigeram*, "horned"—so much so that the MS tradition actually read the latter, only being corrected by an Italian scholar in 1468: Catullus clearly meant to awaken the association in his audience's mind. Cf. Salat 1993, 418–19.

113 The thread here is the ball of twine which Ariadne gave Theseus to ensure his safe return from the maze. (A problem I have never seen confronted is how he found his way *in* correctly to begin with.)

132–201 Ariadne's lament: the longest section of the poem, with, as Godwin reminds us (1995, 151), "no possible source in the tapestry being described."

150 (cf. 181) The relationship is intensified for the sake of dramatic effect. The Minotaur was not Ariadne's full brother *(germanum)*, but her half brother only, his father being the great white bull with which Pasiphaë (Daedalus aiding and abetting) committed her act of miscegenation.

152–53 A deep and universal fear in the ancient world was the fate of a wandering soul if its corpse had not received at least the scatter of earth symbolizing proper burial (well brought out in Sophocles' *Antigone*). An equal (and more immediately understandable) horror was that of becoming mere carrion for birds and beasts of prey to tear and devour (Fordyce 1961, 297; Godwin 1995, 153).

162 Those "white-soled feet" *(candida . . . uestigia)* are interesting. Thomson (1997, 414) says that *candida* "is of course proleptic," i.e., that Ariadne *makes* the feet white by washing them. There is no "of course" about it. What Catullus, rather mischievously, makes Ariadne do, in a context where she sees herself as a willing slave, is to enhance Theseus's opulence by contrast: he doesn't have to walk and work, the soles of his feet are white and unworn. This is not calculated to make the reader like him.

207–50   Theseus's behavior is exactly what Ariadne's curse had sought (200–201), and Zeus/Jupiter had approved (205–206). Seldom can divine retribution have been so promptly enforced.

221–37   Thomson (1997, 419) appositely cites Freya Stark, *The Lycian Shore* (1956, 38), on the sponge fishers of Kalymnos: when they had sailed, their wives on the quayside exchanged their white headscarves for black ones, and wore these till their husbands returned safely.

251–264   Ariadne's "rescue," Catullus is implying, was not a peaceful affair, and in a sense victimized her almost as much as Theseus had done: what choice did she have but to submit to Iacchus's advances? Note also that all the emphasis in Catullus's description of this rout is on its *noise*—something hardly to be gotten from a tapestry. At 259, Mulroy (2002, 73) points out that there is just such a wicker basket represented on the great fresco of the Villa of the Mysteries outside Pompeii, with a (partially concealed) phallus in it.

267–77   Despite the supposed intercourse between men and gods in these mythical times, mere mortals are not invited to the wedding feast, and respectfully depart after viewing the wealth on display in Peleus's palace. Their going is celebrated by Catullus in an elaborate simile that owes something to two such similes in Homer's *Iliad* (4.422–26, 7.63–64).

278–84   Chiron the centaur is invited, not only as the future tutor of the bridal pair's son, Achilles, but as a local Thessalian deity from Mt. Pelion (where his cave was later pointed out, and his supposed descendants, the Chironidae, formed a kind of medical guild). Perhaps most important, he was a personal friend of Peleus, and furnished him with crucial information on how to win his reluctant bride. The flowers he brings to the wedding in Catullus's version are a far cry from the great ash spear which is his gift in Homer's *Iliad* (16.143, 19.390), and which Achilles later wielded.

285–93   The final effect may be of a pleasant green grove shading the palace, but there is something irresistibly grotesque—perhaps deliberately so—about the picture of Penios staggering under the weight of "a giant dendroid bouquet" (Godwin 1995, 163), so out of scale with everything and everyone else.

323–81   Though this wedding song begins (323–36) and ends (372–80) with good wishes to the happy pair, its major theme otherwise is the fate and achievements of the one child born of the marriage, Achilles—a very practical reason for its being delivered by the Fates rather than (as in Euripides' *Iphigenia at Aulis*, 1040ff.) by the Muses: a "song of the Fates" could more easily concentrate on the future than could a normal epithalamium. Cf. Fordyce 1961, 317–18; Godwin 1995, 166.

340–41 Achilles' legendary speed as a runner ("swift-footed" is his regular formulaic epithet in Homer) was, as Catullus makes clear here, also put to good use to make him a famous hunter no less than a warrior (cf. Pind. *Nem.* 3.43–52).

346 The "third in line" from Pelops was Agamemnon, the first and second being Atreus and Thyestes.

357–60 A reference to Achilles' dealings with the Scamander river in Hom. *Il.* 21.

376–77 One of the oddest old wives' tales from the ancient world, confirmed by the third century C.E. poet Nemesianus (2.10; cf. Syndikus 1990, 182 with n. 344; Goold 1989, 254): that the successful consummation of a marriage was proved by an increase in the size of the bride's neck.

382–408 The idea that the gods once enjoyed communion on earth with mortals (in a better and nobler age) goes back to Homer (*Od.* 7.201–206, where King Alcinoüs applies it to his specially favored Phaeacians), and is implied by lyric poets such as Sappho, whose poems envisaged an easy and even teasing personal intimacy— however conceived—between deity and mortal suppliant.

    The degeneration from this happy state of affairs is even more strikingly documented. The *locus classicus* is Hesiod in the *Works and Days* (176–201), who describes his own lifetime in terms of toil, grief, hatred, bitterness, lack of religious reverence, contempt for tradition, and the departure of the last of the immortals, Shame *(Aidôs)* and Nemesis, from earth. In the Hellenistic period the astronomer Aratus echoed Hesiod in his *Phaenomena*, lamenting the loss of the Golden Age and the advent of wars and bloodshed (e.g., at 338–60, that involving Achilles, Godwin 1995, 174).

    The epilogue leaves Catullus's readers—as so often—uneasily conscious of possible ambiguities and ironies. Will Achilles (as Fordyce believes, [1961, 322]) prove to be "the consummation of the heroic age," and, even if he is, can we avoid the dark side of his history? Or is this so-called heroic age being shown up as cruel, bloody-minded, murderous, amoral, and altogether embarrassing in modern, i.e., late Republican Neoteric, terms? Godwin concludes a shrewd analysis (1995, 171–75) with the observation that this "is the last of many paradoxes and ambiguities with which this poem leaves us." The literature on 64 is enormous; for a good selective bibliography see Thomson 1997, 438–43.

65 This poem, together with 66—almost certainly the translation of Callimachus mentioned at 15–16—and 68, was probably an early work, composed in Verona after Catullus's brother's death, but before Catullus himself left for Bithynia in the spring of 57 (Thomson 1997, 444). Sorrow, Catullus asserts, cramps his creativity (1–4, cf. also 68.5–8, 15–26)—or so he says: as with Ovid in his exilic period, the poems themselves show no falling off in that respect. The elegant and

complex structure of 65 (one theme encapsulated inside another) matches, in miniature, the similar format of 64 and 68, thus somewhat subverting the professions of grief with which Catullus addresses Hortalus. It consists of one long sentence—which the parenthetical theme offsets—and is the first poem of the collection as we have it to be written in elegiacs (see introd. pp. 39–41); we do not reach the main verb (*mitto,* "I send") till line 15. Note that the last poem in this group, 116, also has a Callimachean theme. This has been taken as evidence of possible ring closure, implying authorial organization. Skinner (2003, 1–19) sees 65 as an announcement of self-dedication to Callimachean poetics, and 116 as a final admission, in the corrupt world of the dying Republic, that poetics, like patriotism, was not enough.

5–6   It is hard, at first sight, to see what Catullus means here, and even harder not to make the lines sound grotesque in English without losing the image. Only Quinn (1970, 353) bothers to offer a (probably correct) explanation: the "lapping" occurred "at the moment when [Catullus's] brother stepped into the waters of forgetfulness, to board Charon's boat." Cf. Prop. 4.11.15–16.

12–14   The "Daulian nightingale" was Procne, wife of King Tereus of Daulis: for the peculiarly grisly myth to which Catullus is referring, see glossary s.v. Itylus. As Wray points out (2001, 197ff.) Catullus's self-identification with Procne is one of the most overt examples of feminization he provides.

19–24   This delightful and unexpected simile brings a complete change of mood to the last lines of an otherwise rather grey and strained note of apology; it also gives the lie, by implication, to Catullus's profession of poetic impotence. Elaborate interpretations (e.g., Quinn's, 1970, 354) relating it to Catullus's exchange with Hortalus, are unnecessary. As Godwin sees (1995, 180), the only excuse it needs is that of embarrassment. There is also a hint (as so often in Catullus) of innocence lost (Petrini 1997, 15–17).

66   This translation of Callimachus's poem on the lock of Berenice is, not surprisingly, an Alexandrian *tour de force*. It also depends on a complex, not to say scandalous, historical background, on which see the notes to 11–12 and 27–28 below, together with glossary s.vv. Ptolemy and Berenice, as well as Marinone 1997, 13–26. Surviving fragments of the original Greek elegy by Callimachus, from book 4 of his *Aitia,* are available in Kroll (1922, 298–300, text and commentary), Godwin (1995, 227–29, text and translation), Fordyce (1961, 409–10, text only) and Goold (1989, 223, translation only). The poem is narrated by Berenice's lost lock of hair after its elevation to the heavens (see glossary s.v. Conon). It was promised by Berenice as a sacrifice to ensure the safe return of her newlywed husband, Ptolemy III Euergetes, from his Syrian campaign. He duly came back, and the lock was cut off and dedicated. Soon afterwards it mysteriously vanished.

As befitted a poem originally published as part of Callimachus's *Aitia* ("Causes," "Origins"), 66 offers an etiological explanation of the star cluster still known as the Coma Berenices. Catullus preserves Callimachus's Alexandrian allusions (mythological, astronomical and historical), his sentimental playfulness, and his dabbling in erotic psychology (something at which Catullus is both subtler and more insightful). Cf. Thomson 1997, 448; Fordyce 1961, 328–29; and particularly Godwin 1995, 182–83 for the "burlesque of human feelings" which the lock, as narrator, so slyly achieves. (The Latin for "tress" or "lock," *coma*, is feminine, whereas its Greek equivalent, *plókamos*, is masculine. Catullus clearly took advantage of this grammatical accident to give *his* lock a feminine persona.) It is worth bearing in mind that the Callimachean original, as a court poem, reflects the serious politico-religious question of whether Ptolemy III and Berenice II should add themselves to the ruler cult involving Alexander and Ptolemy's own immediate predecessors, the Sibling Gods *(Theoi Adelphoi)*, Ptolemy II and Arsinoë II. Cf. Tatum 1997, 490–92.

5–6   "She of the crossways" is Trivia, and, by association via Hecate and Diana, the Moon (Selene), whose mythical affair with the young shepherd Endymion in a cave on Mt. Latmos in Caria was used as an etiological explanation of the moon's monthly disappearance: the lady was away in that Carian cave, making love.

11–12   The circumstances that led to Ptolemy's invasion of Syria are quintessentially Hellenistic, that is, both complicated and dynastically ad hominem. His sister, Berenice Syra ("the Syrian"), had in 251 married, *en secondes noces*—second marriages were always risky in Hellenistic royal politics—the Seleucid monarch Antiochus II Theos, whose first wife Laodice had already borne him five children, including the heir presumptive, Seleucus II Kallinikos (who actually succeeded in 245). Laodice had been divorced, exiled, and given a small fief in Asia Minor with her sons, Seleucus and Antiochus Hierax ("The Hawk"). Berenice Syra then bore the elderly Antiochus a son of her own. On his death in 246, there were thus two competing queens with male offspring, though Berenice's was still an infant. Seeing at once the danger she was in, Berenice appealed from Antioch to her brother in Egypt; but before Ptolemy could get to her, Laodice's agents had swiftly moved in and assassinated both Berenice herself and her child. Thus Ptolemy's invasion was not merely a case of territorial acquisitiveness, or a new ruler's muscle-flexing to prove himself, but in a very real sense an act of dynastic and familial vengeance. Money, too, was involved; Berenice had brought Antiochus II a substantial dowry, now clearly lost to Laodice and her supporters. See Green 1993, 148–150.

15   Despite Thomson's arguments (1997, 452), like Courtney (2000, 49–50), I cannot tolerate the reading *parentum* here: the meaning is so clearly that the frustration—immediate, personal, physical, not in some remote theoretical future involving children, which in any case the bride's tears do nothing to prevent, impregnation be-

ing no respecter of mere antipathy—is the frustration experienced by *husbands*, especially by new bridegrooms, rather than *parents* (who are hardly privy to what goes on inside the bridal chamber: Thomson's scenario (1997, 212 n. 233) to preserve both *parentum* and *intra* has them listening at the keyhole while their daughter is deflowered; if this is a Danish custom I don't want to know about it). I therefore, with some diffidence, suggest, and translate, the emendation *mariti*. (Munro's *an quod auentum*, which has the same aim, is simply not Latin, while Richmond's *prementum*, preferred by Courtney, is scarcely less awkward.) Callimachus's text is no help here, since what it makes clear is that this reflection on bridal psychology was a gratuitous insertion by Catullus: there is no room for it in the original.

21–22   Berenice and Ptolemy, though not in fact brother and sister—they were actually no more than half cousins —are often so described in inscriptions, in accordance with Egyptian protocol (Fordyce 1961, 332). The lock is being mischievous: could Berenice's tears have been occasioned by *sisterly* love? Cf. Thomson 1997, 449; Godwin 1995, 186.

27–28   Berenice II (not to be confused with Berenice Syra) was the child of Magas of Cyrene. His aim in betrothing this daughter to Ptolemy III was to reunite Cyrene and Egypt after his death. However, his widow, Apame, daughter of Antiochus I, had other ideas (presumably including the continued independence of Cyrene), and so found a son-in-law preferable to her in Macedonia: Demetrius, known as "the Fair," son of Demetrius Poliorcetes ("the Besieger"). Preferable in every sense: he married Berenice, but became her mother Apame's lover. Berenice, a girl not to be trifled with, caught them *flagrante delicto* and had Demetrius executed on the spot (Just. 26.3.2–8). Having thus summarily dealt with one husband, she was ready—haloed with what was seen as "a heroic exploit on the part of a girl defending her outraged virtue" (Thomson 1997, 449)—to fulfill her father's original marital plans for her. Demetrius died in 250; Ptolemy finally married her in 247/6, while still co-ruler with his father, Ptolemy II Philadelphos. As both Callimachus and Catullus make clear, the appeal to him from his embattled sister, Berenice Syra, in Antioch literally interrupted the honeymoon.

35–36   Ptolemy's achievements were exaggerated at the time (Green 1993, 150 with n. 90), but he did occupy Antioch, and, more important, acquired its port of Seleucia (Polyb. 5.58.10ff.). His self-promoted triumphal march to the Euphrates and the gateway of India (accepted without question by Fordyce [1961, 333] and Godwin [1995, 187]) is probably fictional propaganda.

43–46   What Catullus refers to here, with hyperbolic exaggeration (probably borrowed from Callimachus, but the papyrus is defective at this point) is the episode described by Herodotus (7.22–24) when, in 483, Xerxes had a canal dug through the Athos peninsula after his son-in-law, Mardonios, lost a flotilla while attempting to round it during a storm. It should be noted that (i) Mt. Athos, at 6,350 feet, is not the highest peak in Greece, or even in the general area: Olympus, Parnassus, Oeta, and the Pindus are all higher; and (ii) the canal was in fact nowhere near the mountain itself, let alone through it, but (very sensibly) at the narrowest and flattest point of the peninsula, a little east of Acanthus.

52–56   A nice case of intense Alexandrian allusiveness. "Memnon's sibling" was Zephyrus, the West Wind, both being offspring of the Dawn (Eos, Aurora); Zephyrus was frequently represented as a winged horse. His connection with Arsinoë II, Ptolemy II's posthumously divinized queen, is via the eponymous Zephyrion, near Canopus and Alexandria, a site founded by Locrians, where Arsinoë had a shrine in her capacity as the deified avatar of Aphrodite/Venus (just as elsewhere she was revered as the incarnation of Isis).

65–68   The astronomy is accurate: the Coma Berenices is, in fact, adjacent to Virgo, Leo, Boötes, the Corona Borealis (i.e., Ariadne's Crown) and Ursa Major (glossary s.v. Callisto). See Marinone 1997, 245ff.

69–70   The gods are visualized as walking on the "floor of heaven" (Godwin 1995, 191; Fordyce 1961, 338), and hence trampling the lock when its constellation is high; by dawn it will have descended in its revolution to "grey Tethys," i.e., Ocean by metonymy, since Tethys was Ocean's wife.

71   The "Rhamnusian Maiden" is Nemesis, who had a famous shrine at Rhamnous in Attica, and was the goddess, and in a sense the embodiment, of divine displeasure or indignation. The lock fears her censure because of its ingratitude at its new honor (catasterization), and its wish instead to be reunited with its mistress's head.

76–77, 82–83, 91   The repeated allusions to perfume in connection with Berenice II are in part explained by a statement in Athenaeus (15.689A), where we learn that Berenice actively encouraged the cosmetics industry in Alexandria, and had been interested in it even while still a young girl in Cyrene (82–83 and 91 sound like promotional boosts). At 77–78 we should be hard put to it to figure out what was going on did we not have Callimachus's Greek to guide us: Lobel's emendation *uilia* ("cheap," "frugal") depends on it (the Greek is *litá, λιτά*). Courtney (2000, 50) explains, with admirable concision: "Callimachus is drawing a contrast between the simple oil once used by his tomboy (25–28) while still unmarried, and the compounded perfumes which married women habitually used, but of which this lock was deprived because it was cut off immediately after the marriage." But Catullus has no corresponding epithet to represent Callimachus's γυναικείων (*gynaikeiôn*, "proper to [adult, married] women"): certainly not *omnibus* ("all"), the reading of the MS tradition. Hence Skutsch's emendation, which I adopt (and translate) with misgivings; it produces the right sense, but I find it hard to imagine how Catullus's original text could have been so radically distorted. Holford-Strevens (1988, 170) argues that Catullus simply failed to spot the antithesis and mistranslated his original: this, on reflection, I fear may well be the truth.

94 Explanations for this line are numerous, varied, and mostly jejune. Some involve textual emendation. See, for example, Kroll 1922, 212; Quinn 1970, 367–68; Fordyce 1961, 340–41; Godwin 1995, 192–93; Thomson 1997, 462–63. The point to bear in mind is that Orion does *not* shine next to Aquarius, but at a distance of about 120 degrees from it (for astronomical data see now Marinone 1997, 245–59). In other words, what we have here is that familiar rhetorical trope, an *adynaton*, or "impossibility," of which the logic is, "If X [an impossibility] happens, then so can Y." The common run of stars, the lock concludes, are about as likely to share its privileges as is Orion to change its position in the sky and end up next to Aquarius. This interpretation, accepted most recently (1970) by Kidd, involves no change to the MS tradition, simply some careful punctuation.

67 After a talking tress, a positively garrulous house door; frequently apostrophized in love elegy, here it talks back. I find it hard to believe that the juxtaposition (whoever arranged the collection) was not deliberate, especially since what we have here is surely a kind of mini-mime, designed for oral presentation (Wiseman 1985, 128). The initial address (1–2) in the Latin, with its feminine inflections, leads us to expect an address to a respectable wife: instead we get the house-door-as-female-slave. Contrasts are numerous and piquant: as Godwin says (1995, 195), "the idyllic marriage of Berenice and her heroic husband [and cf. Laodamia and Protesilaus in 68.73–84, 105–108] is in stark contrast to the nameless adulteress in 67 whose nominal husband is ridiculously impotent and whose past is anything but fragrant." Catullus was clearly dealing with a scandal well known to the members of his Verona circle, but which remains obscure to us. Yet he hoped to be read by a wider audience and to survive for posterity, so unless this was a purely private lampoon, included by some editor in error after Catullus's death, we have to assume that half the fun for the poet was leaving a row of tantalizing clues for reader or listener to piece together. Analysis in Carratello (1992, 188–95).

What, then, is the story ("predictably racy but maddeningly confused in its details," [Skinner 2003, 46])? The house door (depicted throughout as a typical talkative, knowing slave) belongs to a house in Verona (34), now owned by Caecilius (9), but formerly by an elderly gentleman named Balbus (3). On the latter's death, his son married (Badian's neat emendation of *pacta* for *facta*, plus the restoration of the MS reading *est* for the Aldine's *es*, saves us from having to produce a contorted explanation for why the *door* should now consider itself married). The door *qua* servant does not get on well with the son (5, 7–8). There was a scandal (9–14), which, we gather (19ff.) involved the wife, who probably truthfully claimed that her previous marriage had not been consummated (19–22), but was reported to have had intercourse with her father-in-law (23–28), and with other characters—two named—in Brescia/Brixia, presumably her previous home (31–36). The door claims to have heard all this from her gossiping with the servants (37–49).

The difficulties, such as they are, have been for the most part created by modern scholars. There is no reason to identify Caecilius either with Balbus *fils*, or with the mysterious ginger-eyebrowed gentleman of line 46 (cf. Godwin [1995, 194], who adds to the confusion by his claim that Quinn and Goold identify the father and son of 1–6 with those of 20–27, which they do not). Neither the wife, nor her earlier husband and father-in-law, nor the rufous stranger are named, or really need to be. The door simply has a new master, and seeks, nervously, to justify its own rather patchy record. Like its keeper, it is the guardian of virtue in wives and daughters: hence the chorus of blame (9–14) when the house's mistress goes astray.

37–40 The objection severely strains our suspension of disbelief, even though chiefly directed at the door's immobility (which was never in doubt). But the objector is also represented as addressing a door that, he supposes, can't hear gossip (39). Not a bit of it: listening to gossip, the door snaps back promptly (41–44), is what it's good at, and more fool the wife for supposing (as most of us might in the circumstances) that doors had no ears or tongues. Catullus's mischief is here really rattling the bars. He is also (Wray 2001, 138–43) camouflaging the fact that he's eavesdropping.

45–48 More important than the tall ginger-eyebrowed fellow's identity—not, certainly, Rufus (= *rosso*, "reddish," Carratello [1992, 193–94])—is just what he's supposed to have been up to. Goold's (1989, 256) is the likeliest interpretation: "he had been taken to court for attempting to secure possession of his father-in-law's estate by feigning the birth of a son to his wife." Compare the situation described in 68.119–24. Alternatively (Godwin 1995, 202), he could have been the victim of a fraudulent claim of impregnation, though I find this less likely (as does Kroll 1922, 218). In either case, what lurks behind the whole scenario (Skinner 2003, 48–49) is a *lack of heirs*, and the devices used to claim inheritance. A recently introduced legal change had "allowed blood relatives of the deceased on either side to supersede members of the wider *gens* as claimants to the estate in cases of intestacy." Cf. Gardner 1998, 25–34. The implication in 67 would seem to be that adultery and infertility are linked (perhaps by way of repeated abortions), so that failure to produce an heir, resulting in the transfer of the house to new owners, is the result of the wife's lifestyle.

68A and B We are faced here, to begin with, by a problem of unity. This is partly the fault of the MS archetype, which ran together quite a few of the poems in the collection, including the final sixteen (Wiseman 1974, 89), thus creating a precedent for editors. Also to blame is the similarity, or identity, of the addressees, variously reported, with a bewildering number of MS variants, as Allius, Mallius, Manlius, Malius, or Alius (? A.N. Other!?) throughout. However, Mallius/Manlius predominates in a (1–40) and Allius in b (41–160). There are other factors suggesting that 68a and b should be treated separately, and that the similarity or (as I would argue) identity of the addressees need not imply a unity of poetic structure. Kroll (1922, 218ff.) argues for unity, as more recently do Williams (1968, 229–31), Quinn (1970, 373ff.), and Godwin (1995, 203–207).

68a (1–40) takes the shape of a letter to a friend, "informal in style and indeed sometimes little more than versified prose" (Fordyce 1961, 341). The addressee has asked for literary and personal comfort: he is miserable, his love life (5–6) is in a bad way. Catullus responds that he too is miserable (19ff.) on account of his brother's death, and that grief—together with his lack of a library in Verona— makes it impossible for him to supply the poetic comfort asked for. The poem is thus one form of a rhetorical *recusatio*, i.e., the polite refusal, with explanation, of an unwelcome request.

In 68b (41–160), however, the situation is quite different right from the start, and all the many ingenious rhetorical and thematic attempts to cobble the two poems together must be regarded as suspect (Arkins 1994, 223–25; D'Anna 1999, 235ff.). In Skinner's formulation (2003, 42) he "has initiated a poetic *ludus*," which of course begs the question of historicity. Here Catullus is, from the first lines, not inarticulate with grief, but positively bursting to talk; further, until the short *envoi* (149–60) he refers to his addressee (Allius) in the third person, rather than addressing him directly as in 68a. The bulk of the poem describes Allius's kindness in lending Catullus and his lover (surely, here, Lesbia) a house in which to make love (and let Catullus indulge a fantasy of marriage: cf. above, note on 64, and introd. ad fin.). The technique is as ornate and larded with myth as that of 68a is plain; the structure is symmetrical and complete in itself (Skinner 1972, 509). Where the tone is elevated one suspects irony and tongue-in-cheek mock heroics (cf. Ackroyd-Cross 1997, 117). There is no evidence whatsoever that Catullus has suddenly changed his mind, and produced a poem to comfort Allius or Mallius/ Manlius in his distress. Indeed, there is no suggestion that the addressee *is* distressed, and a fairly broad hint (155) that his love life is, or is presumed to be, in good order. While this does not necessarily mean that the addressees are different individuals, it does strongly imply that the two poems—if addressed to the same person—must be dated to different occasions, both of them subsequent to the death of Catullus's brother in (most probably) 60. As Thomson says (1997, 474), 68a is "in no way structurally determined" by 68b. See also the note on 20–24 below, and the well-argued case against unity by D'Anna (1999, 235ff.).

I am working from the assumption (Wiseman 1974, 102–103; Newman 1990, 228–29; et al.) that the addressee in both poems is L. Manlius Torquatus, the bridegroom in the epithalamium of 61, and that in 68b the use of the (fairly transparent) alias, Allius, is to avoid embarrassment through publicizing the loan of a house for an adulterous affair with a lady of good family. From 155–56 it looks as though Catullus is writing 68b at, or very soon after, the time of Manlius's wedding (also dated to 60), and is harking back to a time (? in 61) when his own affair with Lesbia was new. (It is indeed possible that the bulk of 68b had been composed before Catullus's brother's death, and that lines 91–100 were patched in afterwards.) 68a will then be somewhat later, perhaps early in 59, when Manlius (as we might have anticipated from 61.135ff.) is experiencing marital problems, and Catullus is in Verona to deal with the familial repercussions of his brother's death—not to mention the equally problematic consequences, after March, of Clodia's widowhood. (Quinn [1972, 179–96] reaches a similar chronology, but on different grounds.)

I propose this simply as a translator's working hypothesis, well aware that of all Catullan problems, that of 68 is among the most obdurate (cf. Skinner 2003, xi and passim); as Wiseman (1974, 77) says, "no solution has yet been proposed which commands immediate assent, and there seems no likelihood that any solution ever will."

15 The "white gown of manhood" was the *toga uirilis*, assumed at about the age of sixteen in place of the purple-edged children's garment.

17–18 The goddess is still Venus: ever since Sappho's day the oxymoron of bitter-sweetness had been applied to the effects of love.

20–24 These lines are virtually identical with 92–96, and an additional argument (Fordyce 1961, 343) against 68a and b having been sent on the same occasion, even if they shared the same addressee.

27–30 Goold (1989, 257), with exemplary common sense, gives a convincing explanation of this much-debated quatrain: Manlius, writing from Rome, "is insisting that in Verona Catullus, like other young aristocrats, could not engage in amorous pursuits with the same freedom possible in the capital." This is just the kind of practical remark one would expect from a man who had very probably already lent Catullus a country house (67–68) in which to conduct his clandestine affair.

41–42 The goddesses invoked here are the Muses, who are to see that the addressee's kindnesses are preserved for posterity (43–44), and publicize them as widely as possible (45–46). Nor is there much doubt as to the addressee's identity. In 41 the phrase *m(e)' Allius*, with its elision, "approximates to the colloquial pronunciation of Manlius" (Goold 1989, 257).

51–66 Catullus's love life, with its intertwined splendors and miseries, is here given the high—and conventional—literary treatment, complete with grandiose comparisons. As so often, artifice and emotion, for the modern reader, tend to cancel one another out. How far Catullus did this kind of thing tongue-in-cheek, as a self-mocking exercise, and how far he was in agonized earnest, it is impossible to tell at so vast a remove, though the hyperbolic similes (he's hot as volcanic lava, as a boiling thermal spring) are suggestive (Skinner 2003, 43). The extended image of the mountain stream (56–63) has given rise to much scholarly debate, involving varieties of punctuation and, at 63, textual emendation (*ac* for *hic)*. The problem is this: does the image of the stream refer (a) back to Catullus's tears, or (b) forward to Allius's help? The main arguments in favor of (a) are (i) that Catullus normally used *qualis* (as here at 57) when referring back; and (ii) that the emendation *ac* for *hic* or *hec* at 63 is "unwarranted and palaeographically unconvincing" (Thomson 1997, 481; other arguments from imagery in Vandiver 2000, 151ff.). But (a) produces, at best, a lopsided rhetorical mess; *qualis* at 57 is nicely picked up by *tale* at 66; and even if we accept (a), *hic* at 63 remains awkward and disjunctive, as does the brief concluding simile thus created. I therefore accept (b), and punctuate accordingly. For a good discussion of the basic problems, see Fordyce 1961, 350–51; and cf. Godwin 1995, 214–15.

70–72   Lesbia/Clodia, arriving like a numinous vision in a cloud of heightened expectation (see Lyne 1980, 55) is left with her foot on the threshold till 131. As Skinner says (2003, 52), "the frame freezes cinematographically, and dissolves to Laodamia's union." The reader has to remember 61.159–61, where the bride of the generous house lender receives prayers for a good-omened crossing of her own threshold. (Catullus doubtless also meant to recall, with mordent irony, those less than idyllic comings and goings across another threshold, recounted with such salacious relish by the talkative house door of 67.) Has Lesbia courted bad luck by actually touching the door-sill (Quinn 1970, 385)? What follows, from the marriage of Laodamia to the Trojan War and Catullus's brother's death, hardly sets the stage for a long and peaceful cohabitation, and is indeed (Lyne 1980, 57–59) a deliberate and realistic dismantling of the dream, for which the comparison to Laodamia—who "brings with her a story peculiarly burdened with separation, death, and an end to (sexual and artistic) creative power" (Janan 1994, 121)—is all too apposite. (For an acute analysis of the various analogies, see Feeney 1992, 33ff.)

73–78   The detail of the half-finished house goes back as far as Homer (*Il.* 2.695–702). The "sacred victim" at 75 is sometimes wrongly identified with Iphigenia, but clearly in fact refers to a more private dereliction of religious duty by Protesilaus. For Nemesis as the "Rhamnusian Maiden," cf. 64.395 and note.

109–16   The underground drainage shafts and sinkholes near Pheneus in Arcadia were popularly supposed to have been the work of Hercules, who was "Amphitryon's falsely ascribed offspring," being sired in fact by Zeus/Jupiter on Amphitryon's wife in the guise of her husband. (The remarkable—and not so subtly demeaning—

description of Laodamia as being sucked down by her passion like water in the vortex of a sinkhole is, surely, more immediately applicable to Catullus, who thus places himself by implication in the feminine role for which he was twitted by his friends, see 16 and note.) Hercules' fifth labor (at the behest of Eurystheus, his "inferior master") was to kill the man-eating birds that haunted the lake of Stymphalus. His shafts were "unerring" because loosed from a magical bow that never missed its target—and which he bequeathed on his deathbed to Philoctetes, who survived, when marooned on Lemnos, through the use of it. On the completion of his labors, Hercules was admitted to Olympus (115–16) and given Hebe as his bride.

119–24 The legacy hunter *(captator)* was a stock figure, and target, in Roman literature. The elderly grandfather here is circled by predatory relatives since, by a law of 168 B.C.E. (Fordyce 1961, 357), his daughter could not receive more than half the estate by direct bequest; to inherit it all, the legatee had to be male. What Catullus describes was, of course, a way of taking care of his daughter, since (Godwin 1995, 222 with references) "the money would be *de facto* if not *de jure*, in her hands thus."

125–28 Once again, Catullus seems to be following a private and personal agenda, since doves, while regularly described as "models of conjugal fidelity" (Quinn 1970, 391), were not, in Roman literature, treated as examples of wanton and oversexed rapacity—even if their urges were restricted, in contrast to those of the (unnamed) "promiscuous woman" *(multiuola mulier)*, to a single mate. It is hard (cf. Godwin 1995, 223) not, at this point, to think of Lesbia and her three hundred lovers at 11.17–20: not least in view of what follows at 135–40.

135–40 Catullus clearly is, or pictures himself as being, at that stage in his affair with Lesbia where, though fully conscious of her promiscuity, he is prepared to put up with the "occasional lapse" as a man of the world—and in the knowledge that complaint would be counterproductive. The comparison with the Jupiter-Juno relationship is striking on two counts: (a) it at once lifts Lesbia's sexual adventurism to an Olympian (as well as Olympic) level, and (b) it once more compares Catullus to the feminine member of a relationship (above, note to 109–16). In fact Hera/Juno showed herself highly ingenious when it came to payback time for Zeus/Jupiter's affairs (Godwin 1995, 224 cites the cases of Io, Semele, and Alcmena), and Catullus, similarly, was no slouch at lampooning known or suspected rivals, for example, Gellius, Egnatius, and Caelius Rufus.

141a–b Scholars since the Renaissance have rightly postulated a lacuna between lines 141 and 142, which provide a disjunctive sequence that, despite some attempts (see, e.g., Quinn 1970, 393–94), no syntactical ingenuity or textual changes can convincingly bridge. Cautious though I am about filling such presumptive gaps *exempli gratia*, this passage, with its high emotional content, really demands some kind of supplement in translation. The result is a joint effort: 141a is Goold's (1989, 186); 141b is mine, starting from the conviction (cf. Fordyce 1961, 259) that *tolle onus* (142) can *only* mean "take up the load."

142–46   The irony is poignant: after the marital *mésalliance* of Juno and Jupiter comes the acknowledgment that Catullus and Lesbia are not married at all, but restricted to stolen and furtive pleasures. Indeed, a careful study of the sequence strongly suggests that this may have been the *only* complete night they ever spent together. Wiseman observes (1985, 163), "Only now, and only for a moment, do we catch a glimpse of 'Lesbia' as she may have been in life—the adulterous noblewoman cheating her husband again for a night with an adoring lover. How much did it matter to her that he saw her in his fantasy as his bride? He should be glad she found time for him at all."

147–48   Poignant irony again: Catullus will settle for being Lesbia's favorite, but not her only, lover. For the white stone as the equivalent of a "red letter day," see note to 107.

153–54   Themis (here = Justice) is to bring Allius all the blessings proper to the lost Golden Age, when mortals still observed the requirements of piety and reverence (as they no longer do in Catullus's own age; cf. 64.397–408, and note ad loc.).

155–58   This passage (in particular the deeply corrupt line 157) has caused scholars a good deal of trouble (as even my highly selective *apparatus criticus* should make plain). In brief, I assume that the reference at 155 is to Manlius and his new bride, and at 157 I have built on convincing emendations by Scaliger and Wiseman, but with a different purpose. Whereas Scaliger (followed by Lipsius) believed that 157–58 formed part of Catullus's apostrophe to Lesbia, and referred to whoever "introduced you to me" *(nobis te tradidit)*, I take the addressee of these two lines to be Allius (whose name, in the vocative, I insert at the end of line 157; I also accept Wiseman's *uobis* for *nobis*), and that it is he whom Catullus thanks for being the source of all good things, i.e., for bringing him and Lesbia together. It is the friend who introduced Catullus to Allius who is now left anonymous (for some of the identifications proposed, see Godwin 1995, 226), but the distribution of thanks is better balanced. I am not convinced that this is necessarily the correct solution; I merely find it more plausible than the many others I have seen.

69   The identity of this Rufus is not absolutely certain, but it would undoubtedly add to Catullus's elegantly expressed disdain were he Catullus's rival in love, M. Caelius Rufus. A regular argument against the identification (cf. Wiseman 1974, 107; Lee 1990, xxi; Godwin 1995, 3) is that the Rufus of 69 (and, by inference, 71) suffered from gout; but as Mulroy points out (2002, xiii–xiv with n. 10), gout *(podagra)* in antiquity was not restricted to elderly debauchees, but struck the young (such as

Caelius Rufus) no less than the old, mainly through drinking from lead-lined containers. The goat (5–8), of course, is peculiarly appropriate, combining a rank smell with lustfulness.

70   This poem is usually, and I think rightly, taken to refer to Lesbia/Clodia. It would not have been at all surprising had Catullus raised the possibility of marriage (1–2) after her husband Metellus Celer's death in March 59—indeed, it would have been surprising had he not—and equally predictable that his *inamorata*, elusive as always, would waffle: "Yes, you're the person I'd like to *be married to*, but maybe not to *marry*." Cf. Quinn 1970, 398–99. The poem is an adaptation of an epigram by Callimachus (25 Pf.), but Catullus gives it his own characteristic twist, and the notion of writing on the wind (4) seems without ancient parallel. The reference to Jupiter, though proverbial, hardly suggests stability: the god's brief and lustful infidelities were notorious, and Catullus's overall mood is one of cynical resignation, backed up by a handful of stock literary allusions.

71   Despite the reappearance of malodorous armpits, indicating that (? Caelius) Rufus is being attacked again, the identity of the addressee (3), whose rival he is, remains in doubt. Quinn (1970, 400) claims that "both rival and addressee are being got at," and that therefore Catullus cannot be apostrophizing himself: neither point strikes me as valid. If Catullus *is* reflecting on his own position as displaced lover, surely that makes good sense? Not least, the desire to punish them *both* (5–6), one way or another. For further instances of Catullus's self-apostrophizing, cf. 8, 73, and 76.

72   This poem picks up 70 (just as 71 picks up 69), not least through Catullus's repeated (though significantly varied) citation of Lesbia's preference for him (as a lover this time rather than a husband) over Jupiter. What Lesbia is apostrophized as having said in the past ("solum te nosse Catullum") is syntactically ambiguous Latin: is she supposed to have meant (as I take it) that only Catullus understood her, that only she understood Catullus, or even that either was the only person the other understood (Janan 1994, 89)? Did Catullus mean to imply all these alternatives (which the translator into an uninflected language, alas, cannot)? On top of this, the psychology is both subtle and puzzling. The contrast (5–8) between sexual attraction (which can be sharpened by infidelity) and affection (which behavior such as Lesbia's kills through disgust) is beautifully done. But despite the commentators' best efforts (see, e.g., Fordyce 1961, 362–63 and Lyne 1980, 40–41), the likening by Catullus of his love for Lesbia to that of a father for his sons, or for his daughters' husbands, cannot but raise eyebrows, since Catullus's passion, as has been made clear throughout, is highly sexual in content. As Wiseman (1985, 166) says, "What did Aurelius and Furius (poem 16) make of *that?*"

Catullus may be (in one sense he certainly is) trying to separate sex from affection in his mind, and isolate what, for him, makes his relationship with Lesbia unique and special. In an unpublished paper written as a graduate student, Robert Holschuh Simmons of the University of Iowa points out how hard Catullus had to work to find a relationship "to capture a feeling that he has for Lesbia that would not be invested by readers with sexuality;" as he says, "Catullus's poems confirm or suggest incest, or at least sexual activity, between mothers and sons, fathers and daughters, brothers and sisters, nephews and aunts, nephews and uncles and fathers-in-law and daughters-in-law." This obsession needs further exploration (see, e.g., Hickson-Hahn 1998): there is surely more to it than the simple smear technique of political invective postulated by Skinner (2003, 86, 90–91, and elsewhere). Simmons sees 74 as "the common person's response, both right and wrong, to the revolutionary ideas about love that Catullus proposes in 72," and I find this very persuasive. The immediate impression, however—even granted that Catullus is attempting to explore new emotional territory (Lyne 1980, 40)—still remains not only naïve, but downright embarrassing in its awkwardness.

73   "The feeling that we are entitled to be treated decently by those whom we have treated decently is very characteristic of Roman thinking" (Quinn 1970, 403)— all part of that scrupulously maintained profit-and-loss account mentality, as evident in personal friendships as in an individual's dealing with the gods (cf. Skinner 2003, 72–73, and note on 76). This fragment is one of several pieces featuring faithless friends (e.g., 30, 75, 77). Here the disillusion is general and extreme. For the possibility that the (male) friend who occasioned this outburst was Caelius Rufus, see glossary s.v. As Godwin (1999, 188) observes, the unparalleled number of elisions in the Latin of line 6 suggests "that the poet's words are rushing out and finding the constraint of the metre difficult."

74   Gellius is the target in seven poems (cf. glossary s.v.). This one presents a fairly absurd scenario (Godwin 1999, 188), in which, to protect himself against his uncle's moral lectures on sexual impropriety, Gellius seduces his wife, thus forcing Uncle to keep quiet for fear of scandal: the "Holy Child" (the Greco-Egyptian deity, Harpocrates) was portrayed with one finger to his mouth, as though enjoining silence. Even if Gellius now commits *irrumatio* on Uncle (5–6), Uncle will *still* keep quiet, the joke here being that *fellatio* makes conversation difficult in any case. The debased echoes of 72 make this apparently simple squib uneasy reading.

75   Thomson (1997, 498) finds this "an intermediate stage in compression of thought" between 72 and 85 (q.v.). For Fordyce (1961, 365), Catullus's confusion between passion and affection is a "pathetic paradox." Quinn, on the other hand (1970, 405),

sees these lines as "ruthlessly clear-sighted." Take your choice. But the emotional conflict is real (cf. Copley 1949) and expressed with bitter vigor.

76   This is a crucial poem, and Godwin's basic analysis (1999, 191) is very much to the point, together with Lyne's analysis (1980, 29–34) of Catullus's use of terms borrowed from formal diplomacy or even from interstate politics (*amicitia* ["friendship," "alliance"], *foedus* ["solemn treaty," "covenant"]) to hammer out a new vocabulary of the ideal *personal* relationship, the *foedus amicitiae*, a permanent "marriage pact of friendship" (Lyne 1980, 37) based on affection as well as passion. As lines 23–26 make clear, "after all the rhetoric, the medical language and the pious prayers, we are left with a man in love with a woman who does not love him and does not care." The logic of 1–9 is shaky: Catullus seems to be saying (i) that he has been an averagely decent human being (2–4); (ii) that he has acted kindly, both in general (1, 28) and with specific reference to Lesbia (6, 9); (iii) that the memory of his record in this regard should give him pleasure (1, 5–6); (iv) that the investment in an unresponsive person (6, 9) has made all this go for nothing, and so why persist in the relationship (9–12)? The prayer for deliverance (7–25) seems to rest on the expectation that in return for a halfway decent and god-fearing *(pium)* life (3–4, 19), the gods will in fairness rescue him from the passion that he has come to regard as a disease (18–25). As a variation on the usual *do ut des* (tit for tat), profit-and-loss account that a Roman ran with heaven as well as with his fellow men (cf. 73), this does have the merit of originality. But here (as opposed to 8) "it is the gods who keep the accounts" (Quinn 1972, 120). Skinner (2003, 75) may well be right in her supposition that what Catullus is stressing, *inter alia*, is how the established meaning of words such as *foedus* and *pietas* is being "subverted in the course of power struggles among ambitious oligarchs and their supporters."

The medical metaphor (if it *is* entirely metaphorical, which I have always doubted, but see J. Booth 1999, 150ff.) comes across as both vivid (20–22) and disgusting (24); and while it works well as a description of Catullus's hopeless and corrosive relationship with Lesbia, it may well also spring (cf. introd. p. 3) from a chronic physical malaise, very possibly consumption, which Catullus would inevitably come to associate with his ill-fated passion.

77   The medical imagery of 76 persists here, but now in terms of poison (5), plague (6), and gut ache (3), this last, at least, as much metaphorical as actual. Despite the number of "men of senatorial rank who bore the name Rufus" (Thomson 1997, 504), I find it hard not to believe that this accusation of (clearly sexual) betrayal is not addressed to Catullus's rival Caelius Rufus. Quinn (1970, 410) rightly notes the "tortured violence of expression." There is a useful analysis in Pedrick 1993, 177–80, who remarks that Catullus's practice of directly addressing his targets,

"by depriving his audience of the context of the quarrel . . . provokes their curiosity and sends them on a hunt for clues."

78A   The joke, of course, is that Gallus (identity uncertain), while encouraging his dishy nephew to bed another uncle's wife, is forgetting that he himself is also an uncle with a wife: sauce for the goose . . . . Cf. Skinner 2003, 84: "One uncle becomes a paradigm for the other."

78B   Catullus's own sexual exploits with the young (see, e.g., 56) do not stop him from posing as the champion of abused innocence (just as he is equally annoyed at being done out of the profits while serving abroad, and at seeing someone like Mamurra make a good thing out of it: 10, 28, 29). It is difficult to see, as some have done, this fragment as belonging to 80, or to 77, or 91, or indeed to any of the poems in the surviving corpus. The addressee is presumably either a fellator or a cunnilinctor: in both cases contact *per se* is regarded as contagious, so that "pollution can be spread by a social kiss." Consequently (as this AIDS-conscious generation well knows) "what a man does in private is a matter of concern to his associates" (Skinner 2003, 79). We may indeed wonder whether this Roman belief concerning the *os impurum* did not perhaps have some grounding in the physical realities of venereal infection. Cf. the notes on 79 and 80.

79   With its neat pun on the cognomen Pulcher ("pretty"), this squib is one of our most compelling pieces of evidence for identifying Lesbia as Clodia Metelli. Clodia's brother, Publius Clodius Pulcher, reportedly engaged in an incestuous relationship with her (1–2) from an early age (Cic. *Pro Cael.* 32, 36, 78; Plut. *Cic.* 29.3; other references in Godwin 1999, 194; detailed discussion in Tatum 1993, 31ff.; cf. Skinner 2003, 81–82). The point of this particular pretty boy's unkissability—relatives and close friends being often so greeted—is, of course, the implication of his addiction to oral sex.

80   Oral sex is the theme here again, and not just by implication: the crude specificity of the last four lines is highlighted even more by the fake lyricism of the opening. Wray (2001, 157) suggests that Victor (otherwise unknown, and an odd name) may have been a gladiator, thus compounding the charge of passive homosexuality with that of social slumming. There is also a puzzle here (akin to those oddities of natural history reported by Pliny in his *Natural History,* which even the simplest of practical experiments would have proved false). Any Roman who engaged in oral-genital sex must have been perfectly well aware that the habit neither turned his lips white, nor left indelible semen stains behind. How, then, did these absurd beliefs gain currency? One can only guess that the practice was a good deal less widespread than is normally assumed, and that (as always) the majority was ready to

believe the worst of those whose indulgences they did not share. If so, it will have been for their benefit that the writers who perpetuated the myth (and obviously *did* know it was nonsense) kept it alive.

81   Line 1 suggests that the scene is Rome. Thomson (1997, 508) thinks that Juventius's new favorite may have been Aurelius (cf. 15, 16, 21, 23, 24), with a rather forced pun on *inaurata* (4), but this is highly speculative. Provinciality (in the modern sense) (3) is always good for a put-down in this provincial's book, and a sallow-complexioned provincial would be better still. Worst of all, he is not *bellus*, i.e., smart or stylish. The "seaside snooze-pit" was Pisaurum (modern Pesaro), an Umbrian town and former Roman colony on the Adriatic coast. That it was a dead-and-alive hole is shown (Fordyce 1961, 371) by the fact that new settlers were sent out there in 43 B.C.E.; cf. Carratello 1995, 40.

82   What is Catullus asking of Quintius? It is clear that what he finds "dearer than eyes" can only be Lesbia (cf. 104.2); but is Quintius being asked not to steal her (Fordyce 1961, 372; Godwin 1999, 197), or not to interfere between her and Catullus in the sense of trying to free Catullus from a harmful relationship (Quinn 1970, 416–17)? It all hinges on the verb *eripere* (3), and that remains ambiguous enough to make either interpretation possible—which may well have been Catullus's deliberate intention.

83   On the assumption that Lesbia is Clodia Metelli, this poem must be dated earlier than the sudden death of her husband Metellus Celer in March 59. Quinn (1970, 417) wonders whether the affair has in fact begun: does Catullus hopefully interpret the abuse as proof of love, or is it a cover-up for an affair already in full swing? Almost certainly, I would argue, the latter: the cumulative evidence points back to 61 or early 60 as the likeliest date for the assignation arranged by Manlius (cf. 68 and notes ad loc.). In either case, the psychological subtlety (Godwin 1999, 297–98) is considerable: seeming dislike may hide love. Love and hate (cf. 85) are flip sides of the same coin. And the husband may be a mule (3: nice insult, mules being sterile), but he is still, maddeningly, the one officially entitled to Clodia's favors.

84   The joke is one familiar to English upper-class snobs and devotees of *My Fair Lady* (or Bernard Shaw's *Pygmalion*, on which it was based): the British lower classes, London Cockneys in particular, drop their *h*'s. Catullus was only too happy to use the same joke in his day against class-conscious, mostly provincial, *arrivistes* who put the *h*'s back again, often in the wrong places, and overdid it. As Vandiver points out (1990, 338–39), his aspiration was of the Greek sort, implying initial *chi* (the sound is the equivalent of *ch* in Scottish "loch," what Skinner [2003, 165] describes

as "an explosive guttural hiss"). This turns the aspiration of the Ionian Sea into a neat (and untranslatable) pun: it becomes "Chionian" = χιόνεος, "snowy," i.e., chilly. By Catullus's lifetime, the spread of Greek among educated Romans meant that aspirations long lost in primitive Latin were being restored (Fordyce 1961, 373–75), but by no means always correctly. After the Social War (91–89), there were numerous rural Italians on the make in Rome. *Arena* or *harena? Pulcer* or *pulcher?* Arrius (a more serious character than one might suppose from this poem) "was clearly trying to be thoroughly *à la mode* and only succeeded in sounding ridiculous" (Godwin 1999, 199). Note that the message itself (10) is "horrible" *(horribilis)*—i.e., aspirated. See Marshall and Baker 1975, 220ff.

85   There can be few better-known Latin poems than this pungent and desperate distich. Thomson (1997, 514) sees it as "the ultimate stage in a process of condensation of thought and expression" that began with 72 and 75. Logic (2: *nescio*) has failed; all that remains is feeling (2: *sentio*), painful to the point of torture *(excrucior)*. The juxtaposition remains inexplicable, but a brute fact.

86   Here Catullus reveals more characteristics of what educated Romans regarded as an attractive woman (cf. 43 and note): she should be, *inter alia,* fair (i.e., pale-skinned, protected from the sun, not a field-worker), tall, and hold herself erect. (We should not assume from this ideal, tempting though it is to do so, that most Roman girls were short, dark, and slouched.) She was also expected to be not only literate, but versed in literature: a salon queen, in fact.

    1   Catullus's word for "beautiful," *formosa,* he uses here only, yet he would seem to have injected new subtlety into it (for an oversubtle analysis see Nielsen 1994, 258ff.). Before him it was used of anything well-shaped or well-formed of its kind, whether physical or abstract: for example (Fordyce 1961, 378), goats, fish, cylinders, virtue. But for Catullus it meant good looks plus subtle charm, and after him this usage became (Quinn 1970, 423) "one of the hard-worked words in the love-poet's vocabulary." Quintia was good-looking, but lacked that special magic. Lesbia for Catullus incarnates the Sapphic and Hellenistic ideal. Skinner (2003, 98) suggests that "Quintia and Lesbia stand for contrasting approaches to the Latin elegiac distich, one traditional and the other innovative."

87   This belongs to the same disillusioned group as 72, 75, and 85. The mood in which Catullus's own single-minded loyalty is invoked is one not of self-righteousness (Fordyce 1961, 380) but rather of despair. Note the switch in the last line to direct apostrophe: emotion has got the better of third-person distancing. Catullus startles the reader here, brings Lesbia suddenly, and directly, into the reckoning (Lyne 1980, 42).

88   Another of Catullus's satirical sexual squibs that manages without any obscene lan-
guage, and heightens the atmosphere by means of grandiloquent moral and liter-
ary rhetoric. For earlier attacks on Gellius's sexual habits see 74 and 80. From here
to 91 we see a "clustering and ensuing movement towards a final revelation" (Skin-
ner 2003, 86; Hickson-Hahn 1998, 11–16). One suspects exaggeration on Catul-
lus's part, and this poem contains material indicative of just that, in particular the
charge of maternal incest, since Gellius was elsewhere (see glossary s.v.) charged
with the seduction of his *step*-mother, Polla. Line 3 reiterates the charge of 74.
What Godwin (1999, 202) describes as the "autofellation" of the last line mis-
chievously suggests that, since Gellius has seduced everyone else, he might as well
complete the list by knocking off himself.

89   A general round-up of all the previous accusations against Gellius (except that in
80), subsumed to a picture of this sexually indefatigable character wearing himself
to a shadow through his unremitting attentions to a houseful of female relatives.

90   One more twist on the theme of Gellius's alleged incest: he should have been a
Persian Magus, for whom this particular taboo is not only legitimate but a religious
requirement. Thomson (1997, 519–20) proposes that the "fat caul" *(omentum)* ren-
dered down in the flames represents Gellius's "fat" *(pingue)* and un-Callimachean
literary efforts. Despite her theory that from 65 onward Catullus is moving *away*
from the Callimachean aesthetic, Skinner (2003, 87) buys this argument; but (even
without the Callimachean factor) it strikes me as very far-fetched.

91   Here, at last, we arrive at what may well be the true underlying reason for Catul-
lus's animus against Gellius: that though an old friend (Catullus seems to have put
up with his lifestyle quite happily till it impinged on his own), he tried to steal Les-
bia (cf. Tatum 1997, 498). Catullus makes a rueful, mildly sick joke: "I thought *she*
was safe from you, that you only hit on blood relatives." Catullus is flagellating
himself no less than Gellius: what kind of a fool is it who has this sexual monster
for a friend , and then complains about his treachery? Further, just as in the case
of profiteering while on overseas duty (10, 28, 29, 47), Catullus's accusations of
impropriety only surface when he has personal reasons for annoyance. Cf. God-
win 1999, 203 (though, as so often, he takes all this as reason for supposing the
whole episode a mere literary confection).

92   A summation of the thought expressed in 83, but clearly written at a later stage
in the relationship: there is a sense of *continuity* now in Lesbia's bad-mouthing and
Catullus's reactions: each keeps maintaining a position in what has become an es-
tablished affair with a history. These are "the words of a man who is eagerly look-
ing for confirmation of what he feels sure of" (Quinn 1972, 61).

93   Compare 29 and 57. We do not know the occasion of this coolly insulting couplet, the brevity of which hints eloquently at Catullus's degree of disregard for his addressee, but it does look like the response to some kind of overture, and thus probably *not* the famous occasion (Suet. *Div. Jul.* 73) on which Catullus apologized to the great man and was promptly invited to dinner. Earlier or later? Hard to tell. The black-and-white metaphor is impossible to translate in a way that holds all its implications: (i) that Catullus doesn't care to know Caesar *at all;* (ii) that he is indifferent to Caesar's moods, be they sunny or stormy; (iii) that he has no interest (Thomson 1997, 524) in Caesar's sexual preferences, Greek *leukos* (white) indicating homosexuality, and *melas* (black) manly virility (cf. Aristoph. *Thesm.* 30–35, 191). As Skinner says (2003, 110), "the barbed couplet was a ready and valuable counter of political exchange in the late republican period."

94   The first squib attacking "Prick" *(Mentula)*, generally, on account of 29.13 (q.v.), identified as Caesar's chief engineer Mamurra. Here the joke simply depends on the identity of name and function: Prick behaves as pricks will, and suffers appropriate retribution as a result. The proverb implied in line 2 (and which emphasizes the joke still further) is otherwise unknown: that does not necessarily mean that Catullus invented it for the occasion. The saying is the rough equivalent of "Birds of a feather flock together"; *olla* seems to have been a slang term for the vagina, the implication being that loose ladies collect randy men, as the pot its potherbs (cf. Adams 1982, 29, 86–87). Damschen (1998, 175–76) argues that *olla* can also be the anus (for which there is no evidence), and that *(h)olera* ("vegetables") hints at the punishment *per anum* for adultery (see 15 with note) by means of radishes or, as Juvenal knew (10.317), a mullet. Unfortunately, *olera* refers only to green vegetables *(OLD* s.v. *holus)*, not to stiff and phallic roots such as European radishes or parsnips.

95   As all commentators have seen, this neatly symmetrical little poem is a Neoteric literary manifesto, extolling the virtues of brevity, concision, the *mot juste*, learned allusiveness, and carefully structured technique, as against the lengthy, loosely composed, and rhetorically bombastic epic works churned out by devotees of the old post-Ennian tradition—and commending the taste of learned connoisseurs against common or garden public preferences. Cinna's *Smyrna* (for its subject matter see glossary s.v. Smyrna/Myrrha) is contrasted favorably with the wordy effusions of Hortensius, Volusius (cf. 36), and Antimachus. See now Skinner 2003, 114–18.

4   My supplement (the line is missing in the MS tradition) deliberately offers a quite impossible rate of production, five hundred thousand words in one day (as opposed to Munro's more realistic suggestion of one year), in the conviction that this is just the sort of rhetorical exaggeration that Catullus would enjoy.

5 I find Morgan's emendation, *sacras*, for the unmetrical *canas* of the MS tradition, highly convincing, since Aphrodite made love with Adonis at the Satrachus river, which could thus be regarded as her "bride-bath" (Godwin 1999, 206), a fact that would by definition sanctify it.

96 An oddly ambivalent poem of consolation to Calvus on the death of his young wife Quintilia. What, precisely, is the message being sent? 1–2: Catullus offers a faint, conditionally expressed hope that the dead are conscious of living sentiments regarding them. 3–4: Here Catullus specifies some of those sentiments: the recall of old loves, the lament over lost friendships. (Fraenkel [1956, 278–88], surprisingly supported by Fordyce [1961, 385–86], interpreted these lines as referring to Calvus's past marital infidelities, a grotesquely tasteless theory well disposed of by Godwin 1999, 207.)

5–6 If all this is true, surely Quintilia's joy in Calvus's love will eclipse the sorrow she feels at her premature death.

We know from Propertius (2.34.89–90) that Calvus himself wrote an elegy on Quintilia's death, and two fragmentary surviving lines of his seem to belong to it: *cum iam fulua cinis fuero* ("when [or perhaps 'since'] I shall already be brown ash") and *forsitan hoc etiam gaudeat ipsa cinis* ("perhaps my very ashes may rejoice at this too"). These suggest that Quintilia was indeed represented by her husband as being in contact with him from the grave, and also that Catullus may have had the elegy in mind when composing his own *consolatio:* Calvus's *gaudeat* (maybe, potential subjunctive) becomes, for Catullus, *gaudet* (sure fact, indicative), a neat gesture of consolation (Wray 2001, 51–52).

97 Perhaps the most violently obscene of all Catullus's poems: as Thomson (1997, 530) points out, "half of all Catullus's 'taboo' words are to be found here." The vocabulary is notable not only for obscenities, but also for prosaic, rare, and provincial usages, the last from Cisalpine Gaul (Thomson 1997, 530), which suggests an early poem. Whatmough (1956, 49) figured, persuasively, that the *ploxenum* was in fact a dung cart with a wicker container, drawn by the mule; cf. Skinner (2003, 119).

7 Thomson (1997, 531) proposes that the phrase *in aestu* means not, as is generally assumed, "in hot weather," but when the mule (despite being sterile) is "in heat." Godwin (1999, 209) preserves the normal interpretation, but with an extra twist: in summer "the heat dehydrates and so the urine would smell even worse." Add to this the "pungent ammoniac reek of estrus-discharge" (Skinner 2003, 119), and the effect becomes really overpowering.

12 Godwin (1999, 209) assumes that the hangman's sickness is dysentery, and though this would add point to Catullus's comment on anilingus, his epithet for "sick," *aegroti*, remains nonspecific.

98   In this and the previous poem the Roman obsession with the "dirty mouth" *(os im-purum)* is strikingly demonstrated: the dirtiness can be ascribed to physical causes (halitosis, cock sucking, ass kissing) or to the more figurative malaise of filthy language, obscene slander, and the other perquisites of a poisonous tongue. Vettius (if that was his name, the poem will have been written c. 62–59) is attacked by Catullus on both counts. Seneca (*Ep.* 70.20) revealingly compares the gossip's foul tongue to a lavatory sponge.

99   Catullus's promise never to snatch another kiss (15–16) is appropriate in what is not only the longest and most charming, but also (unless we include 103, which is highly doubtful) the last of the poems to or about Juventius. The present apostrophe, however, also contains elements of resentment and bitterness with a disquieting resemblance to those in some of the Lesbia poems. Did Catullus (or his persona, if we choose to play that fainéant card) encourage, if not actively prefer his lovers, of whichever sex, to treat him like dirt? On the face of it, Juventius has behaved to Catullus in much the same way as, and with even greater disdain than, Bosie dealt with Oscar. Excellent analysis by Godwin 1999, 210. Despite its ostensibly light tone, this is a worrying poem.

100   We do not know who Quintius was, and the attraction of identifying this Caelius as M. Caelius Rufus is tempered by (a) the latter's having no known connection with Verona, and (b) the difficulty of finding a time when Catullus's affair with Lesbia was either over or nearly so (5–7), but he could nevertheless greet his ex-rival in love with thanks for his friendly support *during the affair.* (Very early on, perhaps?) Godwin's unsupported claim that Caelius and Quintius are brothers appears to be pure speculation. The last line gives one pause: did this Caelius suffer from impotence, and if so would he thank Catullus for the way his good wishes were expressed? The idioms are interesting: Catullus, deciding on whom to back in this sexual free-for-all, uses the language of punters and the racetrack (C. J. Simpson 1992, 204ff.)

101   One of Catullus's most famous poems and, since it has no sex in it, frequently anthologized in school texts; the occasion may have been during Catullus's journey to Bithynia in 57. Like 96, it assumes the possibility of communication between the living and the dead (Feldherr 2000, 216–20). The conventions of epigrams addressed to the latter were well established in the Greek tradition which Catullus inherited (see, e.g., Book 7 of the *Greek Anthology* for numerous specimens: 7.476, cited by Fordyce [1961, 388], is akin to Catullus's address in spirit). But the emphasis on family tradition is very Roman (Hopkins 1983, 201–202), and the poignancy of Catullus's ineffectual ("all in vain," *nequiquam*) grief is highlighted by the remoteness of his brother's grave in the Troad. His journey is universal-

ized: lines 1–2 recall the opening of the *Odyssey*. Yet Catullus is very vague. We end up with no idea of the tomb itself (tumulus or headstone?), the gifts he brings are not itemized, and there is no invocation of the gods or the dead man's guardian spirits (Gelzer 1992, 26–32). But Feldherr rightly points out (2000, 223) "in how many ways the contrast between the irreversible flow of time and the present instant governs the poem's content." For Skinner (2003, 128), its position in the collection suggests closure "involving the failure of art to bridge the chasm between life and death, the illusory nature of Callimachean poetic immortality."

102   This is Catullus's somewhat baroque way of saying, in effect, "Trust me. I can keep a secret." The rare allusion to Harpocrates (cf. 74.4; readers of 102 could not—cannot—help recalling the related obscene joke in the earlier poem), the Egyptian deity portrayed as a child with a finger to his mouth, as though prescribing silence, is in fact only there as a periphrastic way of assuring the addressee—who *may* be Cornelius Nepos, but this is quite uncertain—that Catullus can keep his mouth shut.

103   Commentators are agreed that Silo (a good free Roman cognomen) was not a real pimp in the technical sense, but merely so termed by Catullus as an insult. One would, nevertheless, expect the insult to bear some relationship to the supposed offense. What, exactly, was the transaction that went sour? On this they are vague, and small wonder. Ten thousand sesterces is "a tidy sum" (Quinn 1970, 443). What had it been paid out for? The description of Silo as "pimp" suggests, in some form, sexual procurement. If Silo was, in fact (see glossary s.v.), acting as guardian for Juventius, then Catullus was willing to pay out a lot of money for the privilege of access to the boy, and the only circumstances that fit this squib are if Silo had taken the money but was proving uncooperative about fulfilling his side of the bargain. However we look at it, this represents a somewhat unpalatable scenario. Cf. the implications of 106.

104   This has to be a fairly early poem, since there exist quite a few late attacks (e.g., most particularly, 11 and 58) which would, in most people's opinion, qualify as "cursing" or "speaking ill of" Lesbia (*maledicere*, 1): cf. Godwin 1999, 214; Thomson 1997, 541. Godwin also stresses the alleged incompatibility of Catullus's attitude here with that in 92, where Lesbia's bad-mouthing of *him* is taken as proof of love. But perhaps Catullus would explain the lines as wrongly interpreted on just that basis? In any case, Whitman's apothegm applies: Catullus in love is quite ready to contradict himself.

105   Mamurra as "Prick" has literary no less than sexual ambitions (57.7), but Catullus uses sexual imagery (i.e., "mount," *scandere*) to describe his assault on the

Muses, and frames his rejection by them in terms of a cliché best known to us from Horace (*Ep.* 1.10.24, *naturam expelles furca* . . . ["you may drive nature out with a pitchfork . . . "]). The use of the spring of Pipla is a recondite allusion in the best Callimachean tradition, while the diminutive *furcillis* ("forklets") conveys a nice picture of the delicate feminine Muses at their business of extrusion.

106   The joke depends on one's remembering that those in the Roman world who were penetrated rather than penetrators were supposed at least to pretend they didn't want it, whereas here we have a rent boy who not only wants to be sold to the highest bidder but thoroughly enjoys the sex too. Or so Catullus infers from seeing him with an auctioneer—which at least one commentator (Quinn 1970, 445, probably recalling the unsavory reputation of Roman auctioneers in general) describes as "a reasonable assumption." Skinner (2003, 131) sees a political allusion here to Clodius's auctioning the exiled Cicero's property, with the "fetching young creature" *(puero bello)* recalling Clodius himself as *pulcher* in 79.

107   The Latin stutters with emotional excitement: elisions pile up, line 3 (if the text is not corrupt) contains a nice asyndeton in *carius auro,* Catullus's incredulous delight at Lesbia's return after estrangement is beautifully conveyed. The white mark for a lucky day was a commonplace cliché (Fordyce 1961, 395), and variously traced to Thracians (Plin.S. *NH* 7.131) or Cretans (Porph. on Hor. *Odes* 1.36) putting a white or a black stone daily in pot or quiver to indicate that day's happiness or unhappiness. On the textual difficulties of 7–8 see D'Angour 2000, 616 with n. 12.

108   The similarity of this bloody-minded invective to that of Ovid's *Ibis* 165–72 has led some to speculate that both Catullus and Ovid were borrowing from the *Ibis* of Callimachus, now lost: Fordyce is rightly suspicious (1961, 396), conceding that this may be the case, but noting demurely that "such commonplace vituperation perhaps need not have so distinguished an ancestry." Godwin (1999, 217) reminds us that this brutal squib is sandwiched between two love poems; but we cannot be sure that the juxtaposition was Catullus's own doing.

109   Inevitably, in English translation this poem looks more optimistic than it does in Latin. The Latin terms for "pact" *(foedus)* and "friendship" *(amicitia)*, especially when juxtaposed, as in the final line, normally mean a *political* alliance or treaty (cf. Vinson 1992, 163ff.), though as we have seen (note to 76; cf. Lyne 1980, 33ff.) Catullus tries to adapt them to a new kind of emotional relationship. But as Godwin asks (1999, 217–18), and Catullus surely wondered apropos his own situation, "Did any *foedus* last for ever? Or any *amicitia*?" And when did the gods ever show interest in promoting the fidelity of mortal lovers? Catullus's poem sub-

verts its own desperate hopes, not least that of "quasi-spousal fidelity" (Skinner 2003, xiv).

110   There is a thematic connection between this poem and 103: Aufillena, too, has re-
neged on a sexual contract. She has not taken money (Thomson 1997, 547 is right
here, against Fordyce 1961, 398 and Godwin 1999, 218), which would class her
among the "honest whores" with whom Catullus compares her unfavorably. But
she *has* taken presents, and in Catullus's book this presumes the acknowledgment
and acceptance of a relationship. Either say No, like a modest lady, he adjures her,
or keep your side of the bargain: otherwise your conduct is worse than that of a
common prostitute (*meretrix*, 6–8). Note that Aufillena at least claims to be free-
born: *ingenuae* (line 5) means this, as well as "frank" or "open." The conventions,
Catullus is arguing, must be observed.

111   This final insult to Aufillena matches those made against Gallus (78) and Gellius
(74, 88, 89), which neither proves nor disproves its factuality. Thomson (1997,
548–49) and Goold (1989, 218–19, 233) both jib at translating *fratres* as "cousins"
rather than "brothers," and Goold uses Wiseman's 1963 emendation *ex patre
concipere* to have Aufillena's incest produce offspring by her father. But *fratres* can,
in fact, be used in the sense of *fratres patrueles*, "cousins" (cf. Plaut. *Poen.* 1069),
and in any case Catullus's marked predilection for gilding (or in this case dirty-
ing) the lily would not hesitate to make mere avuncular incest look like its more
heinous paternal variant.

112   This little epigram has provoked countless interpretations, but seems to me com-
paratively simple. The sense does not call for Haupt's emendation of the MSS' *de-
scendit* to *te scindat* in order to provide a suitably obscene *dénouement*. Of the var-
ious senses of *multus*, a simple one applies here: "a lot of man," i.e., "a macho guy
(homo)." In line 2 Naso may be *multus* still, but—in the Latin sense!—he's no
homo. What he *is* is only made apparent in the very last word of the epigram: *pathi-
cus*, a passive homosexual. Naso stands revealed as that paradoxical character well
known to Juvenal (2.8–23): the "butch" queen, who conceals his fem instincts be-
hind a show of ultramasculinity.

113   Despite Thomson's reservations (1997, 550; cf. also Fordyce 1961, 400), I am con-
vinced by Pleitner's emendation *Mucillam* for *Maeciliam* at line 2. It makes Pom-
pey himself and Caesar the two original lovers, the first of whom divorced her
(see glossary s.v. Mucilla) for adultery with the second. That this was an old ca-
nard when Catullus wrote the squib is irrelevant; the point is Mucilla's continu-
ing sexual activity, despite the passing years (Pompey's first consulship was in 70,
his second in 55, thus the earliest possible date for the poem) and another mar-

riage, to M. Aemilius Scaurus. For the background see glossary s.v. Pompeius
Magnus.

114   Once again, Prick's shortcomings surprise: rather than his sexual activities, at 103
it was his bogus literary aspirations that were attacked, this time it is his spend-
thrift habits. These last far outrun any income he might derive from his country
estate—itself allegedly the product of profiteering on a grand scale (cf. 29). Crit-
icism of this kind of financial irresponsibility is orthodox Epicureanism. The
"bankrupt from Formiae" (41.4, 43.6) was fair game.

115   Prick's pretensions—like those of Trimalchio (Petron. *Sat.* 53)—far outrun the
actuality: seventy-plus acres with some sea hardly stretch up to the Hyperboreans
and Ocean. There seems, at first sight, something overblown about the rhetoric,
and the implication that Prick's prick is his biggest possession of all comes, on this
interpretation, as bathetic exaggeration. But look again. Both *pratum* ("meadow,"
"pasture") and *arua* ("arable land," "land under the plough") are regular Roman
euphemisms for the general area of the female pudenda. The word *maria* is the
plural, not only of *mare* ("sea"), but also of *mas* ("male" or "masculine"). *Iugum*
can mean acreage, but also the "yoke" of sexual subjection. If we read Catullus's
text in this way, Prick has a harem of over seventy women—not to mention
boyfriends on the side—all dominated by his gigantic member (cf. Thomson 1997,
552). I have tried at least to suggest all this double entendre (including the *maria*
pun) in my translation. The heavily alliterated final line is a parody of Ennius (fr.
620 Skutsch): *machina multa minax minitatur maxima muris*, thus allusively com-
paring Mentula's member to a siege ram battering in a city wall.

116   Both Thomson (1997, 554) and Quinn (1970, 455) regard this as an early poem,
the first of those addressed to Gellius, in which he looks back to a time when they
were friends (at least in a literary sense). Macleod (1973b, 308) calls it an "inverted
dedication." Also, interestingly, the hostility that has developed appears to have
been in the first instance that of Gellius towards Catullus rather than vice versa.
How reconciliation was to be achieved by means of translations from Callimachus
we are not told. The implication is that Gellius's own Greek was not up to snuff,
so Catullus's offer might not have been taken entirely in good part. The last line,
intriguingly, can be scanned as either a pentameter or an iambic trimeter of the
kind allowed in comedy (Macleod 1973b, 305), which suggests to Wray (2001, 189)
Catullus's assertion of his ability to master both genres.

     Godwin's efforts (1999, 222–23) to see these lines as offering a (paradoxical)
sense of closure to the whole collection are strained and unconvincing. More at-
tractive is Skinner's argument (2003, 20–28) that Catullus is here renouncing Cal-
limachean aesthetics for more traditional literary (and political) activities, sym-

bolized by the verbal echo in the last line *(tu dabi[s] supplicium)* to the angry words addressed by Romulus in Ennius's *Annales* to his brother Remus after the latter jumped over his half-built city wall *(mi calido dabis sanguine poenas,* 1.94–95 Skutsch). Yet the echo is problematical, and the point of the allusion (if allusion it be) ambiguous. In the last resort I find the earlier consensus, that here we have one more piece of evidence that Catullus was not responsible for the final ordering of his corpus, a good deal more persuasive.

GLOSSARY

ACHAEA, -AN 64.366. Originally a district of southern Thessaly, and in historical times the name of a state in the northeast Peloponnese; but "Achaeans" in Homer and elsewhere, including Catullus's reference here, was employed as a general equivalent for all the Greeks fighting at Troy.

ACHILLES 64.338. The son of Peleus and Thetis (qq.v.), and the most eminent Greek warrior in the Trojan War, Achilles is the central figure of Homer's *Iliad*. Though he killed his Trojan opposite number Hector, and guaranteed a Greek victory, he himself died (as he had foreseen) at the hands of Paris, with the aid of Apollo. See also s.v. Polyxena.

ACME See s.v. Septimius.

ADONIS 29. The young lover of Aphrodite/Venus, often connected with death and rebirth in the natural cycle; but Fordyce (1961, 162) is surely right that at 29.8 "the white dove and Adonis are both Venus's pets."

ADRIA, ADRIATIC 4, 36. As today, the long narrow stretch of sea between the Balkan peninsula and Italy; Adria, then a seaport near the head of the gulf, is now some miles inland.

AEËTES 64.3. Mythical king of the realm of Colchis on the east shore of the Black Sea, father of Medea, and guardian of the fabulous Golden Fleece sought by Jason and the Argonauts.

AEGEUS 64.212. Father of Theseus (q.v.) by Aethra, daughter of King Pittheus of Troezen. When Theseus forgot to change his black sails for white on returning from Crete, Aegeus in despair threw himself from the Acropolis rock.

AEMILIUS   97. It is impossible to identify this Aemilius, not only because of the dearth
of evidence, but on account of the plethora of candidates. We are looking for a
man near Catullus's age, who fancied himself a Don Juan, was inordinately con-
ceited, probably moved in the same circles, and may indeed have been a sexual
rival. The most amusing identification is with the triumvir M. Aemilius Lepidus,
born c. 89 and thus a slightly older contemporary of Catullus, who was related
to Catullus's friend L. Manlius Torquatus, and was regarded as lazy and vain.
But the poem's Aemilius could equally well have been his elder brother, L. Aemi-
lius Paullus, or—perhaps most likely—the poet Aemilius Macer, who wrote di-
dactic works on birds, snakes, and medicinal plants, and hailed from Catullus's
home town of Verona. Quintilian (1.5.8) says Catullus imported the word *plo-
xeni* (6) from the Transpadane region, which would fit the context and suggests
an early poem.

AFRICA   61.199. To Catullus and his contemporaries, the term "Africa" normally meant
the Mediterranean coastal littoral from Egypt through Libya and Cyrenaica as far
as Carthage. Sometimes, however, "Africa" was used to denote the whole conti-
nent, insofar as this was then known.

AGANIPPE   61.30. A celebrated fountain, beside the road approaching the grove of the
Muses on Helicon, supposed to inspire those who drank from it.

ALFENUS VARUS, P.   30. A native of Cremona in Cisalpine Gaul, Alfenus Varus, Porphy-
rio claims (but such smears were common), had a humble start in life, as either a
barber or a cobbler. He rose to become, eventually, the first Cisalpine consul (39).
He studied law under Servius Sulpicius, and invented the title *Digests* for legal ab-
stracts, of which he produced forty books.

"ALLIUS"   See s.v. Manlius Torquatus, L.

AMARYNTHUS   64.395. A town on the west coast of Euboea, about five miles from Ere-
tria, and famous for its sanctuary of Artemis, who was thus referred to as "Amaryn-
thine" or "of Amarynthus."

AMASTRIS   4. The capital of Paphlagonia, on the south coast of the Black Sea, close to the
eastern frontier of Bithynia, and, like neighboring Cytorus (q.v.), the source of
good shipbuilding timber.

AMATHUS   36. A town on the south coast of Cyprus, one of the oldest on the island and al-
legedly autochthonous, Amathus was celebrated for its cult of Aphrodite.

AMEANA 41. Nothing is certain about this woman, except, as we learn from 43.6, that—like so many of Catullus's acquaintances—she was a northerner, from Cisalpine Gaul. Even her name is dubious; it has to be either scribally corrupt or (less probably) archaic or provincial in its spelling. No suggested emendation is convincing. Neudling (1955, 3) is confident that she was a Roman courtesan, but Quinn (1972, 235–36) makes an excellent case for her having been an upper-class lady using the only means left to cover her mounting debts (cf. Sall. *Cat.* 24–25).

AMPHITRYON 68b.111. Son of Alcaeus, king of Tiryns, and married to Alcmene, daughter of Electryon, king of Mycenae. In Amphitryon's absence Zeus, taking on his likeness, bedded and impregnated Alcmene. On his return the next day Amphitryon likewise had intercourse with her. In due course she bore twins, Iphicles by her husband, and the hero Heracles (Hercules) by Zeus.

ANCONA 36. A city on the Adriatic, still with the same name today, located on a promontory at the extreme northern end of Picenum.

ANDROGEOS 64.77. The son of Minos, and a famous wrestler, killed in Attica during the hunting of the Marathon bull. It was as a reprisal for his death that Minos imposed on Athens the annual tribute of youths and maidens destined as fodder for the Minotaur.

ANTIMACHUS 95. Of Colophon, a scholar-poet of the late fifth and early fourth centuries B.C.E., author of, *inter alia*, a twenty-four-book epic *Thebaïd*, clearly designed to rival Homer's *Iliad* (which he also edited, claiming his predecessor as a fellow Colophonian). He also published an elegy, *Lyde*, in two or more books, on his wife or mistress of that name. Despite his erudition and love of obscure myths, which made him a direct ancestor of the Hellenistic literary avant-garde and their successors, the Roman Neoterics, Antimachus was not popular with either group. His poems were too long: Callimachus referred scornfully to "fat inelegant Lyde," and the *Thebaïd* clearly was held to typify the "big book big evil" syndrome.

ANTIUS 44. Unknown. There is a C. Antius Restio represented on coins of 49–45 (Fordyce 1961, 201), who was the author of a sumptuary law which limited the dining-out rights of magistrates (Macrob. 3.17.13, Aul. Gell. 2.24.13). Since Sestius seems to have entertained on a lavish scale, this Antius would have been a suitable target for his attack (Mulroy 2002, 35).

AONIA, -ES 61.27. The Aones (traditionally descended from Aion, son of Poseidon) occupied the rich plain surrounding Thebes in Boeotia. Roman poets were fond of using "Aonia" as a more euphonious synonym for "Boeotia." The Muses, who haunted Mt. Helicon in Boeotia, also sometimes received the epithet.

APHRODITE   See s.v. Venus.

APOLLO (ALSO PHOEBUS)   64.299. Catullus's sole reference to the famous Olympian deity, twin brother of Artemis, is to point out that he was absent from the marriage of Peleus and Thetis, a far from universally accepted view (and for the absence of Artemis there is no support at all).

Why should he thus abstain? As a supporter of Troy, which of course the son of this marriage, Achilles, was fated to overthrow? But, equally, Apollo is fated to slay Achilles. Earlier sources had Apollo not only attending the wedding (Hom. *Il.* 24.63, Pind. *Nem.* 5.41) but also singing, like the Fates in Catullus's poem, of blessings to come (Aesch. fr. 450, Plat. *Rep.* 383b). Thetis thus had reason to complain of his treachery since, granted his divine foresight, he must have known in advance his own role in Achilles' death. Godwin is therefore right when, in an excellent note (1995, 164), he observes that Catullus "shows Apollo either as a god of integrity—or as a god with an already burning hatred of Achilles."

AQUARIUS   66.94. The zodiacal constellation, no. 32 in Ptolemy's star list.

AQUINUS   14. One of the archaizing poets and stuffy annalists whom Catullus never tired of mocking, Aquinus defies identification. If he is the same as the Aquinius mentioned by Cicero (*Tusc.* 5.63), he was not only a bad poet but quite exceptionally conceited.

ARABIA, ARABS   11. Roughly congruent in Catullus's day with the modern Arabian peninsula, Arabia extended north as far as Mesopotamia and the Levantine coastal strip of Syria.

ARGOS, ARGIVE   64.4, 68b.87. A city in the southern part of the Argive plain in the Peloponnese, and in Homer the kingdom of Diomedes. The term is often used in a general sense of the realm of Diomedes' overlord, Agamemnon of Mycenae. In historical times, Argos was a constant rival of Sparta's for control of the Peloponnese.

ARIADNE   64.57, 61, 248, 253; 66.60. Daughter of Minos and Pasiphaë, she fell in love with Theseus and helped him in his endeavor to kill the Minotaur by providing a ball of twine to let him retrace his steps out of the Labyrinth. However, when they fled Crete together, he abandoned her on Dia (q.v.), from where she was rescued by Dionysus. The crown she wore at their wedding was transferred to the heavens as the Corona Borealis (Ptolemy's star chart no. 6).

ARRIUS   84. Convincingly identified as the boring, self-made, wordily prolix orator Q. Arrius wittily dissected by Cicero (*Brut.* 242–43); see now Skinner (2003, 104–107). Since he is there stated to be an adherent of Crassus, it is reasonable to suppose that his posting to Syria took place in 55 as a result of Crassus's incipient Eastern campaign. It also means we have to take him seriously: he had been praetor in 73, and campaigned successfully against Spartacus in 72/1. He was dead before 46 (Neudling 1955, 9). He had stood for the consulship in 59 with the support of Crassus, but was defeated, and took the defeat hard (Cic. *Att.* 2.7.3).

ARSINOË   66.54. Born c. 316, daughter of Ptolemy I Lagos, Alexander's marshal who won Egypt after the king's death, Arsinoë had a colorful marital life. Her first husband (m. 300/299) was another marshal, Lysimachus. On his death in battle (281), she wed her half brother, Ptolemy Keraunos. Murderous and ambitious, she met her match in Keraunos, who killed two of her children and came within an ace of killing her. She fled to Egypt, where she finally married her full brother, Ptolemy II Philadelphos, thus instituting a tradition of royal sibling marriages. After her death (270), she became semidivinized as an avatar of Isis (and, it would seem, of Aphrodite; cf. Zephyrion).

ARTEMIS   See s.v. Diana/Artemis.

ASIA   46, 61.21, 66.36, 68b.89. For Catullus and his Roman contemporaries, this term meant the province of Asia, consisting of coastal Asia Minor from the Hellespont down to Cnidus, and extending inland to the frontiers of Bithynia, Galatia, Lycia, and Pisidia, thus including both central and Hellespontine Phrygia.

ASINIUS MARRUCINUS   12. The black sheep, napkin-pilfering, elder (12.2) brother of Asinius Pollio. The family was not only of plebeian origin (from Teate, some ten miles inland from Aternum on the Adriatic coast south of Picenum), but as recently as 90 had been fighting against Rome on the side of the Latins, in the Social War. "Marrucinus" refers to the territory of the Marrucini, where they lived.

ASINIUS POLLIO, C.   12. Born in 76, and thus, properly, a "boy" *(puer)* in Catullus's friendly reference to him c. 60/59, Asinius Pollio was to become one of the great literary arbiters of the Augustan age. In the Civil Wars, he supported first Caesar, then Antony. In 41 he saved Virgil's property in Cisalpine Gaul from confiscation. Consul in 40, he campaigned in Illyria in 39, was awarded a triumph, and built Rome's first public library with the spoils. Primarily a historian (of the Civil Wars down to Philippi, 60–42), he also wrote tragedies and erotic verse. A friend of Horace as well as of Virgil, and in youth of Cinna as well as Catullus, he was an Atticist as an orator, and notorious for his sharp criticism of other literary figures, particularly for rhetorical excesses: it was he who complained of Livy's provincialism (*Patavinitas*, i.e., "Po-ishness").

ASSYRIA, -AN 66.12, 68b.144. Properly the region beyond the upper Tigris, today eastern Iraq. Roman poets, whose geographical knowledge tended to be hit-and-miss, frequently confused Assyria with Syria (q.v.), the coastal region of the central to northern Levant. This is true of 66.12; 68b.144 remains ambiguous.

ATALANTA 2b. Exposed at birth and reared first by bears, then by woodsmen, the mythical heroine Atalanta decided (perhaps not altogether surprisingly), when she grew up, to remain a virgin huntress. At the Caledonian boar hunt Meleager fell in love with her. At the funeral games for Pelias, she wrestled his son Peleus and beat him. She offered to marry any man who could beat her in a footrace (losers were put to death). Milanion (or Hippomedon: the suitor's name is uncertain) won by dropping golden apples—a well-known love token, cf. 65.19—on the track, which Atalanta stopped to pick up.

ATHOS, MT. 66.46. The easternmost of three long peninsulas running from Chalcidice southeast into the Aegean, Athos terminates in a precipitous mountain over six thousand feet high, today known as the Aghion Oros ("Holy Mountain") and home to a number of Orthodox monasteries. Prior to Xerxes' invasion of 480 B.C.E., the Persians dug a canal through the neck of the peninsula at its narrowest point, a little east of Acanthus, to avoid having to sail round the storm-ridden promontory.

ATTIS 63. In myth, the Phrygian, youthful consort and eunuch devotee of the Anatolian mother goddess Cybelé. Catullus, however, uses a variant version in which Attis is an athletic Greek youth who, in his enthusiasm for the cult, castrates himself and joins the Gallae, only later to bitterly regret his irreversible act. "Attis" was also the generic name for one of these acolytes, so perhaps we are to think of the poem's central figure as *an* Attis (so Kroll 1922, 130), though the personal identification is strongly stressed. In any case this Attis is not the deity.

AUFILLENUS, -A 100, 110, 111. Examples of this rare name are mostly from Catullus's homeland, including two from Verona; it is reasonable to assume that this brother and sister were Veronese, of good family, and (on internal evidence) teenagers at the time of Catullus's poems concerning them.

AURELIUS 11, 15, 16, 21, ?24, ?81. This friend of Catullus's and colleague of M. Furius Bibaculus (q.v.) cannot be identified with any certainty. The *gens Aurelia* was plebeian, of Sabine origin. Its most common branch under the Republic seems to have been that of the Cottae, and many of these migrated to Cisalpine Gaul (Neudling 1955, 19), where Catullus's Aurelius and the poet may have met. A M. Aurelius Cotta, a Pompeian, was praetor in 54 and later served in Sardinia and Africa. He could have been Catullus's Aurelius, but this remains pure speculation.

AURUNCULEIA, JUNIA (? VIBIA)   61.16, 82. Her name is all we know of L. Manlius Torquatus's bride, and as Neudling says (1955, 185), and all scholars agree, "even that poses problems." Both "Junia" and "Aurunculeia" are *gens* names, *gentilicia*, and freeborn Roman women of the Republic did not, for obvious reasons, have two of these. Two suggestions have been made: (i) that she was by birth Aurunculeia, but later passed into the *gens Iulia* by adoption (most recently Fordyce 1961, 237); (ii) that "Junia" was a mistaken scribal correction of the Oscan *praenomen*, "Vibia," (Syme ap. Neudling 1955, 185). Either is possible; (i) is perhaps marginally more likely.

BACCHUS, BACCHANTS   64.61, 251, 390. Roman Bacchus was directly based on Greek Dionysus (also known as Iacchos), and was like him a god of wine, intoxication, and ecstasy, though somewhat more benign, less dangerous in his epiphanies. The same applies to the bacchants—also known as maenads and thyiads (qq.v.)—who escorted him on his revels, hair dishevelled, dancing wildly, each carrying the ivy-twined, pinecone-tipped thyrsus that was, as it were, their wand of office.

BALBUS   67.3. The Balbi were clearly a local family from the Verona/Brescia area, in which the majority of inscriptions referring to them are located (Neudling 1955, 22). More than that we cannot say with any certainty. Neudling (1955, 23) speculates that the younger Balbus of 67 may have been L. Herennius Balbus, in 56 one of the accusers of Caelius Rufus (on whose possible connection with 67.45–48 see note ad loc.).

BATTUS   7, 65. The semilegendary founder and first king of Cyrene. His rather odd name was variously explained as the Libyan word for "king" (Herodotus) or as a nickname, "stammerer." His tomb stood in the city center, and he was the object of a hero cult. The poet-scholar Callimachus claimed descent from him, and thus used his name as a patronymic (65.16).

BERENICE   66.8, 57, 89. Born c. 273, daughter of Magas of Cyrene and Apame, daughter of Antiochus I of Syria, Berenice (II) married Ptolemy III Euergetes (q.v.) in 246, soon after his accession (for the rather grisly antecedent circumstances see note to 66.27–28), and is mostly remembered for the lock of hair she vowed (and subsequently dedicated) to secure victory for her husband during his campaign in Syria against Seleucus II. When the lock vanished, the astronomer Conon affected to rediscover it catasterized as a star cluster between the constellations Leo and Virgo. Berenice survived until the accession of her son Ptolemy IV in 221; one of his first acts, not long after, was to have his mother executed.

BITHYNIA   10, 25, 31. A region of varying size abutting on the coast of northwest Asia Minor. What Catullus and his friends meant by Bithynia was the newly constituted province of Bithynia and Pontus, established by Pompey in 63, and running from the Propontis as far as Trapezus, with Phrygia and Paphlagonia along its southern frontier. Economically prosperous, rich in forests, pasturage, orchards and marble quarries, Bithynia also had a flourishing shipbuilding trade, as well as good harbors and road communications. The proconsuls who governed it in Catullus's time, as well as the *publicani* who farmed the taxes, reckoned to make a very good profit on their term of office, and Catullus's poems about his time there clearly reflect this.

BLACK SEA   See s.v. Pontus.

BOLOGNA/ BONONIA   59. An ancient town about one hundred miles northwest of Ariminum (modern Rimini) on the Via Aemilia. A natural road junction, and originally an Etruscan foundation named Felsina, Bononia afterwards became in turn a Latin colony and a *municipium*.

BOÖTES   66.67. A constellation north of the zodiacal belt (no. 5 in Ptolemy's star chart) including the bright star Arcturus.

BRESCIA/BRIXIA   67.31. A town of Cisalpine Gaul at the foot of the Alps, about fifteen miles west of the southern end of the Lacus Benacus (modern Lago di Garda) and Catullus's Sirmio.

BRITAIN, BRITONS   11, 29, 45. The invasions of Britain by Caesar in 55 and 54 made the island a contemporary talking point (and trope for poets) in the last years of Catullus's life.

CAECILIUS (I)   35. Both the elder and the younger Pliny were Caecilii, and from favored stock transplanted to the new colony of Novum Comum (q.v.) by Caesar in 59: thus several editors have played with the pleasant fancy that this Caecilius, young poet and lover, may have been their ancestor. More tempting is the case of Caecilius Epirota, the freedman of Cicero's correspondent Atticus, who later in life ran a school for poets (Suet. *De Gramm.* 16).

CAECILIUS (II)   67.9. This house owner of Verona cannot be identified, though many Caecilii are recorded from the area, which supports the notion that he was a real person. Della Corte (1989, 229) argues that the Caecilii and the Valerii were Verona's two leading families. Macleod's thesis (1973b, 298ff.) that he was the red-eyebrowed gentleman at the end of the poem is neat, if unprovable; it would explain his mention in line 9, and, for those in the know, give point to the conclusion.

CAECILIUS (III) (Q. CAECILIUS METELLUS CELER)   A rigid and pompous aristocrat from a family rich in consuls but now beginning to disintegrate, Metellus Celer is not an attractive character. Cicero did him political favors, to which he replied with class-based insults. A dyed-in-the-wool optimate, he broke with Pompey when the latter divorced Mucia (Metellus's half sister) for alleged sexual offenses. His marriage of convenience to his cousin Clodia (q.v.) was not a success. Consul in 60, he died, conveniently, in March 59, before he could take up his provincial governorship of Transalpine Gaul. Cicero encouraged the suspicion that Clodia had poisoned him, but this is unlikely.

CAELIUS RUFUS, M.   ?58, 69, 71, ?73, 77, ?100. It is reasonably certain that this is both Catullus's Caelius and his Rufus (with the possible exceptions of 58, 73, and 100). Both the date and place of his birth are disputed; the first could be as early as 88/7 (confirmed by his senatorial career), but is put by the Elder Pliny (*NH* 7.165), probably erroneously, in 82; Interamnia (modern Teramo) has been suggested for the second. His father, an *eques*, sent him c. 72 (Wiseman 1985, 62) to be trained in forensic oratory by Cicero and M. Licinius Crassus. From early youth he was notorious for his dissolute and dandified lifestyle. In 63 he appears as a supporter of Catiline. It was in 59, after his successful prosecution of C. Antonius Hybrida (Wiseman 1985, 64 with n. 54), that he rented the house of P. Clodius Pulcher on the Palatine, to be at the heart of things and run for public office. It was also now that he became involved with Q. Metellus Celer's widow (and Catullus's great love) Clodia, described by Cicero as "the Medea of the Palatine," and by himself, after their affair ended in 56, as "a two-bit Clytemnestra": she seems to have provoked mythical comparisons. Their breakup was partly responsible (contra Dorey) for Clodia's role in having him prosecuted the same year for public violence, including murder; Cicero led for the defense and got him off. (Cf. L. Gellius Poplicola for further ramifications of this case; detailed analysis in Wiseman 1985, 54–91.) In 50 he was aedile, and we have his gossipy letters to Cicero in Cilicia, reporting sexual scandals, and soliciting panthers and cash subventions for his games. He died in 48 after raising an abortive insurrection, cut down by cavalrymen whom he was, characteristically, attempting to bribe. Tall, handsome, well-read, witty, cynical, pragmatic, and unswervingly self-interested, he fit very well into the highly articulate personal politics of his time, and remains, against expectations, a not altogether unsympathetic character. Difficulties of identification are well set out in Arkins (1983, 306ff.).

CAESAR, C. JULIUS   11, 29, 54, 57, 93. Catullus must have known Caesar from an early age, since he was a regular guest and friend at Catullus's father's house in Verona. Caesar's military exploits seem to have excited Catullus's admiration (11.9–12). So perhaps did his rapacious booty hunting as governor of Further Spain in 61 (it is possible that the Spanish tour of duty by Fabullus and Veranius was under Caesar, who enjoyed having literary intellectuals on his staff). Catullus's chief complaints against Caesar (well summarized by Neudling, [1955, 90]) are (i) sexual perversion, a stock charge; (ii) unjustifiable largesse to socially undesirable subordinates; and (iii), the most serious (and best justified) claim, that his progressive exploitation of personal power from the mid-50s was anticonstitutional and aimed at subverting senatorial rule. Yet though Catullus and his circle were firmly against the early triumvirate, in many other ways they shared Caesar's views. His pared-down literary style ("Atticism") matched theirs, as did his Epicurean abhorrence of excessive rhetoric, and he probably knew Philodemus through his father-in-law, L. Calpurnius Piso.

CAESIUS   14. Identity uncertain: several men of this name (some perhaps related) are known to have been friends of Cicero. There was his fellow townsman, M. Caesius from Arpinum, aedile there in 47; L. Caesius, who was with him during his proconsular residence in Cilicia (50); Sex. Caesius, an *eques*, whose honesty he praises; P. Caesius, another *eques* from Ravenna, with whose father he seems to have had a close friendship (the father could have been M. Caesius, praetor in 75). However, the preferred candidate (Neudling 1955, 41) is a T. Caesius, student (along with Alfenus Varus and others) of Servius Sulpicius Rufus, eminent jurist, close friend of Cicero, and (like so many Roman public figures) a dabbler in philosophy and light verse.

CAESONINUS, L. CALPURNIUS PISO   28, 47. About the same age as Cicero, Piso began his career as an adherent of Caesar, who married his daughter Calpurnia (c. 59). He obtained the consulship himself the year after Caesar (58), and in 58/7, as a reward for not backing Cicero against P. Clodius Pulcher, was allotted Macedonia as his province. It was here that Veranius and Fabullus served under him (57–55); there is no evidence that their Spanish tour of duty (?60/59) was with Piso. Their testimony, as reported by Catullus, concerning Piso's rapacity, indiscriminate Don Juanism, and meanness to his staff matches the charges brought against him by Cicero (Neudling 1955, 43). It is significant that he, like Memmius (q.v.) was both a poetaster and an Epicurean; it is highly likely that he was the original owner of the House of the Papyri in Herculaneum, which contained a collection of the works of Philodemus, his mentor. It looks as though in the mid-50s Rome's *jeunesse dorée* sought service with governers known for their Neoteric literary preferences and Epicurean views. It also would seem from Catullus that experience of such persons at first hand tended to be disillusioning. After reluctantly holding the censorship in 50, Piso refused to commit himself in the Civil Wars, and "apparently subsided into a decorous Epicurean retirement" (Neudling 1955, 45), dying c. 43.

CALLIMACHUS 65, 116. The Greek scholar-poet par excellence to whom the Neoterics looked for inspiration and guidance, Callimachus held a senior position in the Alexandrian library, and was in effect a court poet under both Ptolemy II Philadelphos and Ptolemy III Euergetes, from the 280s to the 240s. He believed in scholarly allusiveness coupled with elegant brevity (his aphorism, "Big book, big evil," became famous). Of his eight hundred books (size was a no-no, quantity clearly wasn't), only six *Hymns* and a handful of epigrams survive intact, but we have substantial fragments of his *Aitia* ("Origins") and of his epyllion *Hekale*, as well as enough of his "Lock of Berenice" (fr. 110) to give us a good idea of how Catullus went about translating it in 66.

CALLISTO 66.66. Daughter of Lycaon (or, in other accounts, Nycteus or Ceteus; alternatively, she may have been a nymph). All that is really agreed upon about Callisto is (a) she was a hunting companion of Artemis; (b) Zeus got her pregnant; (c) she was metamorphosed into a she-bear; and (d) she was finally catasterized as the Great Bear constellation (Ursa Major). Whether Zeus, Hera, or Artemis was responsible for (c) and/or (d), and why, is quite uncertain: *quot capita, tot sententiae.*

CALVUS, C. LICINIUS MACER 14, 50, 53, 96. One of Catullus's closest friends, and (by all accounts) the Neoteric poet most akin to him in publications and temperament. Like Catullus, he wrote epithalamia, a mythical epyllion (on Io), elegies, and satirical squibs and epigrams; he also attacked Caesar, referring to Nicomedes of Bithynia as his "sodomizer" *(pedicator)*. Later writers (Horace, Propertius, Ovid, Pliny, Aulus Gellius) not surprisingly bracketed the two poets together. The small, ebullient (53.5), sexually promiscuous (Ovid, *Tr.* 2.431–32), high-strung·Calvus was born in 82, son of the annalist C. Licinius Macer, and died young, not long after Catullus, and certainly before 47. A courtroom lawyer as well as a poet—he and Cicero were well acquainted—Calvus prosecuted P. Vatinius on several occasions, from 58 onwards. In 54 he was busy attacking the Caesarian Drusus and defending Pompey's supporter C. Cato. He left twenty-one books of speeches, now lost. His wife Quintilia (who predeceased him, and for whom he wrote a memorial elegy, cf. 96.6 and Prop. 2.34.89–90) may have been related to Quintilius Varus, Catullus's friend from Cremona (Neudling 1955, 105).

CAMERIUS 55, 58b. The Camerii were Etruscan by origin, but strongly represented in Rome. Neudling (1955, 46) cites an inscription (*CIL* I² 793) of 45/4 describing a

Cornificius (very probably the addressee of 38) whose sister Cornificia is married to a Camerius; ten years earlier this Camerius (if the identification is right) could have been one of Catullus's tight-knit circle of intimates. This kind of intermarriage would, in the circumstances, be very natural.

CANOPUS   66.57. A port in the Egyptian delta, about fifteen miles from Alexandria, at the mouth of the Nile to which it gave its name ("Canopic").

CASTOR   4, 68b.65. Brother of Helen and Pollux (q.v.), son of Leda and Tyndareus (or, alternatively, of Zeus), famous for his skill with horses, as Pollux was for boxing. Both brothers took part in the Calydonian boar hunt and the voyage of the Argonauts. They were widely regarded as the protectors of sailors and sea travellers; their cult came early to Rome, where they were thought to have helped the Romans against the Latins at the battle of Lake Regillus (496 B.C.E.).

CATO   See s.v. Valerius Cato.

CECROPS, CECROPIAN   64.78, 172. One of the first mythical (and supposedly autochthonous) kings of Attica, who gave the country its early name of Cecropia. Though traditionally represented as a snake from the waist down, he was regarded by Athenians as their first tribal ancestor and a great civilizer, who introduced such things as writing and monogamous marriage.

CHALYBES   66 (48). A people located on the southeast coast of the Black Sea (Pontus), between Sinope and Trapezus, and famous, both in legend and history, as early miners and ironworkers.

CHARYBDIS   64.156. A whirlpool or maelstrom in the strait near Sicilian Messana, famous from Homer's *Odyssey,* and seemingly (unlike the rock of Scylla opposite) based on some kind of natural conflict of currents, however exaggerated.

CHIRON   64.278. Son of Kronos and Philyra, Chiron was traditionally the best and wisest of the semi-equine Centaurs dwelling on Mt. Pelion, and the instructor—in hunting, medicine, music, and gymnastics—of the youthful Achilles, as well as being his great-grandfather: Chiron's daughter Endeia was the mother of Peleus (q.v.), whose life Chiron saved.

CICERO, M. TULLIUS   49. Though mentioned directly only once (and then rather ambivalently) by Catullus, the famous orator, politician, and littérateur (106–43 B.C.E.), always a staunch upholder of the senatorial Republic, was intimately connected, personally and through the courts, with many of Catullus's circle, especially during the decade 60–50. In 58 he was briefly exiled (till September 57) through the machinations of P. Clodius Pulcher, and thus probably relished defending Caelius a couple of years later in the case brought by Clodia and her brother. Much of our—arguably exaggerated—knowledge of Clodia derives from his speech (the *Pro Caelio*) written on that occasion. His approval of the Neoterics was guarded, however, and after Catullus's death he voiced his dislike of the extreme preciosity and obscurity associated with the Greek poet Euphorion.

CIEROS   64.35. A Thessalian town (thus in Strabo 9.5.14, C.435: more properly Cierion), roughly in the center of the Thessaliotic plain.

CINNA, C. HELVIUS   10, 95, 113. Cisalpine native of Brescia/Brixia, near Verona, and a close friend of Catullus, Cinna was a notoriously obscure *doctus poeta* in the Neoteric group (Wiseman 1974, 44–58). His work—not least his *Zmyrna* (95: nine years in the making)—needed elucidatory commentaries (in particular one by L. Crassicius [Suet. *De Gramm.* 18]) to be understood. He seems to have begun it c. 64—the year after he acquired the Greek poet Parthenios of Nicaea as a family tutor (Neudling 1955, 79; Suda s.v. *Parthenios*); Parthenius, too, treated the Smyrna/Myrrha myth. Cinna accompanied Catullus to Bithynia and probably sailed home with him in his cutter, complete with litter-bearers and the MS of Aratos's astronomical poem, the *Phainomena*. Tribune (at a latish age) in 44, he was lynched by the mob at Caesar's funeral in mistake for the anti-Caesarian L. Cornelius Cinna (Plut. *Brut.* 20). As Wiseman (1974, 58) says, "it is a particularly brutal irony that in Cinna's case the people accidentally had the last word."

CLODIA METELLI   Born c. 94, second (?) daughter of Ap. Claudius Pulcher, and sister to C. Clodius Pulcher (q.v.), her junior by a couple of years. The date of her marriage to her cousin, Q. Metellus Celer (q.v. s.v. Caecilius III) is unknown: it certainly took place before 62, but how long before, and even if it was her first marriage, remains uncertain. Wiseman (1985, 24) guesses at a betrothal c. 82 and marriage in 79, which seems a little early; 75 might be nearer the mark. (They had a daughter, Metella, who inherited her mother's reputation.) Famous for her beauty (Cicero called her "ox-eyed," Homer's epithet for Hera), she was, despite scholarly doubts (e.g., Wiseman 1985, Skinner 1983) almost certainly the model for Catullus's Lesbia. She probably met him in 61, and their on-again, off-again relationship seems to have lasted almost till Catullus's death c. 54. Her other lovers included M. Caelius Rufus, whom Cicero defended in 56 against charges largely instigated by Clodia herself, making her a laughingstock in the process. Till then she had been constantly involved in political affairs (Skinner 1983, 277ff.); after the trial she vanishes from public life. (For one last glimpse of her, in her fifties, see s.v. Lesbia ad fin.) Much, though by no means all, of the evidence against her was clearly hyped up by her enemies. It used to be the fashion to believe all of it; today conventional wisdom has gone to the other extreme and dismisses it wholesale as fiction. The truth, as always, lies somewhere in the middle. As a high and arrogant aristocrat she pleased herself, in sex as in other matters.

CLODIUS PULCHER, C.　? 79. Born c. 92, youngest child of Ap. Claudius Pulcher. As a lifelong radical aristocrat, he has come down to posterity painted by the propaganda of his enemies as "mad, bad, and dangerous" (to borrow Caroline Lamb's characterization of Byron). For a general effort at rehabilitation, see Tatum 1999: but there is too much hard, factual evidence to avoid the conclusion that, like his notorious sister, Clodius followed his fancy (the charge of incest between them was probably inevitable, and could have been true; cf. 79 with note), and was a ruthless political infighter into the bargain, quite capable of organizing the street brawls in one of which he lost his life (52). As early as 68 we find him inciting the troops of his brother-in-law, L. Licinius Lucullus, to mutiny. In May 61 (the year of his quaestorship), he was on trial for gate-crashing the rites of the Bona Dea disguised as a woman, but got off through bribery. In 59 he got himself adopted into a plebeian *gens* for populist advancement ("Clodius" rather than "Claudius" was the plebeian spelling of his name), and celebrated his election as tribune in 58 with a distribution of free grain and the exile of Cicero. After several years of savaging Pompey (see, e.g., Plut. *Pomp.* 48.7), he did a U-turn and supported both Pompey and Caesar in 55. He was running for the praetorship when he was killed, and the mob which he had used so often during his lifetime responded by burning down the senate house after his death. See also s.v. Lesbia, -us.

CNIDUS　36. Dorian city of southwest Asia Minor, located on a long peninsula in the Gulf of Cos.

CNOSSOS 64.172. A major settlement and palace of Bronze Age Crete, famous in myth as the seat of Minos and location of the Labyrinth that housed the Minotaur.

COLCHIS, COLCHIAN　64.5. A mountain-ringed, roughly triangular delta of well-watered plain (its main river, the Phasis) on the east coast of the Black Sea; in myth the kingdom of Aeëtes, the possessor of the Golden Fleece, and thus the destination of the Argonauts.

COMINIUS　108. Identity doubtful. Cominii turn up frequently both in Cisalpine Gaul and at Rome. Cicero knew of two brothers, P. and C. (or L.) Cominius from Spoletium (modern Spoleto), who in 66 and 65 twice attempted to prosecute a popular ex-tribune, C. Cornelius (too early for this to be the Cornelius of 102, as is sometimes alleged); on the first occasion they were mobbed, on the second they failed to appear, and were said to have been bought off. By 46 P. Cominius was dead. His age would be right for the target of 108, and he was certainly unpopular, but it is hard to see why Catullus should suddenly take against him ten years or more after his cause célèbre was over.

CONON   66 (7). Third century B.C.E. astronomer and mathematician from Samos, friend of Archimedes, and probably a resident scientist of the Alexandrian Museum under Ptolemy II Philadelphos and his successor Ptolemy III Euergetes (q.v.). It was the latter's wife, Berenice, who dedicated a lock of her hair to her husband's military success; when it disappeared, Conon declared it had been catasterized as a star cluster (the "Coma Berenices") between the zodiacal constellations of Leo and Virgo.

CORNELIUS (I) NEPOS   1, ?102. Like Catullus, from Cisalpine Gaul (perhaps a native of Ticinum), but some years older (? c. 110–24 B.C.E.), a close friend of Atticus, and, through him, of Cicero. Nepos kept clear of political life and devoted himself to literature. He wrote an encyclopedic collection of some four hundred lives of prominent men, *De Viris Illustribus*, a three-volume universal history, *Chronica* (1.5), and some light verse. Of the first a little survives, including *Lives* of Cato and Atticus, and the section on "Distinguished Foreign Leaders;" all else is lost. He was an advocate, perhaps even a patron, of the young Neoterics.

CORNELIUS (II)   67.35. The identity of this local adulterer is unknown, but Cornelii were common in Brescia/Brixia, and he may have been from there.

CORNIFICIUS, Q.   38. The youth to whom Catullus turns in distress in 38 (and who may have been his lover, 38.8) has been convincingly identified as Q. Cornificius, orator, rhetorician, poet, and member of Catullus's Neoteric circle (Ovid, *Tr.* 2.435–36). His sister Cornificia (cf. Camerius) was also a poet. He married Catiline's widow in 50, was quaestor in 48 (and thus a supporter of Caesar). After 44, he switched sides (partly as a result of his intimacy with Cicero), and was killed in Africa, deserted by his troops (whom he had contemptuously written off as "hares in helmets," *galeatos lepores*), fighting for the Senate at Utica. As Fordyce says (1961, 183), "he reminds us at once how small Catullus' world was and how little we know of it."

CRANNON   64.36. A Thessalian town southwest of Larissa.

CRETE, -AN   58b; 64.75, 83, 175. The largest island in the Aegean (about one hundred sixty miles in length), and the chief link in the partially submerged landmass extending from Cythera to Kasos, Karpathos, and Rhodes, Crete is still known today as "To Megalónisi" ("The Great Island"). It is rich in ancient mythic tradition (see, e.g., Minos, Pasiphaë, Ariadne, Theseus), a legacy ultimately of its unique Bronze Age Minoan civilization, centered on Cnossos.

CROESUS   115. The last king of independent Lydia (reigned c. 560–546 B.C.E.), he was defeated and captured by Cyrus the Great of Persia. He is regularly used as a proverbial example of vast wealth.

CUPID, LOVE   3, 36, 45, 64.95, 68b.134. Cupid (and Amor, "Love") were the Roman equivalents of Greek Eros: the concept of erotic desire, personified as a mischievous *putto* whose arrows pierced susceptible hearts, inducing passion.

CYBÉBÉ / CYBELÉ   63.9, 12, 35, 67, 75, 83, 90. The great Phrygian mother goddess, whose worship was particularly connected with the mountain regions of Dindymos and Ida, and was associated with the cult of her youthful lover Attis, after whom her priests were named. A goddess of the wild, she was worshipped in ecstatic rituals akin to those of Dionysus. Her cult, as Magna Mater (Great Mother), was brought to Rome at a time of crisis (205/4), but under the Republic remained carefully controlled and limited.

CYCLADES, CYCLADIC ISLES   4. The group of islands in the central Aegean of which the best known are Naxos, Paros, and Mykonos.

CYLLENE, -AN   68b.109. A high mountain (modern Ziria: 7,788 feet) in northeast Arcadia, near the Achaean frontier; celebrated as the birthplace of Hermes.

CYRENE   7. Chief city of the Greek foundation of Cyrenaica on the north African coast, occupying the great promontory immediately west of Libya.

CYTÓRUS   4. A coastal town, backed by a mountain range of the same name, on the south shore of the Black Sea, between Amastris and C. Carambis in Paphlagonia. The whole region was heavily forested (its boxwood was famous), and supplied the local shipbuilding industry.

DARDANIA, -AN   64.367. Part of the Troad (never well defined) which Dardanus obtained by marriage to King Teucer's daughter, Batia, and renamed Dardania; but the name is frequently used by poets, Catullus included, as a generic synonym for Troy or the Trojans.

DAULIS, DAULIAN   65. An ancient settlement in Phocis, near the Boeotian frontier, on the old road from Orchomenos and Chaeronea to Delphi. In mythical times, its king was Tereus, father of Itylus (q.v.).

DELOS, DELIAN 34. The smallest of the Cycladic islands, in the strait between Rheneia and Mykonos, Delos (originally known as Ortygia, Quail Island) early became an international religious sanctuary, chiefly as being the place where Leto gave birth to Apollo and Artemis.

DELPHI, -IAN 64.392. The scenically stunning position of Delphi is in the higher reaches of the Pleistos valley, cupped between the two great rocks of the Phaedriades on the southern reaches of Parnassos, and overlooking the Gulf of Corinth. In antiquity it was known as the navel *(omphalos)* of the world, one of the great Panhellenic sanctuaries, and internationally famous as the site of the Delphic oracle.

DIA 64.52, 121. A small, rocky island about six miles north-northeast of Herakleion and Cnossos on Crete, and clearly the site of Ariadne's abandonment by Theseus according to the earliest legends (it also lies on the direct route from Crete to Piraeus). By the Hellenistic age, however, an alternative version had developed which identified Dia as Naxos, and explained the name change by claiming that Naxos had originally been called Dia, or vice versa. See Thomson (1997, 400–401), who notes the greater suitability of Naxos for the scene of Ariadne's abandonment (sandy beaches, greater distance from Crete, etc.).

DIANA/ARTEMIS 34, 64.395, 66.5. Diana, an Italic goddess of hunting, healing, and the wild, was later, inevitably, identified with Greek Artemis, and also associated with the moon and childbirth. In Catullus's day her shrine and grove at Aricia by the Lago di Nemi were famous, and much visited.

DINDYMOS -ENIAN 35, 63.90. Dindymos (more properly Dindymon) was a mountain above Pessinos in northeast Phrygia, and a famous center of the cult of Cybelé.

DRYADS 64.287. Tree nymphs, originally associated with Arcadia, and (as their name indicates) particularly with oaks. See also Hamadryads.

DYRRACHIUM 36. Formerly Greek Epidamnos, Dyrrhachium (modern Durazzo) was a busy port on the Illyrian coast opposite Brundisium (modern Brindisi).

EGNATIUS 37, 39. The name is probably Samnite in origin, and the *gens Egnatia* is common in Italy during the Republic. Neudling (1955, 58–64, following Baehrens 1885, 219), makes a very plausible case for Catullus's Egnatius having been a Roman citizen, scion of a family that had earlier emigrated to Spain but now returned (hence the characteristic sneers at his Iberian provincialism), and probably to be identified with the Epicurean poet Egnatius, author (like Lucretius) of a didactic *De Rerum Natura*. The cultivation of literary Epicureanism seems to have been a factor uniting the group to which Catullus, Cinna, Caelius Rufus (qq.v.), and their associates belonged.

EMATHIA   64.304. Originally a district of Macedonia west of Pella, but afterwards used by synecdoche as a poetical synonym for all Macedonia, and finally also for Thessaly, which is how both Catullus and, later, Lucan employ it.

ERECHTHEUS   64.211, 229. Together with Cecrops, regarded as the mythical ancestor of the supposedly autochthonous Athenian people, and an early king of Athens.

ERYX, MT.   64.71. A mountain and settlement in western Sicily above Drepana (modern Trapani), famous in antiquity for the cult of Aphrodite/Venus (i.e., Astarte) located there, including the practice of ritual prostitution.

ETHIOPIA, -AN   66.53. A fairly loose term in antiquity, including not only modern Abyssinia but also the Sudan and neighboring regions.

ETNA, MT.   68b.53. The famous, and still active, volcano of eastern Sicily, over ten thousand feet high, located between Tauromenium (modern Taormina) and Catana (modern Catania).

ETRURIA, ETRUSCAN   39. The area of Etruria proper began immediately to the northwest of Rome and extended as far as Liguria, bounded to the west by the Tyrrhenian Sea and to the east by Umbria. The Etruscans were the most important indigenous group in early Italy, with their own language and culture. For a period their Tarquin dynasty ruled in Rome.

EUROTAS, R.   64.89. The central river of Laconia, the Eurotas rises in the mountains south of Megalopolis, and flows the whole length of the plain between the mountain ranges of Parnon and Taygetos, passing through Sparta and debouching in the Aegean at a point northeast of the port of Gytheion.

FABULLUS   12, 13, 28, 47. One of Catullus's most enduring friends, but unidentifiable: his name is Etruscan in origin, and he may have belonged to the Fabii Fabulli, but all we really know about him (and even that has been fiercely debated) is his service with Veranius (q.v.), first in Spain (? 61 or 60, perhaps with Caesar) and later, in all likelihood, in Macedonia under L. Calpurnius Piso Caesoninus (58/7–55).

FALERNIAN   27. A famous vintage wine, so named from the coastal *Falernus ager* in northern Campania, near the Appian Way, where its vineyards were located.

FATES, FORTUNE   64.169, 306, 383; 68b.85. In Roman thought these semipersonified powers of luck and destiny tended to be confused one with the other.

FIRMUM   114. A town in Picenum, about forty miles south of Ancona and six miles inland from the Adriatic, on the rich coastal plain.

FLAVIUS   6. The Flavian *gens* was plebeian, its members widespread in Rome and central Italy during the late Republic. All we can say about Catullus's friend is that in 56 he was young, well off, occupying his own house, probably of good family, and preparing for a public career. Neudling (1955, 67) guesses that he may have been L. Flavius, suffect consul for 33, but he could equally well have been the C. Flavius who in 57 was mentioned by Cicero as a friend of his son-in-law, C. Calpurnius Piso, and who died fighting with Brutus at Philippi in 42.

FORMIAE   41, 43. A flourishing Roman municipal community, on the coast by the Appian Way, about midway between Tarracina and Minturnae and some seventy-five miles from Rome. Formiae was the hometown of Catullus's pet aversion, Mamurra.

FUFIDIUS   54. An acquaintance of both Cicero and Horace, who, in a satire largely devoted to the disadvantages of adultery, mocked Fufidius for his money-lending activities (*Sat.* 1.2.12–17).

FURIES   64.193. Sometimes known as the Erinyes or (euphemistically) as the Eumenides, or "Kindly Ones," the Furies were chthonian agents of retribution for familial offenses, bloodguilt in particular, hounding down the guilty and executing the curses laid on them by those wronged.

FURIUS BIBACULUS, M.   11, 16, 23, 26. The identification of this poet from Cremona as Catullus's Furius is very plausible. He was born in 82 (Jerome puts his birth in 103, but is clearly confusing C. Marius's third consulship with that of his son, also a C. Marius: see Neudling 1955, 71), and thus a year or two younger than Catullus. He was on close terms with Valerius Cato, and attacked both Caesar and, later, Octavian in scurrilous lampoons. He also, however, wrote a historical epic on the former's Gallic campaigns—not very Neoteric, this, but what he and Catullus seem to have shared was a taste for scurrility. Lyne (1978, 171 n. 13) also identifies him with the poet "Alpinus" satirized by Horace (*Sat.* 2.5.40–41, with Acro's commentary); this is plausible.

GALLI,-AE   63. The eunuch priests and acolytes of Cybelé: the feminine form is used by Catullus to emphasize the notion of emasculation. See also s.v. Maenads.

GALLUS   78. Unidentifiable, but probably (like so many of Catullus's characters) to be located, because of his cognomen, in Cisalpine Gaul. Neudling (1955, 74) hazards a guess that he may have been the Caninius Gallus who was tribune of the plebs in 56, "a riotous and troublesome influence."

GAUL, GALLIC   11, 29, 42, 43. Caesar's campaign in 55 must have made Transalpine, or "long-haired" *(comata)* Gaul a talking point among Romans, as Catullus's references suggest.

GELLIUS [POPLICOLA], L.   74, 80, 88, 89, 90, 91, 116. Born c. 80, son of L. Gellius, first consul in the history of the *gens Gellia* (72) he was—contrary to what might have been guessed from Catullus—"indisputably and formidably *nobilis*" (Tatum 1997, 499; cf. Wiseman 1974, 124–29), and thus Catullus's social superior in an uneasy friendship. As a radical young man—Cicero (*Vat.* 4) called him "a revolutionary wet-nurse"—Gellius moved in the group that included both Catullus and M. Caelius Rufus; he, too, enjoyed Clodia's favors (91). In 56 he was involved in the prosecution of Caelius by Clodia and her brother. Caelius was accused, *inter alia*, of defrauding Gellius's stepmother Polla, whom Valerius Maximus (5.9.1) reports that Gellius seduced. Catullus's charges of indiscriminate incest against Gellius thus gain some confirmation. He switched sides during the Civil Wars, and ended up commanding a wing for Antony at Actium in 31. Since he is not heard of again, he probably died in the action.

GOLGI   36, 64.96. A town some ten miles east-northeast of Idalium in central Cyprus, and like it a cult center of Aphrodite, traditionally established even before that of Paphos.

HAEMONIA, -AN   64.287. Poetic synonym for Thessaly, -ian, derived from the eponymous Haemon, son of Pelasgus and father of the equally eponymous Thessalus.

HAMADRYADS   61.23. Wood nymphs whose lives were coexistent with those of the oaks or other lofty wild trees which they inhabited.

HARPOCRATES   74, 102. In Hellenized Egyptian cult, the son of Isis and Serapis, "Horus as child," frequently portrayed, in temples, as an infant with one finger to his lips, enjoining silence.

HEBE   68b.116. Daughter of Zeus and Hera, cupbearer, with Ganymede, for the gods, and the bride reserved for Hercules on his posthumous assumption into the divine Olympian pantheon.

HELEN   68b.87. The femme fatale whose abduction by Paris provoked the Trojan War, Helen was married to Menelaus of Sparta. Her bizarre genesis was from an egg, the result of Zeus as swan fertilizing either Nemesis (q.v.) as goose (the egg being cared for and hatched afterwards by Leda), or else (the better-known version) Leda in her own person. The fact that swans, almost alone among birds, were known to be intromittent may have encouraged this odd myth: egg births are normally restricted to cosmogonies.

HELICON 61.1, 28. A mountain range in southwest Boeotia, forming an eastward spur or extension of Parnassus, between Lake Copaïs and the Corinthian Gulf. Helicon was closely associated with the Muses; they had a sacred grove there, and two fountains, those of Aganippe and Hippocrene, the waters of which, when drunk, were supposed to stimulate inspiration.

HELLESPONT 64.358. The long narrow channel, today the Dardanelles, connecting the Aegean with the Propontis (q.v.).

HERCULES   68b.112. Roman assimilation of the renowned Greek hero Heracles, performer of the Twelve Labors, and after his death inducted to the Olympian pantheon.

HESPER(US)   62.1, 20, 26, 32. The Evening Star, personified as a son of Astraeus and Eos (the Dawn). His parentage is a reflection of the fact that he was, from early times, also identified with the Morning Star.

HOLY CHILD   See s.v. Harpocrates.

HORTENSIUS HORTALUS, Q.   65, ?95. Prominent Roman orator and supporter of the *optimates*, born 114 and died 50/49, thus some thirty years older than Catullus. (Thomson 1997, 526 raises the possibility that Catullus's sometimes Neoteric [65], sometimes prolix [95] friend was not this Hortensius, but his wealthy and profligate son, known to us only from disapproving references in Cicero's letters. My own guess would be that 65 refers to the father, who sympathized with the Neoterics, 95 to the son.) He affected the florid "Asianic" style (though he had never studied in the East), and was an unscrupulous advocate, resorting to both bribery and intimidation. Nevertheless, his defense of Verres in 70 was defeated by Cicero. He dabbled in literature, writing erotic poems among other things (Plin.J. *Ep.* 5.3.5; Ovid *Tr.* 2.441–42), as well as (on a bet) a historical epic about the Marsian War in the style of Ennius (Plut. *Luc.* 1.5), but he affected a distaste for the close study of philosophy. Like his friend L. Licinius Lucullus, he was a famous gourmet.

HYMEN   61, 62. The ancient god of marriage, probably in the first instance extrapolated
from the marriage hymn (Hymenaeus) rather than the other way round. The son
of Apollo and one of the Muses (which one remains uncertain: Catullus, like Cal-
limachus, picked Urania), Hymen was portrayed, not surprisingly, as a good-
looking young man. Mythographers, however, saw him as being of mortal ori-
gin, and told various far-fetched etiological tales about his evolution into a
divinity.

HYPERBOREANS   115. A mythical people, perhaps based on scraps of fact that trickled down
the Baltic amber route, who lived in a kind of Nordic Shangri-la, a terrestrial par-
adise "at the back of the North Wind," and worshipped Apollo, who (surprisingly
for a Mediterranean deity) was reputed to spend his winters there.

HYRCANIA   11. A country to the immediate south of the Caspian Sea, but whether Catul-
lus knew this is dubious. As Fordyce says, Catullus's "notions of the geography
behind these fabulous oriental names are no more precise than those of other Latin
poets" (1961, 126).

IACCHUS   See s.v. Bacchus.

IDA, MT.   63.30, 69. An extended mountain range of the southern Troad, extending west-
ward above the north coast of the Gulf of Adramyttion as far as Assos.

IDALIUM   36, 61.17, 64.96. A town of central Cyprus, ten miles south-southeast of Ledros
(modern Nicosia), and about midway between Temessos and Kition, which later
absorbed it. It had cult centers of Athena and Apollo as well as the better-known
one sacred to Aphrodite.

IDRUS   64.300. Eponymous founder (?) of the town of Idrias in Caria, a cult center of Di-
ana as Hecate (Fordyce 1961, 314–15). Mulroy (2002, 73) identifies Idrus as "a by-
name for Apollo," but does not state his source, and I know of none.

ILIUM   See s.v. Troy.

INDIA, INDIES   11, 45. By Catullus's lifetime, the monsoon sea routes to and from India
were becoming established, and Romans had begun to acquire a reasonable knowl-
edge of the great subcontinent, though myth (e.g., in the Alexander Romance) still
predominated.

IONIAN SEA   84. The stretch of water immediately below the Gulf of Tarentum (modern
Taranto) and the heel of Italy.

IPSIT(H)ILLA   32. The name is otherwise unattested. Suggestions are implausible. For Neudling (1955, 87) she is Hypsicilla/Ipsithilla, i.e., the "little wench" of P. Plautius Hypsaeus, a friend of Libo's and candidate for the praetorship in 56. Quinn (1970, 188) identifies her, via the diminutive/familiar -*illa* name ending, with the "merry maid" (sic) Aurelia Orestilla , who married Catiline (and may have been his illegitimate daughter). For Garrison (1991, 111) she is "an independent courtesan, a hetaera with her own house." As Godwin crisply remarks (1999, 149), no identification is needed to appreciate this "ironical invitation poem in which the invitee invites himself to be invited."

ITONUS   64.228. A town of Phthiotis in Thessaly, with a famous temple of Athena.

ITYLUS   65.14. Itylus or Itys was the son of King Tereus of Daulis by his wife Procne. Tereus raped Procne's sister Philomela, and cut out her tongue to silence her. Philomela wove a representation of the rape into a tapestry, which Procne saw and understood. In her rage, she killed Itylus and served him up as a dish to his father. Tereus found out what she had done. The sisters fled, with Tereus in hot pursuit. But the gods quickly metamorphosed all three of them into birds: Philomela became a swallow, Procne a nightingale (some sources reverse these transformations), and Tereus a hoopoe.

JUNIA   See s.v. Aurunculeia.

JUNO   68b.138. Ancient and important deity in the Roman pantheon, of uncertain origin, but early equated with Greek Hera, and made the consort of Jupiter, with whom and Minerva she formed the "Capitoline Triad." She attracted and assimilated various external cults, including that of Juno Lucina (34), a goddess of childbirth in Latium.

JUPITER, JOVE   7; 55; 64.21, 171; 66.48; 68b.140. Chief deity in the Roman pantheon, with a temple on the Capitoline Hill: generally equated with Greek Zeus.

JUVENTIUS   ?15, ?21, 24, 48, 81, 99, ?103. Catullus's young boyfriend cannot be firmly identified, but the *gens Iuventia*, of Etruscan origin, turns up in Verona (as does the *gens* of Aurelius, see 15 and 16). The Juventii were "an old and well-known consular family at Rome in this period" (Neudling 1955, 94).

LADAS   58b. A Spartan long-distance Olympian runner, whose name became proverbial for speed, and who died in the moment of victory.

LANUVIUM, -AN   39. An ancient city of Latium (modern Lanuvio), about twenty miles from Rome, in the southern Alban Hills, a little off the Appian Way.

LAODAMIA   68b.73, 80, 105. The wife of Protesilaüs (q.v.): inconsolable after his early death in the Trojan War, she had a statue of him made with which she consorted. When her father put a stop to this, she committed suicide.

LARISSA   64.36. In antiquity as today, an important Thessalian town situated in a fertile plain on the south bank of the River Peneius.

LATMOS, MT.   66.5. A mountain range of Caria, about twenty miles inland from Miletus, where, in myth, the Moon kissed the sleeping Endymion.

LEO   66.65. The zodiacal constellation (no. 26 in Ptolemy's star chart) located beyond Virgo and the Lock of Berenice (Coma Berenices; cf. Fordyce 1961, 338, for chart).

LESBIA, -US*   2, 3, 5, 7, 8, 11, 43, 51, 58, 68b.68, 70, 72, 75, 76, 79*, 83, 85, 86, 87, 91, 92, 104, 107, 109. We are told by Apuleius (*Apol.* 10) that Catullus's "Lesbia" was a cryptonym—the only one in his collection—for a woman named Clodia. The only contemporary family known to us which used this plebeian form of the name (rather than Claudius/-a) was that of Appius Claudius Pulcher, consul in 79, who died prematurely, impoverished and out of political favor, leaving three sons and three daughters. The youngest son was P. Clodius Pulcher (q.v.), an unscrupulous aristocratic activist whose "*potentia* was grounded in family strength and his own political investments" (Tatum 1999, 71), and who caused a scandal in 61/60 by gate-crashing the rites of the Bona Dea disguised as a woman (Tatum 1999, 59–88), helped engineer the exile of Cicero (Tatum 1999, 151–58), first attacked and then defended the triumvirate of Caesar, Pompey, and Crassus, and, in January 52, was murdered by T. Annius Milo during a clash between their rival street-gangs.

The first line of Catullus's 79 runs *Lesbius est pulcher*, "Lesbius is pretty." But of course it is very tempting also to take it as saying "'Lesbius' is [P. Clodius] Pulcher." In that case "Lesbia" can be identified as one of the three Clodia sisters. Nor (*pace* Wiseman 1985, 15–53 and elsewhere) is it hard to decide which one. When Catullus's affair with "Lesbia" began, about 61, she was still living with her husband (83). The eldest Clodia's husband died before 61; the youngest was divorced by L. Lucullus for adultery on his return from the East in 66/5. We are left with the most famous and notorious Clodia, scion of a blue-blooded family that had been consular for twelve generations, no less, and thus socially far superior to a provincial rentier whose family was in business. Clodia was the wife of her cousin, Q. Caecilius Metellus Celer, rightly described by Fordyce (1961, xv) as "dull and pompous," a career soldier who was governor of Cisalpine Gaul in 62/1, when Catullus probably first met him and his attractive dark-eyed wife, now in her early thirties, and thus about ten years older than the poet.

Metellus became consul (60/59) but died almost immediately after leaving office. Clodia's behavior, even before his death, had been so scandalous that she was rumored to have poisoned him (it was not long since he had threatened to kill her wayward brother with his own hands unless he behaved himself). In addition to Catullus (if she was in fact "Lesbia;" this identity, still a subject for debate, has been well defended recently by Mulroy 2002, xi–xvii), she took as her lover Catullus's erstwhile friend, M. Caelius Rufus, a good reason for Catullus's later animus against him. She was also suspected of an incestuous relationship with her equally notorious brother. Her character and affairs are luridly depicted by Cicero in his courtroom speech, *Pro Caelio*, in 56, defending Caelius against Clodia's accusations of battery and attempted murder (detailed analysis in Wiseman 1985, 54–91): an exaggerated portrait, but one instantly recognizable from Catullus's picture of her. After this, almost nothing more is heard of her except for Catullus's last desperate poems; and two years later Catullus himself was dead. But a decade later, in May 45, Cicero wanted, through Atticus, to buy her gardens on the Tiber. By then she was in her fifties. She had scads of money, and no need to sell. She was fond of the property, from which in her youth she had eyed attractive young men swimming (Cic. *Att.* 12.42.2). The offer was turned down. "And that is where we leave her, pleasing herself to the last, sumptuous in her park like a dowager duchess" (Wiseman 1985, 53).

LETO   34. Daughter of the Titans, Coeus and Phoebe, and remembered chiefly as the mother of the twins Apollo and Artemis.

LIBO   54. The only plausible candidate advanced as Catullus's target in 54 is the annalist, L. Scribonius Libo, a slightly older contemporary (born c. 90), and trusted adviser of Pompey, whose son Sextus married Libo's daughter c. 56 or 55. This Libo, like M. Caelius Rufus during the same period, spent recklessly to secure political advancement, and incurred huge debts. He stuck with Pompey till the latter's defeat at Pharsalus (48), went into retirement for a while, switched his support to Antony in 35, and became consul with him the following year.

LIBYA, LIBYAN   7, 45, 60. Strictly, the coastal zone of north Africa to the immediate west of Egypt, home of the indigenous Libyans, but frequently extended to take in Cyrenaica, and sometimes the whole North African littoral, from which developed the poetic habit of using "Libya" as a synonym for "Africa."

LICINIUS   See s.v. Calvus.

LIGURIA, -AN   17. A coastal region of northern Italy, between the frontiers of Gaul and Etruria. Originally the Ligurians had extended much further west, as far as Massilia (modern Marseilles); they were famous for their toughness and hardihood.

LOCRIS, LOCRIAN   66.53. A region of central Greece divided into two separate parts: Ozolian Locris lay wedged between Aetolia and Phocis, on the north coast of the Corinthian Gulf, with Naupactus on its west and Delphi to the east; Epicnemidian and Opuntian Locris lay away to the northeast beyond Doris, on the Maliac Gulf, east of Thermopylae.

LYCAON   66.66. Of uncertain parentage; king of Arcadia, and father of numerous sons, as well as of a daughter, Callisto (q.v.).

MAENADS   63.12, 23, 34, 68. In myth, ecstatically inspired, female devotees of the god Dionysus, who accompanied him on his peregrinations. The frenzied tearers and eaters of raw flesh best known from Euripides' *Bacchae* probably belong in this category, and it is what Catullus and similar poets have in mind. But there were actual maenads, too. In the winter of every second year, Greek women initiates took to the mountains for a ritual of wild, nocturnal dancing, ending in exhausted collapse. This kind of maenadism was essentially archaic, and had begun to die out by the Hellenistic period.

MAGUS   90. The Persian Magi were originally reciters of theogonies and guardians of religious oral tradition rather than priests. Later Greco-Roman tradition associated them with astrology and magic (the word derives from them). Strabo reports (15.3.20, C.735) that "it is ancestral custom for these [Magi] to have intercourse with their mothers" (cf. schol. Eur. *Androm.* 173–76).

MAMURRA   29, 41, 57, 94, 105, 114, 115 (treated, with the exception of 41, as a cycle by Deuling 1999, 188ff.). A Roman knight *(eques)* from Formiae, and the chief engineer *(praefectus fabrum)* for Caesar in Gaul from 58. Here, as earlier under Pompey in the Mithridatic War (66), he performed efficiently (a 1,500-foot bridge across the Rhine in ten days was no mean feat) and was amply rewarded: indeed, as Cicero reports (*Att.* 7.7.7), his rich pickings became a public scandal. He must have been with Caesar on the first invasion of Britain in 55, "acquiring further wealth and spending it more quickly than it came" (Neudling 1955, 112, apropos 29). The extravagant luxury of his town house on the Mons Caelia in Rome was notorious. Catullus also suggests he was a sexual libertine, as his nickname for him, "Prick" *(Mentula)*, suggests (94, 105, 114, 115: Holzberg 2002, 203–206 has a good analysis of him under the heading, "Bruder Schwanz"). But he was clearly an effective officer, and as Fordyce says (1961, 160), Catullus's complaints about his feathering his own nest would come better from a critic whose objections elsewhere (10.9–13, 28) were to provincial governors who failed to cut their subordinates, such as Catullus, a big enough share of the loot. Whether the charge of sexual relations with Caesar had substance, or was a mere literary canard on Catullus's part, is impossible to determine.

MANLIUS TORQUATUS, L.   61.19, 208, 214; 68a.11; ?68b.1, 66. Scion of an old and distinguished Roman patrician family, in Catullus's day in danger of becoming extinct (61.204–8) through lack of heirs. Born c. 90/89, he served under Sulla in the East. Early active as a prosecutor in the courts, he was a friend of Hortensius and a literary protégé of Cicero, who portrayed him in the *De Finibus* as an advocate of Epicureanism, and elsewhere described him as "elegant in speech, prudent in judgment, and altogether civilized" (*Brut.* 239). According to the younger Pliny (*Ep.* 5.3.5), he also, like many Roman aristocrats, composed erotic verses. His marriage to Junia Aurunculeia (q.v.) took place about 60 (Neudling 1955, 119). Praetor in 49, he fought against Caesar in the Civil Wars, and, after the senatorial defeat at Thapsus in 46, committed suicide rather than surrender.

MARRUCINUS   See s.v. Asinius.

MARS, MAVORS   64.394. The Roman god of war, next to Jupiter the most important deity in the pantheon. Inevitably, he was equated with Greek Ares, but seems originally to have been an agricultural guardian: for early Romans, fighting and farming always remained in a close nexus.

MEDES, MEDIA   66.43. Originally a mountainous kingdom immediately southwest of the Caspian Sea, flanking Assyria, which it conquered c. 612, Media was in turn absorbed, about the mid-sixth century, into the growing Persian empire of Cyrus the Great.

MELLA, RIVER   67 (32). A peaceful, winding river in Cisalpine Gaul, flowing down from the Alps into the Lombard plain near Brescia (ancient Brixia). Catullus puts its course through the city, whereas in fact it flows about a mile to the west of it. Ellis (1876, 318) speculates that either a branch of the Mella (still so named) once did flow through Brixia, or else that the city extended much further west in Catullus's day.

MEMMIUS, C.   10, 28. Born c. 100/98, he began his career as an adherent of Pompey, and was with him in Spain as quaestor (77). About the same time, he married Sulla's daughter, Fausta Cornelia. As praetor in 58 he fiercely attacked Caesar, and the following year went out as governor of Bithynia, with Catullus on his staff. In 55 he divorced Fausta. In 54 he was reconciled with Caesar and ran, unsuccessfully, for the consulship. In his youth he was an Epicurean (Lucretius dedicated the *De*

Rerum Natura to him, though apparently without snagging him as a patron) and also something of a poetaster: his bias was strongly in favor of Greek literature, and he therefore favored the Neoterics. He also wrote obscene epigrams, and was notorious for his advances to other men's wives. In 52 he was found guilty of electoral corruption and went into exile in Athens, where he seemingly turned against the Epicureans, since Cicero wrote him on their behalf with a request that he not destroy what remained of the philosopher's famous house and garden (*Ad Fam.* 13.1.3–4). He was dead by 46.

MEMNON 66.53. Son of Tithonus and Eos (Dawn personified), and king of Ethiopia. He took a large contingent to Troy to aid Priam, his uncle, and fought with great success, but was finally killed by Achilles in a duel marked by both combatants' mothers, Eos and Thetis, appealing to Zeus on behalf of their respective sons.

MENENIUS 59. Rufa's husband cannot be identified with any confidence, though there was a Menenius proscribed by the triumvirs in 43, who fled to Sicily with the help of a loyal slave who played the part of his master and was killed. Neudling (1955, 130) points out that the *gens Menenia* was old and patrician, but had been virtually in eclipse since the fourth century B.C.E.

MENTULA See s.v. Mamurra.

METELLUS CELER, Q. See s.v. Caecilius (III).

MIDAS 24. Mythical king of Phrygia who, when offered whatever he wanted by Dionysus (as a reward for the safe return of the god's henchman, Silenus), asked that everything he touched should turn to gold. The result was a severe eating and drinking problem. He also, when called upon to judge a musical contest between Apollo and Pan, declared Pan the winner; Apollo, with furious irony, gave him ass's ears by way of revenge.

MINERVA 64.395. Third member of the so-called Capitoline Triad of divinities, along with Jupiter and Juno. Since she was a virgin goddess of learning as well as of arts and crafts, she was very early on identified with Greek Athena.

MINOS 64.61, 85, 248. Mythical king and lawgiver of Crete, son of Lycastus and Ida, and brother of Sarpedon. He is connected with the tradition of Cretan naval conquests in and around the Aegean.

MINOTAUR 64.79. The semi-taurine monster produced by the miscegenation of Minos's wife Pasiphaë with a bull from the sea. It was kept in the Labyrinth, and fed on the flesh of the seven youths and maidens sent annually from Athens in recompense for the death of Minos's son, Androgeos, till finally Theseus killed it.

MUCILLA   113. Diminutive form of Mucia, the daughter of Q. Mucius Scaevola (cos. 95), and cousin to both Q. Metellus Celer (husband of Clodia, cos. 60) and Q. Metellus Nepos (cos. 57). She herself was Pompey's third wife, bearing him two sons (including Sextus Pompeius) and a daughter. Pompey divorced her in 62, after his Eastern campaign, for adultery with Caesar.

MURCIA   25. An obscure minor goddess of sloth: the correction is highly speculative.

MUSES   1, 65, 68a.7, 105. Goddesses, traditionally nine in number, who had music, literature, dance, and, oddly, astronomy under their patronage. Their habitat was Pieria and Olympus. The canonical nine Muses were: (i) Erato, lyric poetry, (ii) Calliope, epic, (iii) Melpomene, tragedy, (iv) Thalia, comedy, (v) Terpsichore, sung lyric and dance, (vi) Clio, history, (vii) Polyhymnia, hymns, (viii) Euterpe, flute playing, (ix) Urania, astronomy.

NASO   112. An unknown character, though the cognomen is not uncommon. Neudling (1955, 131–32) suggests that he may have been Sextus Pompeius, a supporter of Pompey who later took part in the conspiracy againt Caesar.

NEMESIS (SEE ALSO S.V. RHAMNUSIAN)   50. Daughter of Night and (?) Ocean, and closely linked with Aidos (personified Shame). The shrine of Nemesis at Rhamnous (q.v.) was famous from archaic times. From Pindar's day on, she was best known as a relentless avenger of human hubris and wrongdoing.

NEPOS   See s.v. Cornelius Nepos.

NEPTUNE   31; 64.2, 367. Chief Roman/Italic god of water (both fresh and salt), treated in antiquity as the approximate equivalent of Greek Poseidon.

NEREÏDS   64.15, 28. The fifty daughters of the marine deity Nereus and his wife, Doris: generally regarded as the saltwater nymphs of the Mediterranean.

NICAEA   46. The second city of Bithynia (modern Iznik) after the more northerly provincial capital of Nicomedia, Nicaea was founded (?316 B.C.E.) by Alexander's marshal Antigonus One-Eye (Monophthalmos) as Antigoneia, on the site of an earlier Greek settlement by Lake Ascania, but renamed by Lysimachus. It was laid out as an exact square grid, each side being about two miles in length. Its territory was rich, and its summers hot and humid.

NILE, RIVER   11. The central river of Egypt, admired in antiquity for its enormous length, the mystery of its source, and the way its annual inundation shaped and sustained Egyptian civilization.

NONIUS   52. Neudling (1955, 133–34) makes a good case for this having been M. Nonius Sufenas, Sulla's great-nephew, quaestor in 62, tribune in 56, an adherent of Pompey's (both then and during the Civil Wars) and supporter of Caesar and Crassus: probably rewarded with a curule aedileship in 55/4 (Fordyce 1961, 222), and the praetorship in 53/52, since in 51/50 he was a provincial governor (? of Macedonia). But the evidence is shaky: Gruen 1974, 315 n. 24 with references.

NOVUM COMUM   35. Some twenty-eight miles north of Mediolanum (Milan), in the foothills of the Alps, Comum (modern Como) was resettled in 59 B.C.E. by Caesar with five thousand colonists and renamed Novum Comum. The "Novum" was fairly soon abandoned, and 35 is thus probably to be dated in 59 or not long after.

NYMPHS   Young female divinities chiefly associated with rivers, springs, trees, caves and grottoes, mountains, or the sea.

NYSA   64.252. The traditional name of Dionysus's birthplace, or the original home of his cult. Homer placed it on the Thraco-Macedonian border; later traditions put it in Arabia or, more often, in India.

OCEAN   64.30; 66.68, 88, 115. The river thought of, in early Greek mythography, as encircling the world. Ocean(us) was personified as the offspring of Ouranos (Heaven) and Ge or Gaia (Earth), and as the father of the Oceanids and river deities.

OLYMPUS   62.1. The highest mountain in Greece (9,573 feet), on the frontier between Thessaly and Macedonia, and overlooking the Aegean, Olympus was traditionally regarded as the home of the gods.

OPS   64.304. Roman goddess of plenty and fertility; wife of Saturn.

ORCUS   3. The god of the underworld (synonymous with Hades or Dis), or, by extension, the underworld itself.

ORION   66.94. Of uncertain parentage, Orion was a famous hunter, and even more famous for his erotic exploits, including an attempt on Artemis, who killed him (accounts differ as to the circumstances). He was afterwards catasterized into the constellation south of the zodiacal belt, which bears his name (no. 35 in Ptolemy's star catalogue).

OTHO   54. The name is rare in the Republic, but not unknown. Neudling (1955, 135–36) tentatively identifies him as L. Roscius Otho, a tribune who in 63 had passed the *lex Roscia* restoring the first fourteen rows in the theater to the knights *(equites)*. A supporter of Crassus, he had opposed military commissions for Pompey (Gruen 1974, 187), but may have later worked for both men and Caesar.

PADUA   95. Ancient Patavium, about sixty-five miles east of Verona in Cisalpine Gaul, linked to the Adriatic by canal, was a flourishing center of the north Italian wool trade.

PARIS   68b.103. Second son of the Trojan king Priam and his wife, Hecuba, but exposed as a baby because of Hecuba's dream that he would be a firebrand that consumed Troy. Rescued and brought up as a shepherd on Ida, he became the judge in the competition among Hera, Athena, and Aphrodite (to whom he awarded the prize). Recognized by his father when identified by Cassandra, he proceeded to prove the oracle true by his abduction of Menelaus's wife, Helen, which resulted in the Trojan War.

PARNASSUS, MT.   64.390. A twin-peaked and massive mountain range, a southeast spur of the Pindus range, rising to some 7,500 feet, and extending from north of Delphi to the Corinthian Gulf. For the Greeks it was the haunt of Dionysus and his maenads. It was the Roman poets who associated it with Apollo and the Muses. Today it is a popular ski resort.

PARTHIA, PARTHIANS   11. Originally a small upland territory southeast of the Caspian Sea, ringed with mountains or desert, in Catullus's lifetime Parthia was the ruler of an empire stretching from the Euphrates to the Indus, with its capital at Ecbatana. The Parthians were skilled fighters, who made excellent use of heavy cavalry and mounted archers.

PASITHEA   63.43. An obscure figure of mythology: according to Homer (*Il.* 14.247ff.) one of the Graces, given as wife to Hypnos (Sleep) by Hera. Catullus seems here to be showing off the Alexandrian erudition that got him the epithet *doctus* ("learned").

PEGASUS   58b. The winged horse created from the drops of blood when Perseus decapitated the Gorgon Medusa, Pegasus was ridden by Bellerophon when he fought and conquered the Chimaera.

PELEUS   64.18, 26, 43, 301, 336, 382. Son of Aeacus, king of Aegina, and Endeia. Exiled by his father for fratricide, he went to Phthia where he was purified by Eurytion and married his daughter, Antigone. He then took part in the Calydonian boar hunt with his father-in-law, and accidentally killed him with his spear. After fleeing to Iolcos, he was purified a second time by Pelias's son Acastus; he also wrestled with Atalanta at Pelias's funeral games. Acastus's wife, Astydamia, fell in love with him; when he rejected her advances she informed Antigone that he was to marry Acastus's daughter, Sterope. Antigone hanged herself. Nothing daunted, Astydamia told Acastus that Peleus had tried to rape her. Acastus, uncomfortable at the thought of killing a man he had purified, took Peleus hunting on Mt. Pelion and took his sword while he slept, hoping he would become a prey to wild beasts. Instead, lucky as always, Peleus not only had his sword returned by Chiron, but was chosen to marry Thetis (q.v.). On his record he would not seem a good prospect as a husband for a mortal, let alone a goddess, and his bride's unwillingness to accept him is more than understandable. The marriage, though it produced Achilles, was not a success, though Peleus in extreme old age seems to have been reunited with Thetis.

PELION, MT.   64.1, 279. Pelion is a long mountain range, rising to about 5,300 feet and stretching right down the Magnesian peninsula, from immediately south of Ossa to the east side of the Gulf of Pagasae. A large cave near its summit was traditionally the home of Chiron the centaur. It is still thickly tree-clad, with oaks, planes, and chestnuts as well as pines; the area remains one of the most attractive in Greece.

PELOPS   64.346. Son of Tantalus and father of Atreus. To win the hand of Hippodamia, daughter of Oenomaüs of Pisa by Olympia, Pelops had to win a chariot race against her father (who, some sources say, fancied her himself). The penalty for failure (and there had been many such) was death. Pelops ensured victory by bribing Myrtilus, Oenomaüs's charioteer, to loosen the linchpin of one wheel in his master's chariot. However, after winning, he reneged on his promise (hence Catullus's "perjured"), and killed Myrtilus. Either Oenomaüs or Myrtilus, or both, cursed Pelops before dying. Rather unfairly, the curse skipped a generation, landing on Atreus. Pelops himself prospered, gaining mastery of the Olympic Games, and siring half a dozen sons on his expensive bride.

PENELOPE   61.220. The proverbially patient wife of Odysseus, she held out against the impetrative suitors of Ithaca till the return of her husband, after his ten years' absence in the Trojan War, and ten more spent wandering round the Mediterranean, more off than on the map.

PENÍOS   64.285. The eponymous god of the river of that name (more commonly Peneios), which winds its way across northeast Thessaly seawards through the vale of Tempe.

PERSEUS   58b. Mythical son of Danaë by Zeus (who appeared to her as, or in, a shower of gold). Among his many adventures was the acquisition of the Gorgon Medusa's head. To help defeat her, he received, *inter alia*, a pair of winged sandals from the nymphs, which enabled him to outpace the Gorgon in the air. See also s.v. Pegasus.

PERSIA, -AN   90. Originally the kingdom of Persis (Parsa) in the uplands to the south of the Zagros Mountains, but expanded to take in Media, Babylon, and other eastern realms (as well as western Asia Minor) under the Achaemenid dynasty founded by Cyrus the Great in the mid-sixth century B.C.E., and afterwards conquered by Alexander of Macedon (356–323).

PHAËTHON   64.291. Son of Helios, the sun god, by the Oceanid Clymene, wife of Merops. When Phaëthon learned his parentage, he sought out Helios in his palace and asked, as a special favor, to drive the solar chariot across the heavens for one day. But he was not strong enough to control the horses, which bolted with him and came almost close enough to earth to set it on fire. Zeus killed Phaëthon with a thunderbolt, and his charred body fell into the River Eridanos (Po), where his mourning sisters were turned into poplars and their tears into drops of amber.

PHARSALUS, PHARSALIAN   64.37. A strategically located and well-fortified hilltop city of southern Thessaly, close to the frontier with Phthiotis, with a fertile plain below it and easy access to the main north-south and east-west land routes of mainland Greece. These factors are responsible for its unbroken survival from prehistoric times until today.

PHASIS   64.3. The major river (modern Rioni) flowing through Aeëtes' ancient kingdom of Colchis on the east coast of the Black Sea, debouching near modern Poti.

PHENEUS   68b.109. A town in an enclosed valley southwest of Mt. Cyllene in northeast Arcadia. The waters of the River Olbius were carried out of this valley through a series of sinkholes in the limestone, aided by a canal supposedly excavated by Hercules.

PHILODEMUS   Greek Epicurean philosopher, poet, critic, and polymath (c. 110–c. 40/35 B.C.E.), lived in Rome and Herculaneum from about 75, enjoying the patronage of L. Calpurnius Piso Caesoninus and L. Manlius Torquatus, and the acquaintance of such figures as Cicero and, later, Horace. In addition to philosophical and literary treatises, he wrote highly erotic epigrams, some of which survive. His influence on Catullus and other Neoteric poets was considerable, not least in adapting Epicureanism to the Roman thirst for a public career.

PHOEBUS   See s.v. Apollo.

PHRYGIA, PHRYGIAN   46; 61.18; 63.2, 20, 22, 70; 64.344. The name covered two distinct areas. (a) Greater Phrygia lay in west-central Anatolia (Asia Minor), bounded to the south by Caria and Cilicia, on the west by Mysia, to the east by Galatia and Lycaonia, and in the north by Bithynia. (b) Lesser or Hellespontine Phrygia consisted of western Bithynia and the coastal strip south of the Propontis as far as the Troad. 46 refers to (b), 63 to (a); in 61 and 64 Catullus uses "Phrygian" as a loose synonym for "Trojan."

PHTHIOTIS, -IC   64.35. Phthiotis was a southern district (tetrad) of Thessaly; in fact Tempe (to which Catullus applies the epithet) is in the northernmost part of that state. Fordyce (1961, 283) points out that Callimachus makes a similar error (*Hymn* 4.112), and suggests that this was where Catullus took his information from.

PIPLA   105. Pipla, or Pimpla, a spring dedicated to the Muses, was on an eminence of the same name, on the northern, Pierian, side of Mt. Olympus. Colonel Leake in the nineteenth century identified it as Litókhoro, today the starting point for the ascent to the summit.

PIRAEUS   64.74. The rocky peninsula some five miles southwest of Athens, containing three natural harbors: Zea (Pasalimani) and Munychia (Mikrolimani) in the southeast; Kantharos, known as Megas Limen (the Great Harbor), on the northwest side. Together they formed—as they still do today—one of the largest harbor complexes in the Mediterranean.

PISO   See s.v. Caesoninus.

POLLUX   4, 68b.65. Son of Tyndareus (or Zeus) and Leda, and twin brother to Castor; called in Greece Polydeukes. Together the twins were known as the Dioskouroi, "sons of Zeus," and were best known for their appearances to succor storm-bound sailors (one of their manifestations being Saint Elmo's fire). They were also associated with athletics: Pollux/Polydeukes was a renowned boxer.

POLYXENA   64.368. The youngest daughter of Priam and Hecuba, sacrificed over the tomb of Achilles as a placatory offering to his ghost, and as a "bride" for him in the underworld, thus providing a grim closure to Agamemnon's sacrifice of Iphigenia at Aulis to get a fair wind for Troy: Iphigenia had been brought to Aulis under the impression that she was to marry Achilles.

POMPEIUS MAGNUS, CN.   55, 113. The famous general and politician, born 30 September 106 B.C.E., and thus a coeval of Cicero and slightly older than Caesar. As Neudling says (1955, 142) of both the poems that name him (and several others, e.g., 29 and 54, which may refer to him), "their chronology and significance are inevitably bound up with Catullus's attitude to the first triumvirate." In 62 Pompey returned from his Eastern campaign and won a triumph. He also divorced his third wife, Mucia, for adultery, allegedly with Caesar. Faced with opposition from Lucullus, whose military glory he had stolen, and the tribune M. Porcius Cato (see s.v. Porcius), he nevertheless turned to Caesar, who brokered an agreement between them and M. Crassus in 60/59. Pompey also then married Caesar's daughter, Julia. But his authority was being undermined (he had no army now to back him) and in 58/7 he was attacked by P. Clodius Pulcher. A year later he was given control of the grain supply (again, no army). In 56 the triumvirate was renewed, and Pompey became consul for 55 together with Crassus. Though awarded both Spanish provinces, he governed them through legates, from Rome. Accusations of political negligence and indifference were probably justified. On the excuse of Julia's ill health, he more or less withdrew from public life. Her death, in September 54, must have come at almost the same time as that of Catullus himself. It is against this political background that the poems involving him must be read.

PONTUS, PONTIC 4, 29. The Black Sea, together with its southern coastal regions, from Colchis in the east via Paphlagonia and Cappadocia to the Bosporus, and in poetic usage extending to cover modern Bulgaria and Romania (e.g., Ovid's Tomis) on the west coast.

PORCIUS 47. Was this the M. Porcius Cato who was tribune in 56 (Kroll 1922, Goold 1989)? Possibly, but evidence is wholly lacking. Godwin's comment (1999, 166) is worth noting: "Porcius ('piggy') is an appropriate name for one who dines all evening."

POSTUMIA, -US 27, 67.35. As often with Catullus (cf. Quintia, Aufillena), it looks as though we have to do here with a brother and sister, probably from Brescia, where the name is common, and thus part of Catullus's Cisalpine circle of friends.

PRIAPUS 47. Minor deity whose main function was as guardian of gardens, orchards, flocks and fields. He was normally represented as a scarecrowlike figure with a huge wooden phallus, his weapon against intruders. Short, obscene, ribald poems based on his supposed activities were known as "Priapea."

"PRICK" See s.v. Mamurra.

PROMETHEUS 64.294. Son of the Titan Iapetus, brother of Atlas, and father of Deucalion, he was best known for attempting to trick Zeus over the perquisites of a sacrifice, stealing fire from heaven, and ending up nailed to a rock in the Caucasus for his presumption, where an eagle regularly feasted on his (self-renewing) liver. Some sources, most notably Aeschylus in the *Prometheus Bound* (761–70; cf. Hyg., *Astr.* 2.15) also credit him, rather than Themis, with alerting Zeus to the prophecy that Thetis was destined to bear a son greater than his father, and thus discouraging the Father of Gods and Men from further pursuit of the sea nymph himself. Both as trickster and as a quasi-scientific defier of patriarchal divine authority, he has attracted a modern cult following.

PROPONTIS   4. The modern Sea of Azov, between the Hellespont (Dardanelles) and the Euxine (Black Sea).

PROTESILAÜS   68b.74. A mythical Thessalian warrior, famous (a) for having been the first Greek ashore (as his name implies), and the first casualty, in the Trojan War, killed by Hector; and (b) for the great passion between him and his wife, Laodamia, with whom (most sources assert) he had one night only of married bliss. That either or both were paying the penalty for starting the building of their house (still unfinished at the time of their marriage) before making the proper sacrifice is not attested elsewhere, but is a likely Hellenistic or Neoteric addition to the legend.

PTOLEMY III   66.11, 29, 35. Known as Euergetes, "Benefactor," he was born 284 B.C.E. to Ptolemy II Philadelphos and Arsinoë I, and reigned 247/6–221. He married Berenice II, daughter of Magas of Cyrene (Ptolemy II's half-brother), and Catullus (translating Callimachus) duly glorifies the Syrian campaign he undertook soon after his marriage (for its reasons and details see notes to 66.11–12, 35–36).

QUINTILIA   96. The recently deceased wife (not, as sometimes argued, mistress) of Calvus (q.v.).

QUINTILIUS VARUS   10, 22. The distinguished littérateur, born c. 75 B.C.E., a native of Cremona, friend not only of Virgil and Horace but also of the Epicurean scholar Philodemus. If, as Neudling suggests (1955, 152–53), Calvus's wife Quintilia was his sister, he would then have been Calvus's brother-in-law. It is possible, but not likely, that this Varus is not Quintilius but Alfenus (q.v.), also from Cremona, also a friend of Catullus's (30), and conceivably related to Quintilius.

QUINTIUS, -A   82, 86, 100. Unidentifiable members of Veronese or Brescian society, though most commentators agree that they are probably brother and sister.

RAVIDUS   40. Unidentifiable. Neudling's argument that he was "from the Umbrian territory near Ravenna" (1955) is highly speculative, and that he is Juventius's guest and lover in 81 remains a pure guess.

RHAMNOUS, RHAMNUSIAN   66, 71, 68b.77. A coastal deme in northeast Attica, best known as the site of a famous temple of Nemesis (q.v.), who is frequently identified simply as the "Rhamnusian" maiden or goddess.

RHESUS   58b. A mythical king of Thrace, famous for his swift, snow white chariot horses, and an ally of Priam during the Trojan War. Odysseus and Diomedes slew Rhesus and stole the horses during a raid on his camp.

RHINE [RHENUS], RIVER   11. One of the longest rivers in Europe after the Danube, flowing from Switzerland through Germany to debouch in the North Sea near Rotterdam, and from Catullus's and Caesar's day a major frontier of the Roman empire.

RHODES   4. Largest of the Dodecanese islands, situated in the extreme southeast Aegean, off the coast of Caria, and site of the famous Colossus (in Catullus's day a fallen ruin, but still a tourist attraction).

RHOETEUM, -AN   65. A headland, with a small settlement of the same name, near the entrance to the Hellespont, just north of Ilium; its name is often used by synecdoche as a synonym for Trojan.

ROMULUS/REMUS   28, 29, 34, 49, 58. The mythical wolf-suckled founders of Rome. When Remus mockingly jumped over his brother's half-finished wall, he was killed for his pains. Catullus uses both names as a shorthand for noble Roman ancestry.

RUFA/RUF(UL)US   59. Both are unknown, though the cognomen was common in Cisalpine Gaul, and Quinn (1970, 262) cites a graffito (*CIL* 4.2421) thanking a Rufa for "giving good head" *(bene felas)*. Neudling (1955, 156–57) argues that the names offer a broad hint of incest.

RUSTICUS   54. The name is known in the Republic from coins (e.g., the moneyer M. Aufidius Rusticus, [Thomson 1997, 334]), though more common under the Empire.

SABINE, SABINA   39, 44. The Sabines, a traditionally hardy peasant people, occupied an area to the northeast of Rome, extending northward from the junction of the Anio and Tiber rivers into the Apennine uplands between Umbria and Picenum.

SACAE   11. A race of nomads located to the north of Persia, in the region of modern Tashkent, and described by Arrian as horse-archers.

SALISUBSALIAN   17. This puzzling (but in the context nicely onomatopoeic) word is not otherwise attested, but would seem to refer to a local deity Salisubsalus, probably connected with Mars, whose priests (as the *sali-* portion of the word suggests) were given to leaping rites—appropriate for a strong new bridge.

SAPPHO   35, 51. The famous Greek lyric poet of the late seventh century B.C.E., a native of Lesbos in the northeast Aegean.

SATRACHUS, RIVER   95. A river in Cyprus associated with Smyrna/Myrrha (Ellis 1876, 374), and where Adonis and Aphrodite met to make love.

SATURNALIA   14. A Roman winter festival beginning on 17 December and in Catullus's and Cicero's time lasting for three days, with much eating, drinking, and games playing: during it, presents were exchanged, and slaves were given complete licence, with a mock king or "Lord of Misrule" presiding over the festivities.

SATYRS   64.251. Wild members of Dionysus's rout *(thiasos)*, generally portrayed with goats' hooves: balding. saddle-nosed, permanently ithyphallic, and inflamed by wine.

SCAMANDER, RIVER   64 (357). The river that rises in the Ida range and flows through the plain of Troy to the Hellespont; best known from Homer's *Iliad*, especially from Achilles' fight with the river in book 21.

SCYLLA   60, 64.156. The six-headed monster lurking in wait for unwary sailors in the Straits of Messina, opposite the whirlpool, Charybdis.

SEPTIMIUS   45. Neudling (1955, 158–59) identifies him as the P. Septimius who was M. Terentius Varro's quaestor at some point before 47, and to whom Varro dedicated books 2–4 of his *De Lingua Latina*. For this identification to work, Varro (who became eligible for the praetorship as early as 76) would have had to have held it very late—unlikely, but not impossible.

SERAPIS   10. The cult of this latterly Hellenized Egyptian deity had been introduced to Rome from Ptolemaic Alexandria (where he was the consort of Isis) at some point in the second century B.C.E. See also s.v. Harpocrates.

SESTIUS, P.   44. Politician and orator. In 63 as quaestor he supported Cicero against Catiline. In 56 he was involved with T. Annius Milo in fighting the street-gangs of Clodius, and defended by Cicero, Calvus, and Q. Hortensius Hortalus on the subsequent charge of political violence *(uis)*. Though Cicero later once more defended Sestius (and got him acquitted), the charge this time being electoral corruption, he shared Catullus's contempt for Cicero's rhetorical and literary style.

SICILY, SICILIAN   68b.53. The great island off the toe of Italy, a key source of Roman grain and dairy products.

SILENI   64.251. Like satyrs, members of Dionysus's entourage, generally represented as both ithyphallic and intoxicated, often with tails and hooves, and naked.

SILO   103. Neudling (1955, 163–64) found a family of Juventius in Rome, contemporary with Catullus, who had the cognomen Silo (*CIL* 12.1322); despite the scepticism of Fordyce (1961, 392), it is very tempting to relate this Silo, perhaps as a temporary guardian, to the Iuuentius of whom Catullus was so enamored. The charge of being a pimp *(leno)* would then make good sense.

SIRMIO   31. A narrow rocky point (the modern Sirmione) running out into the south end of the Lago di Garda. The ruins at the so-called grotto of Catullus are not those of Catullus's villa, though (Fordyce 1961, 167) they may occupy the same site. Wiseman (1987, 310–70) has an enchanting mini-monograph, "The Masters of Sirmio," on the vicissitudes of the Valerii Catulli (including the sinister blind monster portrayed by Juvenal) and their wealthy lakeside property. Line 31.12, with its reference to Catullus as "master" *(ero)*, need not necessarily imply that by 56 Catullus's father (as well as his elder brother) was dead and that Catullus had inherited the estate: the term could be purely figurative.

SMYRNA (OR ZMYRNA)   95. In Cypriot myth, daughter of Kinyras and Kenchreïs, also known as Myrrha. She conceived an incestuous passion for her father, was metamorphosed into a myrrh tree, and gave birth to Adonis from the trunk. This is the theme of Cinna's epyllion. The subject was also treated at some length by Ovid in his *Metamorphoses* (10.298–528).

SOCRATION   47. Just possibly a nickname for the Epicurean philosopher and littérateur Philodemus of Gadara, a known intimate of Piso (Goold 1989, 245 and others), but this remains highly speculative. Godwin (1999, 166) suggests that the diminutive (i.e., a pocket, or poor man's, Socrates) is meant to suggest tedious pretentiousness.

SPAIN, SPANISH   9, 12, 25, 37, 39, 64.227. Catullus's interest in the Spanish provinces of Hither and Further Spain seems to have been limited to the reports (and presents) brought back for him by his friends Veranius and Fabullus after their tours of duty there.

STYMPHALUS, -IAN   68b.114. A town in northeast Arcadia, best known for its lake, which was haunted in mythical antiquity by the fierce man-eating birds whose destruction constituted one of Hercules' Twelve Labors.

SUFFENUS   14, 22. Unidentifiable, and unattested elsewhere, though, given the contexts in which he occurs, probably a real person. Goold's suggestion (1989, 240) that the name may be a nickname for Alfenus Varus is unconvincing. Neudling's suggestion (1955, 133–34) of M. Nonius (q.v.) Sufenas has some plausibility.

SULLA [LITTERATOR]   14. Perhaps a nickname for Cornelius Epicadus, a freedman of Sulla and a literary pundit of some standing (Neudling 1955, 165–66; Quinn 1970, 137; Goold 1989, 239). Others (e.g., Thomson 1997, 245) regard him as unidentifiable.

SWAN HILL   67.31. This outcrop above Brescia (Mons Cycneus) got its name from the mythical Ligurian prince Cycnus ("Swan") who, because of his grief for Phaëthon, was metamorphosed into the bird itself (Ovid, *Met.* 2.367–81).

SYRIA   6, 45, 84. The region of the eastern Mediterranean bounded on the north by the Taurus range, on the east by the River Euphrates, to the south by the Arabian desert, and on the west by the Mediterranean itself. Under Rome it was one of the wealthier provinces.

SYRTES   64.156. Two stretches of shallow, shoal-infested, and unusually (for the Mediterranean) tidal coastal waters (the modern gulfs of Gabès and Sidra, in Libya and Tunisia), the Greater and Lesser Syrtes were shunned by ancient voyagers as extremely hazardous.

TAGUS, RIVER   29. One of the largest rivers in Spain and Portugal, famous for its gold-bearing sands, the Tagus (modern Tajo/Tejo) reaches its Atlantic estuary immediately south of Lisbon.

TAPPO   104. Identity uncertain. Tappo is a *cognomen* of the *gens Valeria*, and seems to have Etruscan origins; but it was also the name of a stock character in south Italian farce, and thus here may be used as a nickname for a clownish character.

TAURUS, MT.   64.105. A vast and mostly tree-clad mountain range, up to 7,000 feet in height, running from southwest Asia Minor eastward along the coast of Lycia and Pisidia to Cilicia and beyond.

TELEMACHUS   61.221. Son of Odysseus and Penelope, best known for his role in Homer's *Odyssey*.

TEMPE   64.36, 285. A scenic gorge between Mts. Olympus and Ossa, some seven miles in length and about fifty yards wide, giving the Peneius River an outlet to the sea, and providing the best route out of the Thessalian plain to the northeast.

Tethys   64.29, 66.71, 88. Daughter of Gaia (Earth) and Ouranos (Heaven); married to her brother Ocean, she bore three thousand *(sic)* Oceanids and a variety of river gods.

Teucer, Teucrian   64.344. This Teucer (not to be confused with the Homeric archer, Telamon's son) was sired by the Scamander River on a nymph, Idaea, and his descendants became kings of Troy. Thus "Teucrian" came to be used, by Catullus and others, simply as a poetic synonym for "Trojan."

Thallus   25. The name of this passive but busy homosexual is probably Greek (the word means "a young shoot"), and that of a freedman. Ellis (1876, 65) cites a C. Julius Thallus of unknown date: it would be pleasant to identify him with Catullus's target, and make Caesar his manumitter, but there is no evidence. Cf. Thomson 1997, 266.

Themis   68b.153. A primordial goddess, and according to Hesiod (*Theog.* 901–906), Zeus's second wife: by him she bore several abstractions, including Eunomia (Good Order, the Done Thing), Dike, also known as Astraea (Justice; cf. s.v. Virgo), Eirene (Peace), the Horae (Hours), and the Fates.

Thermopylae   68b.54. The "Hot Gates," so called from the adjacent thermal sulphur springs, a narrow pass between Mt. Kallidromos and the Maliac Gulf, leading from Thessaly into Locris, and the only viable route in antiquity from northern into southern Greece. (Today the waters of the Gulf have retreated several miles.) Thermopylae is chiefly famous for the ultimately unsuccessful holding action fought there in 480 B.C.E. by Spartans and others against Xerxes' invading forces.

Theseus   4.53, 69, 73, 81, 101, 120, 134, 200, 207, 240. Son of Aegeus, king of Attica, by Aethra, daughter of King Pittheus of Troezen, and Athens's most famous legendary hero (Gantz 1993, 249–58, 276–98). Among the various myths associated with him, the most famous (and the one with which Catullus is specifically concerned) is that dealing with his defeat of the Cretan Minotaur, and his subsequent flight with, and abandonment of, Ariadne. The son of king Minos of Crete, Androgeos, had been sent by Aegeus to kill the Marathonian bull (a feat which Theseus subsequently accomplished), but died in the attempt. Minos, in revenge, imposed an annual penalty on Athens of seven youths and seven maidens to be sacrificed to the Minotaur. Theseus finally volunteered to be one of the victims, and on Crete was helped by Minos's daughter, Ariadne, who gave him a ball of thread to let him find his way back out of the Labyrinth where the Minotaur was housed, after killing the monster. Theseus and Ariadne then fled together, but he abandoned her on the island of Dia, from where she was rescued by Dionysus.

Theseus, returning in triumph to Athens, forgot to hoist the white sails that would have signified the success of his mission and his survival, whereupon his father, Aegeus, threw himself from the Acropolis in despair.

THESSALY, -IAN   64.26, 267, 280. A region of eastern central Greece, flanked in the west by Epirus and to the north by Macedonia, with the coastal strip of Magnesia separating it from the Aegean Sea, but with access to the sea through the Gulf of Pagasae. Thessaly consists of two vast plains ringed by mountains (including Ossa and Olympus): it was famous in antiquity for its horses, cattle, wheat, and witches.

THETIS   64.19, 28, 47, 301, 336. A sea nymph, daughter of Nereus and Doris, and thus grand-daughter of Poseidon/Neptune, she was brought up by Zeus's wife, Hera. When she was of age, both Zeus and Poseidon (the latter despite being her grandfather) sought to seduce her. An early version of the myth has her rejecting Zeus to avoid giving offence to Hera, upon which Zeus, in pique, decreed that she must marry a mortal. Pindar gave a new twist to Zeus's motivation (*Isthm.* 8.26–57): the Father of Gods and Men was scared off by Themis's (or Prometheus's) revelation that Thetis was destined to bear a son stronger than his father. In either case, Zeus and Hera decreed that she should marry Peleus. The unwilling bride, capable, like Proteus, of changing her form, tried every trick, but in vain, to elude her destined husband. As Catullus reminds us, the Olympians showed up in force for the wedding. In due course Thetis bore Peleus Achilles, thus fulfilling the prophecy of Themis; but after Peleus interrupted her attempt to make the child immortal through exposure to fire (by burning away his mortality), she left him and returned to the sea, her element. It was by its very nature an ill-fated marriage; however, as Homer testifies, Thetis was devoted to her son, acting as intermediary on his behalf with Zeus, and cleverly persuading Hephaistos to fashion him new armor.

THRACE, THRACIAN   4. The region east of Macedonia extending to the Black Sea, covering present-day Bulgaria, Turkish Thrace, and east Greece beyond the River Struma (Strymon).

THYIADS   64.254, 391. Another name for maenads (q.v.), supposedly derived from the nymph Thyia, said to have been the first to become an orgiastic devotee of Dionysus/Bacchus.

THYONE, -IAN   27. Another name for Semele, the mother of Bacchus.

TIBUR, TIBURTINE   39, 44. Modern Tivoli, lying to the northeast of Rome on the route up the Anio valley to the central Apennines. It retained its independence until 90

B.C.E. A favorite area for out-of-town villas, it served not only Catullus, but also, later, Augustus, and the grandiose tastes of Hadrian.

TRANSPADANA, -ANE   39. The area of Cisalpine Gaul lying (as its name, seen from the Roman viewpoint, implies) north of the River Po.

TRITON   64.395. Originally a son of Poseidon and Amphitrite who lived with them in a submarine palace; later we hear of Tritons in the plural, their main occupations being riding the sea on various marine monsters, and the use of a conch shell as a trumpet.

TROY, TROAD, TROJAN   64.345, 355; 65; 68b.88, 98. The Troad is the northwest corner of Asia Minor, abutting on the Hellespont (Dardanelles), and dominated by the massif of Mt. Ida, with the city of Troy (Ilium) inland from Sigeum.

UMBRIA, UMBRIAN   39. A region of central Italy north of Rome, divided on its west flank from Etruria by the River Tiber, extending east to the Adriatic coast between Ariminum and Ancona, and flanked to the south and southeast by the Sabines' territory and Picenum.

URANIA   61.2. One of the nine Muses, and according to Callimachus (*Aetia* fr. 2a 42–43) the mother of Hymenaeus; his father was Apollo (Pind. fr. 139 Snell). Other Muses cited as his mother include Clio, Terpsichore, and Calliope.

URII   36. Both the name and the location of this haunt of Venus are uncertain. The likeliest identification is with Urion/Uria/Hyria near the Apulian coast, north of Monte Gargano (Thomson 1997, 298–99).

VALERIUS CATO, P.   56. Like Catullus (to whom, as another member of the *gens Valeria*, he was related) a native of Cisalpine Gaul, and born c. 90. He was (contrary to some rumors) freeborn, but lost his patrimony during the Sullan proscriptions. Suetonius (*De Gramm.* 11) reports that Cinna (q.v.) paid tribute to him for his *Diana*, so he was a Neoteric. Despite great fame—he was known as the "Latin Siren"—he died, at an advanced age, forgotten and destitute. Catullus, in dedicating this singularly improper poem to him, may well have hoped, mischievously, that some would take the addressee to have been a very different Cato, the stern moralist and anti-Caesarian, M. Porcius Cato, who once walked out of a theater rather than watch a striptease act. See also s.v. M. Furius Bibaculus.

VALERIUS CATULLUS, (?) L.   65, 68a.20, 68b.91, 101. Catullus's passionately mourned only, and probably elder, brother, who died at some point between 61/60 and 58/7 in the Troad, like Catullus at a very young age (see introd. p. 3 for the possibility that both brothers were consumptive). Lines 68.22 and 94 suggest that he died childless. The patrician *gens Valeria* was prominent in northern Italy during the last century of the Republic, and the Valerii Catulli survived well into the Empire (Neudling 1955, 177).

VARUS   See s.v. Quintilius Varus.

VATINIUS, P.   14, 52, 53. A "new man" *(nouus homo)* from Reate on the Sabine-Umbrian border. Scrofulous, weak-legged, and an inveterate climber who bragged from the start that he would win the consulship (he got it for a few days as a *suffectus* in December 47), Vatinius is not an attractive character. In 59 as tribune he sold his services to Caesar, produced L. Vettius as informer of a supposed optimate plot, including Cicero, against Pompey, and got Caesar a five-year provincial govern-ership of Cisalpine Gaul. Charges of bribery and extortion pursued him every-where; in 54 he was prosecuted—for the third time—by Catullus's friend C. Licinius Calvus for crimes committed during his praetorship the previous year (cf. 14, 53). (This was Catullus's marked anti-Caesarian period.). Reconciled with Cicero (who, in 54, to the astonishment of the respectable, defended him against bribery charges), he steered his way skilfully through the Civil Wars, got a tri-umph 31 December 43, and thereafter vanishes from history.

VENUS   3; 36; 45; 61.17, 61, 195; 64.71, 96; 66.15, 56; 68a.5; 68b.51. The Roman goddess of love, but a latecomer to the Roman pantheon. By the third century B.C.E. she was "the patron of all persuasive seductions, between gods and mortals, and between men and women" (*OCD³* 1587). In Catullus's day, she was regularly claimed as a personal protectress (e.g., by Sulla, Caesar, and Pompey).

VERANIUS   9, 12.28, 47. Catullus's close friend, regularly linked with Fabullus (q.v.), served on the provincial governor's staff in Spain (? 61 or 60, perhaps under Caesar), and very probably also in Macedonia (58/7–55) under L. Calpurnius Piso Caesoni-nus. He seems to have been, like Catullus, from Cisalpine Gaul, and may have been the Veranius who wrote on augury (Neudling 1955, 183).

VERONA   ?17, 35, 67.33, 68a.28, 100. Situated in rich farming and orchard country at the head of the Po Valley, on the River Adige and east of Brescia, Catullus's birth-place lay at the junction of several major thoroughfares, and close to Sirmio and the Lago di Garda.

VETTIUS, ? L.   98. The emendation from "Victius" is uncertain but probable. Cicero (*Pro Cael.* 30) mentions a Vettius as one of Clodia's lovers, a good reason for Catullus to attack him. Whether, as often suggested (Neudling 1955, 186), he is the L. Vettius prominent as an informer between 63 and his death in prison in 59 is quite uncertain.

VIBENNIUS   33. The name of this supposed bath thief suggests an Oscan origin, probably from Etruria or Umbria. It is otherwise unattested during the Republic; some later inscriptions are all from Rome.

VICTOR   80. This hard-worked fellatee is otherwise unknown. Neudling (1955, 187) has the ingenious but highly speculative idea, based on the close association of L. Gellius Poplicola, his fellator, with Clodius Pulcher's circle, that Clodius himself is meant, in the year of his rise to power and exile of Cicero (59/8), and that "Victor" was the nickname this success earned him. Wray (2001, 157) suggests that he may have been a gladiator.

VIRGO   66.65. The zodiacal constellation (no. 27 in Ptolemy's star chart) immediately to the left of the star cluster identified by Conon as the *Coma Berenices* ("Berenice's Lock"), and, beyond that, Leo (chart in Fordyce 1961, 338). As in the case of Berenice, Virgo was the result of catasterism, the constellated virgin in question being Astraea, daughter of Zeus and Themis (q.v.), who lived among men and was the last immortal to quit earth at the onset of the Age of Bronze.

VOLUSIUS   36, 95. The identity of this poetaster is uncertain. He was not (as was once thought) a thinly disguised version of the historian Tanusius (who did not write poetry, and in any case Catullus was not in the habit of disguising his famous targets, least of all under a real name, the holders of which would have good cause for complaint). In fact Volusii were common in Catullus's part of Cisalpine Gaul: the likeliest candidate is Q. Volusius, a wealthy *eques*, Cicero's protégé, and a literary dilettante (Neudling 1955, 188–89).

ZEPHYRION   66.57. A promontory in Lower Egypt, northeast of Alexandria, at the Canopic mouth of the Nile, on which stood a temple dedicated by the Locrians to the deified Arsinoë II as an avatar of Aphrodite.

ZEPHYRUS   66.53. The West Wind personified; like Memnon a son of Eos, the Dawn, and represented as a winged horse. By the Harpy Podagre he sired Xanthos and Balios, the chariot horses of Achilles. Catullus treats him as Arsinoë's "acolyte" because of her epithet *Zephyritis*, "she of Zephyrion" (q.v.).

BIBLIOGRAPHY

EDITIONS, COMMENTARIES, INDICES, BIBLIOGRAPHY

Baehrens, E. 1876. *C. Valerii Catulli Carmina*. Leipzig.

——. 1885. *Catulli Veronensis Liber*. Leipzig.

Ellis, R. 1876. *A Commentary on Catullus*. Oxford. 3rd ed. 1904.

Fordyce, C. J. 1961. *Catullus: A Commentary*. Oxford. 2nd ed. 1973.

Garrison, D. H. 1991. *The Student's Catullus*. Norman, Okla.

Godwin, J. 1995. *Catullus: Poems 61–68*. Warminster.

——. 1999. *Catullus: The Shorter Poems*. Warminster.

Goold, G. P. 1989. *Catullus: Edited with Introduction, Translation, and Notes*. 2nd ed. London.

Harrauer, H. 1979. *A Bibliography to Catullus*. Hildesheim.

Holoka, J. P. 1985. *Gaius Valerius Catullus: A Systematic Bibliography*. New York.

Kroll, W. 1922. *C. Valerius Catullus, herausgegeben und erklärt*. Stuttgart. 7th repr. (with add. including full bibliogr.) 1989.

Lenchantin de Gubernatis, M. 1980. *Il Libro di Catullo*. Turin.

Leon, H. J. 1959/60. A quarter-century of Catullan scholarship, 1934–1959. *CW* 53: 104–13, 141–48, 174–80, 281–82.

Marinone, N. 1997. *Berenice da Callimaco a Catullo: testo critico, traduzione e commento*. 2nd ed. Bologna .

McCarren, V. P. 1977. *A Critical Concordance to Catullus*. Leiden.

Merrill, E. T. 1893. *Catullus*. Boston.

Morisi, L. 1999. *Attis (carmen LXIII): introduzione, testo, traduzione e commento*. Bologna.

Munro, H. A. J. 1879. *Criticisms and Elucidations of Catullus*. London. 2nd ed. 1905.

Mynors, R. A. B. 1958. *C. Valerii Catulli Carmina*. Oxford.

Pighi, G. B. 1961. *Catullo Veronese*. 3 vols. Verona.

Postgate, J. P. 1889. *Gai Valeri Catulli Carmina*. London.

Quinn, K. 1970. *Catullus The Poems: Edited with Introduction, Revised Text, and Commentary*. London.

Scarsi, M. 1992. Rassegna catulliana: (1985–1999). *SLLRH* 6: 204–14.

———. 2000. Rassegna catulliana: (1985–1999). *Boll. di Stud. Lat.* 30: 143–203.

Simpson, F. P. 1879. *Select Poems of Catullus.* London. 2nd ed. 1909.

Syndikus, H. P. 1984. *Die kleinen Gedichte (1–60).* Vol. 1 of *Catull: Eine Interpretation.* Darmstadt.

———. 1987. *Die Epigramme (69–116).* Vol. 3 of *Catull: Eine Interpretation.* Darmstadt.

———. 1990. *Die großen Gedichte (61–68).* Vol. 2 of *Catull: Eine Interpretation.* Darmstadt.

Thomson, D. F. S. 1997. *Catullus: Edited with a Textual and Interpretative Commentary.* *Phoenix* Suppl. 34 (replaces ed. of 1978). Toronto.

———. 1971/72. Recent scholarship on Catullus (1960–1969). *CW* 65: 116–26.

Wetmore, M. N. 1912. *Index Verborum Catullianus.* New Haven.

TRANSLATIONS

Copley, F. O. 1957. *Gaius Valerius Catullus: The Complete Poetry.* Ann Arbor.

Ellis, R. 1871. *The Poems and Fragments of Catullus.* London.

Gregory, H. 1931. *The Poems of Catullus.* New York.

Lee, A. G. 1990. *The Poems of Catullus: Edited with an Introduction, Translation and Brief Notes.* Oxford.

Michie, J. 1969. *The Poems of Catullus.* London.

Mulroy, D. 2002. *The Complete Poetry of Catullus: Translated and with Commentary.* Madison, Wisc.

Myers, R., and R. J. Ormsby. 1972. *Catullus: The Complete Poems for Modern Readers.* London.

Poole, A., and J. Maule, eds. 1995. *The Oxford Book of Classical Verse in Translation.* Oxford.

Raphael, F., and K. McLeish. 1978. *The Poems of Catullus.* London.

Sisson, C. H. 1966. *Catullus.* London.

Swanson, R. A. 1959. *Odi et Amo: The Complete Poetry of Catullus.* New York.

Whigham, P. 1966. *The Poems of Catullus.* Harmondsworth.

Zukofsky, C., and L. Zukofsky. 1969. *Catullus (Gai Valeri Catulli Veronensis Liber).* London.

GENERAL AND MISCELLANEOUS

Ackroyd-Cross, B. G. 1997. Catullus 68, 41–86. *SLLRH* 8: 116–21.

Adams, J. N. 1982. *The Latin Sexual Vocabulary.* Baltimore.

Adler, E. 1981. *Catullan Self-revelation.* New York.

Arduino, M. 1994. Ma Sirmione non deluse Catullo. In *Catullo e Sirmione: società e cultura della Cisalpina alle soglie dell' impero,* N. Criniti, ed., 5–8. Brescia.

Arkins, B. 1982. *Sexuality in Catullus.* Hildesheim.

———. 1983. Caelius and Rufus in Catullus. *Philol.* 127: 306–11.

————. 1994. Textual questions in Catullus. *SLLRH* 7: 211–26.

Aveline, J. 1994. Catullus 32.8: A Jovian boast. *LCM* 19: 122–23.

Badian, E. 1980. The case of the door's marriage (Catullus 67.6). *HSCPh* 84: 81–89.

Bardon, H. 1979. *L'Art de la Composition chez Catulle*. New York.

Batstone, W. W. 1993. Introduction; and Logic, rhetoric and poiesis. *Helios* 20: 83–87, and 143–72.

————. 1998. The programmatic language of Catullus 1. *CPh* 93: 125–35.

Beard, M. 1994. The Roman and the foreign: The cult of the Great Mother. In *Shamanism, History and the State*, ed. N. Thomas and C. Humphrey, 164–90. Ann Arbor.

Beck, J.-W. 1996. *'Lesbia' und 'Juventius': zwei libelli im corpus catullianum*. Göttingen.

Bickel, E. 1949. Catulli in Caesarem carmina. *RhM* 93: 13–20.

————. 1953. Salaputium, mentula salax. *RhM* 96: 94–95.

Blaiklock, E. M. 1959. *The Romanticism of Catullus*. Auckland, NZ.

Blusch, J. 1989. Vielfalt und Einheit: Bemerkungen zur Komposition von Catull c.64. *AuA* 35: 116–30.

Bolgar, R. R. 1954. *The Classical Heritage and its Beneficiaries*. Cambridge.

Booth, A. D. et al. 1958. *Aspects of Translation: Studies in Communication 2*. London.

Booth, J. 1999. All in the mind: Sickness in Cat. 76. In *The Passions in Roman Thought and Literature*, ed. S. M. Braund and C. Gill, 150–168. Cambridge.

Brunt, P. A. 1965. *Amicitia* in the late Roman Republic. *PCPhS*, n.s., 11: 1–20.

————. 1988. *The Fall of the Roman Republic and Related Essays*. Oxford.

Buchheit, V. 1976. Sal et lepos versiculorum (Catull. C.16). *Hermes* 104: 331–47.

Carratello, U. 1992. Le donne veronesi di Catullo. *GIF* 44: 183–201.

————. 1995. Catullo e Giovenzio. *GIF* 47: 27–52.

————. 1996. Il carme 11 di Catullo. *GIF* 48: 55–77.

Clare, R. J. 1996/7. Catullus 64 and the *Argonautica* of Apollonius Rhodius: Allusion and exemplarity. *PCPhS*, n.s., 42: 60–88.

Clausen, W. V. 1964. Callimachus and Latin Poetry. *GRBys* 5: 181–96.

————. 1970. Catullus and Callimachus. *HSCPh* 74: 85–94.

————. 1976. *Catulli Veronensis Liber. CPh* 71: 37–43.

————. 1982. The New Poets and their antecedents. In *The Cambridge History of Classical Literature II: Latin Literature*, ed. E. J. Kenney and W. V. Clausen, 178–206. Cambridge.

Clay, J. S. 1995. Catullus' *Attis* and the Black Hunter. *QUCC* 50: 143–55.

Copley, F. O. 1949. Emotional conflict and its significance in the Lesbia-poems of Catullus. *AJPh* 70: 31–33.

Courtney, E. 2000. Problems in two translations. *Prometheus* 26: 47–51.

Criniti, N., ed. 1994. *Catullo e Sirmione: società e cultura della Cisalpina alle soglie dell' impero*. Brescia.

————, ed. 1999. *Terre nostre Sirmioni: società e cultura della 'Cisalpina' verso il Duemila*. Brescia.

Cupaiuolo, F. 1965. *Studi sull' esametro di Catullo*. Naples.

————. 1994. Struttura e strutture formali del carme 64 di Catullo. *Boll. Stud. Lat.* 24: 432–86.

Cutt, T. 1936. *Metre and Diction in Catullus' Hendecasyllables.* Chicago.

Damschen, G. 1998. Catullus c.94: *Ipsa olera olla legit. Mnem.* 52: 169–76.

D'Angour, A. J. 2000. Catullus 107: A Callimachean reading. *CQ* 50: 615–18.

D'Anna, G. 1994. La concezione etica dell' ultimo Catullo. In *Catullo e Sirmione: società e cultura della Cisalpina alle soglie dell' impero.* ed. N. Criniti, 47–52. Brescia.

————. 1999. Mito ed eros in Catullo: il carme 68. In *Terre nostre Sirmioni: società e cultura della 'Cisalpina' verso il Duemila,* ed. N. Criniti, 235–244. Brescia.

Della Corte, F. 1976. *Personaggi catulliani.* 2nd ed. Florence.

————. 1989. I carmi veronesi di Catullo. *Maia* 41: 229–34.

Dettmer, H. 1997. *Love by the Numbers: Form and Meaning in the Poetry of Catullus.* Lang Classical Studies 10. New York.

Deuling, J. K. 1999. Catullus and Mamurra. *Mnem.* 52: 188–93.

Dorey, T. A. 1958. Cicero, Clodia, and the *pro Caelio. G&R* 5: 175–80.

Duckett, E. S. 1925. *Catullus in English Poetry.* Smith College Classical Studies 6. Northampton, Mass.

Dyer, R. R. 1994. Bedspread for a *Hieros Gamos:* Studies in the iconography and meaning of the ecphrasis in Catullus 64. *SLLRH* 7: 227–55.

Edwards, M. J. 1992. Apples, blood and flowers: Sapphic bridal imagery in Catullus. *SLLRH* 6: 181–203.

Elder, J. P. 1947. Catullus' *Atti. AJPh* 68: 394–403.

Fedeli, P. 1972. *Il Carme 61 di Catullo.* Fribourg.

————. 1983. *Catullus' Carmen 61.* Amsterdam.

Feeney, D. C. 1992. "Shall I compare thee . . . ?" Catullus 68B and the limits of analogy. In *Author and Audience in Latin Literature,* ed. T. Woodman and J. Powell, 33–44. Cambridge.

Feldherr, A. 2000. "Non inter nota sepulcra": Catullus 101 and Roman funerary ritual. *CA* 19: 209–31.

Ferguson, J. 1988. *Catullus. Greece & Rome* New Surveys in the Classics 20. Oxford.

Finamore, J. F. 1984. Catullus 50 and 51: Friendship, love, and *otium. CW* 78: 11–19.

Fitzgerald, W. 1995. *Catullan Provocations: Lyric Poetry and the Drama of Position.* Berkeley.

Forsyth, P. Y. 1990/1. The thematic unity of Catullus 11. *CW* 84: 457–64.

Fraenkel, E. 1955. Vesper adest. *JRS* 45: 1–8.

————. 1956. Catulls Trostgedicht für Calvus. *WS* 69: 278–88.

Fredricksmeyer, E. A. 1985. Catullus to Caecilius on good poetry (c. 35). *AJPh* 106: 213–21.

————. 1993. Method and interpretation: Catullus 11. *Helios* 20: 89–105.

Gaisser, J. H. 1993. *Catullus and his Renaissance Readers.* Oxford.

Gantz, T. 1993. *Early Greek Myth: A Guide to Literary and Artistic Sources.* Baltimore.

Gardner, J. F. 1998. *Family and Familia in Roman Law and Life.* Oxford.

Gelzer, T. 1992. Bemerkungen zu Catull c. 101. *MH* 49: 26–32.

Genovese, E. N. 1974. Symbolism in the *Passer* poems. *Maia* 26: 121–25.

Giardina, G. C. 1974. La composizione del liber e l'itinerario poetico di Catullo. *Philol.* 118: 224–35.

Goldberg, S. 2000. Catullus 42 and the comic legacy. In *Dramatische Wäldchen: Festschrift für Eckard Lefèvre zum 65. Geburtstag*, 475–89. Hildesheim.

Goud, T. 1995. Who speaks the final lines? Catullus 62: Structure and ritual. *Phoenix* 49: 23–32.

Granarolo, J. 1967. *L'Oeuvre de Catulle: Aspects religieux, éthiques, et stylistiques*. Paris.

Gratwick, A. S. 2000. Catullus XXXII. *CQ* 50: 547–51.

———. 2002. *Vale, Patrona Virgo:* The text of Catullus 1.9. *CQ* 52: 305–20.

Green, P. M. 1960. Some versions of Aeschylus: A study of tradition and method in translating classical poetry. In *Essays in Antiquity*, 185–215. London.

———. 1987. Metre, fidelity, sex: The problems confronting a translator of Ovid's love poetry. In *The Tranlator's Art: Essays in Honour of Betty Radice*, ed. W. Radice and B. Reynolds, 92–111. Harmondsworth.

———. 1989. Medium and message reconsidered: The changing functions of classical translation. In *Classical Bearings*, 256–70, 308–13. London.

———. 1993. *Alexander to Actium: The Historical Evolution of the Hellenistic Age*. Rev. ed. Berkeley.

Greene, E. 1998. *The Erotics of Domination: Male Desire and the Mistress in Latin Love Poetry*. Baltimore.

Griffin, J. 1985. *Latin Poets and Roman Life*. London.

Grilli, A. 1994. Catullo tra Celti e Romani. In *Catullo e Sirmione: società e cultura della Cisalpina alle soglie dell'impero*, N. Criniti, ed., 37–46. Brescia.

Gruen, E. S. 1974. *The Last Generation of the Roman Republic*. Paperback repr. with extensive new introd., 1995. Berkeley.

Halporn, J. W., M. Ostwald, and T. G. Rosenmeyer. 1980. *The Meters of Greek and Latin Poetry*. Rev. ed. Norman, Okla.

Harrington, K. P. 1963. *Catullus and his Influence*. New York.

Harrison, S. J. 2001. Fatal attraction: Paris, Helen and the unity of Catullus 51. *CB* 77: 161–67.

Havelock, E. A. 1939. *The Lyric Genius of Catullus*. Oxford.

Heath, J. R. 1986. The supine hero in Catullus 32. *CJ* 82: 28–36.

Hickson, F. V. 1993. *Patruus:* Paragon or pervert? The case of a literary split personality. *Syllecta Classica* 4: 21–26.

Hickson-Hahn, F. V. 1998. What's so funny? Laughter and incest in invective humor. *Syllecta Classica* 9: 1–36.

Highet, G. 1957. *Poets in a Landscape*. New York.

Holford-Strevens, L. 1988. *Aulus Gellius*. London. 2nd ed. 2004.

Holzberg, N. 2000. Lesbia, the poet, and the two faces of Sappho: "womanufacture" in Catullus. *PCPhS* 46: 28–44.

———. 2002. *Catull: der Dichter und sein erotisches Werk*. Munich.

Hopkins, K. 1983. *Death and Renewal*. Cambridge.

Hubbard, T. K. 1983. The Catullan Libellus. *Philologus* 127: 218–37.

Janan, M. 1994. *'When the lamp is shattered': Desire and narrative in Catullus*. Carbondale.

Jenkyns, R. 1982. *Three Classical Poets*. London.

Jocelyn, H. D. 1980. On some unnecessarily indecent interpretations of Catullus 2 and 3. *AJPh* 101: 421–41.

———. 1999. The arrangement and the language of Catullus' so-called *polymetra* with special reference to the sequence 10–11–12. In *Aspects of the Language of Latin Poetry*, ed. J. N. Adams and R. G. Mayer, 335–375. Oxford.

Katz, J. 2000. Egnatius' dental fricatives (c. 39.20). *CPh* 95: 338–48.

Kennedy, D. F. "Cf." : Analogies, relationships, and Catullus 68. In *amor: roma, Love and Latin Literature*, ed. S. M. Braund and R. Mayer, 30–43. Cambridge.

Kenney, E. J., and W. V. Clausen, eds. 1982. *The Cambridge History of Classical Literature II: Latin Literature*. Cambridge.

Khan, A. 1968. Catullus 76: The Summing-up. *Athen.* 46: 54–71.

———. 1969. Image and symbol in Catullus 17. *CPh* 64: 88–97.

Kidd, D. A. 1970. Some problems in Catullus lxvi. *Antichthon* 4: 38–49.

Kirkpatrick, R. S. 1998. Nam unguentum dabo: Cat. 13 and Servius' note on Phaon (*Aen.* 3.279). *CQ* 48: 303–305.

Kraggerud, E. 1993. The spinning Parcae: On Catullus 64. 313. *SO* 68: 32–37.

Krostenko, B. A. 2001. *Cicero, Catullus, and the Language of Social Performance*. Chicago.

Laird, A. 1993. Sounding out ecphrasis: Art and text in Catullus 64. *JRS* 83: 18–30.

Lefèvre, E. 1998. Alexandrinisches und catullisches im Attis-Gedicht (c. 63). *RhM* 141: 308–28.

Leishman, J. B. 1956. *Translating Horace: Thirty Odes Translated into the Original Metres with the Latin Text and an Introductory and Critical Essay*. Oxford.

Levine, P. 1985. Catullus c. 67: The dark side of love and marriage. *CA* 4: 62–71.

———. 1987. Catullus c.100: A potent wish for a "friend" in need. *Maia* 39: 33–39.

Lieberg, G. 1966. Catull c.60 und Ps. Theokrit 23. *Hermes* 94: 115–19.

Lindgren, M. H. 1983. *Non bona dicta:* Obscenity in the poetry of Catullus. MA thesis, U. of Iowa.

Littman, R. J. 1977. The Unguent of Venus: Catullus 13. *Latomus* 36:123–26.

Lyne, R. O. A. M. 1978. The Neoteric poets. *CQ* 28: 167–87.

———. 1980. *The Latin Love Poets: From Catullus to Horace*. Oxford.

Macleod, C. W. 1973a. Catullus 116. *CQ* 23: 304–309.

———. 1973b. Parody and personalities in Catullus. *CQ* 23: 294–303.

Marshall, R. A., and R. J. Baker. 1975. The aspirations of Q. Arrius. *Hist.* 24: 220–31.

Martin, C. 1992. *Catullus*. New Haven.

McDermott, W. C. 1983. Mamurra, Eques Formianus. *RhM* 126: 292–307.

Morelli, A. M. 2001. L'eternità di un istante: Presuppositi ellenistico-romani della poesia leggera di Catullo tra cultura letteraria, epigrafica e 'mondana.' *A&R* 46: 59–79.

Morgan, J. D. 1991. The waters of the Satrachus (Catullus 95.5). *CQ* 41: 252–53.

Most, G. W. 1981. On the arrangement of Catullus' *Carmina Maiora*. *Philologus* 125: 109–25.

Näsström, B. 1989. *The Abhorrence of Love: Studies in Rituals and MysticAspects in Catullus' Poem of Attis.* Uppsala.

Neudling, C. L. 1955. *A Prosopography to Catullus.* Iowa Studies in Classical Philology 12. Oxford.

Newman, J. K. 1990. *Roman Catullus and the Modification of the Alexandrian Sensibility.* Hildesheim.

Nicholson, J. H. 1996/7. Goats and gout in Catullus 71. *CW* 90: 351–61.

Nielsen, R. M. 1994. Catullus 86: Lesbia, beauty, and poetry. *SLLRH* 7: 256–66.

Pedrick, V. 1993. The abusive address and the audience in Catullan poems. *Helios* 20: 173–96.

Perutelli, A. 1996. Il carme 63 di Catullo. *Maia* 48: 255–70.

Petrini, M. 1997. *The Child and the Hero: Coming of Age in Catullus and Vergil.* Ann Arbor.

Pietquin, P. 1986. Analyse du poème 76 de Catulle. *LEC* 54: 351–66.

Putnam, M. C. J. 1961. The art of Catullus 64. *HSCPh* 65: 165–205.

———.1982. Catullus 11: The ironies of integrity. In *Essays in Latin Lyric, Elegy, and Epic*, 13–19. Princeton.

Quinn, K. 1959. *The Catullan Revolution.* Cambridge.

———.1972. *Catullus: An Interpretation.* London.

Radice, W. , and B. Reynolds, eds. 1987. *The Translator's Art: Essays in Honour of Betty Radice.* Harmondsworth.

Radici Colace, P. 1987. Parodie catulliane, ovvero: "quando il poeta si diverte". *GIF* 39: 38–57.

Randall, J. G. 1979. Mistresses' pseudonyms in Latin elegy. *LCM* 4: 37–38.

Raven, D. S. 1965. *Latin Metre.* London.

Rees, R. 1994. Common sense in Catullus 64. *AJPh* 115: 75–88.

Ross, D. O. 1969. *Style and Tradition in Catullus.* Cambridge.

Rudd, N. 1959. Colonia and her bridge. *TAPhA* 90: 305–20.

———. 1986. *Themes in Roman Satire.* London.

Ryan, F. X. 1995. The date of Catullus 52. *Eranos* 93: 113–21.

Saintsbury, G., ed. 1885. *The Works of John Dryden*, vol. 12. Edinburgh.

———. 1906. *A History of English Prosody.* 3 vols. London.

Salat, P. 1993. Catulle 64.105–111. *Latomus* 52: 418–19.

Sarkissian, J. 1983. *Catullus 68: An Interpretation.* Leiden.

Savory, T. 1968. *The Art of Translation.* 2nd ed. London.

Scherf, J. 1996. *Untersuchungen zur antiken Veröffentlichung der Catullgedichte.* Hildesheim.

Schwabe, L. 1862. *Quaestiones Catullianae*, vol. 1. Giessen.

Scullard, H. H. 1982. *From the Gracchi to Nero: A History of Rome from 133 B.C. to A.D. 68.* 5th ed. London.

Segal, C. 1968. Catullus 5 and 7: A study in complementarities. *AJPh* 89: 284–301.

Selver, P. 1966. *The Art of Translating Poetry.* London.

Simpson, C. J. 1992. Catullus 100, Ovid, and the patois of the race track. *SLLRH* 6: 204–14.

Skinner, M. B. 1972. The unity of Catullus 68: The structure of 68a. *TAPhA* 103: 495–512.

————. 1979. Parasites and strange bedfellows: A study in Catullus' poetical imagery. *Ramus* 8: 137–52.

————.1981. *Catullus' Passer: The Arrangement of the Book of Polymetric Poems.* New York.

————.1982. Pretty Lesbius. *TAPhA* 112: 197–208.

————. 1983. Clodia Metelli. *TAPhA* 113: 273–87.

————.1987. Disease imagery in Catullus 76.17–26. *CPh* 82: 230–33.

————.1988. Aesthetic patterning in Catullus: Textual structures, systems of imagery and book arrangements: introduction. *CW* 81: 337–340.

————.1989. *Ut decuit cinaediorem:* Power, gender and urbanity in Catullus 10. *Helios* 16: 7–23.

————.1992. The dynamics of Catullan obscenity: cc. 37, 58, and 11. *Syll.Class.* 3: 1–11.

————.1993. *Ego mulier:* The construction of male sexuality in Catullus. *Helios* 20: 107–30.

————. 2003. *Catullus in Verona: A Reading of the Elegiac Libellus, Poems 65–116.* Columbus, Ohio.

Skutsch, O. 1969. Metrical variations and some textual problems in Catullus. *BICS* 16: 38–43.

Stoessl, F. 1977. *Gaius Valerius Catullus: Mensch, Leben, Dichtung.* Meisenheim am Glan. 2nd ed. 1983.

Stoevesandt, M. 1994/5. Catull 64 und die Ilias: Das Peleus-Thetis-Epyllion im Lichte der neueren Homer-Forschung. *WJA* 20: 167–205.

Stoppard, T. 1997. *The Invention of Love.* 2nd ed. New York.

Svavarsson, S. H. 1999. On Catullus 49. *CJ* 95: 131–38.

Tatum, W. J. 1993. Catullus 79: Personal invective or political discourse? In *Papers of the Leeds International Latin Seminar,* vol. 7, 31–45. Leeds.

————.1997. Friendship, politics and literature in Catullus: Poems 1, 65, and 66.116. *CQ* 47: 482–500.

————.1999. *The Patrician Tribune: Publius Clodius Pulcher.* Chapel Hill.

Thomas, R. F. 1993. Sparrows, hares and doves: A Catullan metaphor and its tradition. *Helios* 20: 131–42.

Thomsen, O. 1992. *Ritual and Desire: Catullus 61 & 62 and Other Ancient Documents on Wedding and Marriage.* Aarhus.

Traina, A. 1994. L'ambiguo sesso: Il c.63 di Catullo. In *Catullo e Sirmione: società e cultura della Cisalpina alle soglie dell'impero,* N. Criniti, ed., 189–98. Brescia.

Treggiari, S. M. 1991. *Roman Marriage: Iusti Coniuges from the Time of Cicero to the Time of Ulpian.* Oxford.

Väisänen, M. 1984. *La Musa Poliedrica: Indagine storica su Catull carm. 4.* Helsinki.

————.1988. *La Musa dalle molte voci: Studio sulle dimensioni storiche dell'arte di Catullo.* Helsinki.

Vandiver, E. 1990. Sound patterns in Catullus 84. *CJ* 85: 337–40.

————.2000. Hot springs, cool rivers, and hidden fires: Heracles in Catullus 68.51–66. *CPh* 95: 151–59.

Vermaseren, M. J. 1977. *Cybele and Attis: The Myth and the Cult.* London.

Vinson, M. 1992. Party politics and the language of love in the Lesbia poems of Catullus. *SLLRH* 6: 163–80.

Weinreich, O. 1959. Catull c.60. *Hermes* 87: 75–90.

Whatmough, J. 1956. *Poetic, Scientific, and Other Forms of Discourse*. Berkeley.

Wheeler, A. L. 1934. *Catullus and the Traditions of Ancient Poetry*. Sather Classical Lectures 9. Berkeley.

Wilkinson, L. P. 1956. Note in *L'Influence grecque sur la poésie latine, de Catulle à Ovide*. Fondation Hardt Entretiens sur l'Antiquité Classique 2, 47. Berne.

Williams, G. 1968. *Tradition and Originality in Roman Poetry*. Oxford.

Wiseman, T. P. 1969. *Catullan Questions*. Leicester.

———.1974. *Cinna the Poet and other Roman Essays*. Leicester.

———.1979. *Clio's Cosmetics*. Leicester.

———.1985. *Catullus and His World: A Reappraisal*. Cambridge.

———.1987. *Roman Studies, Literary and Historical*. Liverpool.

Witke, C. 1968. *Enarratio catulliana: Carmina L, XXX, LXV, LXVIII*. Leiden.

Wray, D. 2001. *Catullus and the Poetics of Roman Manhood*. Cambridge.

Wyke, M. 2002. *The Roman Mistress: Ancient and Modern Representations*. Oxford.

Zucchelli, B. 1994. La cultura della Cisalpina nella tarda repubblica. In *Catullo e Sirmione: società e cultura della Cisalpina alle soglie dell' impero*, N. Criniti, ed., 27–36. Brescia.

INDEX

Garda, Lago di, 49

Garrison, D., 33, 37, 293

Gaul, 2, 3, 57, 75, 216, 221, 230, 275, 296; Cisalpine, 6, 12, 264, 272, 273, 275, 277, 278, 284, 285, 289, 290, 294, 295, 297, 301, 305, 307, 313, 314, 315; Galatia, 304; Transalpine, 222, 279, 290; Transpadana, 313

Gellius, L., 183, 189, 193, 195, 211, 254, 257, 262, 269–70, 279, 290, 315

Genovese, E. N., 213

George III, 1

Giardina, G. C., 18

Gilbert, W. S., xiii

Godwin, J., xii, 39, 215, 218, 220, 223, 226, 233, 241, 244, 257, 264, 269, 274, 293

Golden Age, 255

Golden Fleece, 271, 284

Golgi, 83, 139, 290

Goold, G., 16, 18, 19, 214, 232, 252, 268

Gorgons, 301, 302–3

Graces, the, 301

Gratwick, A. S., 213

Greek Anthology, 213

Greene, E., 214, 215–16

Grote, G., 21

Gytheion, 288

Hades, 300

Hadrian (P. Aelius Hadrianus), 313

Haemonia, -an, 151, 290

Hamadryads, 109, 287, 290

Harpies, 315 (Podagre)

Harpocrates, 183, 203, 257, 266, 290

Harvey, G., 28

Heath, J., 223

Hebe, 177, 290

Hecate, 223, 246, 292

Hector, 271, 306

Hecuba, 301, 304

Helen, 175, 229, 282, 291, 301

Helicon, Mt., 28, 107, 109, 272, 274, 291

Helios, 303

Hellespont, 155, 214, 275, 291, 306, 307, 308, 313

Hephaistos, 231, 312

Hera, 254, 281, 290, 293, 301, 312

Herculaneum, 19, 303; House of the Papyri, 280

Hercules/Heracles, 253–54, 273, 290, 291, 303, 309

Hermes, 286

Herodotus, 247, 277

Herrick, R., 20, 24, 25

Hesiod, 39, 235, 311; *Works & Days*, 244

Hesperus, 123–27, 153, 291

Hildemar of Brescia, 15

Hippocrene, 291

Hippodamia, 302

Hippomedon, 276

Hipponax, 10, 33

Holford-Strevens, L., 15

Holy Child. *See* Harpocrates

Holzberg, N., 213

Homer, 9, 13, 28, 39, 232, 301, 312; *Iliad*, 243, 244, 271, 273, 274, 308; *Odyssey*, 244, 266, 282, 310

Horace (Q. Hor. Flaccus), 2, 9, 10, 14, 26, 33, 36, 216, 223, 275, 281, 289, 303, 306

Hortensius Hortalus, Q., 159, 197, 220, 245, 263, 291, 297, 308

Hubbard, T. K., xv, 18

Hymen[aeus], 107–23, 123–27, 233, 234, 235, 292, 313

Hyperboreans, 209, 292

Hypnos (Sleep), 301

Hyrcania, 57, 292

Iacchus. *See* Bacchus

Iapetus, 305

Ida, Idaea, 298, 311

Ida, Mt., 129, 145, 286, 292, 301, 308, 313

Idalium, 83, 109, 139, 290, 292

Idrus, Idrias, 151, 292

Ilium. *See* Troy

Illyria, 275, 287

India, -an, Indies, Indus, 57, 93, 95, 137, 292, 300, 301

Interamnia, 79

Io, 254

Iolcos, 302

Ionia, -ian, 191; Sea, 261, 292

Iphicles, 273

Iphigenia, 253, 304

Ipsithilla, 79, 223, 293

Isis, 275, 290, 308

Italy, 271, 292, 295

Ithaca, 302

Itonus, 147, 293

Itylus, 159, 245, 286, 293

Iunius Brutus, D., 9; Sempronia, 9

Janan, M., 18, 20

Jason, 232, 241, 271

Jerome, St., 1–2

Jocelyn, H. D., 17, 213

Jonson, Ben, 20

Julia. *See* Pompey

Junia. *See* Aurunculeia

Juno, 177, 223, 254, 255, 293, 298; Lucina, 81, 293

Jupiter/Jove, 51, 103, 135, 143, 145, 151, 157, 163,
    177, 220, 241, 242, 253, 254, 255, 256, 293, 297,
    298

Juvenal (D. Iunius Iuuenalis), 29, 39, 227, 263,
    308

Juventius, 71, 97, 189, 201, 216, ?218, 220, 265,
    266, 293, ?306

Kallidromos, Mt., 311

Kalymnos, 243

Karajan, H. von, 36

Karpathos, 285

Kasos, 285

Keats, J., 21, 23

Kenchreïs, 309

Kinyras, 309

Kipling, R., 238

Kition, 292

Kroll, W., xii, 222

Kronos, 282

Krostenko, B. A., 214, 217, 219

Lachmann, K., 22

Laconia, 288

Ladas, 105, 293

Laevius, 12

Lago di Garda, 214, 223, 278, 308, 314

Lago di Nemi, 287

Lamb, Caroline, 284

Landor, W. S., 20, 21–22

Lanuvium, -an, 87, 293

Laodamia, 175, 249, 253, 254, 294, 306

Laodice I, 246

Larissa, 135, 285, 294

Latimer, D., xv

Latins, Latium, 282, 293

Latmos, Mt., 161, 246, 294

Lattimore, R., 29–30

Leake, Col. W. M., 304

Leda, 282, 291, 304

Ledros (Nicosia), 292

Lee, A. G., xii, 6, 17, 226

Leishman, J. B., 26

Lemnos, 254

Leo, 248, 278, 285, 294

"Lesbia," 2, 4–9, 12, 14, 19, 20, 22–23, 49, 51,
    99, 105, 173–75, 177–79, 181–83, 185, 191, 193,
    ?195, 197, 203, 205–7, 213, 214, 215, 216–17,
    ?222, 224, 228, 231, 232, ?237, 251–55, 256,
    257, 258, 259, ?260, 261, 262, 266, 267, 283,
    294–95; "Lesbius," 187, 259, 267, 284, 294;
    sparrow poems, 45–47, 213

Leto, 81, 295

Levantine region, 274, 276

Lewis, Wyndham, xiii

Lex Clodia, 223

Lex Gabinia Calpurnia, 223

Lex Vatinia, 224

Libo, 101, 229, 293, 295

Libya, Libyan, 51, 93, 107, 272, 277, 286, 295, 310

Licinius. *See* Calvus

Liguria, -an, 288, 295, 310

Lindsay, J., 24

literature, Republican, 9–13; Asianic style, 291;
    Atticism, 275, 280; *ecphrasis,* 239–40; Epicure-
    anism and, 39, 241, 280, 287–88, 297–98, 303;
    epigram, 265; epyllion, 11, 239–44 ; *flagitatio,*
    225; Hellenistic influence on, 220, 231, 233,
    239, 241, 261, 273, 301, 306; myth and, 10, 231;
    Neoterics, 10–13, 14, 97, 220, 224, 225, 227–
    28, 239, 241, 263, 273, 280, 283, 285, 289, 291,
    298, 303 ; satire, 216; social implications of,
    10–11, 244, 258, 280–81

Littman, R. J., 217

Livius Andronicus, 9, 10

Livy (T. Livius), 235, 276

Locris, -ian, 163, 248, 296, 311, 315

Lombardy, 297

Love. *See* Cupid

Lucan (M. Annaeus Lucanus), 39, 288

Lucretius (T. Lucr. Carus), 2, 39, 40, 238, 287, 297–98

Lucullus, L., 5, 284, 291, 294, 305

Lusitania, 75, 222, 310

Lycaon, 163, 281, 296

Lycaonia, 304

Lycastus, 298

Lycia, -an, 275, 310

Lydia -an, 223, 234, 286

Lykambes, 225

Lyne, R. O. A. M., 8, 9, 11, 215, 216

Lysimachus, 275, 299

Macedonia, 11, 216, 227, 247, 280, 288, 300, 312, 314

Macer, C. Licinius, 281

Mackail, J. W., 24

Macleod, C., 218, 279

Maeander, r., 234

Maenads, 129, 131, 157, 277, 289, 296, 301

Magas of Cyrene, 247, 306

Magi, the, 195, 262, 296

magic, hexing, 214, 266, 296

Magna Mater, 286

Magnesia, 302, 312

Malis, Maliac Gulf, 296, 311

Mamurra, 1, 2, 75, 89, 91, 105, 197, 205, 209, 221, 222, 225–56, 230, 231, 237, 259, 263, 266–67, 269, 289, 296–97

Manlius Torquatus, L., 2–3, 35, 109, 123, ?169–79, 225, 233, 251–55, 272, 277, 297, 303

Marathon, 273, 311

Marcius Rex, Q., 5

Mardonius, 247–48

Marius, C., 19, 289

marriage, Roman, 8–9

Marrucini, the, 275

Mars, Mavors, 157, 297, 308

Martial (M. Valerius Martialis), 13, 14, 33

Martin, C., 17

Marvell A., 24

Massilia (Marseilles), 295

Medea, 12, 232, 236, 241, 271

Media, Medes, 163, 297, 303

Mediolanum (Milan), 300

Mediterranean, 299, 304, 310; mockery in, 219

Medusa, 301, 302–3

Megalopolis, 288

Meleager, 276

Meleager of Gadara, 12

Mella, r., 169, 297

Memmius, C., 3, 73, 221, 280, 297–98

Memnon, 163, 248, 298, 315

Menelaus, 291, 301

Menenius, 107, 298

Merops, 303

Mesopotamia, 274

Messana (Messina), 282; Straits of, 308

Metellus Celer, Q., 4, 8, 191, 256, 260, 279, 283, 294–95, 299

Metellus Nepos, Q., 7, 299

metre, 32–41, 269–70; Alcaics, 26, 31; alexandrine, 34 ; choliambic (scazon), 32, 33–34, 215, 220, 222–23, 226; elegiac couplet, 30, 40–41, 245; galliambics, xi, 31–32, 38–39, 237; glyconic/pherecratean, 35–36; greater asclepiad, 36, 222; hendecasyllables, 13, 14, 31–33, 89, 229; hexameter, 10, 11, 28–30, 39–41, 236; iambic tetrameter, 34–35; iambic trimeter, 34; metricized English, 28–29; Neoterics and, 40; priapean, 36; prosody, 27–32; Sapphics, 37–38, 217; Saturnians, 9

Midas, 70, 220, 298

Milanion, 276

Miletus, 294

Milo, T. Annius, 3

Mincio, r., 214

Minerva, 293, 298

Minos, 137, 139, 149, 273, 274, 284, 286, 298–99, 311

Minotaur, 139–41, 241, 242, 273, 274, 284, 298–99, 311

Minturnae, 289

Mithridates VI of Pontus, 11, 222

Mnemosyne, 223

Montaigne, Michel E. de, 20

Most, G., 17

Muci(ll)a. *See* Pompey

Mucius Scaevola, Q., 299

DESIGNER	SANDY DROOKER
COMPOSITOR	INTEGRATED COMPOSITION SYSTEMS
TEXT	FOURNIER
DISPLAY	FOLIO-LIGHT; BAUER TEXT INITIALS
PRINTER AND BINDER	THOMSON-SHORE, INC.